CURIOSITY STUDIES

CURIOSITY STUDIES

A NEW ECOLOGY OF KNOWLEDGE

Perry Zurn *and*
Arjun Shankar, Editors

Foreword by Pam Grossman and John L. Jackson Jr.
Afterword by Helga Nowotny

UNIVERSITY OF MINNESOTA PRESS
MINNEAPOLIS
LONDON

The University of Minnesota Press gratefully acknowledges support for the open-access version of this book from American University Library, Colgate University, the Annenberg School for Communication at the University of Pennsylvania, and the American Philosophical Association.

"Self-portrait as a Karen" is reprinted from Kay Gabriel, *Elegy Department Spring* (BOAAT Press, 2017) by permission of the poet.

Copyright 2020 by the Regents of the University of Minnesota

All rights reserved. No part of this publication may be reproduced, stored in a retrieval system, or transmitted, in any form or by any means, electronic, mechanical, photocopying, recording, or otherwise, without the prior written permission of the publisher.

Published by the University of Minnesota Press
111 Third Avenue South, Suite 290
Minneapolis, MN 55401-2520
http://www.upress.umn.edu

ISBN 978-1-5179-0539-2 (hc)
ISBN 978-1-5179-0540-8 (pb)

A Cataloging-in-Publication record for this book is available from the Library of Congress.

The University of Minnesota is an equal-opportunity educator and employer.

UMP LSI

Contents

Foreword   *Pam Grossman and John L. Jackson Jr.*   vii

Introduction: What Is Curiosity Studies?
Perry Zurn and Arjun Shankar   xi

Part I. Interrogating the Scientific Enterprise

1. Exploring the Costs of Curiosity: An Environmental Scientist's
   Dilemma   *Seeta Sistla*   3

2. Curious Ecologies of Knowledge: More-Than-Human
   Anthropology   *Heather Anne Swanson*   15

3. Curiosity, Ethics, and the Medical Management of Intersex
   Anatomies   *Ellen K. Feder*   37

Part II. Relearning How We Learn

4. A Network Science of the Practice of Curiosity
   Danielle S. Bassett   57

5. Why Should This Be So? The Waxing and Waning of
   Children's Curiosity   *Susan Engel*   75

6. The Dude Abides, or Why Curiosity Is Important for
   Education Today   *Tyson E. Lewis*   91

7. "The Campus Is Sick": Capitalist Curiosity and Student
   Mental Health   *Arjun Shankar*   106

Part III. Reimagining How We Relate

8. Autism, Neurodiversity, and Curiosity *Kristina T. Johnson* 129

9. Obstacles to Curiosity and Concern: Exploring the Racist Imagination *Narendra Keval* 147

10. Curious Entanglements: Opacity and Ethical Relation in Latina/o Aesthetics *Christina León* 167

11. Transsexuality, the Curio, and the Transgender Tipping Point *Amy Marvin* 188

Part IV. Deconstructing the Status Quo

12. Peeping and Transgression: Curiosity and Collecting in English Literature *Barbara M. Benedict* 209

13. Curiosity and Political Resistance *Perry Zurn* 227

14. Curiosity at the End of the World: Women, Fiction, Electricity *Hilary M. Schor* 246

Conclusion: On Teaching Curiosity
Arjun Shankar and Perry Zurn 269

Afterword *Helga Nowotny* 291

Acknowledgments 295

Contributors 299

Index 303

Foreword

Pam Grossman and John L. Jackson Jr.

Research is formalized curiosity. It is poking and prying with a purpose.

—Zora Neale Hurston

Curiosity should be the heart of any educational institution. Indeed, it can be argued that curiosity drives the generation of new knowledge. An urge to wonder, to ponder the hows and whys of existence, has fueled the creation of questions and conceptual formations from physics to philosophy. Even still, universities sometimes seem more comfortable using the language of innovation rather than invoking what might be deemed the more frivolous mien of curiosity. Academicians often cite innovation as a kind of mantra and institutional goal more often than they overtly reference curiosity as a foundational principle for any life of the mind. Maybe that's because innovation seems more substantive and precise, not to mention more hardwired to assumptions about technological transformation and interdisciplinary engagement—as opposed to supporting the potentially rambling machinations of an unchecked commitment to just being intellectually curious. Curiosity begs questions. It demands more specificity. Curiosity about what? Why? To what ends?

Innovation has a telos, a clear objective, goals that predetermine its endgame in ways that are socially conspicuous. Curiosity might be dismissed as more of an aimless journey, a kind of lurching to and fro—without any baked-in presuppositions about transforming the world. It could just mean being nosy or meddlesome. There's a proverbial saying about curiosity finishing off felines for good reason. (With eight more lives to spare, a cat might be able to afford more inquisitive lollygagging and snooping around than humans can safely endure.)

Curiosity is often a private affair, driven by a desire to delve deeper, without a premeditated endpoint. In contrast, most deployments of the term innovation already presume a ready on-ramp to the market, a mechanism whereby price tags are always already hanging off innovators' prescient creations. From certain angles, "innovation" can look like a kind of Trojan Horse for ultimately commercial concerns, not all the time but in ways that take pride of place when laying out institutional or individual priorities. Innovation is perceived as lucrative, dollar signs dancing like sugar plums in everyone's heads. And not simply or selfishly for those behind said innovations. Material gains redound to a larger swath of beneficiaries—maybe even to humanity itself. That explains why there can be an ethical valence to preferring innovation over curiosity. The former is decidedly social; its "good" is ultimately public. The latter seems personal, egoistic, or even antisocial in its privileging of an interiorized purpose and ambition that may not have any obvious social applicability. Whereas innovation comes off as univocally constructive and justifiable, not all forms of curiosity are built that same way. Most get dismissed as distractions while a rare and few others, carefully cultivated, are the would-be elixirs without which anything worthy of the term innovation could never come to be.

In thinking with the critical group of scholars assembled in this volume to help us consider more deeply and carefully what curiosity entails, the specter of innovation is a powerful foil for these collective endeavors. Curiosity doesn't necessarily lead to innovation. Innovation is assumed to play the role of domesticating curiosity, placing its indifferent ethos in service to the public good. Indeed, the very phrase Curiosity Studies might feel implausible, or at least counterintuitive; curiosity is too undisciplined and free-flowing for the kind of systematic and disciplinary approach that its adjectival placement before the idea of organized academic scholarship seems to imply. Can curiosity be disciplined by the academy and become amenable to scholarly inquiry?

Curiosity is one of those words that is all the more intriguing because we take it for granted, because we assume we know what it means. Arjun Shankar and Perry Zurn, former postdocs at the University of Pennsylvania (thanks to generous support from the Center for Curiosity in New York City), have asked a stellar group of thinkers from a variety of disciplines/fields to assist us in our aim to get a lot more curious about the idea of curiosity itself. What does it open up, and what does its evocation occlude? What differentiates curiosity from imagination or creativity? Can curiosity be cultivated

Foreword

or foreclosed? If nothing else, this anthology helps to demonstrate that curiosity is not just a potentially powerful first step in learning and producing new things, a lapdog to innovation's profitable mandates, but also a fascinating notion to examine just for the sake of doing so—even if the only way this undertaking might come to matter (in the academy and beyond) is if it proves to be a groundbreaking way of reimagining what we think curiosity to be in the first place.

We're confident that this collection of essays will inspire you to reconsider curiosity as a fundamental and all-too-often neglected element of what it means to be a human being.

Introduction

What Is Curiosity Studies?

Perry Zurn and Arjun Shankar

Curiosity is a many-splendored thing. In contemporary U.S. culture, for example,[1] its references are as wildly disparate as they are insightful. There is the *Curiosity* Mars Rover, launched in 2011 and still wandering the surface of the red planet, searching for evidence of life. There is the "Curiosity" Discovery Channel series and Curiosity.com, each of which collates bite-size bits of information, uniquely packaged to enhance precisely what is strange and exciting about them. The term "curiosity" appears, over and over again, in educational philosophies and university mission statements, and in talk of innovation and creativity across the business and technology sectors. And, of course, it appears in everyday conversations, more times than we realize: "I'm curious," "I'm just curious." Across popular culture, curiosity is largely defanged and commodified. There is Curious George, Curiosity Cola, and Steel Reserve's 2018 ad for its 8 percent alcohol energy drink Blue Razz: "Curious Is Calling." Not to mention Britney Spears's 1999 hit, "I'm So Curious." As such, curiosity is often taken as a mere superficial interest. Even in its most banal moments, however, curiosity is something more. From science, technology, and education to the consumption of goods and media icons, curiosity somehow consistently drives us to take risks, pushing past what exists to stand on the precipice of the possible.

Perhaps this is why Barack Obama, in his first inaugural speech, identified curiosity—alongside honesty and courage—as an American value on which the country's success depends.[2] At its best, curiosity fuels an openness to difference and a drive toward innovation that together equip us to pursue a more intellectually vibrant and equitable world. Unfortunately, many assess our present political milieu to be markedly, and increasingly, "incurious."[3] The Trump administration's resistance to different perspectives, scientific inquiry, and the habit of asking deep, transformative questions has arguably reinforced some of the worst sorts of sexist and xenophobic rhetoric, policy, and behavior.

Given such high stakes, we, the editors and contributors of *Curiosity Studies: A New Ecology of Knowledge,* find the study of curiosity to be of urgent importance. Curiosity is not an empty, untethered cultural feature of our contemporary era but one of the most important political tools we have at our disposal. There is, in fact, a logic evident in its material and discursive, linguistic and praxiological appearances. That is, despite its various forms and distinguishable types,[4] its simulations and its knockoffs, curiosity is a coherent and powerful phenomenon. It therefore constitutes a proper object of study all its own. Here we bring together fourteen scholars with disparate expertise to establish *curiosity studies* as a unique field of scholarly inquiry. Drawing authors from philosophy, history, literature, ethnic studies, gender studies, education, anthropology, psychology and psychoanalysis, ecology, biomedicine, neuroscience, physics, and visual art, this book stages a transdisciplinary conversation about what curiosity is and what resources it holds for human and ecological flourishing. As such, the book is the first Anglophone, broadly cross-disciplinary interrogation of the concept and future of curiosity.[5] In an age in which human curiosity is at a crossroads—at once more powerful, and yet systematically hypercommodified and curtailed, than ever before—not to mention an age in which the reality of animal curiosity and the possibility of artificially intelligent curiosity is increasingly felt, this book equips us to live critically and creatively in what might be called our new Age of Curiosity.

In what follows, we intervene in the long history of the study of curiosity to propose *curiosity studies* proper. Such a field, we argue, traverses the many disciplinary and experiential contexts in which curiosity appears, in order to generate theories, analytics, and practices of curiosity that are as complex and ubiquitous as the phenomenon of curiosity itself. Assuming an ecology of knowledge framework, which expressly resists academic silos and intellectual monocultures, we envision curiosity studies as an unbounded inquiry built on three simple principles: (1) Curiosity is multiple; its markers shift across history, geography, species, social identities, institutions, contexts, and circumstances; therefore it requires immensely flexible analytic attention; (2) Curiosity is praxiological; far from something that is simply felt, curiosity is something that is done, expressed in behaviors, habits, architectures, and movements across physical, conceptual, and social space; and (3) Curiosity is political; its manifestations within sociocultural worlds are marked by inherited hierarchies of value among scientific methodologies, people groups, and ideologies. And yet, precisely because it is multiple, praxiological, and political, curiosity bears a keen subversive potential. It has the capacity to upend what we know, how we learn, how we relate, and what we can change. Curiosity has the capacity to become radical, to get at the root of things. We therefore propose curiosity studies not only as a field of scholarship but as a way of reimagining the world, both within the classroom and far beyond it.

A Brief History of Curiosity

While curiosity studies might be new, the study of curiosity is thousands of years old.[6] In the Western tradition, beginning in the ancient period, curiosity was, by turns, celebrated for its capacity to generate knowledge and castigated for its tendency to fuel merely meddlesome inquiry. The Greek terms *polypragmosune* and *periergia*—later translated into the Latin as *curiositas*—first carried this dual meaning, referring both to an interest in what is beyond oneself (e.g., other people and the natural world) as well as to what is outside one's proper purview (e.g., the private, the secret, the forbidden, the foreign).[7] Thus while Seneca claimed that curiosity about nature is of critical importance in one's own ethical development,[8] Plutarch insisted that curiosity, particularly when directed at other people's business, bankrupts the soul.[9] Similarly, Aristotle recommended that one be studious about one thing *(monopragmosune)* rather than interested in many things,[10] while Plato argued that curious people, whose appetite for knowledge often rules them, suffer from an imbalance in the three parts of their soul: reason, spirit, and appetite.[11] Over time, this ambiguous or two-toned assessment of curiosity was largely bifurcated into a medieval concern with curiosity as a vice and a modern embrace of curiosity as a key instrument in social and scientific advancement.

The medieval period was marked by a robust suspicion of curiosity, as a source of social fissures and spiritual fragmentation. Saint Augustine set a

Neoplatonic, Christian tone for the era when he catalogued curiosity as a "lust of the eyes,"[12] active on both the sensual and intellective registers. For him, this devilish curiosity attaches to the natural (whether the principles of nature or the behaviors of natural creatures), the supernatural (astrology, necromancy, religious signs and wonders), and the aesthetic (fashion, fantasy, theater). Against the vice of *curiositas,* he recommended the virtue of *studiositas,*[13] or the careful application of oneself to well-circumscribed intellectual work. Isidore of Seville and Gregory the Great would later taxonomize the vice of curiosity—a wandering mind—as a descendant of melancholy or sloth.[14] And later still, Thomas Aquinas would taxonomize studiousness as a form of temperance, marking its superiority over an intemperate curiosity.[15] The weight of these classifications led, on the one hand, to twelfth-century Benedictine Bernard of Clairvaux's advice to renounce curiosity, having instead one's "head bent and eyes fixed on the ground,"[16] and, on the other, to fourteenth-century priest Richard de Bury's treatise *Philobiblon,* a painstaking defense of his own curious habit of collecting books, which had garnered him intense critique from the church.[17]

Particularly at its inception, the modern period was characterized by a suspicion of tradition, a need for independent thought, and a renewed commitment to the secular pursuit of human progress. Here, the first sense of ancient curiosity—as natural and studious—resurfaces with a vengeance. While Réné Descartes still thinks of curiosity—with its interest in minutiae—as fundamentally scholastic, he insists that a certain wonder is necessary for the work of reason, knowledge, and the good of humankind.[18] For the most part, other modern thinkers recognize "curiosity" as that intellectual instrument crucial to the service of human development and civilization. Thomas Hobbes, for example, defines curiosity as "the love of the knowledge of causes."[19] For David Hume, curiosity is "the love of truth."[20] For John Locke, curiosity is an "appetite for knowledge,"[21] to be nurtured in young and old alike. While for Jean-Jacques Rousseau, curiosity is "a principle natural to the human heart," which must be carefully trained to achieve its promise.[22] And what is that promise? In the modern era, curiosity becomes not only rational, disciplined, and controlled, but also useful, productive of scientific knowledge and civic good.

Today, in post-Enlightenment Western culture, curiosity is largely understood and studied in a modern sense. Educators, psychologists, and neuroscientists consistently explore curiosity as the cornerstone of inquiry and innovation. And yet, with the rise of digital technologies and social media, we are also seeing a renewed concern with curiosity's propensity for distraction and superficiality, reminiscent of ancient and medieval insights. Increased political turmoil on both the national and global stage, moreover, has generated fresh interest in curiosity's capacity to undermine the status quo, and therefore the power of the powerful, especially when curiosity is wielded by those who are otherwise perceived as disempowered.

Given both the long tradition of studying curiosity and the fact that age-old questions regarding curiosity's function and value are alive and well today, we believe curiosity studies is best undertaken as a collaborative venture with historical and political sensitivities. It must begin by recognizing that the conceptualization and mobilization of curiosity in our present era is rooted in material conditions and legacies. And it must proceed with a multiscalar analysis through cross-disciplinary, pluri-vector conversations. As various fields deepen their analysis of curiosity along these tracks and begin to draw from one another, a new ecosystem of curiosity can flourish, accountable to historico-political and transdisciplinary ecologies of knowledge.

An Ecology of Knowledge Framework

The term "ecology of knowledge," popularized by Charles Rosenberg in the 1970's,[23] refers to the way in which knowledge functions in and as a dynamic, multilayered environment. Developing in concert with systems thinking, complexity theory, and network science, the knowledge ecology framework refuses to consider the production of knowledge in isolation—limited to a particular scientist, lab, discipline, or research vector—but rather analyzes it through interaction: the interactions among languages, histories, materials, institutions, publishing norms, funding sources, social groups, the natural environment, and the like.[24] While there is a debate over whether the term "ecology" functions here as a metaphor or an analogy,[25] scholars agree that the term does provide a helpful analytical model. Ecology, stemming from the Greek words *oikos* and *logos,* refers to the study of habitation, both where one dwells and what habits mark that dwelling. When applied to the study of curiosity, the ecology of knowledge framework attends less to what curiosity *is* than to how curiosity is practiced, when and where it gets problematized, and why its features change. As such, an ecological view of curiosity aids in the development of a functional, political, and cross-disciplinary account.

The ecology of knowledge framework is predicated on complementary critiques of science and politics. Working, on the one hand, against an abstract, positivist, reductionist science and, on the other, against the political systems of capitalism, patriarchy, and colonialism, the ecology of knowledge rejects what Boaventura de Sousa Santos calls the "epistemological fascism"[26] that promotes "monopol[ies]"[27] and "monoculture[s]"[28] of knowledge. It attends instead to the "intricate interrelationships" that produce intertwined bodies of knowledge—relationships appearing among individuals, artefacts, organizations, and environments,[29] and at the level of labs, subfields, disciplines, colleges, and the academy itself, especially in its contemporary Western guise. As such, rather than analyzing isolates, an ecological perspective focuses on a network of connections, a web of interdependencies, and circulations of exchange. It does so for the purpose of enhancing a plurality of knowledges and knowledge-production practices across sociocultural and historical locales. It therefore preserves bio-, cultural, and epistemic diversity in the knowledge enterprise,[30] often doing so expressly in the service of "social" and "cognitive justice."[31] Some locate this justice in the democracy of ideas that can result from deconstructing academic silos and intellectual monocultures.[32] Others insist that ideal knowledge-formations be evaluated not for their bald equality but rather for their pragmatic efficacy[33] in "guarantee[ing] the greatest level of participation" by relevant stakeholders.[34]

For a number of reasons, an ecology-of-knowledge approach provides an ideal framework for the new field of curiosity studies. On the one hand, this framework reflects the kinesthetic signature of curiosity itself. If anything, curiosity is inherently dynamic and expansive, jumping from one sphere of inquiry to another, one detail or vantage point to another. Much like curiosity, an ecology-of-knowledge approach moves brazenly across boundaries, irrespective of established conceptual, architectural, and disciplinary norms. On the other hand, such a framework also pushes the study of curiosity to better track the kinesthetic signature of curiosity writ large. That is, it equips scholars to study curiosity *curiously*. Rather than succumbing to parochial border wars and aspirations to disciplinary purity, an ecological study of curiosity is capable of perceiving, appreciating, and perturbing as-yet-unimaginable connections and crosscurrents of inquiry.

From a knowledge-ecology perspective, the study of curiosity must honor the material and discursive enmeshments of both the science and social practice of curiosity. At the very least, this requires rooting curiosity studies in political and cross-disciplinary accounts. First, it must refuse the common presumption that curiosity is an ahistorical, value-neutral human capacity. Instead, it must acknowledge the historical matrices—and the clash of social values—in which curiosity has been conceived and mobilized, reproduced or revolutionized. It needs to account for what today's curiosity has inherited and what it has occluded. It needs to ask: Who can be curious, within what contexts, why, and how? For whom is curiosity valorized? How have different functions of curiosity been historically gendered and racialized? Why are Western modalities of curiosity valued over their non-Western correlates? For that matter, what does it mean for Obama to claim curiosity as an American value or for journalists to claim that Trump is dangerously incurious? And what is at stake in reserving curiosity for the human, rather than acknowledging it in animal, vegetal, computational, or extraterrestrial contexts? In asking precisely these sociopolitical questions and more, the present volume positions curiosity studies beyond the traditional anthropocentric, Enlightenment frameworks that continue to haunt much of our scholarly discourses.

Second, an ecologically informed curiosity studies must refuse the common assumption that curiosity is a monadic unit, accessible by any one method of analysis. This means curiosity studies must not locate the proper study of curiosity exclusively in the hard sciences, but in fact reject the onto-epistemological division between the human, social, and natural sciences. Instead, it must nurture computational and behavioral perspectives alongside decolonial and feminist theoretical approaches. In fact, curiosity studies requires interdisciplinary and transdisciplinary modes of inquiry. Interdisciplinary work on curiosity combines discrete concepts, theories, or methods from different disciplines in order to develop a unique scholarly contribution. Transdisciplinary work on curiosity goes even further. Capitalizing on the multiple resonances and tensions in the word "trans"—the transitive and transversal, the transient and transitional, and the transgressive—transdisciplinary analyses not only crisscross disciplinary norms and positions but condition a rich differentiation of concepts, court prescient if impermanent perspectives, precondition paradigm shifts, and politicize the everyday. As such, these analyses recontour the terrain across which curiosity can be explored. Indeed, insofar as curiosity challenges sociodisciplinary boundaries, an ecologically oriented curiosity studies must work in a space liminal to existing fields.

The ecological approach foregrounds the interdeterminacy, contingency, and heterogeneity of knowledge production. Knowledge of curiosity exists in ecosystems, in which information, ideas, experiences, and embodiments cross-fertilize and feed one another. Our commitment to historicizing and politicizing the concept of curiosity, as well as staging interdisciplinary and transdisciplinary conversations, honors the epistemic ecologies that subtend the very possibility of curiosity studies. It is our hope that the new ecologies of curiosity to follow will be new in both a descriptive and a normative sense. That is, they will be as fresh intellectually as they are forward-looking politically.

Science, Education, Relationships, and Change

If one were to think of important contributions to the study of curiosity today, one might think of work done in history or literature, in psychology or neuroscience. One might turn, for example, to Neil Kenny's *Curiosity in Early Modern Europe: Word Histories,* to Hilary Schor's *Curious Subjects: Women and the Trials of Realism,* or to empirical studies by Min Jeong Kang or Charan Ranganath. Rather than focus on isolated contributions from distinct fields, however, we have chosen, in *Curiosity Studies*, to analyze elements of curiosity that have been problematized across disciplinary vectors and historical terrains. We focus specifically on curiosity's role in scientific inquiry, educational practice, social relations, and the power of transformation. By clustering chapters around these themes, *Curiosity Studies* builds on contemporary scholarship and pushes a series of material, multiscalar, and political analyses in fresh, new directions.

Curiosity—as a desire to see, to understand, and to know—is perhaps most consistently and richly considered in relationship to the sciences, broadly construed. As historians of science such as Sander Bais, Philip Ball, and Roger Wagner put it,[35] science is fueled by curiosity, a curiosity for which "nothing [is] too trivial or obscure."[36] And yet the capaciousness of curiosity paradoxically produces its own constraints. The history of science is, if nothing else, one of interminable struggle between forces that liberate curiosity and forces that discipline and direct it. What is more, the very practice of curiosity at once transgresses physical and conceptual boundaries[37] and (re)constructs them. This can be seen not only in bioethical debates

Introduction   xix

over biotechnologies but also across the literature on curiosity, travel, and collections. On the heels of the medieval *curiosi*,[38] for example, who traveled in search of secular knowledge, rose the modern *ars apodemica* (or art of traveling) not only for anthropological and geographical information gathering[39] but also for cultural exploration and ultimately colonization, imperialism, and globalization.[40] Such curious travel resulted in collections of curiosities, which slowly symbolized the advancement of scientific knowledge.[41] These collections often included books (especially dictionaries),[42] but were also interpreted through books,[43] which constructed simultaneously the modern liberal subject of Enlightenment rationality and the paradoxically exotic, mystical, and primitive Orient.[44] The curiosity at work in the scientific enterprise thus has a propensity for but also produces the forbidden.[45] And all of this is determined by political structures and sociocultural values, as well as determinative of those same structures and values.

Curiosity—as a prompt to learning, growth, and exploration—is also commonly analyzed in scholarship on education.[46] This effort to map the inquiring mind relies in great part on the pragmatist philosophy of William James and John Dewey, for whom curiosity is a natural "impulse,"[47] an "expression of an abundant organic energy"[48] that, while shared among all creatures, becomes uniquely human insofar as it serves sophisticated cognition and higher-order problem solving. Developing through behavioral psychology and neuroscience—across thinkers such as Daniel Berlyne, Harry Fowler, George Lowenstein, Charles Spielberger and Laura Starr, Jacqueline Gottlieb, and Celeste Kidd[49]—curiosity has been defined and measured in relation to interest, motivation, attention, arousal, anxiety, and creativity. Much of this tradition assumes a universal human subject and simplified manifestations of curiosity: for example, raising a hand, turning an eye, asking a question, or expressing interest in trivia. Some such studies have historically given rise to troublesome claims that, for example, female students are less curious than their male counterparts because they raise their hands less often.[50] As a corrective, it is important not only to analyze the changing morphology of curiosity across childhood development and adulthood, as Susan Engel and Todd Kashdan do,[51] but also to account for the effects of social inequalities on the practice and perception of curiosity. Scholars might take inspiration from radical pedagogue Paulo Freire, for whom curiosity, as a "restless questioning," equips people not only "to produce something together" but to "resist together."[52] Accounting for curiosity as a sociopolitical practice of resistance involves diversifying not only the methods and modes of inquiry but how those modes are identified and valued.[53]

Curiosity—as an interest in the new, the foreign, and the forbidden—has long had a bearing on the interpretation of cultural differences and the structure of social inequalities. While some scholarship has diagnosed curiosity's complicity in exoticization and orientalism, especially through colonial travel and imperial collections,[54] most scholarship in this vein has centered on women, both as subjects and objects of curiosity. In early modern Europe, just as curiosity is being retooled into its rational, disciplined, and masculine guise, its more uncouth elements—gossip, distraction, transgression—are transferred to a new conceptual domicile: female and/or feminine curiosity. As Barbara Benedict, Neil Kenny, and Line Cottegnies et al. demonstrate, albeit in different respects, such curiosity—taken to signal sexual, cultural, and intellectual ambition—was perceived as impertinent and punishable.[55] The winds turn a bit with the development of the modern realist novel, whose heroine's practice of curiosity helped construct the modern feminist subject.[56] Indeed, Laura Mulvey and Cynthia Enloe have since developed an account of an expressly feminist curiosity, which involves women taking themselves as their own subjects and objects of curiosity.[57] Insofar as curiosity is never abstracted from social life, its practice either supports or challenges the reigning forms of knowledge production (and, in our case, the primacy of a white, Eurocentric, cis-male discourse). Whether it polarizes the abled and disabled communities, a la Rosemarie Garland-Thomson,[58] or reduces polarization across racial difference, a la Narendra Keval,[59] curiosity can entrench or invert sociopolitical hierarchies.

Finally, curiosity—as a drive to transgress, to refuse, and to create—is sometimes considered in relation to social change and transformation. From early myths of Eve and Pandora, Prometheus and Odysseus, curiosity is inherently disobedient, crossing boundaries and borders in its furious press toward the end of the world and beyond. It was Friedrich Nietzsche who memorably insisted that "the great liberation" would one day be characterized by a "vehement, dangerous curiosity."[60] As adventurous as it is insubordinate,[61] curiosity is, for Michel Foucault, "a certain determination to throw off familiar ways of thought and to look at the same things in a different way."[62] This is not only an irreverence for common concepts or mores but a commitment to the struggle, a la Freire, for freedom for all. Such a task involves

Introduction   xxi

deconstructing the status quo,[63] pitting a curiosity of resistance against an institutionalized system of meaning-making and meaning-building. Sometimes, it involves setting curiosities at war.[64] Today our era is marked, Helga Nowotny argues, by the "taming" or "domestication" of curiosity in a neoliberal academy, which subjects the progress of science to the privatization and propertization of a market economy.[65] And yet, it is precisely today that we need a wild, unbroken curiosity. We need, in Anna Tsing's words, a "radical curiosity" about "multispecies worlds,"[66] one that notices what has gone unnoticed, what has fallen outside the frame of our epistemic and material values. This is "the first requirement," she insists, "of collaborative survival in precarious times."[67] How, indeed, might we harness the power of curiosity for change?

Contributions to the Conversation

Curiosity Studies first formalizes and then contributes to these ongoing conversations. It does so by staging—across its four parts—cross-disciplinary investigations into curiosity's increasingly complicated role in the processes of knowing, learning, relating, and changing.

In Part I, "Interrogating the Scientific Enterprise," authors explore the promise and limits of scientific inquiry and method, from its modern inception to its future life. Seeta Sistla, in "Exploring the Costs of Curiosity: An Environmental Scientist's Dilemma," opens with a clarion call to reassess our overreliance on resource-demanding technologies in scientific research. Against an environmentally irresponsible curiosity, she challenges us to refashion our curiosity in concert with Earth's ecologies. As if in response, Heather Anne Swanson, in "Curious Ecologies of Knowledge: More-Than-Human Anthropology," argues that traditional methodologies have to be reimagined if natural and social scientists are to be responsive to and responsible for a more-than-human world. She specifically proposes a multispecies anthropology that relinquishes *curiosity-about* and embraces *curiosity-with*. Likewise, Ellen K. Feder, in "Curiosity, Ethics, and the Medical Management of Intersex Anatomies," insists that, while an objectifying medico-scientific curiosity has, on the whole, caused irreparable harm to the intersex community, there is another form of curiosity—modeled by some doctors and intersex people themselves—that facilitates understanding, respect, and care. This first section significantly complicates the simple celebration of scientific curiosity on new twenty-first-century fronts, insisting on greater ecological awareness, self-reflexivity, and participatory research protocols.

In Part II, "Relearning How We Learn," authors explore recent advances in our understanding of the contours of curiosity in human learning. Danielle S. Bassett, in "A Network Science of the Practice of Curiosity," offers a novel theory of curiosity as a practice of building knowledge networks, a practice traceable in neural connectivity patterns as well as evident in linguistic behaviors. This work promises to enhance education and work settings, where greater facilitation of such patterns and behaviors is required. For Susan Engel, in "Why Should This Be So? The Waxing and Waning of Children's Curiosity," any encouragement of curiosity in educational settings needs to account for the developmental changes in children's curiosity—and presumably adults' curiosity—across time. This task is frustrated, however, by schools and colleges in which certain forms of curiosity are celebrated over others. Taking equal inspiration from aesthetic theory and *The Big Lebowski,* Tyson E. Lewis, in "The Dude Abides, or Why Curiosity is Important for Education Today," for example, argues that real curiosity is not actually serious at all but involves an atypical, "distracted" learning style that, although commonly disciplined and punished, should be encouraged in all of our classrooms and among our students. Last, Arjun Shankar, in "'The Campus Is Sick': Capitalist Curiosity and Student Mental Health," turns to diagnose the plight of curiosity in U.S. higher education. After exploring the affective costs of an overdetermined, ruthlessly pragmatic, neoliberal curiosity, he suggests that a return to a deinstrumentalized and open curiosity that is squarely situated in a student's desire for knowledge is crucial to student mental health. This section clearly pushes discussions of curiosity and education into important new terrains.

In Part III, "Reimagining How We Relate," authors investigate the centrality of curiosity both to the tensions that divide communities—whether over race, ethnicity, gender, or disability—and to the attentions that can heal them. Kristina T. Johnson, in "Autism, Neurodiversity, and Curiosity," opens the cluster by insisting that curiosity studies needs to get more curious about neuroatypical individuals and their curiosity. For Johnson, recognizing curiosity in autistic children, for example, requires entirely new research designs capable of formalizing the neural and motor movement coincident with autistic children's "affinities," or special interests. In a related argument, Narendra Keval, in "Obstacles to Curiosity and Concern: Exploring the Racist

Imagination," argues it is precisely curiosity that can disarm racist states of mind and reopen the psyche to our shared humanity, even our shared curiosity. Analyzing aesthetic productions of *latinidad,* Christina León, in "Curious Entanglements: Opacity and Ethical Relation in Latina/o Aesthetics," shows that such a radical curiosity (rather than a racist, stereotyping one) is ready to sit with uncertainty and unknowing. In doing so, she argues, curiosity can initiate real relationality across the most intransigent differences. Finally, Amy Marvin, in "Transsexuality, the Curio, and the Transgender Tipping Point," after warning that recent media attention has functioned to "curiotize" trans people, reducing them to merely the objects of public curiosity, recommends another sort of curiosity—a reopening one—that instead honors trans experience in all its social and historical complexity. This section highlights the importance of engaging and recognizing curiosity responsibly across our human differences.

In Part IV, "Deconstructing the Status Quo," authors reflect on the radical potential and continued promise of curiosity. Barbara M. Benedict, in "Peeping and Transgression: Curiosity and Collecting in English Literature," explains how curiosity can represent simultaneously the promise of freedom and the threat of danger by locating curiosity in the transgressive: the transgressive phenomena that provoke inquiry and the transgressive character of that inquiry itself. Perry Zurn, in "Curiosity and Political Resistance," then analyzes curiosity as a force of social transformation through political resistance. He does so by investigating the conditions of creative exploration, especially among marginalized groups, and the forces that frustrate that exploration. Hilary M. Schor, in "Curiosity at the End of the World: Women, Fiction, Electricity," then turns to think about the future. If, as she suggests, the novel is the modern curiosity-cabinet—or that *story* is the genre of curiosity par excellence—it will be curious storytelling that equips us to function within a palimpsest of cultures as we press on toward the end of the world. This final section, then, at once affirms and deepens our hope for curiosity today.

Finally, in the Conclusion, "On Teaching Curiosity," we as editors return to discuss both the rationale and the methods for teaching this ambivalent, complex, and multiscalar phenomenon called curiosity. We draw out the tensions between teaching curiosity as subject matter, as pedagogical approach, and as an inspiration for research. Furthermore, we explore precisely how these newly invigorated conversations around curiosity's role in science, education, relationships, and change may not only transform our classrooms but also our ways of being together in the world. In doing so we aim to encourage not only traditional and nontraditional students—but really everyone—to develop their capacities to conscientiously deploy radical curiosity on an everyday basis, in their everyday lives.

Future Directions

Historically, the study of curiosity has been responsive to and yet ultimately unequal to the task of quantifying and qualifying curiosity in its distinctive manifestations and across different milieus. This is perhaps inescapable, reflecting an admixture of human finitude and fallibility. Today, although we are equipped as never before to assess the shifting parameters of curiosity and the inherited or newly acquired delimitations of our understanding, the technologization of knowledge has introduced a fundamental anachronism in that pursuit. What we are curious about, with whom, and how we pursue that curiosity is changing faster than ever before. In this vein and insofar as curiosity precisely clambers after the unknown, it is important to recognize that the very future of curiosity studies should be as yet unimaginable and therefore indeterminable. Nevertheless, it is possible to peer just over the horizon of our present context and location, to correct for currently identifiable limitations, and to risk a wager on new frontiers in the study of curiosity.

It is perhaps appropriate in a U.S. context to begin with the recognition that indigenous curiosity has been and continues to be suppressed, despite the efforts of some exemplary practitioners—for example, Sandy Grande, Erica Violet Lee, Robin Wall Kimmerer, and Kyle Whyte. In this context, curiosity studies ought to develop in tandem with decolonial feminist science studies. Turning from the local to the global, it is imperative that greater attention be paid to non-Western histories of and approaches to curiosity.[68] Might, for example, the turn to mindfulness be a turn to a new series of curious practices? The pedagogical implications of "Eastern" philosophies, alongside developments in network neuroscience and the recognition of neuroatypical expressions of curiosity, have the potential to significantly transform educational norms. In a digital age, it is also critical to account for how human–computer interaction and artificial intelligence[69]—let alone revolutions in social media—refashion the terrain of curiosity. Cross-cultural analyses of curiosity are also sorely lacking, as are concerted efforts to understand the role of curiosity in religious beliefs and practices (e.g., prayer, meditation, fellowship).[70] Moreover, as antidote to the immense attention paid to children's curiosity, it is important to inquire into curiosity across the lifespan, especially among the aging. Finally, in an increasingly polarized, war-torn, disease-ridden, and environmentally devastated world, we need to ask what curiosity's role might be in peacebuilding for sustainable futures.

Curiosity Studies is a groundbreaking book about the nature, promise, and pitfalls of curiosity in the twenty-first century. It is radically imaginative and full of unexpected twists and turns. Its insights are as invigorating as they are haunting. We invite readers to approach the text quizzically. Maintain a mind flexible enough to follow the trail of ideas, to leap between writing styles, and to hazard a mélange of methodologies. Keep a hawk's-eye out for the multiplicity of curiosity, the way it resurfaces in a network of practices. And stay alive to its social investments and political potential. Take up the quest of curiosity bravely. And let *Curiosity Studies* be just one stop along the way, one moment in a long journey of exploration and transformation.

Notes

1. While we here acknowledge our location as U.S. scholars, we later interrogate the U.S.-centrism so common in the study of curiosity.

2. Barack Obama, "Inaugural Address," Grant Park, Chicago: January 20, 2009.

3. See, for example, Sarah Vowell, "The Danger of an Incurious President," *New York Times,* August 9, 2017, https://www.nytimes.com/2017/08/09/opinion/trump-fire-fury-north-korea.html.

4. See, for example, Perry Zurn, "Busybody, Hunter, Dancer: Three Historical Models of Curiosity," in *Toward New Philosophical Explorations of the Epistemic Desire to Know: Just Curious about Curiosity,* ed. Marianna Papastephanou (Cambridge, U.K.: Cambridge Scholars Press, 2019), 26–49.

5. To our knowledge, the only comparable text is the anthology *La curiosité: Vestiges du savoir,* edited by Nicole Czechowski (Paris: Autrement, 1993). Where *La curiosité* relies most heavily on the humanities, however, *Curiosity Studies* canvasses a broader and more balanced array of disciplines to collate twenty-first-century discussions. There are also more circumscribed collections that, while interdisciplinary, nevertheless focus on field hubs relevant to their topics—e.g., Nicole Jacques-Chaquin and Sophie Houdard, eds., *Curiosité et libido sciendi de la Renaissance aux lumières* (Paris: ENS Editions, 1998); Line Cottegnies, Sandrine Parageau, and John J. Thompson, eds., *Women and Curiosity in Early Modern England and France* (Boston: Brill,

2016); Ilhan Inan et al., eds., *The Moral Psychology of Curiosity* (Lanham, Md.: Rowman and Littlefield, 2018); Goren Gordon, ed., *The New Science of Curiosity* (New York: Nova, 2018); and Marianna Papastephanou, ed., *Toward New Philosophical Explorations of the Epistemic Desire to Know: Just Curious about Curiosity* (Cambridge, U.K.: Cambridge Scholars Press, 2019).

6. For the most extensive philosophical history of curiosity to date, see Hans Blumenberg, *The Legitimacy of the Modern Age,* trans. Robert M. Wallace (1966; Cambridge, Mass.: MIT Press, 1983), part 3.

7. Matthew Leigh, *From Polypragmon to Curiosus: Ancient Concepts of Curious and Meddlesome Behavior* (Oxford: Oxford University Press, 2013).

8. Seneca, *Naturales Questiones* (Cambridge, Mass.: Harvard University Press, 1972), 1.12.

9. Plutarch, "On Being a Busybody," in *Moralia VI* (Cambridge, Mass.: Harvard University Press, 2005), 515d.

10. Aristotle, *Politics* (Cambridge, Mass.: Loeb Classical Library, 1932), 4.12.4.1299b.

11. Plato, *The Republic* (Cambridge, Mass.: Loeb Classical Library, 2013), 4.444b.

12. Augustine, *The Confessions* (Cambridge, Mass.: Loeb Classical Library, 2014), 10.35.

13. Augustine, "De utilitate credendi," in *Augustine: Earlier Writings,* trans. J. H. S. Burleigh (Philadelphia: Westminster Press, 1953).

14. Isidore of Seville, *De summo bono*, Latin edition (Nabu Press, 2011), 2.37; Gregory the Great, *Moralia* (Collegeville, Minn.: Liturgical Press, 2014), 31.45.88.

15. Thomas Aquinas, *Summa theologica* (1274; New York: Benziger Brothers, 1947–48), 2.2.167.1–2.

16. Bernard of Clairvaux, *The Rule of St. Benedict* (Collegeville, Minn.: Liturgical Press, 2018), c7.

17. See Christian Zacher, *Curiosity and Pilgrimage: The Literature of Discovery in Fourteenth-Century England* (Baltimore, Md.: Johns Hopkins University Press, 1976), chapter 4.

18. René Descartes, "The Search for Truth," in *The Philosophical Writings of Descartes II,* trans. John Cottingham, Robert Stoothoff, and Dugald Murdoch (Cambridge: Cambridge University Press, 1984), 400–420.

19. Thomas Hobbes, *Leviathan,* ed. Edwin Curley (1651; Indianapolis: Hackett Press, 1994), 11.24–25.

20. David Hume, *A Treatise on Human Nature* (1739; Oxford: Oxford University Press, 2000), 2.3.10.

21. John Locke, *Some Thoughts Concerning Education*, ed. John William Adamson (1693; New York: Dover, 2007), §118.

22. Jean-Jacques Rousseau, *Emile, or On Education,* trans. Allan Bloom (1762; New York: Basic Books: 1979), 167.

23. Charles E. Rosenberg, "Towards an Ecology of Knowledge: Discipline, Context, and History," in *The Organization of Knowledge in Modern America, 1860–1920,* ed. Alexandra Oleson and John Voss (Baltimore, Md.: Johns Hopkins University Press,

1979), 440–55. An even earlier iteration, "ecology of ideas," was developed by Gregory Bateson in *Steps to an Ecology of Mind* (New York: Chandler, 1972).

24. Atsushi Akera, "Constructing a Representation for an Ecology of Knowledge: Methodological Advances in the Integration of Knowledge and Its Various Contexts," *Social Studies of Science* 37, no. 3 (2007): 418; Peter J. Taylor, "Mapping Ecologists' Ecologies of Knowledge," *PSA: Proceedings of the Biennial Meeting of the Philosophy of Science Association* 2 (1990): 97.

25. For a metaphorical interpretation, see Atsushi Akera, "The Circulation of Knowledge, Institutional Ecologies, and the History of Computing," *IEEE Annals of the History of Computing* 26, no. 3 (2004): 86–88. For an analogical interpretation, see Susan Leigh Star, *Ecologies of Knowledge: Work and Politics in Science and Technology* (New York: State University of New York Press, 1995).

26. Boaventura de Sousa Santos, "A Non-Occidentalist West? Learned Ignorance and Ecology of Knowledge," *Theory, Culture and Society* 26, nos. 7–8 (2009): 117.

27. Boaventura de Sousa Santos, "Beyond Abyssal Thinking: From Global Lines to Ecologies of Knowledge," *Review* 30, no. 1 (2007): 69.

28. de Sousa Santos, "Beyond Abyssal Thinking," 76; Daniel Coleman, "Toward an Indigenist Ecology of Knowledges for Canadian Literary Studies," *Studies in Canadian Literature* 37, no. 2 (2012): 5–31; Silvia Elisabeth Moraes and Ludmila de Almeida Freire, "The University Curriculum and the Ecology of Knowledges towards Building a Planetary Citizenship," *Transnational Curriculum Inquiry* 13, no. 1 (2016): 39.

29. Eve Mitleton-Kelly, "Organisation as Co-evolving Complex Adaptive Systems" (lecture, British Academy of Management Conference, September 8–12, 1997, London, UK).

30. Kay Milton, "Ecologies: Anthropology, Culture, and the Environment," *International Social Science Journal* 49, no. 154 (1997): 494; de Sousa Santos, "Beyond Abyssal Thinking," 67.

31. De Sousa Santos, "Beyond Abyssal Thinking," 69; de Sousa Santos, "A Non-Occidentalist West?," 117; Boaventura de Sousa Santos, *Epistemologies of the South: Justice against Epistemicide* (New York: Routledge, 2016), 13.

32. Star, "Introduction," in *Ecologies of Knowledge*, 27; Moraes and de Almeida Freire, "The University Curriculum," 52.

33. Milton, "Ecologies: Anthropology, Culture, and the Environment," 494; de Sousa Santos, "Beyond Abyssal Thinking," 72.

34. de Sousa Santos, "Beyond Abyssal Thinking," 73.

35. Sander Bais, *In Praise of Science: Curiosity, Understanding, and Progress* (Cambridge, Mass.: MIT Press, 2010); Philip Ball, *Curiosity: How Science Became Interested in Everything* (Chicago: University of Chicago Press, 2012); Roger Wagner, *The Penultimate Curiosity: How Science Swims in the Slipstream of Ultimate Questions* (Oxford: Oxford University Press, 2016).

36. Ball, *Curiosity*, vii.

37. See, for example, Daniel Gade, *Curiosity, Inquiry, and the Geographical Imagination* (New York: Peter Lang, 2011).

38. Zacher, *Curiosity and Pilgrimage*.

39. Justin Stagl, *A History of Curiosity: The Theory of Travel, 1550–1800* (Poststrasse, Sw.: Harwood Academic, 1995).

40. Nigel Leask, *Curiosity and the Aesthetics of Travel Writing, 1770–1840* (Oxford: Oxford University Press, 2002).

41. Krzysztof Pomian, *Collectors and Curiosities: Paris and Venice, 1500–1800* (Cambridge, U.K.: Polity Press, 1990).

42. John Considine, *Small Dictionaries and Curiosity: Lexicography and Fieldwork in Post-Medieval Europe* (Oxford: Oxford University Press, 2017).

43. Marjorie Swann, *Curiosities and Texts: The Culture of Collecting in Early Modern Europe* (Philadelphia: University of Pennsylvania Press, 2001).

44. David L. Martin, *Curious Visions of Modernity: Enchantment, Magic, and the Sacred* (Cambridge, Mass.: MIT Press, 2011).

45. Roger Shattuck, *Forbidden Knowledge: From Prometheus to Pornography* (New York: Harcourt, 1996).

46. See, for example, Arjun Shankar and Mariam Durrani, "Curiosity and Education: A White Paper" (Center for Curiosity, New York, 2013), accessed July 27, 2018. http://centerforcuriosity.com/wp-content/uploads/bsk-pdf-manager/WhitePaper-CuriosityandEducation__2.pdf.

47. William James, *Talks to Teachers on Psychology and to Students on Some of Life's Ideals* (1899; New York: Dover, 2001), 24; cf. Ross Posnock, *The Trial of Curiosity: Henry James, William James, and the Challenge of Modernity* (Oxford: Oxford University Press, 1991).

48. John Dewey, *How We Think* (New York: Dover, 1997), 31.

49. Daniel Berlyne, *Conflict, Arousal, and Curiosity* (New York: McGraw-Hill, 1960); Harry Fowler, *Curiosity and Exploratory Behavior* (New York: Macmillan, 1965); George Lowenstein, "The Psychology of Curiosity: A Review and Reinterpretation," *Psychological Bulletin* 116 (1994): 75–98; Charles Spielberger and Laura Starr, "Curiosity and Exploratory Behavior," in *Motivation: Theory and Research*, ed. Harold O'Neal Jr. and Michael Drillings (New York: Routledge, 2009), 221–44; Celeste Kidd and Benjamin Y. Hayden, "The Psychology of Neuroscience," *Neuron* 88, no. 3 (2015): 449–60.

50. See, for example, Hasida Ben-Zurn and Moshe Zeidner, "Sex Differences in Anxiety, Curiosity, and Anger: A Cross-Cultural Study," *Sex Roles* 19, nos. 5–6 (1988): 335–46; Ruth A. Peters, "Effects of Anxiety, Curiosity, and Perceived Instructor Threat on Student Verbal Behavior in the College Classroom," *Journal of Educational Psychology* 70, no. 3 (1978): 388–95.

51. Susan Engel, *The Hungry Mind: The Origins of Curiosity in Childhood* (Cambridge, Mass.: Harvard University Press, 2015); Todd Kashdan et al., "The Five-Dimensional Curiosity Scale: Capturing the Bandwidth of Curiosity and Identifying Four Unique Subgroups of Curious People," *Journal of Research in Personality* 73 (2018): 130–49.

52. Paulo Freire, *Pedagogy of Freedom: Ethics, Democracy, and Civic Courage* (New York: Rowman and Littlefield, 2001), 37, 69. See also the commentary by Tyson Lewis, *The Aesthetics of Education: Theatre, Curiosity, and Politics in the Work of Jacques Rancière and Paulo Freire* (London: Bloomsbury, 2012).

53. See, for example, Arjun Shankar, "Listening to Images, Participatory Pedagogy, and Anthropological (Re-)Inventions," *American Anthropologist* 121, no. 1 (2019): 229–42.

54. Leask, *Curiosity*; Martin, *Curious Visions of Modernity*.

55. Barbara Benedict, *Curiosity: A Cultural History of Early Modern Inquiry* (Chicago: University of Chicago Press, 2001), chapter 3; Neil Kenny, *The Use of Curiosity in Early Modern France and Germany* (Oxford: Oxford University Press, 2004), parts 4 and 5; Cottegnies, Parageau, and Thompson, *Women and Curiosity*.

56. Hilary Schor, *Curious Subjects: Women and the Trials of Realism* (Oxford: Oxford University Press, 2013).

57. Laura Mulvey, "Pandora's Box: Topographies of Curiosity," in *Fetishism and Curiosity* (Bloomington: Indiana University Press, 1996), 53–64; Cynthia Enloe, *The Curious Feminist: Searching for Women in a New Age of Empire* (Berkeley: University of California Press, 2004).

58. Rosemarie Garland-Thomson, *Staring: How We Look* (Oxford: Oxford University Press, 2009).

59. Narendra Keval, *Racist States of Mind: Understanding the Perversion of Curiosity and Concern* (London: Karnac, 2016).

60. Friedrich Nietzsche, *Human, All Too Human*, trans. R. J. Hollingdale (1878, Cambridge: Cambridge University Press, 1996), preface to part 1, §3.

61. For an unsustainable distinction between a masculine, adventurous curiosity and a feminine, disobedient curiosity, see Victoria Reid, *André Gide and Curiosity* (New York: Rodopi, 2009).

62. Michel Foucault, "The Masked Philosopher," in *Ethics, Subjectivity, Truth* (1980; New York: New Press, 1997), 325.

63. Perry Zurn, "The Curiosity at Work in Deconstruction," *Journal of French and Francophone Philosophy* 26, no. 1 (2018): 65–87.

64. Perry Zurn, "Curiosities at War: The Police and Prison Resistance after May '68," *Modern and Contemporary France* 26, no. 2 (2018): 179–91.

65. Helga Nowotny, *Insatiable Curiosity: Innovation in a Fragile Future*, trans. Mitch Cohen (Cambridge, Mass.: MIT Press, 2008).

66. Anna Tsing, *The Mushroom at the End of the World: On the Possibility of Life in Capitalist Ruins* (Princeton, N.J.: Princeton University Press, 2015), 144, 281.

67. Tsing, 2.

68. This might include Kunimasa Sato, "Socratic Examplars: Considering the Traditional Japanese Idea of Exemplars in Learning," in *The Moral Psychology of Curiosity*, ed. Inan et al.; Ian James Kidd, "Asking the Right Questions? Confucian Curiosity and Moral Self-Cultivation," in *The Moral Psychology of Curiosity*, ed. Inan et al.; and Rāmapratāpa Vedālankāra, *Camatkāravicāracarcā* (Hośyārapuram, Pañjāba:

Viśveśvarānanda-Vaidika-Śodha-Samsthānam, 2004), a text on the concept of curiosity in Sanskrit poems.

69. Pierre-Yves Oudeyer, Jacqueline Gottlieb, and Manuel Lopes, "Intrinsic Motivation, Curiosity, and Learning: Theory and Applications in Educational Technologies," *Progress in Brain Research* 229 (2016): 257–84.

70. See, for example, Tanya Luhrmann's "Spiritual Curiosity and the Experience of God," Templeton Grant, https://www.templeton.org/grant/spiritual-curiosity-and-the-experience-of-god.

PART I

Interrogating the Scientific Enterprise

1

Exploring the Costs
of Curiosity

An Environmental Scientist's Dilemma

Seeta Sistla

Set in a New England forest among the dying stands of eastern hemlock *(Tsuga canadensis),* the large glass reagent bottles filled with moss, soil, water, and bits of the plant debris stood perched on a stand made of salvaged wood. It is doubtful that any previous user of the bottles would have envisioned their most recent fate. The bottles, once the repository of research reagents, had undertaken a new livelihood as the home for an ecosystem in miniature on the brink of collapse. They were now part of an exhibit blending artistic interventions with the findings of scores of environmental scientists showing that the hemlock, a long-lived foundation evergreen tree of the eastern United States, is rapidly disappearing under the combined pressures of the tiny hemlock woolly adelgid *(Adelges tsugae)* insect, which was accidentally introduced from Asia in the 1950s, and ever-warming winters that no longer suppress the insect's population.

The artist—a visiting scholar to the research forest hosting the exhibit—identified both the enormity of scientific research available on this landscape under change, as well as the wealth of discarded or forgotten scientific materials available for his reenvisioning. The artistic creations told the story not only of a forest "in hospice" but also of the tools and techniques scientists have used to study it and surrounding ecosystems. In their construction and placement, the pieces inevitably also commented on the scientific debris of these research projects: from roads and power lines (infrastructure built to access sites of particular scientific interest), to flagging tape markers, tubes, plastic peeping through the leaf litter, and instrumentation left behind with intent or in error during the rush to complete experiments. Or perhaps simply forgotten bits of experimental remains as scientists joined and left projects that outlived the abrupt project stints that now define many research careers.

Who knows? I pondered the familiarity of ecological experimental designs gone astray in this unusual artistic enterprise. But the day passed and I returned to my own work as an ecosystem ecologist at a nearby college. And thoughts of eco-trash grew distant as the daily concerns of my own scientific agenda resurfaced. Months later, an offhanded remark from a PhD student whose research also centered on samples derived from this forest pushed me to further reflect on this uncomfortable question. *"I'm not excited about the new position because I will not fly. . . . And traveling to the East Coast by train will take over three days."* Assuming the student and I shared an apprehension of flying, I responded in kind, only to be told it was neither fear nor the long wait times that detracted her, but rather the extraordinary environmental footprint that air travel necessarily entails.

Her sentiment surprised me. As an environmental scientist, it is rare to hear a remark on the ecological cost of the research livelihood. In this age of increasing environmental urgency, a tension has grown between the pressure to produce high-quality, informative data that uses novel methods and experimental manipulations while also developing and executing ethical frameworks for ecological research. But why am I able to remain a passive participant in this process? Is this environmental cost a necessary price to pay for satisfying scientific curiosity?

Curiosity is foundational to science. Scientific curiosity, characterized by information-seeking specific behaviors, is recognized to be distinct from "common curiosity," which reflects the excitement (or irritation) that is stirred by novelty.[1] Scientific curiosity drives us to mechanistically understand the world through the construction and testing of falsifiable theories via systematic and repeatable observation, measurement, and experimentation.[2] While scientific curiosity is arguably an innate component of the human condition, the twentieth century is hallmarked by the growth of professional scientists.[3] This expansion in scientific resources and researchers has paralleled exceptional rates of technological advancement and growth in our fundamental understanding of the natural world. It is unlikely that even the most insightful scientists and futurists of the early twentieth century would have even remotely foreshadowed the massive expansions across all fields of

Exploring the Costs of Curiosity 5

science and technology. In less than a century, the collective scientific endeavor has yielded incredible insights and developments ranging from the discovery of the structure of DNA, to the internet, to fundamental shifts in our understanding of the physical processes that govern the universe.[4]

Intriguingly, despite the tremendous growth in the scientific community and the financial investment in research, the early twentieth-century explosion of "big scientific ideas"—innovations that fundamentally shifted our understanding of the natural world—appears to be decelerating.[5] This shift is reflective of increasing recognition that the development of formal institutions and scientific bureaucratization is a double-edged sword. On one side, the expansion beyond the elite to fully immerse oneself in scientific research has resulted in a democratization of the scientific process and accelerated the rate of scientific discovery. On the other hand, the growth of the scientific enterprise drives an industrialization of knowledge production that creates a milieu of resource competition among an ever-expanding population of scientists. As the scientific workforce continues to grow more quickly than the stable job pool for the professional scientist of the twenty-first century, researchers are often valued through the length of their publication list and proposals funded, at a cost of time allocated toward reflection, quality control, and scientific risk-taking.[6]

Thus, to obtain and maintain one's position within a professionalized community, scientists face mounting pressure to consistently publish novel research and secure funding through highly bureaucratic schemes.[7] As such, the modern scientific enterprise is now shaped by a surplus population of scientists who work not only to satisfy their scientific curiosity but also under the pressure of sustained competition. If the professionalization of science repurposes scientific curiosity away from creative exploration, what are the costs of this retooling? Across the sciences, the rise of "groupthink" behavior, the increasing need for scientific self-promotion, and a stymieing of "risky" research that pushes forward radically new directions in lieu of incremental (but publishable) additions to the core knowledge base is a noted cost of twenty-first-century science.[8]

Beyond the cost to creativity, what are the additional costs of this intersection between scientific curiosity and scientific professionalization? The accelerated growth of the scientific enterprise has also expanded the potential to experiment. From characterization of microbial genetic material in plastic test tubes, to travel to field sites and conferences, to extensive manipulations of ecosystems designed to test the implications of invasive species and climate warming, scientists can manipulate, document, and alter the natural world to an unprecedented extent and rate. When scientists are pressed to accelerate the production of novel, publishable data sets using cutting-edge techniques and experimentation, is there also a more subtle but pernicious rise in the resource use entwined in carrying out these studies?

History is rife with ethical questions that challenge the methods and justifications for scientific inquiry. In particular, where human and animal subjects are concerned, the risk of harm has guided the development of review boards and guidelines for experimentations and scientific conduct.[9] Iconic examples extend across an array of subjects centered in the biomedical and social sciences: from moral questions regarding research conducted on unknowing subjects to debates over the development of technologies such as nuclear power and weapons, genetic modification of organisms, cloning, and stem cells.

While ethical quandaries are an inherent facet (either explicitly or implicitly) of scientific investigation, post–World War II revelations spurred an era of ethical conduct codification and governmental regulation of research practices. Public disclosure of research atrocities, including experiments committed by Nazi doctors on nonconsenting prisoners, the U.S. Public Health Service's syphilis study on low-income African American males who were unknowingly infected with syphilis and monitored for four decades while treatment was withheld, and the widespread prescribing of teratogen thalidomide for pregnancy-related nausea in the 1950s and 1960s spurred a sea change in the limits on scientific curiosity.[10] Responding to these concerns, a suite of research ethics fields (e.g., biological, medical, technological) and governance structures (e.g., institutional review boards, mandated training and monitoring for science students and researchers in responsible research conduct) have emerged to address the moral issues entwined in experimental conduct and technologies development.[11]

These ethical fields and frameworks have helped to guide and limit the extent of experimentation—in essence, putting a constraint on scientific curiosity in its modern incarnations. Notably, the subject of concern in these ethical paradigms is most often human and, to a lesser extent, nonhuman animals. While the biomedical and social sciences are hallmarked for their connection to ethics, environmental research poses challenging and diverse ethical quandaries ranging from public welfare to the well-being of nonhuman organisms, communities, and ecosystems. Further, although many countries have enacted legislation and institutional-review processes to minimize harm to animals in laboratory and field research, these protocols and norms vary by regulating body, species, and country.[12] These requirements tend to focus on vertebrates and other charismatic species,[13] but rarely require researchers to consider impacts on other species, biological communities, or ecosystems.

The field of environmental ethics, which largely focuses on the philosophical and ethical justification for species conservation and recovery, as well as the preservation of ecosystems,[14] has added to our conceptualization of the valuation of nature. Yet the ethical concerns of environmental scientists remain seldom recognized within and outside of the field.[15] Paralleling the rapid rise of the environmental sciences, ecological ethics has emerged as a framework to address this deficit. Drawing from environmental ethics, research ethics, and professional ethics, ecological ethics provides a potential structure for environmental scientists to pragmatically identify ethical issues, weigh ethical considerations, and improve ethical decision-making in the design and conduct of ecological-research and conservation-management agendas.[16]

In recent years, a small, but growing number of researchers have recognized cases that highlight the typically overlooked costs of environmental science research.[17] At the species-level, these scholars have pointed to the unintended consequences of collecting fauna and flora. There is a long history of collecting organisms as curiosities for food, amusement, and scientific investigation that has fundamentally shaped our understanding of global biodiversity.[18] However, the scientific practice of cataloging the natural world into "voucher specimens" (and even human intrusion through observation alone) may also have deleterious effects on fragile populations. Taxa as varied as birds, highly endemic plants, and amphibians have all been further threatened with extinction following the overzealous collection by scientists.[19] In an era of unprecedented threats to entire habitats and ecosystems, some researchers have further questioned the fundamental efficacy of scientific voucher collections.[20]

Scaling up, field studies and ecosystem manipulations can have dramatic and potentially irreversible ecological consequences.[21] Environmental scientists often implement large-scale experiments to identify the effects of abiotic and biotic changes (such as the invasion of the woolly adelgid) on ecosystem-level properties. How does a scientist define and weigh the ethical considerations, for example, of experimentally deforesting an entire watershed?[22] While in situ experimentation is fundamental to the development of modern ecological insights and environmental science more generally, how to meaningfully and systematically identify and weigh the impacts and benefits of environmental science research remains a conceptual and logistical hurdle.

These challenges include determining how to identify whether environmental damage from an experiment would be reversible or not and how to weigh the scale of experimentation footprint relative to the possible return of, for example, a new conception of ecosystem or organismal function, or the development of better-informed regulations on development. How much and what kinds of data are necessary, and how will this information be incorporated into the broader scientific community's knowledge base? Even data themselves can become a cost. If the integrity of the data is not maintained, if data are not interpreted and published, if changing data interpretation and publication norms mean that new media and new statistical techniques make early interpretations obsolete, what is the future of that information (let alone the true cost of its production)? Scientific continuity falters under a weight of data. How much of modern science is the reemergence of old studies and questions in new experiments, subdisciplines, and journals?[23]

Despite these myriad considerations, the prevalence of environmental costs carried by research arguably could be at least partly mitigated through more thoughtfully scrutinized experimental design, implementation, and dissemination paradigms. Yet the incorporation of an ecological ethics framework into the environmental scientist's toolkit remains a rarity. Again, I find myself asking, "Why?"

I am an environmental scientist of the twenty-first century. Thus I am a scientist studying the natural world in an era of unprecedented environmental change, where the distinction between "human" and "natural" processes has become increasingly challenging to identify. While early natural scientists may have been wholly concerned with identifying these laws in their most innate form, the exponential growth of the human footprint upon the environment has yielded no natural system untouched by human influence. Reflecting this era of unprecedented environmental change shaped by extraordinary pollutant levels, climate change, biodiversity loss, and the reshaping of ecosystems globally through human use, the natural sciences have grown multiple fields centered on understanding environmental systems and their responses to these massive perturbations.

My own curiosity to understand the mechanisms that drive the natural world has been inevitably shaped by the anthropogenic forces that ripple through every aspect of the Earth system. As an ecologist, many studies I have learned from and worked with involve a brute force approach to understanding the mechanisms of the natural world and their response to anthropogenic global-change pressures. Over a decade ago, in the forest where art pieces now stand, scientists tested the ecosystem effects of slowly dying, adelgid-infested hemlocks by girdling one living stand—that is, severing its vascular system—while preemptively clear-cutting a neighboring stand.[24] Curious about the inevitable, can we gain knowledge that will inform our governance of the land? And does this knowledge justify a preemptive strike to eradicate a forest stand?

As my own scientific career has progressed, I have become less certain of the answer. Ethical conduct in environmental science is complicated by both its philosophical and practical contexts. The incidental costs of research do not present a paradigmatic moral problem. They lack the framework whereby one actor intentionally harms another, both the actors and the harm are clearly identifiable, and there is a close spatial and temporal coupling of the agent and recipient of harm, as well as the harmful act in itself.[25] This decoupling, combined with the growth of groupthink and group norms for research conduct, allows for a passive neglect of the harms researchers might inadvertently create through their activities. In contrast to the research reforms of the twentieth century that were marked by concern for human welfare, the cost of scientific curiosity is thus difficult for the actor—the scientist—to identify in part because of its morally opaque nature.

While still sparsely found among the multitude of publications lamenting the challenges faced by environmental scientists and other researchers in an era of academic contraction and declining research funding, others have pinpointed the tension between embodying environmental stewardship and the professional obligations of an environmental researcher. After calculating that the American Geophysical Union's Fall Meeting—the world's largest annual international gathering of Earth and space scientists—accounted for five millionths of total global anthropogenic emissions from fossil fuels in 2012, an emerita professor of paleoclimatology boldly argued that the social and scientific connections gained from this event did not justify its environmental costs.[26] In critiquing what she assessed to be a disproportionate carbon footprint of such large and travel-intensive scientific meetings, Parrish also suggested that scientific bodies must rapidly reshape the nature of their meetings to reduce carbon-intensive travel by embracing technologies that support remote meeting platforms. Reflecting on the teachings of Rabbi Hillel the Elder, this senior scientist provocatively asked her community: "If not us, who? If not now, when?"[27]

Such observations are not limited to dialogue between members of the scientific community in specialty journals. When the *Washington Post* reported in 2016 that, for the third consecutive year, annual fossil fuel emissions had not grown, the phenomenon was showcased as an environmental success story reflecting the data analysis of "a massive study . . . written by no less than 67 researchers from an army of institutions."[28] Readers of the article posted a variety of comments about the findings and the climate science enterprise more generally, of which a particular string caught my attention.

I read that there are thousands upon thousands of people who jetted into Marrakesh to attend the climate conference. These are all people who get taxpayer-funded grants to live on while they study the climate and jet around the world to attend conferences. Makes me all warm inside to know this. —rand49er

It's like having a friend come to you and say that getting fake tans from tanning beds causes skin cancer. You remark that he looks awfully tan, and he says, "[Y]es, that's because I use a tanning bed." You say, "But I thought you just said that tanning beds cause cancer." "Yep, they do—it's known science. Well, I'm off to the tanning bed!" I would doubt the tanning beds really cause cancer. Likewise, I'll start [to] believe that burning fossil fuels are dooming the planet when the people who swear that burning carbon fuels are dooming the planet start ACTING like burning fossil fuels are dooming the planet. —mackbuckets

These are false analogies used to make a specious argument. That is, no one would use a tanning bed as a way of working to reduce the use of tanning beds. The current transportation system depends upon fossil fuels and we must use that system to try to carry out the mission of bringing change, which includes meeting in person to share and develop information and build relationships

Exploring the Costs of Curiosity

that improve our understanding of the risks, the chances of reducing emissions, and our abilities to mitigate impacts. —FungibleTruth

As a scientist who travels for meetings and research campaigns, my initial instincts (perhaps for personal preservation) drew me to agree with FungibleTruth. Yet the comments of mackbuckets and rand49er are not so easily brushed aside. The fundamental question remains: How might we ensure that the environmental costs of scientific endeavors yield a net ecological benefit without compromising scientific curiosity (and professional advancement)? In order to be more readily accepted by the public and better aligned with our collective understanding of the anthropogenic nature of modern environmental change, this tension of seeming hypocrisy that is alluded to in the *Washington Post* article comments demands careful consideration and honest discussion from within the environmental science community. But are we ready to have this conversation?

Responding to the recent call by Jane Lubchenco, former administrator of the National Oceanic and Atmospheric Agency, for environmental scientists to "make a quantum leap into relevance,"[29] a group of four firmly established environmental scientists wrote an opinion piece in *The Chronicle of Higher Education* stressing that junior researchers must rediscover their scientific curiosity.[30] These scholars recognized the misalignment of academic vetting with the pursuit of scientific curiosity and ultimately, the ability of scientists to make the quantum leaps that our rapidly changing biosphere demands. They suggest building a scientific career around the pursuit for sustained discovery coupled with intellectual fulfillment and societal influence, but they also recognize that the success of this imperative rests upon a restructuring of the current metrics of scientific success. A lofty call to action. What will be the cost of inaction?

I have come to reflect upon my own research decisions as inevitably shaped by the scientific paradigms and norms within which I have developed. My scientific curiosity is also governed by the professionalization of the scientific enterprise. As such, I am challenged to conceive novel research questions, employ innovative methodologies, produce data sets, publish peer-reviewed articles, and disseminate my findings while building and retaining my professional networks largely through air travel. Most recently, I find myself weighing a field season in the Arctic and the travel for various meetings that looms ahead. To go opens up the potential for new discoveries, a strengthening of my scientific network, and the growth of intellectual capital. To stay suggests that the environmental costs of travel, field, and laboratory work may not justify these benefits.

Working within this context, even if a strong ethical framework for environmental science can be identified, is self-regulation of scientific conduct reasonable to expect in an era of hypercompetitive and individualistic professional science? Should, for example, one be more conservative in their travel for field research and meetings? And what would be the cost of such a decision for fulfilling one's scientific curiosity and activities? Fundamentally, can actions that come at a high cost to scientific curiosity be separated from those that come at a high cost to the professional demands of the modern scientific enterprise?

Notes

1. Jaimie Jirout and David Klahr, "Children's Scientific Curiosity: In Search of an Operational Definition of an Elusive Concept," *Developmental Review* 32, no. 2 (2012): 125–60, https://doi.org/10.1016/j.dr.2012.04.002.

2. Stephen E. Toulmin, "The Evolutionary Development of Natural Science," *American Scientist* 55, no. 4 (1967): 456–71, https://www.jstor.org/stable/27837039.

3. Giovanni Frazzetto, "The Changing Identity of the Scientist," *EMBO Reports* 5, no. 1 (2004): 16–18, https://doi.org/10.1038/sj.embor.7400063; Peder Olesen Larsen and Markus von Ins, "The Rate of Growth in Scientific Publication and the Decline in Coverage Provided by Science Citation Index," *Scientometrics,* 84, no. 3 (2010): 575–603, https://doi.org/10.1007/s11192-010-0202-z.

4. Frazzetto, "Changing Identity"; Donald Geman and Stuart Geman, "Opinion: Science in the Age of Selfies," *Proceedings of the National Academy of Sciences* 113, no. 34 (2016): 9384–87, https://doi.org/10.1073/pnas.1609793113.

5. Geman and Geman, "Opinion."

6. Geman and Geman.

7. Frazzetto, "Changing Identity"; Peter A. Lawrence, "The Mismeasurement of Science," *Current Biology* 17, no. 15 (2007): R583–R585, https://doi.org/10.1016/j.cub.2007.06.014.

8. Geman and Geman, "Opinion"; Larsen and von Ins, "Rate of Growth."

9. Barry Bozeman and Paul Hirsch, "Science Ethics as a Bureaucratic Problem: IRBs, Rules, and Failures of Control," *Policy Sciences* 38, no. 4 (2005): 269–91, https://doi.org/10.1007/s11077-006-9010-y.

10. Bozeman and Hirsch.

11. Kirsten M. Parris et al., "Assessing Ethical Trade-Offs in Ecological Field Studies," *Journal of Applied Ecology* 47, no. 1 (2010): 227–34, https://doi.org/10.1111/j.1365-2664.2009.01755.x.

Exploring the Costs of Curiosity

12. Mark J. Costello et al., "Field Work Ethics in Biological Research," *Biological Conservation* 203 (2016): 268–71, https://doi.org/10.1016/j.biocon.2016.10.008.

13. Ioan Fazey, Joern Fischer, and David B. Lindenmayer, "What Do Conservation Biologists Publish?" *Biological Conservation* 124, no. 1 (2005): 63–73, http://doi.org/10.1016/j.biocon.2005.01.013.

14. Parris et al., "Assessing Ethical Trade-Offs."

15. Ben A. Minteer and James P. Collins, "Ecological Ethics: Building a New Tool Kit for Ecologists and Biodiversity Managers," *Conservation Biology* 19, no. 6 (2005): 1803–12, https://doi.org/10.1111/j.1523-1739.2005.00281.x; Parris et al., "Assessing Ethical Trade-Offs."

16. G. K. D. Crozier and Albrecht I. Schulte-Hostedde, "Towards Improving the Ethics of Ecological Research," *Science and Engineering Ethics* 21, no. 3 (2015): 577–94, https://doi.org/10.1007/s11948-014-9558-4; Ben A. Minteer and James P. Collins, "Why We Need an 'Ecological Ethics,'" *Frontiers in Ecology and the Environment* 3, no. 6 (2005): 332–37.

17. Costello et al., "Field Work Ethics"; Crozier and Schulte-Hostedde, "Ethics of Ecological Research;" Elizabeth J. Farnsworth and Judy Rosovsky, "The Ethics of Ecological Field Experimentation," *Conservation Biology* 7, no. 3 (1993): 463–72; https://doi.org/10.1046/j.1523-1739.1993.07030463.x; Minteer and Collins, "'Ecological Ethics'"; Ben A. Minteer and James P. Collins, "From Environmental to Ecological Ethics: Toward a Practical Ethics for Ecologists and Conservationists," *Science and Engineering Ethics* 14, no. 4 (2008): 483–501, https://doi.org/10.1007/s11948-008-9087-0.

18. Farnsworth and Rosovsky, "Ethics."

19. Farnsworth and Rosovsky; Ben A. Minteer et al., "Avoiding (Re)extinction," *Science* 344, no. 6181 (2014): 260–61, https://doi.org/10.1126/science.1250953.

20. Jared M. Diamond, "Justifiable Killing of Birds?" *Nature* 330, no. 6147 (1987): 423–23, https://doi.org/10.1038/330423a0.

21. Farnsworth and Rosovsky, "Ethics."

22. Gene E. Likens et al., "Effects of Forest Cutting and Herbicide Treatment on Nutrient Budgets in the Hubbard Brook Watershed-Ecosystem," *Ecological Monographs* 40, no. 1 (1970): 23–47, https://doi.org/10.2307/1942440.

23. Aaron M. Ellison, "Decomposition and Memory," in *Forest under Story: Creative Inquiry in an Old-Growth Forest,* ed. Nathaniel Brodie, Charles Goodrich, and Frederick J. Swanson, 77–83 (Seattle: University of Washington Press, 2016).

24. Aaron M. Ellison et al., "Experimentally Testing the Role of Foundation Species in Forests: The Harvard Forest Hemlock Removal Experiment," *Methods in Ecology and Evolution* 1, no. 2 (2010): 168–79, https://doi.org/10.1111/j.2041-210X.2010.00025.x.

25. Dale Jamieson, "The Moral and Political Challenges of Climate Change," in *Creating a Climate for Change: Communicating Climate Change and Facilitating Social Change,* ed. Susanne Moser and Lisa Dilling, 475–82 (Cambridge: Cambridge University Press, 2008).

26. Judith Totman Parrish, "Should AGU Have Fly-In Meetings Anymore?" *Eos* 98 (2017). https://doi.org/10.1029/2017EO089361.

27. Parrish.

28. Chris Mooney, "Stunningly Good News for the Planet: Carbon Emissions Were Flat for the Third Straight Year," *Washington Post,* November 13, 2013.

29. Jane Lubchenco, "Environmental Science in a Post-truth World," *Frontiers in Ecology and the Environment* 15, no. 1 (2017): 3, https://doi.org/10.1002/fee.1454.

30. Emily S. Bernhardt et al., "Rethinking the Scientific Career," *Chronicle of Higher Education,* October 3, 2017.

2

Curious Ecologies of Knowledge

More-Than-Human Anthropology

Heather Anne Swanson

How is one to be a curious anthropologist in a more-than-human world? Anthropology has long defined itself as the study of human lifeways. Yet in the past two decades, new conversations within the discipline—particularly in relation to the Anthropocene and multispecies anthropology—have raised questions and frictions about the scope, modes, and objects of anthropological curiosity. The goal of this chapter is to explore the tensions that manifest when anthropologists seek to be more curious about nonhuman worlds and environmental concerns while simultaneously holding on to existing disciplinary commitments. How, within renewed dialogues between anthropology and the natural sciences, do anthropologists find themselves pulled into new intradisciplinary debates over the shape, possibilities, and limits of anthropological curiosity?

As a discipline, anthropology is closely tied to its ethnographic field methods, which fundamentally depend on the participation of others in the research process. Anthropological inquiry is typically not a process of formal hypothesis testing. While anthropologists begin a research project with ideas, goals, and questions, they assume that the trajectory of their research—and indeed their fundamental interests—will be substantially shaped by their field encounters. This approach to fieldwork and anthropological knowledge-making hinges on flexible forms of curiosity that aim less to answer predefined research questions than to foster new ones. In short, in good fieldwork, one must open oneself to the curiosities of others and allow them to alter one's own. But how can this imperative to be responsive

16 Heather Anne Swanson

to others' curiosities be enacted within anthropological inquiries that engage more-than-human worlds? Is it possible to be curious about organisms, such as animals, plants, and fungi, in a specifically anthropological mode?

Unexpected *Intradisciplinary* Differences

These are questions that emerged within a collaborative, interdisciplinary field research project at a former brown coal mining site in western Denmark, in which the author was a participant. The field project is a central component of a larger research effort called Aarhus University Research on the Anthropocene (AURA), headed by anthropologist Anna Tsing.[1] One of AURA's ambitions has been to experiment with new knowledge-making practices for the Anthropocene.[2] The group's premise is that the Anthropocene, a term used here to draw attention to the proliferation of environmental damage, calls out for new interdisciplinary modes of inquiry—and for new curiosities. AURA specifically selected an abandoned brown coal mining landscape as our central analytical unit in order to explore how humans and non-humans inhabit industrial ruins. The project asserted that the insights of social and natural scientists are jointly needed to understand the more-than-human relations in such sites, as well as to develop better practices for living on a damaged planet.[3] One of its goals was to publish joint articles in which natural- and social-scientist coauthors worked together to ask and address questions in ways not possible from a single field—a goal partially realized via a special issue on the brown coal mining project in the *Journal of Ethnobiology*.[4]

Such cross-disciplinary collaborations have a history of difficulties, often foundering on debates about scientific objectivity, reality, and knowledge-making. Thus, rather than seek epistemological consensus from the get-go, the AURA project proposed that interdisciplinary collaboration might best begin from natural and social scientists' *overlapping curiosities* about lively multispecies worlds. As part of this project, its anthropologists (including the author) conducted fieldwork alongside and in dialogue with a number of natural scientists from fields such as ecology, zoology, and mycology. Our team's approach is a self-declared "rubber boots method," a kind of "slow science"[5] where we meet *in* the field and discuss *what* we notice when conducting fieldwork. The project predicted that anthropologists and biologists would see different things when they engaged in what Tsing calls "the arts of noticing"—the situated and sensuous acts of observing, taking notes, drawing, and discussing as we repeatedly walk the site together.[6] The phrase "rubber boots," coined by project member Bubandt, signaled that our goal was to get curious by getting into the dirt and mud of the field.[7] By discussing their different field observations, our diverse team members would stretch and expand each other's curiosities. By relying on joint, exploratory fieldwork rather than discussions about already conceptualized research endeavors, we hoped to spark new forms of enthusiasm along with novel research questions, objects, and approaches.

The project sought to draw on what some of its members saw as the similar field sensibilities of anthropology and natural history. Both practices center embodied modes of noticing and description and favor the slow emergence of more focused questions from the observation of patterns. At some level, we expected a certain degree of methodological tension between our team's anthropologists and biologists. While all of our biologists were curious natural historians, they were accustomed to a scholarly world that favors more rigid experimental design over more open-ended observation. What caught us off guard, however, were the frictions that emerged *among the project's anthropologists*. While all of the anthropologists agreed on the *importance* of curiosity as a fundamental disciplinary value, we diverged on *which* curiosities to cultivate and *how* to do so. AURA anthropologists were collectively excited to see how they might work together with natural scientists to explore the lives of nonhumans within anthropogenic, or human-disturbed, landscapes. For too long, they agreed, anthropologists have completely ignored how being human is a multispecies relationship.[8] How might attention to such nonhuman relations help anthropologists better understand the ecological worlds of which people are a part and on which they depend?

Yet some of the AURA anthropologists were concerned about the modes of anthropological practice and fieldwork curiosity that seemed to unfold from our intense focus on collaboration with natural scientists, experimentation with natural history observation, and the ways that our conversations about tree roots and fungi made these entities seem rather similar to the objects of standard biological research. Were we just aligning our curiosities and categories with those of natural scientists? Were we ignoring the anthropological imperative to be responsive to the curiosities of those we encountered in the field? It seemed irresponsible, they argued, to consider scientists as collaborators while positioning local people primarily as data providers. It felt antithetical to anthropological practice to seek to satisfy one's own interests. Doesn't anthropology call for more responsive and dialogic forms of curiosity?

This chapter aims to explore these substantial, yet respectful, disagreements within the AURA group. It argues that they at once show us the heterogeneity of anthropological curiosities and illustrate the tensions among them within the growing field of more-than-human scholarship. The chapter begins by outlining some of the anthropological histories of different modes of curiosity. It then returns to the brown coal mining site in more depth to trace the conflicting curiosities that manifested in our field encounters with a mushroom. The methodological challenges of multispecies work that it describes demand what Haraway has called "staying with the trouble"[9]—an approach that acknowledges different sets of compelling, embodied commitments that "require action and respect without resolution."[10] Overall, this chapter does not present settled positions on how to be curious but highlights a few of the challenges of more-than-human curiosity in the humanities and social sciences that leave many scholars—including the author and other AURA members—with ongoing and unresolvable uncertainties. It is important for me to note that, while I often use the term "we" in this chapter to indicate the collective work from which it emerged, the descriptions and interpretations in this chapter reflect my particular (and perhaps even idiosyncratic) understandings of AURA events rather than a shared group narrative. While my accounts are overly simplistic and fail to capture the full range of AURA concerns, I nonetheless hope they might offer a prompt for further conversations.

Questioning Anthropological Curiosities

In themselves, debates about *how to be curious as an anthropologist* are nothing new. Anthropology has been simultaneously characterized by celebration of the expansive nature of the discipline's curiosities and intense disagreements about their politics and limits. The imperative to pay attention to *everything* human is rooted in the origins of the discipline. Consider, for example, the classic village study that structured much nineteenth- and twentieth-century anthropological practice. Because village studies demanded that scholars collect a wide range of information about topics as diverse as demography, gender, childrearing, labor, exchange, agriculture, hunting, and spiritual practices, anthropologists were trained to be "expert generalists" with broad curiosities—researchers holistically interested in all aspects of a given community's way of life. In this sense, expansive curiosity has long been a core methodological stance for the discipline.

Yet despite its importance in fieldwork practice, curiosity as such remains curiously unexamined in anthropology. Late twentieth- and twenty-first-century anthropologists have written surprisingly few analytical texts that address curiosity as a theme. Instead, curiosity more often crops up implicitly in methodological texts that stress the importance of being alert to surprises during fieldwork or of the need to collect ethnographic data on topics far beyond one's formal research question. Mentions of curiosity also make their way into hagiographic descriptions of famous anthropologists, where it is celebrated as a key trait for scholars working in the field. One powerful example is a 2002 speech at the centennial anniversary for the Department of Anthropology at the University of California, Berkeley, during which Karl Kroeber described the curiosity of his father and department founder, Alfred Kroeber, at length:

> Once, when I was in the Navy, I visited my parents with a sailor friend, who, when we were back on the bus, asked me, "Is there *anything* your father doesn't get interested in?" I remember from an earlier time when a family of bats took up residence in vines near the front door of our home on Arch Street, Alfred immediately became intrigued with how little he understood bat sexuality and the nurturing of young when upside down. Curiosity, I judge from him, is essentially immediate, a response to the specific: What goes on here? How does *this* work? Curiosity is wonder at a material fact suddenly observed, or about an idea that has just occurred in thought or conversation. Curiosity borders on nosiness because it begins with and never turns away from the physical world in its full sensuousness, even though curiosity expands most fully when penetrating into intellectual activity. True curiosity seeks an explanation for oneself: one satisfies one's own curiosity, not somebody else's. This accounts for its link both to prying into what is none of your damned business and to its childlike innocence.[11]

This description of Kroeber depicts several persistent ideals of anthropological curiosity—an embrace of a childlike wonder, a willingness to be nosy, and a belief that seemingly frivolous inquiries constitute serious intellectual work.

Yet at the same time, a number of anthropologists have worried that such curiosities are largely sanitized versions of deeply colonial desires. The description above depicts an atomized curiosity, rooted in an individual's desire to know. One might call this *curiosity about* (in contrast to *curiosity with*). It is a gaze that has violently objectified others—and one that has been problematically foundational within the history of anthropology. Focused on places outside Euro-America, anthropological curiosities have been inextricably linked to exoticism—to an interest in "primitive others"—and its ethnographic collection practices have produced curio displays designed to titillate European audiences. Like other imperial collecting practices, such as the assembly of plant specimens and the creation of botanical gardens, anthropology sprang from the curiosities of white European men that emerged within their encounters with colonial worlds. These curiosities, often couched in languages of a distant observer contributing to a neutral science, were—of course—far from innocent: they legitimized the measuring of human head shapes for the making of racial typologies and the robbing of graves for the creation of archeological collections. They also provided valuable information about the social organization of non-Western people that directly aided the expansion of colonial powers.[12] While curiosity was portrayed as an innocent drive or a valued technique to unlock and illuminate the wonders of the world, it was clearly anything but.[13] Ethnographic research repeatedly produced so-called objective descriptions of cultures that explained peoples' practices and defined their identities without their participation or consent—and without realizing the anthropologists' and the discipline's own situatedness.

In the late 1980s and 1990s, during the discipline's "crisis of representation," anthropological scholars began to deeply question not only their research and writing practices but also their curiosities and desires.[14] A growing number of anthropologists argued that the kinds of curiosity that Kroeber's son celebrates above were unresponsive to colonial histories and unacceptable within the discipline. Anthropologist Vincent Crapanzano, for example, critiqued the asymmetries produced between ethnographers and "natives" when anthropologists assume that their interests and analyses are somehow more important or more correct than those of their informants. Crapanzano problematized standard anthropological analyses as "a sort of asymmetrical we-relationship with the anthropologist behind and above the native, hidden but at the top of the hierarchy of understanding."[15] When anthropologists' analyses and curiosities determined the descriptions of people and their worlds, they perpetuated colonialist dynamics. Such critiques of anthropological practice foregrounded important questions of *how one might be curious in noncolonial ways.* How could anthropologists engage with often marginalized subjects as coanalysts rather than as objects of study? How could they follow others' interests rather than allow Western scholarship to wholly determine what counts as interesting? Through such questions, anthropologists began to ask how they might move toward more collaborative curiosities, allowing their work to be shaped not only by their own curiosities but also by those of others.

Multispecies Curiosities

The rise of multispecies anthropology has only further complicated such questions about appropriate modes of curiosity within the discipline.[16] This subfield has argued for more attention to nonhumans within the humanities and social sciences as an antidote to these disciplines' alleged blindness to more-than-human worlds. Many multispecies scholars see increased curiosity about more-than-human relationships—among anthropologists as well as Euro-American publics—as a crucial political practice for addressing ongoing wanton extraction and ecological damage. Responsibility toward other beings lies in one's ability to *respond* to them, multispecies scholars have argued—and for this, curiosity is key.

The work of science-studies scholar Donna Haraway has been especially important to this line of thinking. In *When Species Meet,* Haraway puts curiosity about her dog at the center of multispecies practice. In the act of loving and living with her dog Cayenne, Haraway finds herself compelled to ask: "Whom and what do I touch when I touch my dog?"[17] When she does, the simple act of touching her Australian shepherd pulls her not only toward a wide range of curiosities—about dog breeding and genetics, practices of training and cross-species communication, and the forms of Australian settler colonialism that she and her dog jointly inherit—but also toward *a mode of curiosity* in which Haraway allows her inquiries to be fundamentally shaped by her relations with her dog rather than by her "own" interests.

For Haraway, this kind of expansive curiosity must be actively cultivated, especially among humanists and social scientists, who are not accustomed to being interested in more-than-human others. She highlights its centrality via her critique of philosopher Jacques Derrida's *The Animal That Therefore I Am (More to Follow)*.[18] While Derrida begins this lecture on categorical boundaries between human and animal with a description of being naked in his bathroom with his cat, the cat quickly disappears from the lecture as he turns to more abstract musings. Haraway criticizes Derrida for failing to take his cat seriously:

> With his cat, Derrida failed a simple obligation of companion species; he did not become curious about what the cat might actually be doing, feeling, thinking, or perhaps making available to him in looking back at him that morning. Derrida is among the most curious of men. . . . What happened that morning was, to me, shocking because of what I know this philosopher can do. Incurious, he missed a possible invitation, a possible introduction to other-worlding.[19]

According to Haraway, Derrida shied away from curiosity about his cat and his relations with it and retreated into the comforts of established patterns of scholarship that do not work across nature–culture divides:

> Therefore, as a philosopher he knew nothing more from, about, and with the cat at the end of the morning than he knew at the beginning. . . . Actually to respond to the cat's response to his presence would have required his joining that flawed but rich philosophical canon to the risky project of asking what this cat on this morning cared about, what these bodily postures and visual entanglements might mean and might invite, as well as reading what people who study cats have to say and delving into the developing knowledges of both cat-cat and cat-human behavioral semiotics when species meet.[20]

Contra Derrida, Haraway calls for humanists and social scientists to be more responsive to and curious about nonhuman others, be they cats, dogs, or any other creature. What is essential about the curiosity that Haraway proposes is its willingness to allow one's interests to be captured by another across species differences. In her case, her love for her dog torques disciplinary boundaries by leading her to learn from dog trainers and canine geneticists as well as philosophers.

These new collaborators have been especially important in multispecies scholarship, where many of the beings involved are not very amenable to classic social science techniques, such as interviewing and participant observation. Multispecies anthropologists have often addressed such concerns by attempting to expand their modes of inquiry and observation, including by working with animal trainers and ethologists, in the case of mammals and birds; botanists and ecologists, in the case of plants, fungi, and insects; and a host of other observers such as hunters, gatherers, farmers, and naturalists, regardless of kind.[21]

Enacting Curiosities at the Brown Coal Beds

The AURA brown coal mining project—with its focus on cross-species interactions in a heavily disturbed landscape—found itself pulled in different directions in the midst of these scholarly trends. In line with Haraway, some members wanted to kindle Krober's childlike wonder and allow their passions to be captured by particular nonhumans, which would then drive their methods and modes of inquiry. But others, often referencing an overlapping set of texts, emphasized other curiosities and concerns. Because practices of hubris and imperialist knowledge-making have contributed so significantly to ecological damage, they wanted to be curious about new modes of scholarship that questioned their own curiosities and were willing to see them as a possible problem as well as a solution. Drawing on the critiques in line with Crapanzano, as well as feminist Science and Technology Studies (STS) scholars such as Helen Verran, they wanted to democratize knowledge-making and scholarly analysis by allowing their curiosities about the site to be fundamentally guided by fieldwork as a dialogic social practice. While we had different dispositions and interests prior to our collaborative fieldwork, these contrasting approaches only coalesced within our field encounters—that is, within the mangle of anthropological field practice.[22]

The Danish brown coal bed area—where our group worked—was a former mining site, primarily active from 1940 to 1970.[23] Mining intensified in the area when World War II made the import of coal difficult and heightened the need for a sovereign national source of energy. Although brown coal is a relatively inefficient fuel, entrepreneurs and Danish state agencies systematized its exploitation, and the intensive digging that followed literally upended the area, leaving barren sand dunes and unstable ground with frequent landslides and quicksand.[24] The mining required pumping away groundwater, but once the pumps were turned off after the digging, the water seeped back in, exacerbating ground instabilities and making the terrain unstable for industrial forestry or agriculture. The area has thus been largely commercially unused—a rare thing in a densely populated country like Denmark.

Today the mining site is characterized by a mix of lakes, bare sand, and patchy forest, some of which had been originally planted to stabilize the postmining sands and provide shelter for wildlife.[25] Traffic is only allowed on designated pathways, since the lakes (water-filled former mining pits) have soft, collapsing banks that make it dangerous to go off-road. Among the lakes are a few patches of agricultural land where owners grow crops, primarily potatoes. Wildlife species, most prominently deer, thrive in the area due to its relative desertedness, as do recreational hunters who actively feed the herds while trying to keep other people from disturbing them. Danish authorities carefully manage the area, some of which is, in fact, designated for recreational use and intended to encourage visitors to enjoy the forest and learn about its mining history. Even though the brown coal site is rather small in scale (only 16 km^2), it is thus a complex ecology, crisscrossed by diverse human interventions, animal life, and plant growth.

All of the anthropologists were fascinated by the site, which we saw as a place for open experimentation. We were committed to avoiding the predefinition of research objects or questions, expecting that—per common anthropological practice—we would develop them within the flux of fieldwork. Yet we quickly found that we differed in our assumptions about the processes through which research objects would emerge. Part of the group imagined that our research objects would emerge from natural history–style observations of nonhuman species in this human-disturbed place. With scientist guides, shovels, and sample bags, they sought to develop modes of *attunement* with other organisms to explore how they express themselves and participate in world-making. Their goal was to move from a methodological focus on language to a focus on form—on the shapes of more-than-human bodies and the patterns of their interactions and movements—in order to better understand how humans and other beings make particular sites together.

Other members of the group shared this goal of more-than-human attention, but they imagined a somewhat different research process: they anticipated that more-than-human research objects would develop out of a process of following the interests and practices of people in the field, including residents and scientists, who were actively using and exploring the landscape. They emphasized *co-analysis* and sought to develop a research practice that would follow others' curiosities about the more-than-human landscape with which they engage. They were deeply curious about how anthropological methods, in a broad sense, might expand existing descriptions of more-than-human relations.

In the following section, I discuss two different field practices—one involving a fungus *(Paxillus involutus)* and the other a potato starch factory—that raised substantial debate within our group. Together, the two practices and our responses to them show how different and heterogeneous forms of anthropological curiosity arose within our experiments to develop multispecies methods for the Anthropocene.

Field Encounters

Collectively we wanted to explore how humans and nonhumans came to inhabit the postindustrial ruins of the former mining site in the particular ways that they did. As we walked through the site, we encountered heaps of overburden, a discarded washing machine, an old Bible, deer-hunting towers, trees stripped of bark, mowed grassy fields, local residents who were managing their land for hunting, mushroom pickers, and much more. One of the entities we kept stumbling across was a fungus that one of our members recognized as *Paxillus involutus.* A highly common fungus in Denmark, *Paxillus* came to capture the curiosities of some of our members and to occupy a central place in our discussion of multispecies curiosities. We often saw *Paxillus* near the pine trees that were swiftly recolonizing the former mining site. Was this fungus somehow aiding these trees in turning the site's barren sands and coal tailings into a forest? Was it a key actor in enabling new forms of living in this damaged place?

Some of our members knew from previous experiences in the U.S. West that mycorrhizal fungi often partner with trees to allow their roots to grow in relatively poor soils. Might this fungus be part of a similar arrangement here? After repeatedly observing the fungus and pine together, some members of our team (led by Tsing and Gan) decided to dig into the soil to see if the roots and fungi were relating to each other below ground. With shovels and hand lenses, they were able to see that the fungi and roots were indeed

Figure 2.1. *Paxillus involutus* at the Danish brown coal field site. Photograph by Anna Tsing.

entangled with each other. It appeared that the fungi were helping the pine trees to revegetate these highly disturbed landscapes by assisting them in extracting nutrients from the brown coal fragments left behind at the end of mining.[26]

Some of our group members were especially interested in this partnership because it was a novel one—this particular species of pine had been imported from the United States and was not native to Denmark. These were not two species that had coevolved together over a long period of time but ones who had quickly come to work together. We were also awed by what this partnership had facilitated. With the fungus, the tree had become able to spread rapidly across the sandy ground, changing it from blowing dunes into an emerging forest ecology that drew not only deer and wolves but also new landowners who sought to use the area for hunting. We were deeply curious about the hunters/landowners and the ways they used the area, and it seemed important to us to trace the ways that their patterns were intertwined with (and dependent on) those of nonhumans such as trees and fungi.

The multispecies approach that evolved in this case began from curiosities about the prevalence of the fungus and its potential for nurturing trees in poor soil and then led us to probe how it might vitally contribute to making the postmining brown coal site livable for others. Practices of looking underground, sketching roots, and analyzing DNA became techniques for understanding how trees and fungi navigate a site remade by particular patterns of land ownership, mining, and hunting. By examining roots and fungi, the group members who were excited about exploring *Paxillus* saw themselves as extending anthropology's methods while staying with its commitments to empirical observation and openness to surprise. In this vein, their work on *Paxillus*–pine relations could be seen as a new form of natural history description attentive to interactions that are not "natural" in a simplistic use of the term but instead a knot of anthropogenic and more-than-human relations. Methodologically and analytically, the fungal group (and some other AURA members, including the author) aimed to engage the techniques of natural history not as a singular white colonial legacy but as a set of overlapping and heterogeneous practices through which people everywhere engage with the natural world around them.[27] The aim was to use observation, sketching, collection, and probing to attune oneself with the lifeworlds of fungi, tree roots, and other nonhuman beings.

The interest in *Paxillus* also drew members of the AURA team into relations with mycologists, who were also interested in both observing fungi in the field and further querying them in lab contexts. One of the AURA members also spent time in dialogue with a molecular biologist, resulting in DNA analysis of fungal samples from the fieldwork site.[28] Yet while some group members were excited by these investigations, others on the team saw them as anthropologically unproductive. We often conducted fieldwork alongside biologists and mycologists, and they aided us in seeing patterns in fungi, trees, and deer behavior. While everyone agreed that the scientists in our group were generous and kind interlocutors, some of the anthropologists worried about the dynamics of our cross-disciplinary collaborations, which seemed to focus predominately on what anthropologists could learn from biologists rather than from truly dialogic encounters. When we focused on *Paxillus* and pine with natural scientists, were anthropologists merely handing over our curiosities to science?

Some group members worried that the anthropologists were simply repeating known biological information rather than using anthropological insights and methods to thicken the story of the *Paxillus*. Were we contributing anything *anthropological* to conversations about the fungus, or were we simply reproducing scientific practices and confirming already-known fungal traits? In their attempts to become curious about nonhumans, were anthropologists jettisoning their disciplinary commitments in toto? In their efforts to attune themselves to fungal bodies, were they simply becoming biologists rather than using anthropology to enrich conversations about more-than-human worlds?

In addition to the challenges of establishing mutual analytic processes with natural scientists and natural science practices, there was also the challenge of doing so with nonhuman organisms. On one hand, anthropologists have been highly critical of the objectivizing gaze of the white-coated male scientist and its conceptions of knowledge-making as a dispassionate, disengaged process. Haraway has called this form of objectivity a "God-trick," in which the scientist takes the place of the omniscient deity, able to see and judge all without acknowledging their own entanglements with the world.[29] Yet while feminist scholars have critiqued forms of science that create a "view from nowhere," they have embraced notions of situated knowledges, where researchers come to know something partially and in entangled relation with it.[30]

Some of the AURA members saw fungal observation as an engaged and situated act. Lying on the ground, probing into the soil, and glimpsing its more-than-human relations seemed to offer insights more attuned to the world-making projects of trees and fungi than established anthropological approaches that focus on how people encounter and classify these organisms (usually in their above-ground incarnations as leaves and mushrooms). While they indeed read scientific articles about trees and fungi and collaborated with a mycologist and molecular biologist, they saw their practice as a different and anthropologically inspired mode of noticing that emerged from involving themselves with the dynamics of the landscape as much as they could. Rather than a view from nowhere, they saw their work as a messy and muddy encounter. They also saw themselves as surrendering their curiosities to fungi and pines—in that their questions about these relations were dynamic ones responsive to their field engagements with these others.

However, some AURA anthropologists were not fully convinced. The enthusiastic natural history passions of some of the group members often appeared dangerously close to a rekindling of the colonial modes of curiosity within which those practices had initially emerged. Despite the emphasis on attunement, the observations of fungi often seemed more monologic than dialogic, with human eyes peering down at these other beings. Were there any situations in which observation could actually be dialogic? Fungi were responsive to humans and others in that their patterns of growth clearly responded to conditions in which people had been involved—such as soil type and the presence of tree roots. But the temporalities of their responsiveness limited possibilities of dialogue within research encounters. Given such challenges, was there any possibility—in line with anthropological commitments—to be *curious with* a fungus in a co-analytic sense? If co-analysis and dialogue are at the heart of anthropology, were our efforts to focus on *Paxillus* and use scientific methods to engage them pulling us toward modes of curiosity that run counter to anthropological commitments?

We also stumbled into questions about the role of the brown coal field site in our research. With our abilities to be in dialogue with the fungus seriously constrained by our different modes of being and our onto-epistemological dialogues with scientists limited by the challenges of disciplinary difference, it often seemed that we were seeking to develop our research questions in relation to general and abstract scientific literatures rather than in relation to the field itself. This seemed to run counter to grounded anthropological methods, which posit that larger research interests should be emergent from a site, not applied to it. If ethnographic fieldwork is supposed to be directed by encounters in the field, is *Paxillus* a possible object of anthropological curiosity—given the specificities of the AURA project?

Some of us wondered if our efforts to study *Paxillus* were turning the lively, relational, and relentlessly specific "field" of anthropology into a more general and less engaged space. In learning the biological names for fungal species and listening to biologists' explanations of general processes, were we learning anything specific to this site? Was a research effort that began from such generalities responding to natural science—as a discipline—rather than to the field?

Calls for a Different Approach

In the midst of such concerns, two of our team members set out a different approach to curiosity—one that inspired and challenged others. Drawing on a practice that they had previously called "lateral theorization,"[31] they proposed that we allow research objects and trajectories to emerge through *shared analytical work* with the people one encounters in the field. Their proposal was to allow anthropological curiosities to be codirected by other people in a more radical way than scholars usually permit. Their ambition was for anthropologists to let go of a priori assumptions of what might constitute interesting objects of study and to allow fieldwork to be fundamentally conversational and dialogic. The participation of others in anthropological knowledge-making, then, means not that they provide bits and pieces of "data" to address the researcher's questions and curiosities but that the anthropologist and collaborator generate objects of interest and modes of analysis together.[32]

They were as interested in probing questions of more-than-human relations as were the fungal group, but they specifically foregrounded the question of what *anthropological* methods might contribute to their study. By first paying attention to the curiosities of human others, these AURA members made their way to a local high-tech food factory that processes and modifies starch from potatoes—a place that the fungally curious team members had not noticed.[33] A potato farmer with agricultural fields located in and at the outskirts of the brown coal beds had encouraged them to visit the factory. They met him on his farm during a 2014 field trip after they had heard that he was very outspoken about the increased number of deer in the area, cherished as wild game by some and seen as an unwelcome nuisance by others. The population of deer had grown huge, the farmer told us, especially the number of females, as hunters were primarily interested in shooting males with antlers. After voicing complaints about the deer that entered his potato fields and ate the leaves of his crop, he turned to a topic that clearly enthused and animated him: the wonders of his potatoes, a special type particularly rich in carbohydrates that was not meant for direct consumption. Rather than so-called food potatoes, his were designed to become starch. He told the AURA members that, through the high-tech processes in the nearby factory, these potatoes could be turned into ingredients for all kinds of products that needed starch for the right texture. They could even find their way into gummy bears, substituting for their usual pig-derived gelatin and thus making the candy exportable to Arab countries.[34]

When these AURA team members handed over their analysis to the farmer's curiosities, they were drawn into worlds that the others missed. When they followed the farmer's suggestion to visit the factory, they found still more curious people. The factory salesman greeted them with a box full of test products that contained starch from the local potatoes. There were diet products in which fats were replaced with a particular modified starch, fruit gums of different hardnesses, and a chunk of cheese in which potato starch had been substituted for the expensive casein from milk. The pair of

AURA members who visited the factory were fascinated by this creativity, along with the starch's wide-ranging global relations, as described by the salesman: markets, tariff barriers, the European Union, a worldwide taste for instant noodles, a failed tapioca harvest in South East Asia a few years ago, the importance of storage facilities, and the charm of local farmers who came on their tractors to the factory. The potatoes seemed to contain unlimited possibilities for the producers—and for analysis. Thinking and analyzing together with the farmer and the salesman, these members developed a *shared* curiosity about what the potatoes could become as they were transformed into new substances and entities, such as the factory's registered trademarked starch-binding products—each with their own qualities and multispecies entanglements.[35]

These group members felt strongly that these stories of living together in industrial landscapes were highly relevant to AURA conversations about land use and multispecies histories. Furthermore, they seemed to be a place from which to build an *anthropological* contribution to such topics—one that engaged more-than-human worlds without abandoning anthropological methods. As many AURA members noted, it was difficult to explore *Paxillus* in traditional anthropological fieldwork encounters because none of the human interlocutors at the site seemed to care much about it or even pay attention to it. Landowners simply did not evoke it in interviews or walks across the site. Even when our team pointed out the fungus to local residents, they did not see it as important or interesting: it became something of a dead end. For AURA anthropologists who felt strongly that anthropology should be a practice of *curiosity with,* it was difficult to see a way to be directly and responsibly *curious with* a fungus within the scope of anthropological methods. In contrast, following the lead of humans who make a business out of potatoes opened other possible modes of multispecies ethnography. While the natural scientists collaborating with AURA seemed most interested in developing research questions in relation to general processes and categories, the potato farmer embraced analytical curiosity that moved outward from the specific potatoes at the former brown coal site. By engaging the curiosities of the humans they met in relation to the specific nonhumans in the field, this approach maintained the kind of intimate, co-analytic process that many in the AURA group saw as integral to anthropology.

While other AURA members saw such research as a contribution to the overall brown coal project, they did not see its immediate relevance for their efforts to expand multispecies curiosities. The fungus-focused AURA faction worried that the lateral approach used at the potato starch factory might overly limit scholars' curiosities by demanding that their research object be determined by the curiosities of the people whom they encounter in the field. Of course, they were very interested in the observations of locals who were themselves curious about nonhuman species; they saw hunters and farmers as keen observers of deer behavior, for example, and they were attentive to their insights. But many crucial more-than-human relations, like those of the fungus, went largely unnoticed by locals. Why should the group limit itself to their curiosities and thus ignore important beings and processes to which they don't happen to pay attention? For some, organismal names and generalized scientific knowledges served as tools for noticing the specific more-than-human relations at the site, rather than a priori explanatory categories that blocked curiosities. When no one gave much attention to the particular *Paxillus* at the brown coal site, it still seemed possible to some to encounter them in their ethnographic particularity by repurposing scientific knowledges and practices that tend to traffic in generalities.

Ongoing Challenges

I have presented some of the tensions that seemed to emerge in the field among the AURA anthropologists (as I came to understand them) in an attempt to illustrate the ways that curiosity, methods, and disciplinary critique are bound up with each other. The AURA group seemed to widely agree that anthropological knowledge should be coproduced in transformative field encounters. But coproduced among whom and in what ways? And how much dialogue is necessary for coproduction or codirection? These questions become particularly acute when anthropological imperatives are joined to multispecies research. Within natural history–style observation practices, the *Paxillus* certainly raised new and unexpected questions for the anthropologists through its patterns of growth. Yet engaging in a practice of collaborative curiosity with a fungus is clearly very different from doing so with farmers. Could one be *laterally curious* well enough with a fungus to meet the dialogic commitments of anthropology? Were we merely cultivating our "own" individualized curiosities about fungi, or were our inquires at least partially coproduced with the fungi? Were our collaborations with natural scientists leading us away from core anthropological practices of curiosity and back toward more detached, objectifying ones? Such questions remain unresolved for the AURA group—and within multispecies anthropology more generally.

Yet the encounters described above show us the importance of thinking curiosity together with modes of critique. The two approaches of fungal curiosity/attunement and lateral curiosity/co-analysis emerged out of AURA members' concerns about and critiques of existing anthropological curiosities—about their blindnesses to human entanglements with other species and about the ways that their analytical moves sometimes continue to take colonialist/masculinist forms. Both of these approaches offer new modes of curiosity in relation to disciplinary histories that they seek to inherit and remake.

The point of this chapter is not to argue for either mode of curiosity or method but to demonstrate why they need to be considered—and enacted—together. Multispecies anthropology makes much-needed interventions by positing curiosity and noticing as antidotes to blindness about nonhumans. It is a key project of becoming responsive to more-than-human worlds. While lateral curiosity does not reject such an effort, it slows it down and trips it up in important ways. It firmly asserts that there is no external, objective position from which to be curious.[36] In this way, relentless curiosity becomes a method that ensures one is always uncertain about who one is and with whom one is being curious. It is a practice that raises essential questions about the hubris of analyzing, critiquing, and being *curious about* others from an ostensible outside.

The challenge of building an anthropology that is at once alert to nonhuman worlds and the practices of *curiosity with* is profound: by describing the AURA group's concrete tensions and disagreements over how to be *curious with* potatoes and mushrooms, this chapter hopes to spark additional grounded conversations at this interface. In the case of domestic mammals (like Haraway's dog), many anthropologists readily see the possibilities of having their curiosities fundamentally shaped by a nonhuman being, such that one is *curious with* rather than about that being. In practice, multispecies anthropology in relation to such animals has often allowed scholars to skirt the questions of responsive curiosity that the *Paxillus* forced the AURA group to confront directly. The AURA project offers no final answers in this regard: its members remain unsettled about how to become co-curious with a fungus. What kinds of possibilities do natural science techniques and collaborations offer for anthropologists who seek to be co-curious with beings very unlike themselves? What are the conditions for being *curious with* and not merely *curious about* nonhuman others who are so different from people that anthropological practices of dialogue and co-analysis become difficult to enact? Within this endless profusion of questions and challenges, perhaps the only thing that can be said with certainty is that there is a need for more attention to curiosities and the curious ecologies of knowledge-making with which they are entangled.

Notes

This chapter draws extensively on conversations, disagreements, and exchanges with Frida Hastrup and Nathalia Brichet. I am grateful for their generosity throughout the difficult process of producing this piece. I would also like to thank the Aarhus University Research on the Anthropocene (AURA) project, funded by the Danish National Research Foundation. All of the group's members have contributed to this piece—directly or indirectly. Special thanks are due to project leader Anna Tsing for sparking the group's explorations at the brown coal site and for her comments on an earlier draft of this chapter, as well as to co-leader Nils Bubandt for his work on rubber boots methods. Jennifer Deger also kindly discussed anthropological curiosities with me at length.

1. See http://anthropocene.au.dk/.

2. For one description of this concept, see Paul J. Crutzen and Eugene F. Stoermer, "The Anthropocene," *Global Change Newsletter* 41 (2000): 17–18.

3. Anna Tsing et al., *Arts of Living on a Damaged Planet* (Minneapolis: University of Minnesota Press, 2017).

4. Nils Bubandt and Anna Tsing, eds., "Feral Dynamics of Post-Industrial Ruin: An Introduction," *Journal of Ethnobiology* 38, no. 1 (2018).

5. Isabelle Stengers, "Another Science Is Possible! A Plea for Slow Science" (Chair Willy Calewaert Inaugural Lecture, Université Libre de Bruxelles, December 13, 2011).

6. Anna Tsing, *The Mushroom at the End of the World: On the Possibility of Life in Capitalist Ruins* (Princeton, N.J.: Princeton University Press, 2015).

7. I thank Nils Bubandt for coining this our "rubber boots" approach.

8. Anna Tsing, "Unruly Edges: Mushrooms as Companion Species," *Environmental Humanities* 1 (2012): 141–54.

9. Donna Haraway, *Staying with the Trouble* (Durham, N.C.: Duke University Press, 2016).

10. Donna Haraway, *When Species Meet* (Minneapolis: University of Minnesota Press, 2008), 300.

11. Karl Kroeber, "Curious Profession: Alfred Kroeber and Anthropological History," *Boundary 2* 30, no. 3 (2003): 153.

12. See, for example, Michael Taussig, *Mimesis and Alterity: A Particular History of the Senses* (New York: Routledge, 1993).

13. See, for example, Helen Verran, *Science and an African Logic* (Chicago: University of Chicago Press, 2001).

14. See, for example, James Clifford and George Marcus, eds., *Writing Culture: The Poetics and Politics of Ethnography* (Berkeley: University of California Press, 1986).

15. Vincent Crapanzano, "Hermes' Dilemma: The Masking of Subversion in Ethnographic Description," in *Writing Culture: The Poetics and Politics of Ethnography,* ed. James Clifford James and George Marcus, 74 (Berkeley: University of California Press, 1986).

16. Heather Anne Swanson, "Key Concepts Entries: Multi-Species Research," in *Sage Encyclopedia of Research Methods*, 2019.

17. Donna Haraway, *When Species Meet* (Minneapolis: University of Minnesota Press, 2008), 3.

18. Jacques Derrida, *The Animal That Therefore I Am* (New York: Fordham University Press, 2008).

19. Haraway, *When Species Meet,* 20–21.

20. Haraway, 22.

21. Heather Swanson, "Methods for Multispecies Anthropology: Analysis of Salmon Otoliths and Scales," *Social Analysis* 61, no. 2 (2017).

22. Andrew Pickering, *The Mangle of Practice: Time, Agency, and Science* (Chicago: University of Chicago Press, 1995).

23. Jan Svendsen, *Det brune guld* (Brande, Den.: DialogForum, 2007). See also the journal special issue on the AURA brown coal field site: Bubandt and Tsing, "Feral Dynamics."

24. See Mathilde Højrup and Heather Swanson, "The Making of Unstable Ground: The Anthropogenic Geologies of Søby, Denmark," *Journal of Ethnobiology* 38, no. 1 (2018): 24–38; Nathalia Brichet and Frida Hastrup, "Industrious Landscaping: The Making and Managing of Natural Resources at Søby Brown Coal Beds," *Journal of Ethnobiology* 38, no. 1 (2018): 8–23.

25. George Schlätzer, "Some Experiences with Various Species in Danish Reclamation Work," in *Ecology and Reclamation of Devastated Land,* ed. Russell Hutnik and Grant Davis, 2:33–64 (New York: Gordon Breach, 1973); Poul Moller Sørensen, *Søby brunkulslejer: Helhedsplanlægning—botanisk registrering,* Gruppen for by- og landskabsplanlægning (Kolding, Den.: Gruppen for by- og landskabsplanlægning, 1984).

26. Elaine Gan, Anna Tsing, and Daniel Sullivan, "Using Natural History in the Study of Industrial Ruins," *Journal of Ethnobiology* 38, no. 1: 39–54 (2018), https://doi.org/10.2993/0278-0771-38.1.039.

27. Anna Tsing. "More-Than-Human Sociality: A Call for Critical Description," in *Anthropology and Nature,* ed. Kirsten Hastrup, 37–52. New York: Routledge, 2013.

28. See the online supplement to Gan, Tsing, and Sullivan, "Using Natural History," titled "Mushrooms and Mycorrhiza: Paxillus, Pisolithus, and Pines; What Can DNA Tell Us?" for more detailed information about DNA analysis in this project.

29. Donna Haraway, "Situated Knowledges: The Science Question in Feminism and the Privilege of Partial Perspective," *Feminist Studies* 14, no. 3 (1988): 575–99.

30. Haraway, 575–99. See also Karen Barad, *Meeting the Universe Halfway* (Durham, N.C.: Duke University Press, 2007).

31. Frida Hastrup, "Shady Plantations. Theorizing Shelter in Coastal Tamil Nadu," *Anthropological Theory* 11, no. 4 (2011): 425–39.

32. Brichet and Hastrup, "Industrious Landscaping."

33. Frida Hastrup and Nathalia Brichet, "Antropocæne monstre og vidundere: Kartofler, samarbejdsformer og globale forbindelser i et dansk ruinlandskab," *Kulturstudier* 7, no. 1 (2016): 19–33, http://tidsskriftetkulturstudier.dk/tidsskriftet/vol2016/1-juli/antropocaene-monstre-og-vidundere/.

34. Hastrup and Brichet.

35. Hastrup and Brichet.

36. Brichet and Hastrup, "Industrious Landscaping."

3

Curiosity, Ethics, and the Medical Management of Intersex Anatomies

Ellen K. Feder

All human beings by nature desire to know.

—Aristotle, *Metaphysics*

It's easy to take for granted the desire for knowledge, what Aristotle saw as a fundamental part of human life. Awakened, as Descartes wrote, by "wonder," the first of the passions of the soul,[1] curiosity is celebrated as central to children's learning and character development. Curiosity is valued across the lifespan, institutionalized in the most esteemed centers of learning and investigation. But this curiosity, associated with the expansion of understanding and ethical sensitivity, has another side. In the psychoanalytic terms of Melanie Klein, the "epistemophilic impulse" is linked from the start with an obverse "sadism."[2] In the frustration of the desire for knowledge and the pleasure that wonder brings there lies a destructive potential. Klein's observation about the positive and negative expressions of epistemophilia provides a helpful starting place from which to consider very different expressions of curiosity we find in the history of the medical management of intersex anatomies.

Intersex anatomies are neither clearly male nor female and so challenge conceptions of sex difference as simply or unassailably dimorphic. The destructive effects of a negative or objectifying curiosity are readily apparent in the narratives that have been produced over the last twenty-five years by adults who, as infants, young children, or teens, experienced "corrective" genital surgeries and other unnecessary normalizing interventions. The positive sort of curiosity Aristotle identified as the beginning of philosophy may not be apparent in these narratives, describing, as they do, the impact of decisions made by physicians certain of the need to change intersex anatomies and confident in the therapeutic promise of their treatment. Each narrative constitutes an invitation to be curious about the experience of those who have been subjected to practices that physicians have promoted—without evidence of "success"—for more than five decades.

Examining the medicalization of intersex bodies and the resistance it produced through the lens of curiosity has led many to look at the history of psychologist John Money's role in the development of the protocol that became the "standard of care." Indeed, the damning history of Money's role has been a keen object of study in the critical literature concerning the medical management of intersex since the birth of intersex activism in 1993. Focusing particularly on the curiosity that appears to have animated Money's inquiries into intersex bodies and lives may enrich our understanding of and appreciation for the moral violation that has seen increasing recognition. It may also present some surprises that challenge settled beliefs. If we find that criticism of Money's role has neglected positive aspects of his work that exemplify the best qualities of curiosity, we may better appreciate the reverberating consequences of a refusal to be curious. I want to be clear that my aim is not to excuse Money's actions. We must not minimize the harm to which his work has contributed and that persists after his death. Rather, I propose to follow the hunch that the more complicated picture of Money that closer examination reveals may offer insight into the promise of curiosity awakened on the one hand and the perilous risks of its suppression on the other.

Subjects of Curiosity

When I began to consider the place of curiosity in the context of the medicalization of intersex, what came immediately to mind was image after image of medical students and residents gathered around an infant, child, or adolescent in a hospital room or surgical theater. When aspiring and new physicians are led—"paraded," as a number of individuals have put it[3]—through rounds to inspect atypical sex anatomies, their supervisors do not intend for physicians-in-training to be surprised in the ways that Descartes identifies with the passion of wonder. Medicine is not, or at least not at this moment, creative, wonder-filled, scientific inquiry, but what we might see as

Curiosity, Ethics, and Intersex Anatomies 39

a highly skilled trade, one that puts a high premium, furthermore, on "dispassion" in practitioners. And yet physicians are interested in seeing intersex anatomies, or other sorts of unusual anatomies, precisely because they are not common; they are, in other words, "objects of curiosity." Wonder may be prompted by an encounter with what is unexpected or simply experienced for the first time, but wonder comes from "noticing" rarity. Having already taken note of the rarity of intersex anatomies, medicine is no longer caught up in the wonder that feeds curiosity but in the sort of investigation and understanding whose aim is building knowledge.

Narratives by intersex individuals—those that inaugurated an activist movement of resistance,[4] and continue to appear in print[5] and online,[6] attest to the harms of being the objects of "a kind of prurient curiosity," as Iris Marion Young put it, "that convert[s] the openness of wonder into a dominative desire to know."[7] Individuals' accounts of their experience as patients emphasize the effects of their subjection to a medical gaze that has made curiosities of their bodies. In the clinic and surgical theater, their anatomies are exposed to examination; in the lab, blood and saliva are magnified to explain the bodies' secrets. But such examination, one might reasonably observe, is the work of clinical medicine and research that aims to improve care for patients.

What appears to distinguish the medical management of intersex, however, is the startling lack of curiosity specialists in the standard of care for intersex anatomies have demonstrated in response to stories of individuals who have spoken up about their experiences. Far from the "success stories" that multiple case studies in the medical literature represented, intersex individuals—among them the very patients depicted in the literature[8]—have conveyed how medical interventions have damaged their bodies and spirits. Individuals report chronic pain or dysfunction resulting from unnecessary surgeries to remove or reshape genitals that didn't conform to standards for assigned gender. Loss of reproductive function following gonadectomy was seen as critical to the successful sex assignment of some; in others, being a suitable woman justified clitorectomy. Many speak of trauma resulting from having their medical histories concealed from them, or because they recall too clearly the experience of clinical examinations intended to educate medical students and residents. As one former patient wrote, "I still struggle to understand how it can be that medical professionals who seemed so interested in my care could have been so unaware of how their treatment had hurt me."[9] Wouldn't physicians want to know about the outcomes of treatment they have recommended or themselves administered?

Painful and consistent, these stories are also, perhaps especially for those who encounter them for the first time, surprising. First there is the "fact" of intersex, the recognition that there are bodies that fall outside the norm of sexual difference. We learn then of the harms entailed by the medical management of these bodies. These are not only physical harms, which are substantial, but also psychological harms that originate in the secrecy and silence—and often outright deception, both of children and their parents—that has characterized the treatment of intersex bodies since the 1950s. Surprising, too, are the repeated opportunities and attendant failures by physicians and parents to recognize the wrong of these practices in the face of these testimonies and now, in the increasing number of international statements condemning them.[10] Indeed, that there has appeared to be no reduction in these practices worldwide in the face of these statements is itself cause for wonder: How can it be that a practice can at once appear wrong to so many, and yet necessary (and so, a right or "good" action) for others, and especially for the physicians and parents responsible for the well-being of children in their care?

Perhaps more vexing still is the question of how physicians have remained confident in the standard of care even as they failed to engage in follow-up studies of their work.[11] If information concerning how patients have fared over the long-term is inadequate, how could they provide assurances to anxious parents who had been informed that their children's futures depended on surgical or hormonal intervention?

Investigation—or the lack of investigation—of outcomes has been among the thorniest of problems for supporters of the standard of care. When questions about the lack of evidence of putative success of normalizing interventions were first raised in the mid-1990s, specialists balked: It wasn't clear, after all, how much patients knew about their diagnoses or the surgeries or treatments they had undergone.[12] Even the parents who had consented to procedures might not be fully aware of the details of surgeries that had taken place in the 1960s and 1970s. Daunting ethical problems in conducting outcomes research came to present apparently insurmountable barriers even for physicians who recognized the benefit of robust follow-up, even if only to substantiate their convictions that "their" patients would be counted among the "happy silent majority"; surely the positive results they could demonstrate should discredit the "unhappy vocal minority" whose stories were raising doubts about the standard of care. Despite the absence of evidence supporting the standard of care, most physicians have continued as they have, apparently relying on the rationale for normalizing interventions formalized at Johns Hopkins University in the mid-1950s by psychologist John Money and his mentors, Joan and John Hampson. While there have been some changes in the standard of care beginning at the turn of the twenty-first century (most notably regarding the routine reassignment of male children with micropenises to female),[13] proponents of cosmetic surgical intervention remain committed to resisting efforts—ethical, political, and legal—to alter the standard of care.[14]

The Origins of the Standard of Care

I am hardly alone in the confusion I have experienced in the face of the abiding confidence specialists demonstrate with respect to the importance of ensuring that the anatomies of children match their sex of assignment. After all, the validity of the standard of care would seem to have been seriously undermined, if not destroyed, following the 1997 revelation of Money's prolonged deception regarding what was reported to have been the successful sex reassignment of an identical twin (known as "the case of John/Joan").[15] Certainly I was curious about the motivation of those specialists whose commitment to the standard of care appeared unchanged in the years following Money's marginalization in medical discussions of care for children with atypical sex anatomies. But, in reflecting on the subject of curiosity, I realized that I had not been curious about John Money.

On the one hand, that lack of curiosity isn't especially surprising. He makes an excellent villain, as has been demonstrated in the book that journalist John Colapinto wrote after publishing the breaking story in *Rolling Stone*. Colapinto described how "Joan" (Brenda Reimer) had been living for some time as a man, now called David, who had married and was raising two children. A few years later, there was the BBC documentary, *Dr. Money and the Boy with No Penis* that described David Reimer's suicide. His death, the narrator intones:

> was more than just a human tragedy. It was also a devastating blow to the reputation of the psychologist whose groundbreaking research on David had

42 Ellen K. Feder

influenced a whole generation of scientists. Because some say that it was his unflinching belief in his theories that may have ultimately led to David's death.[16]

It doesn't seem quite right to claim that it was Money's "belief" in his theories that resulted in the death of David Reimer. The story that garnered Money so much renown (including a story in *Time* magazine) seems more like a function of a hunger for recognition so deep as to overwhelm other, also human needs, such as the ethical "pull" to tell the truth.

The demonization of Money satisfies the narrative arc of the tragic story of David Reimer and his family, as well as the stories of so many who have been affected by the medical management of atypical sex anatomies. My own discussions of Money's work have not been particularly nuanced with respect to his role in formalizing the medical approach to managing atypical sex anatomies in children. I have highlighted the apparent contradiction between the rationale for these protocols—which promote surgery to ensure psychosexual health—and his conclusions based on the study of 10 individuals and 238 case histories presented in his doctoral dissertation. One might suppose that "the paradox of hermaphroditism" in these 248 cases would create, he wrote,

> a fertile source of psychosis and neurosis. The evidence, however, shows that the incidence of the so-called functional psychoses in the most ambisexual of the hermaphrodites—those who could not help but be aware that they were sexually equivocal—was extraordinarily low.[17]

Where Colapinto and many following him see in this passage and the contradictions it reveals a culpable hypocrisy, Alison Redick's study of the development of the Johns Hopkins protocols and especially of Money's role, provides another view. She argues that the evidence Money gathered in his dissertation research did not upset his own suppositions about what has been figured as Money's focus on the imperative to make intersex bodies conform to a social order organized by a rigid division of sex. Rather, the individuals with intersex who might appear to be the subject of his research were for Money a means of finally settling debates about sexual difference; rearing, he claimed, "trumped all" other influences, including the activity of hormones. The fact that the majority of "hermaphrodites" who had not been subject to surgical intervention accepted their gender assignments without psychological disturbance provided ample evidence for this conclusion.

Money's theoretical analysis appears from Redick's reading to have more sophistication than it did when subsequently presented—including by Money himself—and taken up by specialists in the care of children with atypical sex anatomies. In his earliest work, Money's research posed a challenge to the mind/body dualism that shaped motivation theory and behavior.[18] His conviction that "human psychology would always assume either a masculine or feminine gender orientation" was neither a matter of "biology" nor of "society" but was a product of a multipart feedback system beginning in utero[19] and continuing through early childhood.[20] This was true not only in the case of the majority of individuals who accepted their gender assignment but also, Money argued, in the cases of the forty-one individuals he documents (forty of whom had initially been assigned female) who failed to accept their assignment "despite the amputation of their phalluses in many cases."[21] Second, Money's work aimed to challenge the view of prevailing psychoanalytic theory locating psychological disturbance in psychosexual aberration, specifically in homosexual orientation.[22]

If psychopathology and sex difference figured importantly in Money's dissertation, it was not because he was interested in shaping medical practice as he would shortly come to do; at this stage, Money's dissertation may be viewed principally as a theoretical work notable for the radically new understanding of "gender" introduced there, and elaborated in his better-known published works. Hermaphroditism lies at the center of this work because "hermaphrodites," as he wrote in 1952, "provide invaluable material for the comparative study of bodily form and physiology, rearing, and psychosexual orientation."[23]

Indeed, it was this theoretical rationale that Lawson Wilkins, the "father" of pediatric endocrinology, sought in Money and his mentors, Joan and John Hampson, when he offered Money a fellowship at Johns Hopkins. Wilkins had become acquainted with Money as he was completing his dissertation. Some of Money's cases, in fact, had come from Wilkins's clinic, where Wilkins had, only the year before Money's arrival in 1951, confirmed and was then refining the lifesaving use of cortisol for the treatment of salt-losing congenital adrenal hyperplasia, the most common condition resulting in atypical sex anatomies in genetic females.[24] At Johns Hopkins, Money appears no longer to have been involved in the initial investigation and testing of theories but was instead engaged in the formalization and defense of a theoretical framework. He turned, in other words, from a project that now strikes me as characterized by curiosity in the positive sense—namely, in asking new questions in the face of surprising phenomena—and came to occupy a role at Johns Hopkins where his function was to consolidate and advance a theoretical framework in the service of developing the new field of pediatric endocrinology at a leading medical institution.

Investigating John Money

I was initially moved to question the soundness of my previous reflections on Money and his legacy after reading a narrative prepared by "Peggy Cadet," which complicates the picture of Money I had formed. Now a middle-aged woman, Cadet had initially been raised as a boy, but had struggled with that assignment throughout her childhood and young adulthood. She recalls that when she was around twenty-one, she gained access to the medical record of a younger cousin, then twelve years old, with whom she shared an intersex condition. The record contained "the verbatim transcript" of her cousin's interview with Money who, Cadet writes, offered sympathetic advice, and explained clearly and frankly to her cousin that he had choices: "Money not only told my cousin that he could change to being a girl instead of having a mastectomy, he gave him explicit information about intercourse, erotic sensation, homosexuality, transsexualism . . . all presented in language geared to a 12 year old's understanding."[25] These were choices that had never been presented to Cadet. "Ironically," she writes, "the counselor I was seeing at that time cited Money's ideas as the rationale for my not having been informed in the same way as a child." Though Money has been "vilified for promoting a policy of secrecy and non–disclosure for intersexed patients . . . in the case of my cousin, it appeared that he actually provided the sort of information and education intersex activists have argued for."[26]

Cadet's narrative finds significant confirmation in the memories of Tiger Devore, one of the very first intersex activists and a clinical psychologist who sought a fellowship with Money as Devore was completing his PhD in psychology. Despite enduring nearly annual surgeries for "hypospadias repair"[27] throughout his childhood and young adulthood, Devore had never met anyone who shared his experiences. He saw the prospect of that changing when, as a graduate student, he attended a lecture at UCLA by psychologist Robert

Stoller. Having encountered the diagnostic term hypospadias only in his own medical records, Devore describes what seemed like a kind of thrill on seeing, projected on the screen, his diagnosis, along with others describing different conditions that were not yet known—at least outside of the halls of the clinic—by the term "intersex." The promise of learning about others like himself who had been born with sex anatomies judged in need of "correction" led him to ask for Stoller's help in recommending him for a position in Money's clinic.

Devore's account provides a view of Money that helps us join together some of the stray pieces in what is emerging as the larger, more complicated puzzle that is John Money, his work, and his legacy. "He really cared about his patients," Devore recounts. "He connected with them and met them without judgment." Well aware of the harm that Money's work has done—and open about his deep disagreements with Money, both during his fellowship and long since, Devore recalls the compassion Money displayed toward his patients. By his account, the empathic concern Money demonstrated was a product of his genuinely nonjudgmental curiosity about the lives of many of those who came to the clinic, whose bodies or desires were taken at that time to be "pathological." Like Cadet, Devore also recalls Money's efforts to help his patients make adjustments that could provide them the space to express their desires and more safely make their way in the world.

Money extended a warm welcome to his trainee, who made clear in his communications not only his qualifications to work at Johns Hopkins but his specific motivation for seeking a position in Money's clinic. Devore reports that Money was openly enthusiastic about having someone with an intersex condition as a clinical intern. Perhaps not surprisingly, Money saw in Devore an opportunity to extend his own renown. Money arranged for Devore to be featured with him on a 1984 Baltimore talk show—they were interviewed by Oprah Winfrey on "People Are Talking"—which Money heralded as the first television appearance by an intersex person speaking about their identity and experience. At the same time that Money sought to capitalize on his student's willingness to make public appearances and so, we may speculate, imply Devore's endorsement of Money's work at Johns Hopkins, Money also took seriously his responsibility as a supervisor, encouraging in Devore the curiosity that appears to have characterized Money's early research, and that, according to Devore, was so evident in his clinical work with older teenagers and adults. This curiosity extended both to the clinic's patients and to Devore himself.

Devore's reflections on what he saw of Money's clinical work provide a better sense of why many of Money's students and junior colleagues were so devoted to him during his life and remain eager to defend his work after his death. In what is at least partly an effort to reckon with the uneasy legacy of Money's aspiration to create "a comprehensive map of sex, gender, and sexuality," the editors and coauthors of *Fuckology: Critical Essays on John Money's Diagnostic Concepts* observe the strident defense of Money mounted by former students and collaborators.[28] Among them is Anke Erhardt, who emphasized in a heartfelt obituary Money's wide-ranging contributions: He was a founding member of the new field of psychoendocrinology, responsible for important changes to the treatment of variations in anatomy and desires. It was Money who popularized the term "paraphilias" to replace the pejorative "perversions," and introduced "sexual orientation" to replace "sexual preference." This change was crucial for Money, according to Erhardt, "because our attractions are not completely voluntary nor simply matters of free choice or taste."[29] Erhardt was at pains to highlight the contributions that Money had made to the lives and self-conceptions of those who would become his harshest critics.

Erhardt was not alone. A few years before Money's death, Money's colleague Vern Bullough had similarly characterized Money as "one of the great pioneers of American sexology."[30] Bullough laments especially the way that the Joan/John case had been represented and received. Attempting to reduce the unfortunate "blot on his career" left by the public revelation of David Reimer's rejection of his assignment (Reimer's suicide occurred the year after Bullough's "Contributions"), Bullough suggests that Money's critics have been unfair or even disingenuous in their condemnation, pointing readers to Money and Erhardt's caution that successful reassignment is contingent on the "clear and unambiguous signals about the new identity" parents in particular must convey to a child born with atypical sex.[31] Interestingly, Bullough implicates not only David Reimer's parents for supposedly undermining the treatment designed to help him adjust to life without a penis but also suggests, as Peggy Cadet suspected, that specialists in the care of children with intersex conditions have themselves failed to heed Money's cautions, simplifying and thus distorting Money's recommendations in ways that do not accurately reflect the subtlety and complexity of

Curiosity, Ethics, and Intersex Anatomies

the protocols he promoted.[32] It is not Money who is to blame, Bullough suggests, for the criticisms made by the Intersex Society of North America (to which Bullough appears somewhat sympathetic); rather, Money appears to be a kind of straw man or scapegoat in a set of widespread and frustrated demands to resolve the mysterious challenges posed by biology and society to which, Bullough tells us, "there is no easy answer."[33] The "real" John Money, both Bullough and Erhardt insist, was a deeply curious, even courageous student of the human embodied condition, one who contributed to a radical rethinking of assumptions about gender and sexuality.

In his characterization of Money's work, Bullough rightly emphasizes the significant social, psychological, and legal challenges posed by discomfort with or intolerance of variations in sexual anatomies, identities, and desires that are taken to be outside a rigid norm, and the serious personal risks assumed—voluntarily or otherwise—by those individuals whose identities and desires fall outside this standard. In her tribute, Erhardt emphasizes how Money's "deep empathy and passionate caring for patients with anomalies of their sex organs, their sexuality, and their gender remained a haven for many people for decades. Many felt that he was unique in his understanding, expertise, and knowledge, and tolerance and counseling."[34] While Bullough is rather forthright about Money's personal shortcomings, calling attention to his occasional displays of obstinacy and even arrogance,[35] both Bullough and Erhardt aim to defend their teacher, colleague, and friend, and decry the misrepresentation of Money's work and the marring of his legacy that both hope will be eventually redeemed. Erhardt recounts how, in the last years of his life, Money was "deeply affected" by the "attacks" he had suffered to his reputation:

> I tried to reassure him that he would share the fate of many truly pioneering giants in science, namely, that we were experiencing a swinging of the pendulum that ultimately would swing back and that his work would find the proper place in history. Indeed, the pendulum has started to swing back to give John Money the proper credit for his extraordinary contribution to the field of psychoendocrinology and sex research.[36]

Erhardt's promise that his contributions would, in time, receive proper recognition may have seemed far-fetched before his death. However, the critical essays in *Fuckology* provide some hope for the redemption Money and his supporters believe is his due. The volume's title may strike a reader as disparaging of Money's work. But Money himself coined the term to name the field of inquiry in which he placed his work. Eventually called sexology (of which psychoendocrinology, another neologism, would be a part), this new field combined a number of existing medical and psychological areas, but would also work to challenge societal taboos.[37]

The slow and difficult work of challenging social taboos that have damaged the spirits of those whose desires or anatomies do not fit the norm seems an unassailable good that requires the sort of curiosity that Money appears to have demonstrated in the clinic. But the legacy of deception that Money left cannot be so readily dismissed as those of other pioneers of science and the human condition to which Erhardt may believe Money should be compared.[38]

When I asked him how it could be that Money appeared to have two faces, Devore responded without hesitation that the tension between the sort of open curiosity Money demonstrated toward his older teen and adult patients and the stubborn defense of his academic work came from "the institution." Devore takes his teacher's aspiration to create a comprehensive, "Linnean" taxonomy[39] of sex, gender, and desire as a means with which he would "find distinction." Recognition of the sort Money sought—to be "the first," "the best," "the most influential"—required not only the shaping of a classificatory/theoretical apparatus but clinical evidence, and so "proof" of its success.

At an institution that prided itself on being world-class, professional respect and renown were valued above all else. Reflecting on his experience with Money at Johns Hopkins University, Devore credits his teacher with providing both a model for the compassionate clinician Devore has proved to be over the last two decades and a cautionary tale that made the practice of academic psychology, which demands the blurring of lines between research subjects and patients, unappealing to him.

From Devore's account, perhaps we may affirm that Money did, indeed, exhibit an admirable curiosity, a generous and compassionate curiosity, which provided Devore and Money's patients a "haven" in a world too fearful or threatened to tolerate or support their bodily and affectional deviation from some fantasied norm. But that same curiosity served also to elicit the details that would help Money to lay out what he believed would prove a master design of human identity and desire that, at this sociohistorical moment, insisted on surgically creating "normal" bodies from "abnormal" ones. Money and a growing body of specialists, whose initial members were trained at Johns Hopkins, applied the protocols he helped to formalize and shaped the standard of care not only in the United States but throughout the West. Intersex patients, then, were both radically affirmed and tragically damaged by Money's work, which contained both genuine curiosity and powerful drives to normalization.

That Money's name and theory no longer appear in defense of contemporary practice should itself occasion wonder. There is ample evidence of his role in the history of harms resulting from the formalization of the protocols practiced at Johns Hopkins under the guidance of Lawson Wilkins, and then in the work of his protégés, many of whom remain leaders in the field today. And yet, invocation of Money's work may now be deployed to distinguish past practices from the present. Changes resulting from the "dramatic failures"[40] of the optimal gender approach, so publicly on display in the case of John/Joan and privately manifest in the experience of many former patients and their physicians[41] in routine reassignments of male children with micropenises, have been offered as an implicit defense of present practices. Few physicians openly defend the standard of care today, and ethical defenses have been and remain thin. Today any open justification focuses on "parental rights"—informed, presumably, by medical guidance—to make decisions on behalf of children,[42] rather than the health and well-being of the patient. Why, we must ask, would physicians who had understood the harm of these interventions in the past resist recognition of the harm that continues? What does that resistance serve? Perhaps an answer lies in the risks, both to one's professional position and to one's self-respect, that Money himself may well have seen in the potential revelation of the truth of his most famous patient.

Curiosity's End

The institutional recognition John Money sought comes not from what Aristotle called "the desire for knowledge" but from the belief that knowledge has been finally attained. What is celebrated, and rewarded, in such institutional recognition is not a spirit of inquiry, but its conclusion. Reflecting on the value assigned to this achievement, we may recognize another dimension of the ethical violation entailed by the standard of care, and the

50   Ellen K. Feder

end of curiosity it seems to promise—namely, the crushing silence experienced by many individuals subjected to the standard of care. This silence was not simply a refusal to or proscription against talking about a child's physical difference but also a stifling of a desire to know. The standard of care was designed expressly and intentionally to foreclose questions not only about a child's unusual anatomy, or what that might mean about that child's desires, but also about the very fact of intersex. But if this intention was shaped by a paternalistic effort to prevent discomfort or doubt in the child, and perhaps especially in the child's parents, these interventions also had the effect of stifling a curiosity about oneself and one's world that is at the heart of wonder.

If there is a positive lesson to take from Money's work, it lies in the creative and life-affirming value in the curiosity that could be both welcomed and encouraged in teens like Peggy Cadet's cousin and adults like Tiger Devore. Understanding how curiosity's stifling can so brutally encumber the prospects for a well-lived life, Devore would go on to build a life's work in its encouragement, supporting and fostering a movement of individuals who would find, in the reclamation of curiosity, a righteous anger and new prospects for the wonder, the desire, and the delight that the revelation of injustice may bring.

Notes

Perry Zurn and Arjun Shankar's invitation to participate in the "Curiosity across the Disciplines" symposium sparked my thinking about curiosity, and I am grateful for the thoughtful comments and criticisms they have provided since the event. Special thanks to Jameson Garland, Alice Dreger, Eileen Findlay, and Andrea Tschemplik for their careful readings and suggestions.

1. Marguerite La Caze, *Wonder and Generosity: Their Role in Ethics and Politics* (Albany: State University of New York Press, 2013), 13.

2. Melanie Klein, "Early Stages of the Oedipus Complex," in *Love, Guilt and Reparation and Other Works, 1921–1945* (1928; New York: Free Press, 1975), 187–88.

3. Konrad Blair, "When Doctors Get It Wrong," *Narrative Inquiry in Bioethics* 5, no. 2 (2015): 89–92; Laura Inter, "Finding My Compass," *Narrative Inquiry in Bioethics* 5, no. 2 (2015): 95–98; Lynnell Stephani Long, "Still I Rise," *Narrative Inquiry in Bioethics* 5, no. 2 (2015): 100–103.

4. Cheryl Chase and Martha Coventry, eds., "Intersex Awakening," special issue of *Chrysalis: The Journal of Transgressive Identities* 2, no. 5 (1997); Alice Domurat Dreger, ed., *Ethics in the Age of Intersex* (Hagerstown, Ms.: University Publishing Group, 1999).

Curiosity, Ethics, and Intersex Anatomies   51

5. See, for example, Tiffany Jones et al., *Intersex: Stories and Statistics from Australia* (London: Open Book, 2016); Georgiann Davis and Ellen K. Feder, eds., "Intersex" Narrative Symposium, *Narrative Inquiry in Bioethics* 5, no. 2 (2015): 87–150.

6. See, for example, Jim Ambrose, The Interface Project: Stories of People Born with Intersex Traits (2012), https://www.interfaceproject.org/stories.

7. Iris Marion Young, *Intersecting Voices: Dilemmas of Gender, Political Philosophy, and Policy* (Princeton, N.J.: Princeton University Press, 1997), 56.

8. See, for example, Karen A. Walsh, "'Normalizing' Intersex Didn't Feel Normal or Honest to Me," *Narrative Inquiry in Bioethics* 5, no. 2 (2015): 119–22.

9. Blair, "When Doctors Get It Wrong," 7.

10. See, for example, Human Rights Watch, "'I Want to Be Like Nature Made Me': Medically Unnecessary Surgeries on Intersex Children in the U.S.," July 25, 2017, https://www.hrw.org/report/2017/07/25/i-want-be-nature-made-me/medically-unnecessary-surgeries-intersex-children-us; Parliamentary Assembly of the Council of Europe, "Promoting the Human Rights of and Eliminating Discrimination against Intersex People," (2017), Resolution 2191, http://assembly.coe.int/nw/xml/XRef/Xref-XML2HTML-en.asp?fileid=24232&lang=en; European Union Agency for Fundamental Rights, "The Fundamental Rights Situation of Intersex People," April 2015, http://fra.europa.eu/en/publication/2015/fundamental-rights-situation-intersex-people; United Nations Human Rights Council, "Report of the Special Rapporteur on Torture and Other Cruel, Inhuman or Degrading Treatment or Punishment, Juan E. Méndez" (2013), A/HRC/22/53.

11. Sarah M. Creighton et al., "Childhood Surgery for Ambiguous Genitalia: Glimpses of Practice Changes or More of the Same?" *Psychology and Sexuality* 5, no. 1 (2014): 36, 38; Lih-Mei Liao, Dan Wood, and Sarah M. Creighton, "Parental Choice on Normalizing Cosmetic Genital Surgery," *BMJ* 351 (2015).

12. Creighton et al. "Childhood Surgery for Ambiguous Genitalia," 36.

13. Peter Lee and Christopher Houk, "Surgical, Medical and Psychological Dilemmas of Sex Reassignment: Report of a 46, XY Patient Assigned Female at Birth," *Journal of Pediatric Endocrinology and Metabolism* 19 (2006): 111–14.

14. Milton Diamond and Jameson Garland, "Evidence Regarding Cosmetic and Medically Unnecessary Surgery on Infants," *Journal of Pediatric Urology* 10 (2014): 2–7.

15. Milton Diamond and Keith Sigmundson, "Sex Reassignment at Birth: Long-Term Review and Clinical Application," *Archives of Pediatric and Adolescent Medicine* 15, no. 11 (1997): 298–304; John Colapinto, "The True Story of John/Joan," *Rolling Stone,* December 11, 1997, 54–97.

16. BBC TV, "Dr. Money and the Boy with No Penis" (London: British Broadcasting Corporation, 2004).

17. John Money, "Hermaphroditism: An Inquiry into the Nature of a Human Paradox," PhD diss., Harvard University, 1952, 6.

18. Alison Redick, "American History XY: The Medical Treatment of Intersex, 1916–1955," PhD diss., New York University, 2004, 22, 171–72.

19. That the process of "sexual identity" begins in utero, with the influence of fetal hormones, has been a controversial point. Biologist Milton Diamond, who was primarily responsible for the eventual revelation of David Reimer's rejection of his gender assignment as a girl, criticized Money's claim that fetal hormones had little influence on "erotic orientation." But Money's research before this time affirmed this view, and indeed, several years after his dissertation research, and without any reference to Diamond, Money affirmed the influence of "fetal gonadal hormones" on the shaping of "neural pathways." See also John Money, *Sin, Science, and the Sex Police: Essays on Sexology and Sexosophy* (Amherst: Prometheus Books, 1998). Money's claims, as the editors of *Fuckology* observe, were "often brazenly inconsistent." Lisa Downing, Iain Morland, and Nikki Sullivan, *Fuckology: Critical Essays on John's Money's Diagnostic Concepts* (Chicago: University of Chicago Press, 2015), 9. And yet following this discussion can be complicated by the various ways that "sexual identity" is taken and so confused by authors and critics. In Money's claims that sex hormones do not influence "erotic inclination," he appears to separate, as some of his critics and subsequent defenders do not, the various components of "sexual identity."

20. Redick, "American History XY," 22, 166–67, 172. See also Iain Morland, "Cybernetic Sexology," in Downing, Morland, and Sullivan, *Fuckology*, 113–14.

21. Redick, "American History XY," 26.

22. Redick, 161.

23. Money, "Hermaphroditism," 10.

24. Sandra Eder, "The Volatility of Sex: Intersexuality, Gender and Clinical Practice in the 1950s," *Gender and History* 22, no. 3 (2010): 692–707; Downing, Morland, and Sullivan, *Fuckology*, 4.

25. The record of Cadet's cousin is echoed in a chapter written by Money that appears in a medical textbook on pediatric endocrinology. In a section on counseling patients, Money emphasizes the need to provide information to young patients that does not promote "the trauma of ignorance" and that avoids "the intolerable burden of feeling implicitly accused and blameworthy" for one's difference. Money, *Sin, Science*, 331–32.

26. Peggy Cadet, "Solving the Jigsaw Puzzle," *Narrative Inquiry in Bioethics* 5, no. 2 (2015): E1–E3, https://muse.jhu.edu/article/589226/pdf.

27. Hypospadias describes a penis with a urinary meatus (opening) at the underside or base of the penis rather than at the tip, which is typical. Hypospadias surgeries are the most frequent pediatric urological surgeries and are usually regarded as "routine," despite a high rate of repeat surgeries and the risk of resulting in what specialists continue to refer to as "hypospadias cripples" in the medical literature. See, for example, Nauman A. Gill and Abdul Hameed, "Management of Hypospadias Cripples with Two-Staged Bracka's Technique," *Journal of Plastic, Aesthetic, and Reconstructive Surgery* 64, no. 1 (2011): 91–96.

28. Downing, Morland, and Sullivan, *Fuckology*, 189.

29. Anke A. Erhardt, "John Money, Ph.D.," *Journal of Sex Research* 44, no. 2 (2007): 223–24.

Curiosity, Ethics, and Intersex Anatomies   53

30. Vern Bullough, "The Contributions of John Money: A Personal View," *Journal of Sex Research* 40, no. 3 (2003): 230.

31. John Money and Anke A. Ehrhardt, *Man and Woman, Boy and Girl* (Baltimore, Md.: Johns Hopkins University Press, 1972), 173; see also Money, *Sin, Science*, 318–19.

32. Bullough, "The Contributions of John Money," 233.

33. Bullough, 234.

34. Erhardt, "John Money, Ph.D.," 224.

35. Bullough, "The Contributions of John Money," 235.

36. Erhardt, "John Money, Ph.D.," 224.

37. Downing, Morland, and Sullivan, *Fuckology*, 2.

38. Among such cases of "truly pioneering giants of science," whose reputations have suffered the sort of vicissitudes Erhardt evokes in her assurances to Money, the thinker who may come most readily to a philosopher's mind is Aristotle. There is good reason to reject any such comparison out of hand. Aristotle's role as a pioneer is unparalleled; his work has been foundational to every single discipline, including Money's. (It is owing to Aristotle's creative contribution to every recognized discipline, after all, that recipients of the highest certification of educational achievement are awarded a "doctor of philosophy.") Despite Aristotle's undeniable contribution, history has seen the rise and dramatic fall, and rise again, of Aristotle's stature in a number of fields. The narrower comparison to Aristotle's work in natural science may hold up better, as biologist Armand Marie Leroi has detailed in *Aristotle's Lagoon: How Aristotle Invented Science* (New York: Viking, 2014).

Leroi's generous re-creation of Aristotle's investigations on Lesbos urges us to set aside any errors regarding function or classification the philosopher made in order to focus on the care and insight Aristotle's meticulous observations of the natural world demonstrate. Supporters of Money today may want to take the Reimer case as an error, perhaps not exactly like the mistakes that Aristotle made about cuttlefish, eels, or women (See Leroi's *Aristotle's Lagoon*). But if the difference between these errors is not plain to them, then perhaps we are met with another case of the ethical danger presented by the absence (or suppression) of curiosity.

39. Downing, Morland, and Sullivan, *Fuckology*, 2.

40. Jakub Mieszczak, Christopher P. Houk, and Peter A. Lee, "Assignment of the Sex of Rearing in the Neonate with a Disorder of Sex Development," *Current Opinion in Pediatrics* 21 (2009): 542.

41. See, for example, Lee and Houk, "Sex Reassignment."

42. See Claudia Wiesemann et al., "Ethical Principles and Recommendations for the Medical Management of Differences of Sex Development (DSD)/Intersex in Children and Adolescents," *European Journal of Pediatrics* 169, no. 6 (2010): 671–79; Mieszczak, Houk, and Lee, "Sex Development," 545.

PART II

Relearning How We Learn

4

A Network Science of the Practice of Curiosity

Danielle S. Bassett

Curiosity is not an accidental isolated possession; it is a necessary consequence of the fact that an experience is a moving, changing thing, involving all kinds of connections with other things. Curiosity is but the tendency to make these conditions perceptible.

In other words, knowledge is a perception of those connections of an object which determine its applicability in a given situation. . . . Thus, we get at a new event indirectly instead of immediately—by invention, ingenuity, resourcefulness. An ideally perfect knowledge would represent such a network of interconnections that any past experience would offer a point of advantage from which to get at the problem presented in a new experience.

—John Dewey, *Democracy and Education*

What we know today about the neural basis of curiosity has capitalized on conceptual frameworks and empirical advances across many fields of science. The disciplines that have contributed the most to this conversation in recent years include biology, psychology, neurology, and psychiatry, spanning the gamut from basic science to clinical medicine. Although an exact definition of curiosity from a neuroscience perspective has remained elusive,[1] most scientists and practitioners would agree that curiosity is accompanied by some sort of information-seeking behavior.[2] A particularly important characteristic of this behavior is that it appears to be internally motivated,[3] meaning that no one forces a person to be curious. Naturally then, the scientific study of curiosity tends to uncover the motivations for and neural correlates of information-seeking behavior.[4]

One manner in which to formalize this study is to examine perturbations of curious thought, which—as it turns out—occur quite ubiquitously in the world we know. By studying how curious thought is modulated by natural or unnatural factors, one can begin to infer underlying mechanisms. A canonical example of a natural perturbation of curious thought is normative neurodevelopment: as children grow from infants to adults, the type of curious thought they produce appears to change in kind. In young children,[5] information seeking can amount to heightened attention and focus on objects that are "bright, vivid, startling,"[6] while in older adults, information seeking is naturally accompanied by voluntary movements (of the eye or body) to gain more knowledge. One might envision the infant obsessed with the cotton-stuffed ball, with colorful velvet patches on the outside, and a rich smattering of various sorts of ribbons attached with teeth-resistant stitching; and one might contrast this parochial vision with that of a graduate student entering the Ren Library at Trinity College, Cambridge, seeking a definitive tome on "neurons, networks, and nebulae."[7] In other words, information seeking can be distinguished based on the types of information that the subject seeks.

Likewise, information seeking can also be characterized by the manner in which the information is sought. Indeed, the practice of curiosity can differ across individuals,[8] may change with age and cognitive development,[9] and is likely impacted by stress and socioeconomic status,[10] as well as prior experience. Intuitively, the practice of curiosity could be impatient or enduring. It could involve seeking completely unknown information or vaguely familiar information. It could involve gathering the new information and keeping it logged separately like bits of trivia, or it could involve determining the links between bits of information, fitting them into one's existing body of knowledge. While these manners of curiosity are intuitive, it remains difficult to precisely define them, categorize them into classes, write down mathematical formulations for their nature, and form generative models for their processes. In other words, we lack a science of the practice of curiosity.

In this chapter we develop the conceptual foundations for such a science. We suggest that the practice of curiosity can be defined as knowledge network building. This proposition offers an interdisciplinary perspective on curiosity that is informed by neuroscience, psychology, linguistics, and network science. By drawing on concepts and tools across these disciplines, we suggest that knowledge can be represented mathematically as a network. While prior scholarship has focused on definitions of curiosity more akin to the force that enables us to seek knowledge, we focus on the manner of network growth in our minds and the potential to quantitatively characterize and mathematically model that growth using tools from network science. The proposal formalizes many of the intuitions that we have about the practice of curiosity, and by that formalization provides the foundations from which to construct explicit hypotheses that can be tested empirically in humans.

The chapter is organized as follows. In the first section, we define what a network is both conceptually and mathematically. In the second section, we discuss how networks can be used to represent knowledge, and we review key efforts in the study of language networks, semantic networks, and concept networks. In the third section, we outline the general idea of network building, and we review models of network growth from various fields of biology, including genetics, vasculature, and neuroscience. In the fourth section, we unpack more explicitly the bridge between the practice of curiosity and models of network growth, placing special emphasis on how this intersection can be informed by theories of learning and education. In the fifth section, we highlight several future directions in empirical science, mathematics, and their intersection that could further inform a science of the practice of curiosity, and in the last section, we conclude.

What Is a Network?

To make the notion of knowledge network building concrete, we must first clarify what we mean by a network. A network is a representation of a complex system, which in turn is a system that is composed of many interacting parts and in which the pattern of interactions is far from homogeneous and therefore defies simpler modeling efforts.[11] Specifically, a network is a representation in which the system's components are represented by network nodes, and a relationship between two components is represented by an edge (or a link) between two nodes. Commonly, network representations are encoded in a graph $G=(V,E)$ with vertices V representing nodes and edges E representing relationships between them (see Figure 4.1).[12] Further, a common storage object for a graph is an adjacency matrix, which is an N-by-N matrix A, where N is the number of nodes in the network, whose element A_{ij} indicates the strength of connectivity between node i and node j. Naturally then, networks are an excellent way in which to represent and probe relational data.[13]

Figure 4.1. A network is often encoded in a graph, in which a system's parts are represented by nodes (circles), and in which relations between parts are represented by edges (lines). Art by J. K. Rofling, www.jkrofling.com.

Historically, network representations have been commonly exercised in the context of social groups, largely in an effort to understand patterns of social interactions,[14] quantify the influence of a single individual on collective behavior,[15] and predict voting patterns or political tumult.[16] Across these efforts, it has proven critical to carefully consider the definition of network nodes.[17] While a single person is perhaps the clear initial choice for a network node, there are arguments both to choose larger components (extraperson objects such as groups, parties, communities, or countries) or smaller components (intraperson characteristics including brains or brain areas driving social behaviors). Indeed, the choice of what constitutes a node depends on the scientific question at hand; some levels of description will be more or less

A Network Science of the Practice of Curiosity   61

sensitive to the phenomenon of interest. In other words, the term "social network" may be a misnomer for a multiscale network system that can be interrogated either in a scale-specific manner or in a cross-scale manner.

Importantly, the concept of a multiscale network is not only relevant for the historical fodder of network science (social networks) but also particularly appropriate for the organ that produces our curiosity: the human brain.[18] Network representations of the brain usually begin with a subdivision of the cortical and subcortical tissue into parcels, which are thought to perform different functions, and whose boundaries are defined by anatomical[19] or functional markers.[20] These parcels are then connected with one another either using estimates of hardwired connections, as defined by imaging markers of white-matter tracts, or by estimates of functional connections, as defined by similarities in the time-dependent activity traces measured from pairs of parcels.[21] Expanding this representation to a multiscale network enables us to capture interactions between neural units defined across both spatial and temporal scales. Intuitively, these networks then represent the patterns of interactions between functional units of the brain that enable the complex patterns of thought characteristic of humans. Indeed, individual differences in the architecture of these brain networks across people have been linked to individual differences in openness to experience,[22] creativity,[23] and information-seeking behaviors.[24]

Knowledge as a Network

The multiscale network housed inside of the human skull enables us to acquire knowledge, learn new languages, and build conceptual frameworks and theories to explain the world around us. While the *Oxford English Dictionary* provides a quite general account of knowledge as "the sum of what is known,"[25] Webster's 1828 *Dictionary of the English Language* more specifically claims that knowledge is "a clear and certain perception of that which exists, or of truth and fact; *the perception of the connection* and agreement, or disagreement and repugnancy *of our ideas*."[26] Indeed, knowledge is quite naturally thought of as a set of ideas and a pattern of connections between those ideas. That is, we do not simply hold disconnected concepts in our minds; instead, we hold concepts and their relationships.

Perhaps the simplest illustration of this networked nature of knowledge is evident when considering language. Language is composed of units defined over different temporal scales, including phonemes, syllables, and supra-syllabic objects, each of which is represented and processed in different areas of the brain.[27] At the finest level of phonemes, pairs of phonemes are found beside one another with some specific probability, and the set of probabilities defines a network architecture for the language. The rules by which these probabilities are defined are the topic of a large body of work in artificial grammars.[28] At the coarser level of phonological word-forms, or lexemes, one can similarly construct a network representation by linking lexemes, if they are phonological neighbors of each other in the adult lexicon.[29] The structure of this network has specific implications for the process of retrieving word-forms from the mental lexicon, and also motivates questions regarding the mechanisms that might lead to certain network structures.[30]

While phonological neighborhood is a natural metric by which to link units of language, its relationship to knowledge per se is arguably rather tenuous. Closer to our focus are semantic networks, which represent semantic relations between concepts: for example, mammal (node) is (edge) an animal (node).[31] Early efforts argued that these networks are tree-like structures with connections determined by class-inclusion relations,[32] while later work argued that such strict hierarchical structures may not be relevant for a large majority of concepts.[33] Since those early efforts, data continue to mount supporting the notion that semantic networks are not particularly tree-like,[34] but instead have a small-world organization (local clustering accompanied by a few long-distance connections), and a scale-free organization (most nodes having relatively few connections and a few nodes having many connections).[35] Both this clustering and heterogeneity are thought to impact the formation and search of semantic memory.[36] One can expand on the simple semantic network by adding causal links between concepts; this extension takes concepts organized into categories and enables causal inference, causal reasoning, and causal perception from them.[37]

The number of possible semantic relations between concepts is massive. This fact increases the potential complexity of semantic networks and can hamper simple interpretations of that complexity. A more tractable place to start is to choose a single relation, or a set of similar relations, and study the network architectures that emerge. For example, one might wish to study the network of concepts in which words are represented as network nodes, and two words are connected with one another if they share similar

A Network Science of the Practice of Curiosity   63

meaning. Technically speaking this approach moves us from networks of semantic relatedness (broadly defined) to networks of semantic similarity.[38] A strict way to construct this network is to use information regarding synonyms in a dictionary or thesaurus; alternatively, one can perform laboratory experiments in which one asks a human participant to list a sequence of words in which each word is related to the next by meaning.[39]

Indeed, this discussion naturally raises the question of how to measure the knowledge network of a single individual, with the eventual goal of understanding how their knowledge network might be built through the practice of curiosity. Intuitively, individual semantic networks can be observed and measured through either verbal or written form. Verbal assessments include free association tasks,[40] or asking participants to produce narratives or stories, with or without visual prompts such as pictures. The structure of these narratives can provide insights not only into healthy cognition but also into the minds of those with cognitive impairments or mental health disorders.[41] An alternative to verbal measurements is to use written forms, such as stories, blogs, articles, or books. Common network representations of these data include word co-occurrence networks,[42] where words are represented as network nodes and two words are connected with one another if they are less than x words away from one another in the text; here, x is a threshold that is often chosen in the range of two to ten. Other measures of word-to-word relations beyond co-occurrence have also proven useful, and many computational algorithms have been devised to build such networks from large corpora.

Network Building: Models of Network Growth

While the previous section described the existence of knowledge networks, both in the population at large and in individual humans, it did not address the question of how those networks are built. Indeed, how does one build any sort of network? Intuitively, one might imagine that to build or grow a network, one must have a rule for choosing nodes to add to the network and a rule for choosing how to link those new nodes to existing nodes in the network (see Figure 4.2). In addition, one might consider whether or not older nodes or older edges die out after a certain time has elapsed, or after a certain amount of growth has occurred. These ideas lead to questions of conservation: are there energetic, spatial, or other constraints on the system that inform the rules of network growth?

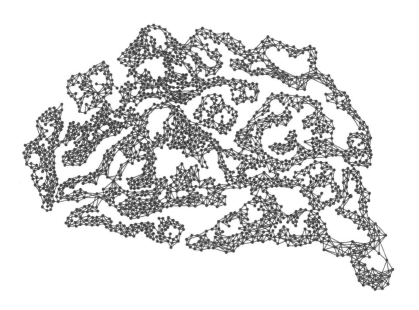

Figure 4.2. Knowledge networks can be built in a purposeful manner, with explicit rules for choosing nodes to add to the network and for choosing how to link those new nodes to existing nodes in the network. This figure is an artist's rendition of the knowledge network created by a daydream, where the meandering nature of thought produces a network with loopy structure. Art by J. K. Rofling, www.jkrofling.com.

As one might imagine, the answers to these questions may vary from system to system; rules may depend on the purposes of the network, on persistent pressures from evolution, and on transient demands from the environment. Some of the simplest growth models, however, ignore physical constraints and simply follow a set of abstract topological rules. For example, the Barabási-Albert model (also known as the *preferential attachment* model) begins with a single edge connecting two nodes, and then iteratively adds a single node to the network by linking the new node to m existing nodes, with a preference for nodes of high degree.[43] This growth model tends to form networks with highly skewed distributions of degree (the number of edges each node has): a scale-free distribution, in fact, whereby most nodes have relatively few connections and a few nodes have many connections.

A recent extension of the Barabási-Albert model is the affinity model, which is designed to create more explicit hierarchical structure in the network by assigning each node an affinity parameter, and then linking nodes with similar affinity parameters.[44]

While these growing models create networks with architectural features that are commonly observed in concept networks—such as local clustering and skewed degree distributions—they do not explicitly account for realistic constraints in the environment or in the mind of the thinker. Two particularly salient examples of network growth models, which do account for realistic constraints, address the development of neural and vasculature systems. In neural systems a common observation is that neurons are more likely to connect to one another if they are close in physical space.[45] A natural model for this process is the distance drop-off growth model, which distributes nodes uniformly at random in a physical space, and then connects nodes to one another according to a probability that is a function of node–node distance.[46] This model creates degree distributions that are consistent with empirical data, and also recapitulates observed patterns of assortative mixing:[47] nodes with high degree (also called hubs) tend to connect to other nodes of high degree. While this and similar models focus solely on the growth of nodes and edges in a single system, models of vasculature have coupled models of underlying tissue growth, with the overlaid vasculature network growth. Notably, recent work demonstrates that the growth of the underlying tissue, coupled to the dynamical equations for network development, can explain the emergence of highly optimized transport networks in animal and leaf vasculature.[48]

Thus a variety of network growth models span those that evolve by abstract topological rules and those that evolve by physically or biologically motivated rules. Do these notions help us in constructing growth models for knowledge networks? This question has been most actively addressed in the context of semantic networks. For example, Steyvers and Tenebaum suggest a simple model for semantic growth in which new words or concepts are added to the network in such a way as to differentiate the connectivity pattern of an existing node,[49] generating both small-world architecture and scale-free degree distributions. Interestingly, this model suggests a mechanism for the effects of learning history variables (age of acquisition, usage frequency) on behavioral performance in semantic processing tasks. In a similar spirit, Hills et al. consider the learning of word association networks

66 Danielle S. Bassett

and demonstrate that a preferential attachment model incorporating word frequency, number of phonological neighbors, and connectedness of the new word to words in the learning environment offered a reasonable fit to a data set of noun acquisition from children under thirty months of age.[50] While both models are described as generically applicable across individuals in the broader population, it is also of interest to examine if and how individual differences in semantic networks are correlated with individual differences in the participant's personality or creativity,[51] under the assumption that the manner in which an individual interacts with the world may impact their network's growth.

Bridging the Practice of Curiosity with Models of Network Growth

While growth models exist for semantic networks, no current efforts address the active growth of knowledge networks through the practice of curiosity. And what is the practice of curiosity? Can one practice curiosity? Many studies operate under the idea that curiosity is an innate or default state: a capacity that is best characterized as a trait of a person, or the common mode in which the person operates.[52] This notion is similar to the notion that a person has a natural level of self-assurance, irritableness, or self-referential processing, also referred to as *mindfulness*. Yet, in truth, self-assurance and irritability can vary over short timescales, and mindfulness is far from fixed in a single person. In fact, mindfulness training can fundamentally alter a person's patterns of thought, leading to a change in their decision-making,[53] working memory, spatial memory, verbal fluency,[54] and cognitive flexibility,[55] by altering the activity of specific areas of the brain.[56] Similarly, curiosity can be argued to be far from fixed in a person, but instead can wax and wane naturally from moment to moment.[57] Furthermore, curiosity can be modulated by external factors including those present in learning environments.[58] The fact that curiosity can vary and be varied opens the possibility of practicing curiosity with the aim of self-betterment.

Here we define the practice of curiosity as the performance of mental tasks characteristic of curious thought. Just as in mindfulness training where one practices a certain set of mental states and transitions (or lack of transitions) between them, so in curiosity training one practices mental states of curiosity, and mental state transitions following a line of inquiry. Moreover, one might practice choosing the objects of curiosity, following patterns of curious search, and making time and space in one's life to act on one's information-seeking proclivities. Metaphorically, one walks along one's network of knowledge and seeks to build new webs, add new edges, add new nodes, or leap into the black (or blank) space beyond one's knowledge in the hopes of landing on some deliciously unexpected idea (see Figure 4.3). The manner in which we walk, build, and leap may be informed by our personalities, our educational experiences and learning capacities, and other characteristics that differ from person to person.

Building network growth models for the practice of curiosity then entails several distinct ingredients. First, one must determine the type of node one seeks; while semantic networks are arguably the most common knowledge network studied in the current literature, one could argue that the ideas one tends to search for in curious acts are often larger than a single concept. Second, one must determine the type and distance of links one is willing to make: How distinct may two ideas be for one to still acknowledge their relationship? Third, one must determine the manner of incorporating the

Figure 4.3. One can walk along one's network of knowledge, deciding to build a steady path or to leap to a new space in the hopes of landing on an unexpected idea. Art by J. K. Rofling, www.jkrofling.com.

new node and edge into the existing knowledge network (if at all): What sort of architecture does one wish to build? Is it dense or sparse? Ordered or disordered? Low-dimensional or high-dimensional? The answers to these questions require some explicit notions of distance, geometry, and space: the distance between ideas, the geometry of the network, and the space in which the network exists.[59] Building on the work of Peter Gärdenfors, one can ask: "What is the geometry of curious thought?[60] And how does it relate to one's own conceptual space?"[61] Such a space may even be poetic.[62]

The geometry of the network that one builds may depend on processes of implicit learning that occur as we watch others perform acts of curiosity, either by visual or auditory observation or by reading their written work. One of the most commonly studied forms of implicit learning is known as statistical learning,[63] whereby we acquire knowledge about statistical regularities in our environment. The neural computations supporting this type of learning can facilitate either the encoding of pairwise relationships between objects or concepts or higher order relational patterns between them.[64] In the context of learning the practice of curiosity from others,[65] this human capacity could manifest in acquiring knowledge about the types of ideas others search for, how they connect them, and, over time, how these small steps lead to the growth of knowledge networks. Learning the practice of curiosity can be strengthened further through so-called reinforcement learning processes, where one is explicitly told by another that one has responded correctly.[66] This confirmation of accuracy can reinforce the learned behavior; one's nature or idea may be validated as "curious" by another person.

The notion of learning the practice of curiosity from others naturally motivates a discussion of education and educational forms. In the common forms of education, is the practice of curiosity taught? Does one learn what category of nodes to look for, what types of edges to draw, and what sort of networks to build? Of course, it is entirely possible that a teacher or professor lecturing in front of a class for a semester may be able to impart some knowledge about the practice of curiosity, as a byproduct of demonstrating their own. But perhaps the more natural means of transferring a mode of knowledge network building is by mentorship or apprenticeship. Here, the one-on-one nature of the interaction can denoise the mentee's observed statistical regularities, perhaps leading to a swifter and more accurate acquisition of the knowledge offered.

Future Directions

While previous sections have laid out a framework for a network science of the practice of curiosity, many questions remain that directly motivate ongoing and future empirical research. The first and most natural place to begin is to empirically characterize the objects of curiosity that individuals seek—whether they be concepts or causal relations, ideas or principles, and whether they be crystalized or hazy, simple or complex. The second objective is to empirically measure the relationships that humans seek to make between those objects of curiosity, and the third is to characterize the evolution of the participant's knowledge network as they build. It seems natural to tackle these challenges both over short time scales in living subjects (in the course of a traditional laboratory experiment) and over long time scales in deceased (or merely absent) subjects, by examining the evolution of their written work. Collectively, such studies would provide insights into the manner of network evolution that accompanies the practice of curiosity.

To complement these empirical measurements, one needs to build fundamental theories and mathematical models to explain the observations. Specifically, one needs to use these empirical measurements to determine the parameters and rules of network growth models characteristic of a cohort of participants, as well as variations in those parameters or rules that are representative of individual people. It is possible that the rules by which we build semantic networks are similar to the rules by which we build knowledge networks through acts of curiosity. However, it is also possible that curiosity enables us to reach farther for ideas than we would naturally—to seek, search, and track with greater fervor and with greater dedication than would otherwise be our want, leading us to stretch out tendrils into the knowledge network space that would otherwise remain tight local neighborhoods. A careful blend of theory and experiment could prove or disprove this inkling.

In this chapter we have described a formalism embedded in the natural sciences in which to study the thoughts and acts of curiosity. We described the mathematical notion of a network or graph and how it can be used to represent information about different sorts of knowledge, from grammars to semantics. We then described models of network growth and their relation to the evolution of semantic networks, which parsimoniously capture complex patterns of relationships between concepts. We then defined the

70 Danielle S. Bassett

practice of curiosity and described how it can be characterized as a purposeful growth of one's knowledge network, which can be influenced by one's personality, learning capacity, and educational experiences. We suggested that further developing, empirically testing, and validating a network science of the practice of curiosity could inform not only an individual's internal practice but also educational practices at large. We look forward to future efforts clarifying these ideas.

Notes

The author is grateful to (i) Perry Zurn for inspirational discussions that were instrumental in the formulation of these ideas, (ii) Arjun Shankar and Perry Zurn for helpful comments on earlier versions of this manuscript, (iii) the Center for Curiosity at the University of Pennsylvania, which motivated the author to devote time to developing the ideas put forth in this chapter, and (iv) Brennan Klein for illustrations.

1. Celeste Kidd and Benjamin Y. Hayden, "The Psychology and Neuroscience of Curiosity," *Neuron* 88, no. 3 (2015): 449–60.

2. Jacqueline Gottlieb et al., "Attention, Reward, and Information Seeking," *Journal of Neuroscience* 34, no. 46 (2014): 15497–504.

3. George Loewenstein, "The Psychology of Curiosity: A Review and Reinterpretation," *Psychological Bulletin* 116 (1994): 75–98; Pierre-Yves Oudeyer and Frederic Kaplan, "What Is Intrinsic Motivation? A Typology of Computational Approaches," *Frontiers in Neurorobotics* 1, no. 6 (2007).

4. Geoffrey K. Adams et al., "Neuroethology of Decision-Making," *Current Opinion in Neurobiology* 22, no. 6 (2012): 982–89.

5. G. Stanley Hall and Theodate L. Smith, "Curiosity and Interest," *Pedagogical Seminary* 10 (1903): 315–58.

6. William James, *Talks to Teachers on Psychology: And to Students on Some of Life's Ideals* (New York: Henry Holt, 1899).

7. Michael Taylor and Angeles I. Diaz, "On the Deduction of Galactic Abundances with Evolutionary Neural Networks," in Antonella Vallenari et al., "Stars to Galaxies: Building the Pieces to Build up the Universe," *ASP Conference Series* 374 (2007).

8. Teresa M. Amabile et al., "The Work Preference Inventory: Assessing Intrinsic and Extrinsic Motivational Orientations," *Journal of Personality and Social Psychology* 66, no. 5 (1994): 950–67.

9. Angelina R. Sutin et al., "Sex Differences in Resting-State Neural Correlates of Openness to Experience among Older Adults," *Cerebral Cortex* 19, no. 12 (2009): 2797–802.

10. Josephine D. Arasteh, "Creativity and Related Processes in the Young Child: A Review of the Literature," *Journal of Genetic Psychology* 112(1st half) (1968): 77–108.

A Network Science of the Practice of Curiosity 71

11. Mark E. J. Newman, "Complex Systems: A Survey," *American Journal of Physics* 79 (2011): 800–810.

12. Béla Bollobás, *Modern Graph Theory* (New York: Springer, 2002).

13. Mark E. J. Newman, *Networks: An Introduction* (Oxford: Oxford University Press, 2010).

14. Duncan J. Watts and Steven H. Strogatz, "Collective Dynamics of 'Small-World' Networks," *Nature* 393, no. 6684 (1998): 440–42.

15. Filippo Radicchi and Claudio Castellano, "Fundamental Difference between Superblockers and Superspreaders in Networks," *Physics Review E* 5, no. 1 (2017), https://journals.aps.org/pre/abstract/10.1103/PhysRevE.95.012318.

16. Sandra González-Bailón et al., "The Dynamics of Protest Recruitment through an Online Network," *Scientific Reports* 1 (2011): 197.

17. Carter T. Butts, "Revisiting the Foundations of Network Analysis," *Science* 325, no. 5939 (2009): 414–16.

18. Richard F. Betzel and Danielle S. Bassett, "Multi-scale Brain Networks," *Neuroimage* 160 (2017): 73–83.

19. Korbinian Brodmann, *Vergleichende Lokalisationslehre der Grosshirnrinde* (Leipzig, Ger.: Johann Ambrosius Barth, 1909).

20. Matthew F. Glasser et al., "A Multi-modal Parcellation of Human Cerebral Cortex," *Nature* 536, no. 7615 (2016): 171–78.

21. Edward T. Bullmore and Danielle S. Bassett, "Brain Graphs: Graphical Models of the Human Brain Connectome," *Annual Review of Clinical Psychology* 7 (2011): 113–40.

22. Roger E. Beaty et al., "Personality and Complex Brain Networks: The Role of Openness to Experience in Default Network Efficiency," *Human Brain Mapping* 37, no. 2 (2016): 773–79.

23. Roger E. Beaty et al., "Default and Executive Network Coupling Supports Creative Idea Production," *Scientific Reports* 5 (2015): 10964.

24. Aaron M. Scherer, Bradley C. Taber-Thomas, and Daniel Tranel, "A Neuropsychological Investigation of Decisional Certainty," *Neuropsychologia* 70 (2015): 206–13.

25. *Oxford English Dictionary,* accessed July 14, 2010, http://oxforddictionaries .com.

26. Daniel Webster, *American Dictionary of the English Language* (1828), Foundation for American Christian Education, facsimile of 1st edition (June 1, 1967), emphasis added.

27. Maya Brainard et al., "Distinct Representations of Phonemes, Syllables, and Supra-Syllabic Sequences in the Speech Production Network," *Neuroimage* 50, no. 2 (2010): 626–38.

28. W. Tecumseh Fitch and Angela D. Friederici, "Artificial Grammar Learning Meets Formal Language Theory: An Overview," *Philosophical Transactions of the Royal Society of London B: Biological Sciences* 367, no. 1598 (2012): 1933–55.

29. Paul A. Luce and David B. Pisoni, "Recognizing Spoken Words: The Neighborhood Activation Model," *Ear and Hearing* 19, no. 1 (1998): 1–36.

30. Michael S. Vitevitch, "What Can Graph Theory Tell Us about Word Learning and Lexical Retrieval?" *Journal of Speech, Language, and Hearing Research* 51, no. 2 (2008): 408–22.

31. John F. Sowa, "Semantic Networks," in Stuart C. Shapiro, *Encyclopedia of Artificial Intelligence* (New York: Wiley-Interscience, 1987).

32. Allan M. Collins and M. Ross Quillian, "Retrieval Time from Semantic Memory," *Journal of Verbal Learning and Verbal Behavior* 8 (1969): 240–48.

33. Frank C. Keil, *Semantic and Conceptual Development: An Ontological Perspective* (Cambridge, Mass.: Harvard University Press, 1979); Dan I. Slobin, "Cognitive Prerequisites for the Acquisition of Grammar," in *Studies of Child Language Development,* ed. Charles A. Ferguson and Dan I. Slobin, (New York: Holt, Rinehart and Winston, 1973), 173–208.

34. Michael E. Bales and Stephen B. Johnson, "Graph Theoretic Modeling of Large-Scale Semantic Networks," *Journal of Biomedical Informatics* 39, no. 4 (2006): 451–64.

35. Mark Steyvers and Joshua B. Tenenbaum, "The Large-Scale Structure of Semantic Networks: Statistical Analyses and a Model of Semantic Growth," *Cognitive Science* 29, no. 1 (2005): 41–78.

36. John R. Anderson, *Learning and Memory: An Integrated Approach,* 2nd ed. (New York: Wiley, 2000).

37. David Danks, *Unifying the Mind: Cognitive Representations as Graphical Models* (Cambridge, Mass.: MIT Press, 2014).

38. Sebastien Harispe et al., "Semantic Similarity from Natural Language and Ontology Analysis," *Synthesis Lectures on Human Language Technologies* 8, no. 1 (2015): 1–254.

39. Yoed N. Kenett et al., "Global and Local Features of Semantic Networks: Evidence from the Hebrew Mental Lexicon," *PLoS One* 6, no. 8 (2011), https://journals.plos.org/plosone/article?id=10.1371/journal.pone.0023912.

40. Douglas L. Nelson and Ningchuan Zhang, "The Ties That Bind What Is Known to the Recall of What Is New," *Psychonomic Bulletin and Review* 7, no. 4 (2000): 604–17.

41. Michelle Lee et al., "What's the Story? A Computational Analysis of Narrative Competence in Autism," *Autism* (2017), https://www.ncbi.nlm.nih.gov/pubmed/280 95705; Kelly Renz et al., "On-line Story Representation in Boys with Attention Deficit Hyperactivity Disorder," *Journal of Abnormal Child Psychology* 31, no. 1 (2003): 93–104; Claudia Drummond et al., "Deficits in Narrative Discourse Elicited by Visual Stimuli Are Already Present in Patients with Mild Cognitive Impairment," *Frontiers in Aging Neuroscience* 7 (2015): 96; Manfred Spitzer, "Associative Networks, Formal Thought Disorders and Schizophrenia: On the Experimental Psychopathology of Speech-Dependent Thought Processes," *Der Nervenarzt* 64, no. 3 (1993): 147–59.

A Network Science of the Practice of Curiosity   73

42. Angeliki Lazaridou, Marco Marelli, and Marco Baroni, "Multimodal Word Meaning Induction from Minimal Exposure to Natural Text," *Cognitive Science* 41, S4, 677–705.

43. Reka Z. Albert and Albert L. Barabási, "Statistical Mechanics of Complex Networks," *Reviews of Modern Physics* 74 (2002): 47–97.

44. Florian Klimm et al., "Resolving Structural Variability in Network Models and the Brain," *PLoS Computational Biology* 10. no. 3 (2014), https://journals.plos.org/ploscompbiol/article?id=10.1371/journal.pcbi.1003491.

45. Danielle S. Bassett and Edward T. Bullmore, "Small-World Brain Networks Revisited," *Neuroscientist* 23, no. 5 (2017): 499–516.

46. Albert and Barabási, "Statistical Mechanics of Complex Networks."

47. Mark E. Newman, "Assortative Mixing in Networks," *Physical Review Letters* 89, no. 20 (2002), https://journals.aps.org/prl/abstract/10.1103/PhysRevLett.89.208701.

48. Henrik Ronellenfitsch and Eleni Katifori, "Global Optimization, Local Adaptation, and the Role of Growth in Distribution Networks," *Physical Review Letters* 117, no. 13 (2016), https://journals.aps.org/prl/abstract/10.1103/PhysRevLett.117.138301.

49. Steyvers and Tenenbaum, "Large-Scale Structure."

50. Thomas T. Hills et al., "Longitudinal Analysis of Early Semantic Networks: Preferential Attachment or Preferential Acquisition?" *Psychological Science* 20, no. 6 (2009): 729–39.

51. Yoed N. Kenett, David Anaki, and Mariam Faust, "Investigating the Structure of Semantic Networks In Low and High Creative Persons," *Frontiers in Human Neuroscience* 8 (2014): 407.

52. Jordan A. Litman and Charles D. Spielberger, "Measuring Epistemic Curiosity and Its Diversive and Specific Components," *Journal of Personality Assessment* 80, no. 1 (2003): 75–86.

53. Ulrich Kirk et al., "Mindfulness Training Increases Cooperative Decision Making in Economic Exchanges: Evidence from fMRI," *Neuroimage* 138 (2016): 274–83.

54. Victoria L. Ives-Deliperi et al., "The Effects of Mindfulness-Based Cognitive Therapy in Patients with Bipolar Disorder: A Controlled Functional MRI Investigation," *Journal of Affective Disorders* 150, no. 3 (2013): 1152–57.

55. Jonathan K. Lee and Susan M. Orsillo, "Investigating Cognitive Flexibility as a Potential Mechanism of Mindfulness in Generalized Anxiety Disorder," *Journal of Behavioral Therapy and Experimental Psychiatry* 45, no. 1 (2014): 208–16.

56. Hannah J. Scheibner et al., "Internal and External Attention and the Default Mode Network," *Neuroimage* 148 (2017): 381–89.

57. Robert Sternszus, Alenoush Saroyan, and Yvonne Steinert, "Describing Medical Student Curiosity across a Four Year Curriculum: An Exploratory Study," *Medical Teacher* 39, no. 4 (2017): 377–82.

58. Raakhi K. Tripathi et al., "Development of Active Learning Modules in Pharmacology for Small Group Teaching," *Education for Health* 28, no. 1 (2015): 46–51; Yair Berson and Shaul Oreg, "The Role of School Principals in Shaping Children's Values," *Psychological Science* 27, no. 12 (2016): 1539–49.

59. Dominic Widdows, *Geometry and Meaning* (Stanford, Calif.: CSLI, 2004).

60. Peter Gärdenfors, *Conceptual Spaces: The Geometry of Thought* (Cambridge, Mass.: MIT Press, 2004).

61. Peter Gärdenfors, *The Geometry of Meaning: Semantics Based on Conceptual Spaces* (Cambridge, Mass.: MIT Press, 2014).

62. Gaston Bachelard, *The Poetics of Space* (Paris: Presses Universitaires de France, 1958).

63. Patrick Rebuschat and John N. Williams, *Statistical Learning and Language Acquisition* (Boston, Mass.: Walter de Gruyter, 2012).

64. Elisabeth A. Karuza, Sharon L. Thompson-Schill, and Danielle S. Bassett, "Local Patterns to Global Architectures: Influences of Network Topology on Human Learning," *Trends in Cognitive Science* 20, no. 8 (2016): 629–40.

65. Susan Engel, *The Hungry Mind: The Origins of Curiosity in Childhood* (Cambridge, Mass.: Harvard University Press, 2015).

66. Wolfram Schultz, "Neuronal Reward and Decision Signals: From Theories to Data," *Physiological Reviews* 95, no. 3 (2015): 853–951.

5

Why Should This Be So?

The Waxing and Waning of Children's Curiosity

Susan Engel

A small boy, playing out in the woods behind his home, came across a bug in the dirt. He stooped down to examine it more closely. Like children everywhere, looking wasn't enough. He picked it up to study its interesting shape, little legs, and odd movements. But then, out of the corner of his eye, he saw another bug quite different from the first one, on the ground nearby. He had to have that one too. Not ready to give up the first bug, but needing both hands to capture the second bug, he did what many curious children might do under the circumstances: he popped it into his mouth for safe keeping. But as it turned out, that wasn't so safe. In an act of instant self-defense, the bug squirted an unpleasant liquid onto the boy's inner cheeks and tongue. Unpleasant, but not poisonous. The little boy survived his encounter with the two bugs. Years later, facing another intriguing source of mystery involving wild creatures, he wrote this:

> The naturalist, looking at the inhabitants of these volcanic islands in the Pacific, distant several hundred miles from the continent, yet feels that he is standing on American land. Why should this be so? Why should the species which are supposed to have been created in the Galapagos Archipelago, and nowhere else, bear so plain a stamp of affinity to those created in America?[1]

When people think about Darwin, they are likely to focus on what made him exceptional: his brilliance, intellectual bravery, and vision. And it's tempting to try and identify glimmers of Darwin, the towering adult scientist in Darwin, the little boy. His biography makes it clear that even as a young child he had a formidable intellect and an appetite for exploring the natural world. Beyond

76   Susan Engel

these stable internal characteristics, it is also clear that his mature accom-
plishments rested in part on other benefits as well: wealth and opportunities
to travel and to study. Those features may help explain what set him apart
from the average child or adult. But asking what set him apart from others
may be less fruitful than trying to identify other more common aspects of his
experience, which help explain his sustained inquiry and intellectual industry.
By understanding these, we may get a better sense of the potential for more
"ordinary" children to develop into inquisitive and thoughtful adults. You
don't need to be Darwin to be curious and eager to solve intellectual puzzles.
This chapter is about the path that leads children to become curious adults.

Curious at Birth

Though few ever achieve what Darwin did, in one essential way, almost all
very young children are like the very young Darwin: they are indefatigable
explorers. This tremendous appetite for discovery begins with a very powerful and simple mechanism universal to human babies. They are predisposed
to look for regularity and familiarity in everyday life.[2] They know the difference between the face of someone they have already seen and that of a
stranger; they notice the difference between the sound of their mother's
voice (which they were exposed to in utero) and that of someone new; and
when shown pictures or patterns that are different from the one they have
been shown before, their breathing and heartbeat change, and their skin
produces more moisture. They not only show surprise and momentary tension when they encounter something new, they also do things differently in
the presence of novelty. Specifically, they look longer, studying whatever is
new or unexpected.[3] This attention to novelty is the foundation of curiosity,
and helps explain why babies and young children learn more than they ever
will again in their lives. The tendency to devote intellectual resources to the
unfamiliar powers the enormous advances children make by the time they
are five. Needless to say, it also helps explain why babies and toddlers seem
curious so much of the time. A great deal of their daily lives entails encoun-
tering things they haven't yet experienced: any number of animals, new
people, most foods, and 101 other small changes to the routines that make
up a very young child's day. They quickly absorb most of these new things
into their schema—that is, the cognitive scripts that guide them through

Why Should This Be So?   77

daily life get more flexible and complex. For example, by the time children are four they can tell you what they usually have for breakfast, and they can also tell you what they have for breakfast on holidays, or when it's especially hot outside. Their mental models include the fixed and variable elements of scripts for everyday experience.

The novel becomes familiar, leaving them ready and willing to respond to the next new thing. They are curious because so much of daily life entails novelty and, throughout the life span, curiosity is based on this one simple mechanism: the urge to explain the unexpected and resolve uncertainty. This also explains why, as children get older, curiosity becomes somewhat less ubiquitous. More and more of their everyday experiences are folded into schema that render breakfast, a trip to the grocery store or park, nap time, and a visit from neighbors unexceptional and unlikely to spark their curiosity. As this happens, more children begin to show specific curiosity for domains or events that grab their interest.

For instance, consider Owen at eighteen months. When his father brought him to the rooftop of their Brooklyn, New York, apartment building, he wandered around, glancing quickly at various things: a rooftop box garden, some pails, an old deck chair, and some curled sheets of tar paper. But these objects, possibly fascinating to another child, were too familiar to Owen to warrant examination. However, there was something he hadn't seen before. A metal spout, attached to a small water tower, gushing water into a plastic tray on the floor of the rooftop. The moment he spotted it, he rushed over to it immediately, stood watching it for a moment, then crouched down, leaned in, and did what any toddler might do: he stuck his tongue out to explore the water more thoroughly. For the next eight months, he couldn't pass a waterspout without wanting to watch it, touch it, and, most of all, lick it. For a period of time, waterspouts elicited far more exploration from Owen than many other more common daily objects and events.

But such vivid demonstration of curiosity becomes rarer as children leave toddlerhood behind. Because at the same time that curiosity narrows, it also becomes harder for the observer to see. By the time children are three or four, they are somewhat less intrepid and indiscriminate in their physical investigations. However, as physical inquiry wanes, another process for gathering information enters the scene. Children learn to ask questions. And when it comes to curiosity, language is a game changer.

78 Susan Engel

The Language of Inquiry

Babies and toddlers can watch, touch, tinker, open, taste, and experiment with the physical world. But they are more limited when it comes to finding out about the unseen world: both physical (e.g., bacteria, why smoke goes up a chimney, and why heat melts ice but hardens eggs) as well as cultural (e.g., why humans poop inside and pets do not, what people mean when they say someone has passed on, and what a ghost is). Here, questions are the sine qua non of human curiosity. They allow children to ask about a vastly larger, more complex range of topics, and to ask for many more kinds of information. They ask not just what something is but what it was like before, why people view it a certain way, or what others know and think about something.

When psychologists Barbara Tizard and Martin Hughes recorded three-year-olds in their homes, they found that children ask, on average, 26 questions per hour.[4] Of those questions, two-thirds were to gain information.

That means that most children were asking a question every two minutes or so. But just as important, the majority of those questions were aimed at gaining information about the world (rather than, say, seeking attention or permission). In a more recent study, Michele Chouinard studied the language of four children over a period of four years.[5] One of her subjects asked, on average, 104 questions per hour. That child, in other words, was asking more than 2 questions per minute. Chouinard's young subjects ask three times as many questions aimed at getting new information as they did other kinds of questions. Children not only use questions to find out about the world, they typically want more than names of objects, or simple information. They want explanations. Drawing on the language used by children in a nursery school in Cambridge, England, during the 1920's, Nathan Isaacs argued that, contrary to the prevalent view of children as focused only on the here and now, a closer examination of their questions showed that many children were interested in a much deeper, less concrete kind of knowledge.[6] The children in his sample weren't only asking "what, where, and when" questions but, just as often, "why" questions. He argued that young children's why questions reflect an eagerness to understand phenomena that cannot be explained by their existing knowledge. Thus, even at three, children have some sense of when their knowledge is insufficient and use questions to fill in the gap. Their impulse to do so is quite strong as well.

Why Should This Be So?

Paul Harris has argued that children's persistence in the face of incomplete or unsatisfactory answers is evidence that their questions serve an important epistemological function and reflect an underlying drive for understanding.[7] They use questions in order to explain the mysteries of everyday life, and they are assertive and deliberate inquisitors as they seek intellectual satisfaction. Consider the following exchange between a three-year-old child and her mother:

> C H I L D : Why the dog poops outside?
> M O T H E R : Because that's what animals do.
> C H I L D : Why don't we poop outside?
> M O T H E R : Because we're people.
> C H I L D : But you said people were animals.
> M O T H E R : Yeah, but people have houses.
> C H I L D : But this is Lucky's house too, right?
> M O T H E R : Yes, but even so, Lucky's a dog.
> C H I L D : But they don't like to poop in a toilet?
> M O T H E R : I don't know. Lucky's never tried it.
> C H I L D : But he might like it, right?

The little girl takes six turns during this exchange, and five of those turns contain questions. Not only that, the questions are not only responsive to the mother's answers, they are related to one another, revealing a fairly systematic search for an explanation of two discrepant ideas: (1) dogs and humans are alike in that they are both animals, but (2) they don't poop in the same place. Her sequence of questions reveals her need for something beyond simple or discrete pieces of information. It dawns on her that something doesn't make sense. We know from her argument that she has been told that dogs and people form some kind of conceptual group (you said people are animals). Thus, it follows that the same rules might apply. Yet in this instance, they are different. People poop in bathrooms, Lucky poops outside. She keeps delving deeper when her mother's answers don't fully satisfy her need for an explanation.

In sum, once children can use questions to satisfy their curiosity, a whole new world opens up to us as researchers and to them as investigators. They can ask about things beyond the here and now, they can directly seek explanations, and they can inquire about knowledge that is socially constructed.

80 Susan Engel

Probing Ideas

When you put all the records and diaries of children's questions (collected over a period of one hundred years by approximately seven different scholars) side by side and examine them, an intriguing ambiguity arises. Many of the earlier scholars noted the unusual and often surprising nature of young children's questions: "Does God exist?"; "Why don't we see two things out of our two eyes?" But as Paul Harris notes, those examples are much more interesting to discuss than questions like, "What are we having for dinner?" "What's this called?" or even, "Why does the dog poop outside?" which may be more common.[8] But comparing the various data in terms of whether they are grand or prosaic obscures an interesting and possibly more developmentally important question: the degree to which the child's question gathers information for an underlying abstract idea. On this dimension, it seems that when children are as young as three they begin collecting information for fairly abstract problems.

For instance, take this description from Tizard and Hugh's data:

[R U T H] was bending over so that her mother could wipe her bottom. In this position, her mother could not see her head:

C : Mummy, you lost me.

M : I have lost you, yeah.

C : Can you only see my bottom and legs?

M : That's right.

C : And shoes and pants.

M : That's right. Stand up straight.

C : Here I am.

M : That's nice. There she is, back again. Off you go![9]

This example demonstrates two important features of young children's questions. First, the question emerges in an unexpected situation, quite spontaneously, apropos of leaning over and realizing that the view from upside down is different. She must have also realized that when her view changed, her mother's view also changed, and she began to wonder about it. This kind of momentary oddity is exactly what leads to brief moments of curiosity, like Ruth's, but also bigger, more extended stretches of curiosity as well. But the second thing that's interesting about it is that it pertains to an issue much larger than what her mother can see of her when she's bent over. It suggests she's thinking about the idea of different people's perspectives. Not only have most researchers focused on children's questions about the here and now, they've also tended to focus on the very concrete nature of children's questions: how an object works, why something is classified in a certain way, and even how something came to be. But when you sift through all the different data, it becomes clear that children increasingly use questions to ask about fairly abstract problems, such as the problem of perspective.

Consider, for instance, the following exchange, which I overheard while traveling in an airplane:

> A little girl, about age four, was nestled next to her mother, in the seat in front of me. She was peering out of the airplane window, far down below at the ground and said, "Mommy, there's probably a little kid down there asking her mommy if there is a kid up here in a plane. And is her mommy going to say, 'Yes, there is a child up there'?"

As with Ruth, this little girl seems to have suddenly realized that all the way down on the ground there might be another person, who views the situation from a very different perspective. She seems to be toying with the intriguing idea that two people can be experiencing the very same moment in ways that are both different and very much the same. The idea, or question, underlying her question is both abstract and profound. And though, in the stream of conversation, it floats right by (as I recall, her mother simply said, "Yep, that's right Sweetie"), it does two things, one for the researcher and another for the girl. For the researcher, it suggests that seemingly fleeting moments of curiosity may indicate a more sustained and intellectually significant interest on the part of a young child. For the girl, it's a chance to collect information on a topic she may be mulling over, however sporadically and implicitly.

Both young girls, the one looking through her legs and the one on the airplane, are pursuing puzzles, however casually, that jump out at them during regular life. But a puzzle such as the possibility for people's simultaneous but opposite experience (the view from under one's legs, or from an airplane) can become something more crafted and deliberate as children get older. This move toward a more deliberate and sustained pursuit of information first shows up as a sequence of questions or investigations that unfold over time. Needless to say, gathering evidence of such sustained inquiry requires tracking children's questions in their everyday lives and over time. Luckily there are such data.

Years ago two developmental psychologists, Brian MacWhinney and Catherine Snow, began collecting all the diaries parents had kept of their children's language and all the recordings psychologists had made of children going about their daily lives and put them into an online data bank, which they called CHILDES.[10] When my students and I looked at those diaries and recordings, we found plenty of evidence that children do in fact focus in on particular things that puzzle them. When they are playing, eating dinner, and riding in the car, they ask questions, muse, and speculate about their chosen topic—death, consciousness, how one's voice can be saved on a machine and replayed, to give just a few examples. Take Laura, for instance, who periodically mused aloud about death. In the following exchange, she has just heard that her pet bird died:

> MOTHER: . . . and he got himself ready to die, Laura.
> MOTHER: He took his nest down and he knew he was dying and he got himself ready.
> LAURA: He knew he was dying?
> MOTHER: Yes.
> FATHER: He knew.
> LAURA: How did he know he was dying?
> MOTHER: He could feel inside.
> FATHER: A feeling in the air.
> LAURA: I don't want to die.
> MOTHER: Mm.
> MOTHER: We're not going to.

A few minutes later, Laura returned to playing on her own with some toys, murmuring, "I wonder what it feels like to be dead." Over the course of two years, Laura engaged in a series of questions about death and dying more than nine times, and that's just in the periodic samples collected for this database. One can imagine that she asked at least as many during times that were not recorded. We are just beginning to investigate how common it is for children to pursue a line of inquiry over time, but the initial data suggests that it's fairly common. That is, curiosity becomes less about a moment of surprise regarding whatever a child encounters and more about the kind of puzzles that engage a person's interest over a matter of days, weeks, or even months. These puzzles may emerge from an interest in a set of objects (for example, dinosaurs, insects, colored yarns and threads, clocks, or objects that defy gravity) and it may emerge from an interest in something more social or cultural (for example, language, social interactions, invisibility, or immortality).

But while virtually all very young children are inquisitive, they don't all remain so. The path that leads from the ubiquitous inquiry of three-year-olds to the selective, probing, and sustained curiosity of the ten- or twenty-year-old is an uncertain one, riddled with potential inhibitors.

The Risks and Rewards of Exploration

Whether these sequences, which unfold over a number of days, weeks, or months, lead to the more crafted and sustained curiosity of which adults are capable depends, in good part, on specific features of the environment. Here I discuss four aspects of everyday situations that play a significant role in determining how curious a person will be by the time she leaves child-hood behind.

First, though curiosity rests on an appetite for the unknown, it depends, paradoxically, on a sense of safety and security. Early on, that sense of safety comes from a child's first relationship: an ongoing and close bond with a primary caregiver.

Visiting orphanages in London during World War II, the physician John Bowlby noticed that the children, though well-fed and tended to, were listless and disengaged to such a degree that they failed to reach standard benchmarks of psychological and physical growth.[11] He reasoned that this was because healthy development required more than food, sleep, and relative safety. Children also needed to be close to one constant caregiver. His observations and insights culminated in his theory of attachment, a pillar of developmental psychology. His student, Mary Ainsworth, and her colleagues took the theory a giant step further by empirically testing variations in children's attachment to a caregiver. They observed individual children (ages nine months to three years) in a room with the mother and some novel toys that were unfamiliar to them. After a few minutes, Ainsworth and her colleagues instructed the mother to leave the room. The researchers recorded the toddlers' reaction to this separation. Most babies cried at this separation. According to attachment theory, such distress is actually a healthy sign of attachment. When the mother returned after a very brief separation, the way that children reacted was key. Most toddlers would typically smile with joy and relief, hurry into their mother's arms for reassurance and comfort, cuddle briefly, and then return to exploring the new toys in the room. But some babies had trouble settling down after the separation. They greeted their mother's return with continued crying, angry looks, and other expressions of distress. Most important, though, when they returned to playing, they had trouble giving the toys their full attention, constantly looking over at or actually returning to their mother, as if for reassurance she wouldn't leave again. This insecure attachment prevented them from fully exploring interesting and new experiences in the immediate environment. In other words, the quality of a child's attachment has a powerful influence on the vigor and depth of her inquiry.

The connection between security and exploration lasts beyond early childhood. In one longitudinal study, Arend and his colleagues assessed the attachment security of two-year-olds.[12] The researchers invited those children back to the lab when they were four and brought them into a room that held a box filled with novel toys. They found that the children who had been rated as securely attached when they were two were the ones who now most eagerly explored the box and its contents, while those two-year-olds who had been rated as insecurely attached seemed timid or reluctant to explore.

It's not a very far stretch to imagine that as children get older the quality of their original attachment might not exert a direct influence on their curiosity, but it might also work more indirectly. As children get older, insecurity seems to limit their curiosity in two ways. Children who are, by virtue of their temperament or early attachment, uneasy in the face of novelty are less likely to ask questions, investigate the world around them, or dive into unfamiliar situations. In addition, even those with a relatively secure and easygoing approach to the world are less likely to explore when they feel scared, whether that fear is caused by angry adults or other unstable or threatening features of the immediate learning environment. One might even imagine that the pressure to "do well," when learning is wrapped up with tests and grades, works against a child's inclination to seek uncertainty. But in addition to a sense of security, children need to feel interest and opportunity.

A wide range of studies has shown that children are more curious when they can interact with things and topics in which they are interested. Sometimes this has to do with the inherent "interest factor" of the material: how complex, surprising, or unusual it is, or how it is intellectually framed. In one experiment, fourth grade children were put into small groups and given a topic to study over several days. In one condition, the groups of children were encouraged to focus on ambiguous and controversial material. In a second condition, children focused on learning the same topics, but conveyed in a more straightforward way. The children in the controversy condition learned more about the topic than the others. They were also more eager to give up a free period to continue studying the topic than those in the more straightforward condition. In other words, ambiguity and controversy led to more learning and more interest in learning. To explore this idea, Schulz and Bonawitz watched children learn about a new toy.[13] In one condition an adult demonstrated the function of the toy, and in another condition children were left to explore the toy without any adult intervention. The children who were first shown the function of the toy explored it on their own far less than those children allowed to examine it without any guidance. In this study, by getting to the "point" of the activity, adults reduced children's interest or motivation in exploration. This is but one example of an increasing body of evidence showing that uncertainty is key to learning.

When my students and I went into classrooms to find out where and when children were expressing curiosity, we noticed that the few places where kids lingered to observe were often the most dynamic places, the places where unexpected and irregular things could happen. Children would often wander over to the aquarium, if there was one.[14] They'd stand there gazing for up to six minutes. They'd track one particular fish. Then they'd look around, behind the coral, or watch the seaweed float and change shape. These habitats offered much more irregular and changeable phenomena than elsewhere in the room. The environmental psychologist Roger Hart has written about this regarding playgrounds for children, arguing that they need natural, complicated, and messy places to play rather than the highly manufactured pristine equipment that often fills the most affluent playgrounds and recess areas.[15]

Some materials, objects, and environments are more interesting because they are richer and more complex. But in addition, not all children are interested in the same things. This sounds so obvious as to be trite, but it's often disregarded: for children to develop their curiosity they need to have access to the particular things that interest them. Research has shown that children express much more curiosity when they are interacting with materials or topics in which they've developed some sustained interest, whether it's bugs, machines, warfare, or clothing.

There is a third feature of the environment that exerts a tremendously strong influence on children's curiosity: the behavior of the adults around them. Unsurprisingly, the simplest and most direct way that adults encourage or discourage children's curiosity is by the way they respond when children ask questions, open things up, and fiddle with objects. In one study, psychologist Bruce Henderson invited children into a room with a box that had several drawers on every side, each containing an interesting and somewhat anomalous object.[16] In one condition, the experimenter smiled and said mildly encouraging things to the children. In another condition, the adult said nothing and kept her face immobile. In a third condition, the experimenter looked disapproving when the child touched the box. Needless to say, children who were encouraged, even mildly, spent more time opening the drawers and explored the objects more fully. In similar studies, when the researchers assessed each child's curiosity as a base trait, those children who seem less curious by nature were even more susceptible to the response of the adults in the room. Thus the lower a child's intrinsic curiosity the more sensitive he or she is to disapproval. A wide range of studies show this same pattern. By the time children go to school, their curiosity waxes and wanes as a function of the feedback they get from the adults around them.

Contrary to popular contemporary conceptions of classrooms, it is not obvious which classrooms might encourage curiosity and which might not. It is not simply that kind teachers encourage curiosity and mean ones do not. In one study, we invited teachers into our lab to help us with a study about how children learn.[17] We provided each teacher with the materials and a worksheet to conduct a science activity called Bouncing Raisins with a child who would be joining them in our lab. The activity involves mixing several ingredients into a beaker, dropping a raisin in, and watching while bubbles form on the surface of the raisin, causing it to rise to the surface. Unbeknown to the participating teachers, the children were in fact our paid confederates, trained to pause in the middle of the activity and drop a Skittle into the mixture. If the teacher asked them what they were doing, they were

Why Should This Be So?   87

trained to answer, "I just wanted to see what would happen." In other words, they expressed curiosity. In one condition, when we explained the activity, we said, "Please use the materials to help your student learn more about science," and as we left them in the room with the child, we said, "Have fun learning about science." In a second condition, we said to teachers "Please use the materials to help your student fill out the worksheet." As we left the room we said, "Have fun filling out the worksheet." The results showed that no matter their age, their level of teaching experience, or their gender, when teachers are encouraged to focus on learning about science, they responded encouragingly to the child's deviation, saying things like, "Oh that's cool. Where'd you get that idea?" But teachers who were encouraged to focus on the worksheet responded quite differently with comments like "No, no. That's not part of the instructions," or "Don't do that."

The data show that the way teachers respond to children's curiosity depends more on their sense of the purpose of the activity than it does on their particular characteristics.

But responding to a child's inquiry is only one way an adult might influence a child. To examine this more closely, we flipped the bouncing raisin study on its head. In this version,[18] we brought children into the lab as real subjects. Each child did the bouncing raisin activity with an experimenter acting in a teacherlike capacity, guiding the child through the steps and the associated worksheet. In one condition, halfway through, the adult suddenly took a Skittle and dropped it into the liquid saying, "Let's just put this in even though it's not on the worksheet. I just want to see what happens." In a second condition, the adult expressed no such curiosity, and simply paused to tidy the materials. Once they had finished the Bouncing Raisins activity, the adult explained that she had to leave the room for a few minutes to get materials for another fun activity. She said to each child, "You wait here. I'll be back in a few minutes. While I'm gone feel free to use the materials some more. You can also draw using these colored pencils and paper. Or you can just hang out and wait. Whatever you want," and left the room. Children who had seen the adult deviate from the task in order to experiment with the Skittle looked carefully at the ingredients, picked them up, stirred the raisin and Skittle around, and talked to themselves aloud about what had happened. Children who had not seen her deviate tended to just stand there. Some whistled, some looked at the ceiling, and one played a game with his zipper. But they did not seem curious about the materials. In other words, it is not only what adults say to children about inquiry, but it's also a question of whether the adults themselves model curiosity.

Why is it that, though nearly all children enjoy a state of almost perpetual wonderment and active exploration before the age of five, by the time they are in sixth grade they show very little curiosity? What was once a ubiquitous and robust characteristic becomes the province of just a few. Nor does this trend turn around even for young people who to go to college.

Until very recently most of the research on the development of curiosity has focused on young children. And yet in the past ten years it has become abundantly clear that college professors are also deeply concerned with their students' curiosity, interested in whether it is too late to spark an appetite for inquiry in the many eighteen-year-olds who appear to have lost any intrinsic curiosity. Time and again professors, upon hearing about my work, approach me to ask if there is a way to "turn curiosity on" in their college students. Needless to say, students are not incapable of learning in the formal sense of acquiring information and skills. Rather, it seems that they tend to do so only for some utilitarian goal: a good grade or a job offer. Rarely, according to my colleagues at a wide range of institutions, do their students seem to thirst for knowledge just because they feel compelled to close an information gap, explain the unexpected, or reduce their own uncertainty within a particular domain.

To learn more about whether college is cultivating the disposition and ability to ask questions, we presented first-year students with a brief and entertaining PowerPoint presentation about a complex and unfamiliar topic: the science of mindfulness.[19] We explained that we needed feedback on the material for a future presentation. At the end of the presentation, we asked each subject if he or she had any questions or comments. A year later we contacted the students and said that, again, we needed some feedback on another presentation. This time the presentation was about executive functioning in childhood. Though there were individual differences between students in terms of the number of questions they asked and the quality of the questions (e.g., whether they were superficial, probed for more information, or explored a deeper implication of the ideas presented), we found no increase in either number or quality of questions between year one and year two. While it may be that it takes more than a year for college to have an impact on this dimension, it may also be that in general students don't become more eager to ask questions or become better at it while in college.

Needless to say, this doesn't tell us much about whether students *can* become more curious at this stage of their development. There is more to be learned.

What Has Darwin Taught Us?

Which brings us full circle to the bug-eating Darwin, who became the question-asking Darwin. Rather than relegate him to the realm of outliers—the unique genius who saw discrepancies and puzzles where others did not—using those puzzles to fuel important investigations, we now can see that most young children engage in some version of bug eating. Almost all humans begin life with an aptitude for noticing the unexpected and pursuing unanticipated phenomena in order to resolve uncertainty. As they become more familiar with more aspects of everyday life, their novelty detection tends to zero in on topics that particularly interest them. They become more surprised by subtler details within a domain, which explains the emergence of specific interests. This explains why one child is curious about bugs, another about the interaction between people, and a third by visual patterns and why, by adulthood, though some people seem more curious than others, no one is curious about everything. Though curiosity narrows its focus, no data have yet suggested that the startling drop in curiosity during the early school years is a necessary byproduct of development. The research is clear that children are sensitive to various aspects of the environment: complexity and ambiguity, a chance to explore the particular materials that interest a given child, encouragement for unscripted inquiry, and role models who exhibit curiosity. A look at contemporary educational practice in this country suggests that very little of the system is designed to foster the development of curiosity. Quite to the contrary, most classrooms lack the kinds of variety and complexity of experience that elicit inquiry. An emphasis on acquiring certain kinds of knowledge and skills has promoted classrooms in which mastery is prized over exploration, certainty over uncertainty, and answers over questions. Which brings us to the next questions research must answer. How long-lasting is the influence of the situational factors we have identified? Can a child whose curiosity has been diminished by the classroom environment become more curious? Is there any age beyond which this is no longer possible? What would we need to do to help the majority of children acquire the habit of asking the question: Why Should This Be So?

Notes

1. Charles Darwin, *On the Origins of Species by Means of Natural Selection*, 1st ed. (London: John Murray, 1859), 397–98.

2. Katherine Nelson, *Event Knowledge: Structure and Function in Development* (Mahwah, N.J.: Lawrence Erlbaum Associates, 1986).

3. Susan Engel, *The Hungry Mind: The Origins of Curiosity in Childhood* (Cambridge, Mass.: Harvard University Press, 2015).

4. Barbara Tizard and Martin Hughes, *Young Children Learning* (1984; John Wiley and Sons, 2008).

5. Michelle M. Chouinard, "Children's Questions: A Mechanism for Development," *Monographs of the Society for Research in Child Development* 72, no. 1 (2007).

6. Susan Isaacs, *Intellectual Growth in Young Children: With an Appendix on Children's "Why" Questions by Nathan Isaacs* (New York: Routledge, 1999).

7. Paul Harris, *Trusting What You're Told: How Children Learn from Others* (Cambridge, Mass.: Harvard University Press, 2012).

8. Harris.

9. Tizard and Hughes, *Young Children Learning*, 127.

10. Brian MacWhinney, *The CHILDES Project: Tools for Analyzing Talk*, 3rd ed. (Mahwah, N.J.: Lawrence Erlbaum, 2000).

11. John Bowlby, *Attachment and Loss* (London: Hogarth, 1969).

12. Richard Arend, Frederick L. Gove, and L. Alan Sroufe, "Continuity of Individual Adaptation from Infancy to Kindergarten: A Predictive Study of Ego Resiliency and Curiosity in Preschoolers," *Child Development* 50, no. 4 (1979): 950–59.

13. Elizabeth Bonawitz et al., "The Double-Edged Sword of Pedagogy: Instruction Limits Spontaneous Exploration and Discovery," *Cognition* 120, no. 3 (2011): 322–30.

14. Engel, *The Hungry Mind*.

15. Roger Hart, *Children's Experience of Place* (New York: Irvington, 1979).

16. Bruce Henderson and Shirley G. Moore, "Children's Responses to Objects Differing in Novelty in Relation to Level of Curiosity and Adult Behavior," *Child Development* (1980): 457–65.

17. Susan Engel and Kellie Randall, "How Teachers Respond to Children's Inquiry," *American Educational Research Journal* 46, no. 1 (2009): 183–202.

18. Susan Engel, "Children's Need to Know: Curiosity in Schools," *Harvard Educational Review* 81, no. 4 (2011): 625–45.

19. Susan Engel, *Does College Change the Way Students Think?* Report to the Spencer Foundation, 2016.

6

The Dude Abides, or Why Curiosity Is Important for Education Today

Tyson E. Lewis

Often when people ask a question (especially students), they preface it with the simple saying, "I am just curious." Such a phrase is more than a mere social lubricant. It also has philosophical implications. For instance, prefacing a question with the phrase "just curious" indicates that what follows is *not really that serious.* The interlocutor is asking on a whim, nothing more than that. Further, this phrase could indicate that the question is *harmless* or of little consequence or not meant to be offensive in any way. This is no grand inquisition. It is a friendly, incidental conversation. For both participants, the stakes are exceedingly low. Such common ways of speaking about curiosity indicate that there is a tendency to reduce it to the level of a secondary, peripheral form of intentionality. There is nothing rigorous about being just curious. It is an occasional, fleeting thought that will not likely matter to any of the participants in the exchange, whatever the results of the question happen to be. Indeed, one can quickly move on without being distressed.

But whereas the common, everyday use of curiosity in the phrase, "I am just curious . . . ," emphasizes the *harmless* nature of curiosity, philosophy finds this seemingly benign appearance a ruse, concealing a very dangerous possibility: when we become just curious, we become distracted from the important questions of life. I am thinking here of a particular strand of philosophy that leads from Augustine (a fourth-century North African Christian theologian) to Martin Heidegger (a twentieth-century German phenomenologist) and up to Bernard Stiegler (a twentieth-century French poststructuralist).

In this chapter I want to focus on the educational implication of this particular line of analysis and see if curiosity has any educational value. Is it ever educationally desirable to be "just curious" about something? I will start with an overview of several philosophical arguments that warn against curiosity as a distraction, in particular those found in the phenomenologies of Augustine and Heidegger. Mis-educative at best, at its worst, curiosity, for these philosophers, can become anti-educative. But here I would like to take a different approach and argue that Augustine, Heidegger, and other contemporary figures have missed something important in their own analyses of curiosity. Instead of seeing the distracted nature of curiosity as a deficit, I want to use Paul North's work on distraction as a starting point for a new philosophy of education that embraces the distracted qualities of curiosity as an asset. As an example of how distraction can educate, I will end with a brief analysis of the Coen brothers' film *The Big Lebowski*. Although not ostensibly about education, I argue that the film has certain educational implications, especially concerning the nature of curiosity's relationship with distraction. In this film the lead character embraces distraction—or what he calls "abiding"—in order to accidently and absentmindedly solve a mystery. In short, this film reveals that there are indeed *positive lessons* from being in a distracted state of mind, and that there should be room in education for daydreaming, flights of fancy, and intellectual wandering even if such activities are not quantifiable in terms of prescribed outcomes or efficient/ effective measures.

Being Attentive to Attentiveness

A number of philosophers are prone to chastise curiosity as a deficient form of engagement with the world. For instance, in the book *Confessions,* Augustine argues that curiosity is a form of distractedness from our search for the Truth. The mind has a tendency, for Augustine, to use the senses of the body for the "satisfaction of its own inquisitiveness."[1] Such curiosity might call itself science but, in reality, it is driven by nothing more than a lust for gratification. For Augustine, there are three problems here. First, curiosity is focused on knowledge acquired through the senses and, in particular, sight. Knowledge acquired through sight is concerned with what is finite, contingent, and therefore mutable rather than what is infinite, absolute, and unchanging. Because of this, curiosity can only lead us away from the Truth.

The Dude Abides 93

Second, curiosity is not driven by pleasure in the Truth (in God's infinite wisdom) but rather by a perverse form of inquisitiveness for its own sake. Indeed, curiosity is uniquely related to sight, and to the pleasure in the act of seeing. The result is knowing for the sake of knowing and a gratification in investigation and discovery as such. Third, the overarching result of this curiosity is an increasing sense of drifting away from God's path to the Truth. As Augustine summarizes, curiosity is a temptation for the mind to wander and as such poses a problem. He confesses that curiosity "might easily hold my attention and distract me from whatever serious thoughts occupied my mind."[2]

This description, I find, resonates with a peculiar moment before Augustine's conversion in which he finds himself truly in a state of indecision. He writes, "So, treating everything as a matter of doubt, as the Academics are generally supposed to do, and hovering between one doctrine and another, I made up my mind at least to leave the Manichees, for while I was in this state of indecision I did not think it right to remain in the sect now that I found the theories of some of the philosophers preferable."[3] In an indecisive state, Augustine is hovering between belief systems rather than subscribing to any one of them. He is curious as to what each system offers him, and he is testing them all out. This state is one akin to wandering about, without the clear direction provided by belief in God. And for Augustine, this state is decisively dangerous, as it could lead the wanderer further and further away from Christ. As such, it appears that curiosity is always on the verge of becoming mis-educative. It is a state that lacks a clear path, a clear light to guide the way, or a voice to call the wanderer back home. It is a state veiled in darkness and silence. Nevertheless, in this darkness and silence, the curious wanderer is also radically exposed to *all* the possibilities of thought without discretion.

But this is precisely what Augustine fears the most. Without the Truth orienting knowledge toward God, knowledge falters and becomes an end in itself. While Augustine admits that it might very well be Truth that "we learn better in a free spirit of curiosity,"[4] this natural predilection is also a sign of our sin and the ultimate form of intellectual distraction and indulgence. Sadly, in Augustine's assessment, teachers fall prey to the trap of curiosity, encouraging students to do well in their studies simply for instrumental reasons. Or they expose students to curiosities (such as Greek myths) without understanding how raising such interests might actually tempt their minds

94 Tyson E. Lewis

to abandon God's Truth. Indeed, Augustine goes so far as to suggest that only God can be a teacher because only God fully understands the Truth. He writes, "My God . . . I believe that it was you who taught me . . . because it is the truth and there is no other teacher of the truth besides yourself."[5] All other teachers are marked by their own curiosities, and thus given to perpetuating distraction. We might say that the original sin of the teacher is precisely the sin of failing to cultivate attentiveness to Truth in his or her students.

Heidegger, a careful reader of Augustine, reiterates many of these claims. In his analytic of the human, Heidegger argues that there are essentially three dimensions of its everydayness: idle talk, ambiguity, and curiosity. While Heidegger is clear that he does not want to judge these dimensions—and thus presents us with a neutral description of how the human gets around in its most banal, day-to-day activities in the world—nevertheless, there are moments in his description that at least warn the reader of the potential downsides of idle talk, ambiguity, and curiosity. Take, for instance, curiosity. According to Heidegger curiosity is, as with Augustine, related to seeing. And like Augustine, Heidegger thinks that when humanity is curious, "it has a tendency to let itself be carried along solely by the looks of the world."[6] Once carried away, humanity can no longer be attentive to the existential question defining the meaning of being and instead dwells on a rather superficial level of experience. Curiosity "concerns itself with seeing, not in order to understand what is seen (that is, to come into a being towards it) but *just* in order to see."[7] Pleasure is pure seeing, and the novelty of seeing overtakes any attentiveness to what is seen. The result is the "constant possibility of *distraction*."[8] The floating, drifting, absentmindedness of curiosity can only leap from one novelty to the next without attunement to being in its Truth. In this suspended, or hovering state, "circumspection has been set free," opening "the possibilities of seeing the 'world' merely as it *looks*."[9] These looks are superficial. Thus curious freedom is the freedom to skim the surface of experience without ever attaching one's being to something meaningful. The uprootedness of humanity means that it leads a distracted existence where it "keeps floating unattached"[10] and aimless, always in danger of being lured by the next curiosity, by the next inauthentic temptation.

Curiosity flees from the experience of being "amazed" or "marveling"[11] at the miracle of being, and therefore our everyday condition is a fundamental threat to our understanding of being. Instead of the experience of wonder,

The Dude Abides   95

which stops humanity in its tracks and forces it to take up the question of its
being, curiosity derails humanity by submerging it in trivial experiences. In
such a state of suspended hovering, the human can never own its experiences, can never really care about anything at all, let alone its relationship
to the question of its own being. This is a vision of humanity's everydayness
as falling away from being. Curiosity has estranged us from a philosophical and educative mood: wonder. Indeed, in *Basic Questions of Philosophy:
Selected "Problems" of "Logic,"* Heidegger traces the slow degeneration of
wonder into curiosity. To do so, he returns to the basic definition of wonder
found in ancient Greek sources. Instead of hovering from one appearance to
the next in a curious state, Heidegger argues that "in wonder, what is most
usual of all and in all, i.e., *everything,* becomes the most unusual. . . . Everything in what is most usual (beings) becomes in wonder the most unusual in
this one respect: that it is what it is."[12] This state of mind is educationally
relevant for Heidegger because it is "the basic disposition that primordially
disposes man into the beginning of thinking."[13] We are no longer distracted
by the flow of beings but rather stop and *think* about the very being of these
beings, what makes them beings at all. This is why the experience of wonder
is, for Heidegger, the most fundamental form of attunement. If curiosity is a
kind of absentminded drifting among beings (lured forever by the appearance of the new), then wonder is the mindfulness of being as such (that
which is not new at all but has always already been there in the background
of our experience as that which makes all experience possible). And when
curiosity becomes our dominant attunement, education is precisely what is
at stake. From the moment that humanity becomes curious, "then in place
of the basic disposition of wonder, the avidity [*Gier* in German is closely
related to the word for curiosity, *Neugier*] for learning and calculation enters
in. Philosophy itself then becomes one institution among others, it becomes
subjected to a goal which is all the more insidious the higher it is . . . 'education.'"[14] Again, echoes of Augustine can be heard here. For both, curiosity
is a temptation because it finds pleasure in learning as such, in seeing as
such. Education is no longer in the service of Truth, does not stay with the
Truth but rather offers restless excitement through continual change.

Taking these warnings seriously, there is a strong movement in educational philosophy to return to the virtues of attentiveness. Informed by the
recent work of Bernard Stiegler, educational theorists argue that the distracted dimension of curiosity is a major danger to youth and to society as a

96 Tyson E. Lewis

whole. Indeed, for Stiegler, without the intellectual capability to be attentive, youth become careless consumers who are lazy, cowardly, irresponsible, and infantile. As opposed to a culture industry that "destroys attention along with the ability to concentrate on an *object* of attention,"[15] "scholarly education . . . consists entirely of psychotechniques for capturing and fashioning attention."[16] Thus instead of the infantile state of interminable immaturity caused by media and consumer culture, scholarly education produces individuals who are mature precisely because of their attentiveness to the self and the world. Here attentiveness means caring for ideas, things, and language so as to *think* them and give them meaning and significance in a world. Importantly, Stiegler avoids any discussion of curiosity in his reconstruction of education as a system for forming attention. This is no coincidence, for curiosity has been linked with precisely the forms of distractedness of which Stiegler is critical. While frequently aligned with inquisitiveness, curiosity is also characterized negatively as something that leads astray. Its educational value is therefore dubious.

In short, there is a philosophical lineage here that questions whether or not "just curious" is educationally relevant. Or, perhaps worse, this same lineage could indicate that "just curious" is a condition that needs to be overcome in order for real, authentic education to happen at all. To call into question this lineage, I want to make a surprising move. I want to leave behind philosophical texts and take a curious leap into the world of film. I want to do so for a simple reason: according to Walter Benjamin in his famous essay "The Work of Art in the Age of Mechanical Reproduction," film is the distracted medium par excellence.[17] As such, if one wants to explore the meaning of distraction, then it is best to go directly to the source.

Rethinking Distraction

OK, I lied a bit. We still have some philosophical setting up that needs to happen before we move on to film. In particular, I want to point to another tradition in philosophy—a minor one—that is interested in distraction as a positive, rather than a negative, state. I want to leverage this minor tradition in order to argue that educationalists should not reject the distracted dimension of curiosity but rather *yield to it*. Instead of disparaging what is most suspect about curiosity, embrace it fully. What would we find in this movement *into* rather than *beyond* the curious? Key to answering this question is liberating curiosity from comparison with attentiveness, therefore thinking it on its own terms (even if these terms are rather distracting).

Distractedness is a marginal mental phenomenon that always tends toward that which is on the verge of or has already disappeared, hence philosophy's suspicions of it. In other words, it always concerns the presence of a nonbeing, a specter, or a nonthought within thought. For Paul North distraction is "a paradoxical capacity to receive non-beings" in the form of daydreams, flights of fancy, and so forth, while at the same time "resist[ing] becoming an object of thought."[18] Distraction happens when the mind lets go of bonds to intellectual structures, determining concepts/categories, and passionate attachments to norms. And when such bonds are loosened, the mind can drift off topic ("Where was I again?"), the eye can be caught by something appearing in our peripheral vision that escapes the mind ("What was that?"), and there can be moments of interruption where the flow of thought gives way to the blankness of no thought ("I seem to have lost my train of thought . . ."). While Stiegler argues that attentiveness is the fulcrum of caring for the world, North argues that attention focuses on stretching out and taking possession of the world *(ad-tenere)*. Attention is therefore concerned with a will to possess that is capable of providing continuity and unity to the self. Distraction on the other hand "gives itself away"[19] and is therefore a form of dispossession. The unity of self provided by attention (as a possession of experience) suddenly loses itself, exposing itself to dispersal.

On North's reading, we can approach Heidegger's theory of curiosity with new eyes and see something that Heidegger himself had missed. In order to guard against the dangers of dissipation and dispersal—as in a curious state of being—Heidegger turns toward an ontology of care. Care steps in to stop the dispersal process and to provide some kind of ontological unity to humanity's everyday being. What is avoided here is, for North, a theory of dispersal–distraction as such—a theory of curiosity that does not fall back on the normative value placed on wholeness, unity, and attentive concentration. What Augustine, Heidegger, and later Stiegler avoid at all costs is a theoretical confrontation with *not caring,* with a kind of being that loses itself in what it yields to, that disperses itself to the margins. This would be a state of being that is careless, directionless, and open to the contingencies of what happens to it. By maximizing distractibility, a carefree life would help throw into high relief the features of curiosity that are *most curious*. I mean this in two senses. First, this life would be curious in that it would be strange, unfamiliar, and perhaps shocking for those of us who value the long-established norms of attention and care. Indeed, such a life might appear meaningless, disorderly, silly, if not a total waste of time. Second, in its dispersion, distracted life would threaten any foundational social system predicated on the predictable certainty and regularity of an attentive, consistent, and unified identity. In this sense, distraction would prove to be the politically anarchic dimension of being "just curious." If philosophy cares about and promotes care for an arche, then the distractive excess of curiosity would threaten this arche with anarchic digression and disorientation.

The Educational Value of Distractedness: A Comparison of Two "Detectives"

The question becomes: How can North be used as a new starting point for theorizing curiosity as an educational virtue without losing curiosity's distracting qualities? Here I will turn to an unlikely example of how the distractible dimension of curiosity can be educational: the Coen brothers' cult classic *The Big Lebowski*.[20] The character referred to as "the Dude" is perpetually distracted and, in this distraction, is open to the contingent flow of experiences as they drift by. He is caught up in things and yields to what appears. Even his speech is infected by the meaningless phrases he haphazardly adopts from the other characters he meets ("in the parlance of our times . . ."). But more important, I argue the form of the film itself is distracted. I will conclude this section by contrasting the content and form of *The Big Lebowski* with another Coen brothers' film, *No Country for Old Men*,[21] which, in many ways, also offers a commentary on curiosity, but this time from an opposing existential angle.

The opening sequence of *The Big Lebowski* summarizes many of these points. The stranger who narrates the story starts with a series of perplexing observations about the curiously enigmatic character of the Dude. "A lot about the Dude didn't make a whole lot of sense," the narrator ponders. The narrator goes on to warn the audience that the Dude might appear to be the "laziest [man] worldwide." Playing in the background of the voice-over is the cowboy classic "Tumbling Tumble Weeds," as sung by Sons of the Pioneers. The song lazily "drifts along" as we literally see a tumbleweed roll aimlessly through Los Angeles (a place that is full of drifters, strangers, displaced peoples, and hapless wanderers). The metaphor is clear: the Dude is a tumbleweed himself—drifting, hovering, aimlessly meandering through life. But what is unique here is that the narrator embraces this condition and even praises it as somehow suitable to the times. Indeed, the rest of the film is a demonstration of what we can yield by fully yielding to a tumbling, distracted form of curiosity.

The rootlessness of the Dude means that he is radically passive, the brunt of a series of misadventures and misunderstandings (his rug is pissed on, his car is stolen, and so forth). And despite all these distractions, the Dude "solves" the crime precisely by not paying attention to it. He almost literally stumbles over the solution to the mystery that defines the dramatic plot of the film. Unlike other famous detectives, the Dude remains absentminded throughout. He admits, "I am adhering to a pretty strict drug regimen to keep my mind limber." The limberness of his mind refers to a state of maximal flexibility wherein tangential and seemingly unrelated bits and pieces of information can hang loosely together. Instead of forcing connections between these fragments, he simply abandons himself to the flow of experiences with a curious ease, and through his misadventures tumbles headlong into various solutions and/or answers to interconnected mysteries.

The proper term to describe this state of maximal distractibility is "abiding." When the stranger tells the Dude to "Take it easy," he replies, "The Dude abides." For North, such abiding could be conceptualized as a particular form of curious yielding.[22] Yielding means giving in but also giving over (as in yielding a crop). Only by yielding to the situation through curiosity, only by abiding through distraction, can the Dude's actions yield anything at all. This is not the picture of the detective who is driven by a will to solve a case, who is characterized by superhuman attentiveness (as in the TV show "Monk" or even Sherlock Holmes), but a kind of absentminded drifter who allows the case to come to him, wash over him in a series of mishaps and comical reversals of fortune. Yielding to these forces with casual, absentminded curiosity produces a yield.

On this reading, the Dude embodies precisely those qualities that the proponents of attentiveness and wonderment abhor. Unlike Stiegler's mature, attentive, and responsible adult, the Dude is immature, inattentive, and irresponsible throughout most of the film. He lacks a job; he is a "bum"; he is a pothead; and he has an abiding personality. And yet, instead of viewing these from the perspective of attentiveness as a normative ideal, the film asks the audience to view distraction on its own terms, and therein find a new kind of intelligence in giving one's self over and giving in to the experiences that float by. Of course, the Dude's narrative begins with a certain desire for compensation after his rug had been mistakenly pissed on, yet it would be incorrect to interpret the film as a series of events centered on his desire to right this particular wrong. Such a reading would be reductive at best as it would take what is merely an accidental (and largely inconsequential) moment that jumpstarts the narrative as an unconscious, motivating force behind all the Dude's actions. Missed here is how the Dude abides, giving way on even this desire in order to be taken up by the world around him. Likewise, it would be wrong to reduce the motive driving the film to the Dude's love of bowling. Although the impending bowling tournament is always in the background of the narrative, providing some kind of continuity to the action, it never happens, and, indeed, this does not seem to matter at all to the Dude, who merely keeps abiding. Thus, it is crucial to note that, in the end, he has no rug, no monetary compensation for the loss of his rug, and no bowling trophy, yet he continues to abide.

Because the film does not satisfy audience expectations to see the Dude at home with a decent rug (what will tie his room together?) or engaged in a hilarious bowling tournament (would the Dude's team win against Jesus Quintana?), many felt that the film was somewhat of a failure.[23] The rug fiasco led nowhere (except to the death of the Dude's friend, Donny) and the bowling tournament never materialized. Even the mystery concerning Bunny Lebowski and her abduction is somewhat of an anticlimax. Thus the fundamental plotlines of the film do not yield to our expectations for any genre of film or, even worse, the film does not yield to our expectations for what a Coen brothers' film should be. The tight, intricate, and driven plots of *Fargo* or *Miller's Crossing* (two more famous Coen films) are missing here, leaving the audience with what seems to be a half-hearted, half-baked try that might have needed a few more drafts before it was screen ready.

But I would suggest another reading. Not only do the characters in the film embody curiosity, the form of the film itself exemplifies the distracted nature of cinema that Benjamin describes. The film is a tumbling tumbleweed, meandering around absentmindedly in the world of the Dude. This is not simply a depiction of abiding but is an abiding form of cinema. The Coen brothers are pulled in this way (to the rug), then in another way (to a kidnapping), then in another (to a bowling tournament). Yet they do not

The Dude Abides 101

follow through on any one of these narratives. Instead, we get a weirdly suspended, hovering, inattentive feeling that fully embraces the distracted and distracting nature of cinema. This is a cinema that is dispossessed of itself (its genre conventions) and dispersed (across a series of plotlines that lead nowhere in particular). The form of the film comes to mimic its content, producing a truly abiding, and thus anarchic, cinematic experience.

I conclude my analysis with a comparison between the Dude and another famous Coen brothers' character: Sheriff Ed Tom Bell in the film *No Country for Old Men*. One of the central mysteries of the film revolves around the killer's preferred weapon: a bolt gun. The gun shoots out a bolt using compressed air. In the film, the hired assassin, Anton Chigurh, employs this device several times to mysteriously kill victims without leaving behind any bullet casings and to break into the house of the protagonist, Llewelyn Moss. Sheriff Bell is informed that a man with a hole in his head without a trace of a bullet was found dead by the side of the road. He subsequently discovers the lock cylinder of Llewelyn's trailer home blown out. The link between these two incidents remains largely undetected by Sheriff Bell throughout the film.

In discussing the danger that Llewelyn is facing with Clara Jean (Llewelyn's wife), Sheriff Bell tells the story of a man who was accidently shot in the arm with a bullet that was intended for a steer. He then concludes with the observation that ranchers now use bolt guns to slaughter their livestock. Clearly shaken by the chilling story, Clara Jean asks Sheriff Bell why he told her the story. He pauses and then answers, "I don't know. My mind wanders."

Like the Dude, Sheriff Bell's mind wanders, indeed he is absentminded, often raising tangential or oblique questions that stupefy his deputy and others. He hits upon the connection between the mysterious blown-out lock cylinder found at a crime scene and the use of a bolt gun. Yet his distraction is not so complete that free association can drift into his conscious mind. The connection found him, yet he could not find it! To use North's language, Sheriff Bell was not willing to yield to his curiously distracted state of mind. Thus the association passed without notice. Indeed, we might argue that because he was so attentive to the situation, he willfully pulled himself out of this loose state of mental wandering back to his job. Stated differently, Sheriff Bell is *too responsible* or *too mature* to solve the mystery. This maturity did not allow him to contemplate the seemingly irrelevant details of his own free association. It is no coincidence that he is an officer of the law, and thus is held to the pressures of institutional norms, values, and practices. He is a representative of the state, and curiosity, as indicated above, is fundamentally disruptive of state power to control and centralize (see Zurn, this volume). The anarchic strain running through curiosity is suspicious to Sheriff Bell (and to others around him) as it might indicate a faltering or falling off the prescribed path. Thus his mind cannot fully embrace the aleatory wandering of the Dude; he cannot abide.

In another scene, Sheriff Bell relates the disturbing story of a couple who rented out a room to senior citizens, tortured them, killed them, and then collected their social security checks. This continued for some time until a neighbor noticed a man wearing a dog collar fleeing the neighbor's house. In disbelief, Sheriff Bell states, "But that's what it took to get someone's attention. Digging graves in the backyard didn't bring any." Sheriff Bell emphasizes the need for attentiveness as a key virtue in taking responsibility for the world. It is the lack of attentiveness that he finds fundamentally disturbing about the current state of affairs, and that is a central reason why he ultimately resigns from being sheriff at the end of the film. Without attentiveness, this is indeed no country for old men.

Toward the end of the film, Sheriff Bell pays a visit to his uncle Ellis, an ex-lawman, to discuss his early retirement from law enforcement. He confesses to his uncle, "I always felt that when I got older God would come into my life somehow, but he didn't." Like Augustine, Sheriff Bell waits for God to *teach* him, to help him see the Truth of the world. Indeed, he is attentively waiting for God's lesson, yet no such lessons reveal themselves. Sheriff Bell is left with only one decision: to retreat from a world that has outmatched him. Unlike the Dude, who is not dependent on a teacher to keep him on the right path or to lead him to Truth, Sheriff Bell remains in a system of hierarchical and centralized dependencies. The result is that he continues to search for a teacher even though he does not need one. In fact, we might make the argument that this search for a teacher or a guide to Truth is precisely the obstacle that hides what his absentminded wandering has already discovered!

Unlike *The Big Lebowski, No Country for Old Men* has one of the Coen brothers' tightly woven and intricate plotlines. Yet it also unravels toward the end, leaving more loose ends than earlier films such as *Miller's Crossing.* After the apparent climax of the film, we have a scene of Sheriff Bell, now retired, recalling two dreams involving his father—a scene that radically slows the pacing of the film and extends for an uncomfortable amount of time. In a state of suspension (a retirement without direction or work), Bell has time to be distracted, to be curious, to freely let his mind wander. Yet he does not know what to do with himself except exist in a state of agitation. He cannot abide. His dreams do not illuminate but rather bother him, once again reminding him of the rootless nature of his current state of existential disorientation in a country that is not meant for old men. Here we find the Coen brothers cinematically exploring a thesis not unlike that offered by Augustine, Heidegger, and Stiegler: that distraction is a deficit, a disconcerting existential break with meaning and continuity that unravels the fabric of our lives, leaving us shipwrecked somewhere in foreign lands. But unlike Augustine, Heidegger, or Stiegler, Bell cannot return or progress toward a state of attentive wonderment. And unlike the Dude, he cannot seem to abide. Distraction is now a fact of the world . . . one that is regrettable, if not nihilistic. The audience is therefore left hanging, without resolution, feeling the dread pass over Bell as if it were their own. Distraction overwhelms and turns into distress. We cannot possess a meaning or a direction in life and are therefore adrift.

In both cases, wandering, absentminded curiosity is infused with distractedness. But whereas one example willingly yields to the yield, the other willfully resists this yield. The first strategy ends in anarchic abiding, the second in fatalistic nihilism. If wonderment is off the table in the Coen universe, then it seems that these are the two political and existential options that remain.

But perhaps there is a deeper and more interesting lesson to be learned here. The audience of these films is itself encouraged to experience the two dialectical sides of curiosity's most troublesome feature: distraction. While certainly most viewers will not exit the theatre consciously contemplating distraction, they nevertheless obliquely experience a cinematic experiment (in both form and content) that might pique their curiosity. What emerges here is a new kind of collectivity: one that is curious about curiosity without being overtly attentive to this curiosity. For instance, *The Big Lebowski* does not ask the audience to care about the Dude or the tangled plot he finds himself in. Rather, it only asks that they find him curious in an absentminded way. And it does so through subtly playing with the inherently distracting qualities already present in the cinematic medium. Rather than merely depicting individual drifters, loners, or rebels, these films produce an experience that *massifies* the problems and possibilities of curiosity's distractibility for their audiences. And in this way, curiosity spreads out, swarms, and multiplies beyond any centralized control. This is the educational and political value of a cinematic experience of curiosity.

Anti-climax: Educational Philosophy as Cinematic

In this sense, film might enable educational philosophers to imagine a new relationship with curiosity. For educational philosophy, there is the potential for a performative contradiction when dealing with curiosity, for how can one be attentive to curiosity without betraying what is most unique about curiosity: its distracted, dispersed qualities. What is philosophical inquiry if not a form of intellectual attentiveness to a concept? Curiosity, which, as North seems to indicate, avoids becoming an object of thought, is therefore a perplexing problem. But perhaps cinema, and in particular, the Coen brothers' films, offers a pedagogical solution to this conundrum. To take a line from the Dude, educational philosophers might opt for abiding as a way to approach curiosity in an inattentively curious way. To do so would mean that educational philosophy about curiosity would have to embody a curious form, one that is fitting for its content. This would not necessarily result in an argument or in a systematic examination of a topic or in a definitive definition or in an operationalized formulation. Rather, it would be a form of writing that wanders, that yields to the features of curiosity that ensure it remains curious. It might also be an irreverent form of writing, one that might risk appearing "silly" or "unprofessional" because of its stylistic quirks or odd, carefree subject matter. Indeed, it would be a decisively *cinematic* form of educational philosophy, one that is distracted all the way down. While the dramatic and sublime qualities of wonder still hold the imagination of philosophers of education, the more mundane, average, and everyday abiding of curiosity's willingness to yield might produce an educational yield all its own, including a new form of writing and thinking that draws inspiration from cinematic experiences of absentmindedness. As the Coen brothers' films remind us, "just curious" does indeed have some merits for education. Instead of the phrase being a mere disclaimer, I feel we should embrace it as a new form of educational life and educational writing with all its problems and possibilities.

Notes

1. Augustine, *Confessions* (London: Penguin Classics, 1961), 241.
2. Augustine, 243.
3. Augustine, 108–9.
4. Augustine, 35.
5. Augustine, 97.
6. Martin Heidegger, *Being and Time* (New York: Harpers Perennial, 2008), 216.
7. Heidegger, 216.
8. Heidegger, 216.
9. Heidegger, 216.
10. Heidegger, 214.
11. Heidegger, 216.
12. Martin Heidegger, *Basic Questions in Philosophy: Selected "Problems" of "Logic"* (Bloomington: Indiana University Press, 1994), 144.
13. Heidegger, 147.
14. Heidegger, 155–56.
15. Bernard Stiegler, *Taking Care of Youth and the Generations* (Stanford, Calif.: Stanford University Press, 2010), 13.
16. Stiegler, 65.
17. Walter Benjamin, *Illuminations: Essays and Reflections* (New York: Shocken Books, 1968).
18. Paul North, *The Problem of Distraction* (Stanford, Calif.: Stanford University Press, 2012), 13.
19. North, 3.
20. Ethan and Joel Coen, dirs., *The Big Lebowski* (Working Title Films, 1998).
21. Ethan and Joel Coen, dirs., *No Country for Old Men* (Scott Ruden Productions, 1998).
22. Paul North, *The Yield: Kafka's Atheological Reformation* (Stanford, Calif.: Stanford University Press, 2015).
23. William Goldman, *Which Lie Did I Tell? More Adventures in the Screen Trade* (New York: Vintage, 2001).

7

"The Campus Is Sick"

Capitalist Curiosity and Student Mental Health

Arjun Shankar

"The campus is sick. That's what I have been saying for a while now. It's sick, very, very sick." I have just met Adam, a fifth-year senior at Hamilton College, for the first time, and I am struck by his candor, how quickly he presses into the issue of college mental health. Adam himself has experienced the pressures of college life, eventually taking a year off after experiencing debilitating depression and suicidal ideation during his junior year. He has since recovered and become one of the most vocal advocates for change on Hamilton's campus.

Hamilton, like nearly every college and university campus in the United States, has seen a steady and ever-more-concerning increase in mental unwellness in students—excess stress, depression, anxiety, suicidal ideation—which has made the college experience less and less like the utopian visions of an elite liberal education.

Millennials, like those who have come to Hamilton's campus, have been characterized as the "anxious generation." Nearly one out of three students experience a depressive state during their college careers. Recent studies have shown that suicidal ideation on university campuses in the United States is over 10 percent and suicide is the second leading cause of death for college-age students.[1] In the fall of 2017, a student on Hamilton's campus took his own life, the second suicide in so many years, setting off a crisis on the campus as students tried to make sense of another tragic death and administrators scrambled to find the best method to provide support for a college community thrown into deep despair.

Hamilton's goals have been to place greater emphasis on counseling and awareness, wanting students to feel less stigmatized and afraid of getting the help and support they need. In many ways, Hamilton, like most universities today, still locates the problem in the individual student, placing the responsibility for their unwellness at their feet and seeking to find ways to mitigate the psychological issues that students experience after the fact. However, as Adam's statement indicates, many students do not see the problem as necessarily located in these individual students. Instead, by locating the sickness in the campus, he is suggesting that the problem is environmental and systemic: about the political and economic landscape of university education in the twenty-first century, the policies that the college puts in place, and the culture that this system produces. Indeed, the problem of student mental unwellness is not unique to Hamilton. Four major suicide clusters have occurred in the past ten years at the University of Pennsylvania, Tulane University, New York University, and Cornell University, each with its own specificity but part of the broader mental unwellness epidemic on campuses across the country. What these tragic events indicate is that the issue of mental unwellness cannot be merely viewed as an issue of individual psychiatric disease, nor is it solely an individual elite university problem. Rather, the issue of mental unwellness in the university must be viewed as a sociocultural problem that is related to the complex political and economic processes that influence how the college/university system functions. *The question is, What practices, policies, and cultural values are producing this campus sickness?*

Much of the data for this chapter was gathered in collaboration with students in a class entitled *Curiosity: An Ethnographic Approach,* in which they shared their perspectives on campus life, the stressors they felt both within and outside of the classroom, and the kinds of structures that facilitated and limited their curiosity. In this chapter, I argue that the rapid increase in mental unwellness on university campuses is directly related to the capitalist sociocultural values produced in and by the current university and college systems. These values curtail students' curiosity, forcing them into regimes of success that dictate what they ought to want to learn and how they ought to want to ask questions. The link between educational success and monetary reward necessarily channels students' curiosity, what Thorstein Veblen might call a pecuniary curiosity but which I am calling here a neoliberal curiosity.[2] A neoliberal curiosity is a form of curiosity that is instrumentalized toward questions that pertain only to monetary success and value as defined by corporate-State interests, carrying with it gendered, sexualized, and racialized norms in the form of competitive "drive." As a result, students continue to experience an increase in the distance between what they want to know (i.e., a self-motivated curiosity) and what they ought to want to know (neoliberal curiosity), which in turn tears them from themselves, producing anxiety, depression, and the like.

I want to be clear that, as an anthropologist of mental health, I am much less concerned with the diagnosis of disease and illness but instead am most interested in the kind of emotional states that are produced within particular social and cultural milieus. That is to say, while medical diagnosis of mental illness is extremely important, I am much more interested in understanding the everyday experience of anxiety, fear, and depression, which may or may not be diagnosed as mental illness in some cases.[3] In so doing, I seek to stay away from the kinds of simplistic binaries between sick/healthy, well/ill, and pathological/normal, which are themselves socially constructed but do little to address the sociocultural and environmental systems that produce social suffering for all individuals along a spectrum, whether deemed medically healthy or not.

In the rest of this chapter, I provide some theoretical starting points for the discussion of curiosity, arguing for an anthropological theory of curiosity as "knowledge-emotion" situated within nested regimes of value. I connect this theoretical discussion with the issue of mental unwellness before progressing into a discussion of how curiosity is commodified within educational discourse, channeling all forms of curiosity toward the singular path of economic mobility and drive. I then analyze interview data with a group of college-age students to provide a deeper perspective on how this particular form of curiosity affects their way of seeing themselves, their goals, and their understanding of success, and, in turn, produces emotional states that are indicative of the kinds of campus sickness Adam alludes to above. In the conclusion, I provide some preliminary thoughts on what college faculty can do while also suggesting several productive avenues for further research into capitalism's effects on student curiosity and mental unwellness.

Theorizing the Anthropology of Value, Curiosity, and Mental Health

I want to begin by positing a framework for an anthropological theory of curiosity. While no anthropological text has taken curiosity as its primary locus of study, most anthropologists acknowledge that curiosity is a constitutive element of social and cultural life.[4] In many references to curiosity, especially in traditional psychology, it is taken as a "universal" trait from which the study of the Other might be undertaken. Methodologically speaking, this characterization could imply that curiosity would manifest similarly across social contexts and would have the same attributes regardless of one's social position. However, as anthropologists, we take issues of culture, social interaction, historical situatedness, and political–economic context not as epiphenomenal to some natural, underlying process but as constitutive of it, making this framing of curiosity not particularly useful for anthropologically grounded empirical research. How, then, might anthropology imagine curiosity as an object of study?

First, I want to suggest that, for anthropological study, curiosity is less about the epistemic (i.e., the acquisition of knowledge) and much more about the emotional value that is associated with learning something new. In other words, we express curiosity as a feeling rather than a state of being *(we feel curious rather than are curious),* and, as such, I want to posit that curiosity is a type of knowledge-emotion that is observable in everyday embodied interaction and situated in sociocultural norms. Within this framework, curiosity is not a static trait that one has or does not have but is rather a constantly shifting relation between the knowledge one acquires and how one feels about the knowledge one acquires. This emotional intensity can be increased or diminished; it can be facilitated or constrained, based on one's position within a complex web of historical, political, economic, and cultural power relations.[5] One might think of curiosity as a sociocultural fact—to borrow from Emile Durkheim—whose form of manifestation, direction, motivations, and constraints shift over time.

From this starting point, an anthropological method would seek to study curiosity not as an abstract concept disembedded from social life. Instead, one way of observing the production of curiosity is to recognize the dominant regimes of value that determine the relative desirability of the knowledge one seeks to acquire and, as important, what knowledge one disregards. Following David Graeber and Paul Kockelman, I define value as socially constituted "ideas about what one ought to want,"[6] a definition that emphasizes "values are not desires; values are a means of determining relative desirability."[7] These determinations of desirability are constrained by "regimes of value" that become entrenched in disparate national, linguistic, and cultural contexts because of historically emplaced relations of power that circulate over greater distances as people, mediatized images, and commodities move in space and time and forge global connections.[8] These regimes of value, in turn, structure feeling, dictating how people feel about their actions based on their relative desirability.

This relation of value and affect inflects any understanding of knowledge and knowledge acquisition: particular forms of knowledge are considered especially valuable within social settings, while others are not. In reality, individuals want to know about a lot of things, minute or grandiose. But regimes of knowledge-value are about what one *ought to want to know*. In this sense, I draw on Michel Foucault's understanding of knowledge as situated in nested regimes of institutional power, which in turn determine what types of knowledge might be valued or not. Foucault argues:

> It is the production of effective instruments for the formation and accumulation of knowledge—methods of observation, techniques of registration, procedures of investigation and research, apparatuses of control. All this means that power, when it is exercised through these subtle mechanisms, cannot but evolve, organize, and put into circulation a knowledge, or rather apparatuses of knowledge.[9]

We might say that regimes of knowledge-value embedded within social institutions and social discourses "structure" what one *ought to want to know* and *how one feels about what one wants to know*.[10] In other words, to speak of knowledge-value-power is to understand that knowledge-values carry incredible affective intensities, especially as they circulate across social fields and among different groups of people.[11]

In other words, how one feels about what one ought to want is one way to see cultural productions of all sorts, including the production of curiosity. Curiosity—how one feels about the knowledge she acquires—is challenged by, or at the very least influenced by, what one ought to want to know. This is perhaps one reason why not all types of knowledge will spark curiosity.

It is within this context that I want to shift to the question of mental health in the university and college system. In the past twenty years, the context of higher education has seen a massive shift in policies and practices that situate learning within a regime of knowledge-value almost completely dictated by the precepts of neoliberal, racialized, and gendered capitalism.[12] As part of the slew of neoliberal free-market reforms of the late 1980s, universities began to shift from what had been, for at least the twenty years prior, a tendency to assert their place as bastions of democratic knowledge production for the common good. As Dana Cloud explains:

> Since the 1990s, administrators have escalated the rhetoric and practices of austerity, claiming budget deficits to deny faculty raises, student scholarships, and staff jobs—all while spending millions on the beautification of campuses and administrative bloat. Meanwhile students left behind by state and university support have taken on impossible amounts of student loan debt that they will never be able to repay.[13]

Indeed, the university has become one of the two or three most entrenched sites of the modern debt economy, forcing students to think about loan repayment even as they leave college for their first jobs. The rules of business have had several other major effects on university practice, including but not limited to (1) tuition at universities rising by 35 percent between 2008 and 2017, (2) adjunct faculty making up over 75 percent of the university workforce (as opposed to almost 75 percent standing faculty in the 1970s), (3) administrative roles mimicking corporate roles and placing the salaries of presidents and deans in line with that of corporate executives, and (4) STEM curricula taking primacy over all humanities and social science courses, and slowly eroding the growth of gender, women's, and ethnic studies programs. Indeed, what Cloud makes clear is that "the emergence of queer theory and sexuality studies, antiracist and women's studies, and the critiques of imperialism that were the result of popular movements of the 1960s have become real threats to the hegemony of right-wing ideas on our campuses—and therefore threats to the restoration of a university system compliant with the imperatives of neoliberal capitalism."[14] It is for this reason that these kinds of critical curricular undertakings had to be eroded.

Inevitably, these massive shifts in knowledge-value have impacted student learning. Most students come into college already deeply indoctrinated into capitalist knowledge-values, inculcated into ideas of achievement, success, and self-worth during a secondary education that emphasizes standardized tests calibrated to those ideas that will make them compliant and productive members of the workforce. Indeed, by the time students leave high school, they are already experiencing much of the stress and anxiety that comes with the discourse on achievement.[15] And the college experience only exacerbates these anxieties as students know that they will be in debt in a cultural milieu that correlates their self-worth directly with their future earning potential after college and contextualizes nearly all learning outcomes and social relations in the context of networking and competitive advantage. What students want to know, in this context, is inevitably forced toward what they ought to want to know: *How do I get a job? What courses do I need to take to get there? How do I get the grades I need? Who do I need to know to get ahead? How do I get a leg up on the competition? How do I pay off my debt?*

Nowhere in such forms of curiosity does the question of what a student wants to learn take primacy or priority. And it is this distance between the active self-determined choice to learn and what one ought to learn based on capitalist regimes of knowledge-value that is at least a partial explanation for the many forms of mental unwellness that students exhibit in college today. Students exhibit such high levels of anxiety based on the tensions produced between what they are expected to value and learn and what they might actually want to learn, some examples of which I will show below.

Finally, I want to emphasize that this regime of knowledge-value is heavily influenced by one's own position in this system and is especially heavily gendered and racialized. In the context of heightened competition, traditional forms of white, cis, heteromasculinity are seen as a necessary social good, as men and women who are willing to be cutthroat and willing to do whatever it takes to win are rewarded both in classrooms, in future job prospects, and in their feelings of self-worth. At the same time, those who have not been bred to thrive in such hypercompetitive environments are left to struggle with their feelings of self-worth and wonder if they have any chance of success in such a system.

In the next section, I want to focus specifically on "curiosity talk" and how the very idea of curiosity is commodified and filters into our university discourse. I will then move into the specificity of student experiences at Hamilton College.

The Commodification of Curiosity

In 2015 I stumbled on an article in the *Harvard Business Review,* "Four Ways to Cultivate a Culture of Curiosity," a title that piqued my own curiosity. In

"The Campus Is Sick" 113

it, Pat Christen, the CEO of HopeLab, a California-based not-for-profit that designs video game technologies for kids, argues that "we look at our culture as a product, just like Re-Mission and Zamzee [video games] are products. . . . And we believe a culture of curiosity is key to innovation."[16]

The article goes on to discuss the methods by which HopeLab seeks to cultivate this curiosity, but I am stuck on this first statement and the many assumptions embedded in it. *What does it mean to consider culture a product? And, moreover, what does it say about how individuals conceive of curiosity?*

On the one hand, Christen's statement reflects the kind of "cultural turn" in public discourse, framing our worldviews on distinctions between us and them, binding culture in a form that has been amply critiqued within anthropology.[17] On the other hand, and more important, "culture as product" suggests that our human norms, values, rituals, practices must be sublimated into the prerequisites of capitalism: culture is what we ought to want only insofar as *culture sells.* In this case, Pat Christen is suggesting that *curiosity* is a commodifiable cultural form. That it has rules and specific practices that we can actualize, and, in so doing, we will become innovators. Innovation is already tied to the question of selling product. An invention will be deterred if the inventor cannot adequately articulate how it is addressing a market's need. In other words, we find in this article a *neoliberal curiosity,* a curiosity whose purpose and emotional resonance is derived from its ability to facilitate free market capitalism. This particular form of curiosity, I would argue, is a very recent one, derived only in a post–Washington Consensus world in which privatization and corporatization have inflected most aspects of knowledge acquisition. *"We believe a culture of curiosity is key to innovation."* Proof, it goes without saying, is when the product sells.

Moreover, this version of curiosity is *cultivatable* and *instrumental.* If we set the right norms, we can produce the particular culture of curiosity we seek. Employees, it is assumed, will feel curious when they feel that wanting to learn and acquire new knowledge will also result in what they *really ought to want*—that is, to innovate and help the company grow.

There is a "trickle-down effect" to this neoliberal curiosity. Take, for example, the University of Pennsylvania's mandate: "Penn has a long and proud tradition of intellectual rigor and pursuit of innovative knowledge . . . . That tradition lives today through the creativity, entrepreneurship, and engagement of our faculty, students, and staff."[18] Deeper in the website, it continues,

"Penn's award-winning educators and scholars encourage students to pursue inquiry and discovery, follow their passions, and address the world's most challenging problems through an interdisciplinary approach."[19]

If there is a form of curiosity in Penn's vision, it is certainly not what we might call a radical curiosity in which boundaries are broken and ideas proliferate ad infinitum. Instead, it is a curiosity already channeled toward problem-solving and entrepreneurial excellence. Students are encouraged to inquire and discover, and even to follow their passions, but only as a subset of the larger innovation-based umbrella. They are simultaneously encouraged, if not outright pressured, to be preprofessional, tying their success to the possibility of making money working at Goldman Sachs or Lehman Brothers or perhaps even as part of an organization like HopeLab after college. In this sense, we might say curiosity as commodity has become the first principle of Penn's education—*it sells to be curious*—but it also means that student curiosity is inherently constrained by the superstructure of entrepreneurialism and innovation rhetoric.[20]

Hamilton College's website takes up the rhetoric of curiosity even more directly. On its homepage, it boldly states "Constantly Curious"[21] with a link to its open curriculum, what it hails as a one-of-a-kind experience for students: "At Hamilton, study what interests you, be accepted for who you are, and prepare to be the person you were meant to become." The open curriculum supposedly allows students to choose classes based on their interests without having to worry about requirements and areas of study that don't seem to fit their goal. Hamilton, in other words, appears to promote free exploration, a curiosity untethered by the precepts of a college curriculum. And yet choice has its own pitfalls for the university student who lives within a neoliberal social order. When one's choices are already tethered to the possibility of job outcomes and future economic potential, it is unlikely that choices are as free-floating as one might imagine. In fact, given the fears of getting lower grades and taking courses that don't seem relevant for one's major, students are, in fact, *less likely to explore*. At the same time, an open curriculum assumes that a student coming to college should already know what they want to do during their college career without the kinds of curricular requirements that might push students to learn in areas that they otherwise may never know that they enjoy. Ironically, then, the open curriculum does not necessarily produce the constantly curious student it purports to.

"The Campus Is Sick" 115

In the rest of this chapter, I will turn to some insights derived in conversation with students who experience the result of this model every day.

Student Life, the Neoliberal University, and Commodified Curiosity

One student at Hamilton, Michael, a senior, began an interview by telling me that he had actually read about the need for curiosity during his job search on Recruiter.com that, he pointed out, hailed curiosity in a fashion almost identical to the *Harvard Business Review,* articulating that it was essential for business success because, along with creativity, it was the basis for innovation.

When discussing this kind of commodification of curiosity, Michael went on to say, *That's just life.* He could not imagine a world in which curiosity, learning, or his future would not or should not be based on his possibilities for economic mobility and, as such, he frankly told me that he made his decisions from this premise without trying to challenge or question any of these assumptions of what he ought to be doing with his life. Of course, he was also well aware of the fact that a curiosity that has been commodified—made instrumental only toward career advancement—actually delimits and inhibits one's ability to explore one's curiosities. Michael continued:

> Students are restricted to thinking about their life after college through goals and achievements versus simply the acquisition of knowledge.... The issue arises when there is unnecessary pressure put on students to find an internship, pick a career, and get a job all while in college. This pressure has the ability to lead kids away from their passions and towards a base level job with minimal connection to their interests. *Ultimately, it is this pressure that creates the fatalist and pragmatic individual.* (Emphasis added)

The linking of fatalism to pragmatism is one preliminary way of understanding how mental unwellness manifests in the student body.[22] To feel a sense of fatality, the idea that this is the way that it must be and that we must accept it with a shrug—*that's life*—has major consequences for how students see themselves and their ability to be themselves and change their surroundings, a literal *tearing from Self* in doing what they ought to want to do. I will return to the issue of feeling unable to make change in the conclusion.

116 Arjun Shankar

A few days later I sat with John, another Hamilton senior, and he started discussing his own dreams for his future as a musician. He was both passionate and dedicated, believing that he could and would become a musician with enough work. John was always asking questions about his craft and areas that might help him toward these goals, whether it was to think mathematically about music or to think about the creative, improvisational sensibility he sought to unleash in himself. And yet, even as he started to speak about his future dreams, he stopped, then restarted, then stopped again. Finally, he told me, without prodding, as if trying to justify his decisions to himself: *"But I still have marketable skills."*

It really does not matter what those marketable skills might be. It was the fact that John felt the need to justify himself in this way, his self-reflexive statement that what he wanted in life, what he was curious about learning, was not what he should want. Recall that knowledge values—what one ought to want to know—are always in relation to our curiosity, and in this example, this splitting of occupational desire from what one *should* desire was the basis for a lot of anxiety, continuously creating a neurosis associated with whether John was doing the right thing even as he pursued his passion. Here, a student who exhibits a curiosity that is not already explicitly commodified is by nature at risk.

John wanted to extend this idea of commodified curiosity beyond the individual student and, in trying to explain why students felt such a deep sense of worry about what they ought to pursue during college, he began thinking about the Hamilton College Career Center:

> Students at Hamilton often treat getting a job as their only goal for post-grad life and, in order to best accomplish that goal, they end up at the career center getting connected to alumni or perfecting their resume, or they end up in the OCC [Oral Communication Center] perfecting their interview styles. These institutions foster pecuniary curiosity because they are all goal-oriented and, instead of asking how specifically you need help, there is a set formula that every student must go through in order to unlock access to more resources.

John placed students' increased anxieties about their future in relation to the strategies employed by the career center, which sought to "help" students graduate from college by stressing specific, identifiable goals that students should pursue. In this institutional context, students' curiosity is channeled toward asking questions regarding resume building, networking, and career advancement. The "set formula" for what students should want in the future, and for how they should get there, alienated students who may have had ideas for present and future success that did not neatly fit into this path. Indeed, even if those in the career center were not actively discouraging students from alternative life choices, the lack of resources for such possibilities suggested that such life choices were too risky to pursue. In other words, this goal-based and risk-free approach to learning had striking secondary effects on student decision-making, creating a situation where they could not sit with any process that took time and did not already include a career end goal in mind or that might produce the possibility of failure based on the set parameters of career advancement.

In this vein, the choices of major and course requirements become key sites for this negotiation, as any "risky" class experience, which could not already be placed neatly into the confines of career goals, needed to be eliminated. Take, for example, Amanda, a senior who had wanted to choose an interdisciplinary major but found herself in a difficult situation almost immediately:

> When I chose my major, I wanted to declare an interdisciplinary major that involved experiential education. Yet I was just beginning to explore this area, so it seemed that I wouldn't be employable without direction. So I declared mathematics so that I could "sell myself" as a math teacher, if I ever needed to. Now I'm in the predicament where the math senior seminar I want to take conflicts with a course I need to take for the education minor. Why, as a sophomore, did I have such difficulty following what I was passionate about?

What students like Amanda are alluding to is the risk–security paradox produced in neoliberal education. When future success, developing the appropriate portfolio, grades, and the like are all primary concerns, students refuse the possibility of taking risks and, in fact, face much higher levels of anxiety when they do take risks. In this case, Amanda refused to take what she perceived as a risky major option—the interdisciplinary major—because she felt it would not be easily decipherable by future employers. This, in turn, made it nearly impossible to explore, be curious, and embed herself in spaces about which she was legitimately excited. Amanda is, unfortunately, one of the more fortunate ones, as she still made the choice of doing *both* the major she wanted to do and the major she ought to want to do, despite the complications therein. In the majority of cases, the anticipation of employability has meant students will refuse any educational opportunity that may feel less certain and less related to expected career outcomes. As such, by *not taking risks*, students fail to develop the very skills during college that would make them feel more secure with the uncertainties that are inevitable during life in and after college.

Amanda continues to reflect on how the college itself facilitates this type of decision-making through the commodification of student success:

> And when students do get jobs, internships, and awards, students are contacted to be featured in a story for the Hamilton News portal. If, as a school, Hamilton can show that students are doing something major, people will come. I have to admit, it is a tactic that works, but, as a student, it makes me feel that if I am not accomplishing some high-profile task, I am not the ideal "Hamilton student." This *exploitation of curiosity* creates a space where students might measure their self-worth by Hamilton News portal standards.

In this situation, success or failure is not based on a student's own interest or on their ability to satiate their curiosity. Instead, all forms of gratification are linked to external forms of success and failure, a paradigm that has major implications, as Amanda notes, for the self-worth of students. But in the case Amanda provides above, the college itself plays a key role in producing this image of success, actively framing how students should see themselves by selecting those who have reached the prescribed standards of achievement. This becomes a constant visible marker, a yardstick of success by which everyone must then compare themselves even though they may not believe in, desire, or receive such accolades.

The tendency toward specified goals in a neoliberal system of inquiry also has a paradoxical relationship to how students experience time. Time, in much of their lives, is experienced through instantaneous gratification. Information at their fingertips, ever-present social relations, and the feeling that they can get any of their desires met with just the click of a button. However, the problem is that *learning* is necessarily time consuming, processual, difficult, and cannot occur instantaneously. This contradiction between students' day-to-day experience of time and the time of learning can

"The Campus Is Sick" 119

be debilitating, causing students to continuously loop into failure narratives. There is no room for idle curiosity in this narrative.

Instead, in the neoliberal college, students are given a massive number of choices as to what kinds of activities they can do both within the classroom and also outside of it. There is an assumption, of course, that *they must choose,* and so students are embedded in a never-ending cycle of doing, as Charlotte tells me:

> In my experience, I think Hamilton students care about being busy. We care about busyness because we consider it a sign of success, and we have turned that positive association with busyness into a competition of who can be the busiest. We think that idle time or time spent doing nothing is wasted time. We try to angle everything we do into something done for a purpose. Even time spent socializing or time spent doing something for pleasure is for the purpose of de-stressing or not letting yourself burn out. We don't have the time to take a chance on some activity that is potentially a waste of time. We put activities into two categories: work or rest from work. I don't even think the categorization is inherently a bad thing, but the focus on categorizing is exhausting and limits my desire to try new things for the sake of trying something new.

I am struck by Charlotte's explicit attention to the lack of idle time, the loss of the ability to wander, explore, and question without purpose. In Veblen's discussion of capitalist university productions, he too laments this loss of *idle curiosity,* what he believed should be the ultimate purpose of university life but that had, as Charlotte too notes, been completely subsumed by the need to instrumentalize questions toward goals.[23]

This competitive behavior—pushing oneself to the limit, playing hard and working hard—was heavily racialized and gendered. Indeed, when I spoke with young white men like Michael and John, who shrugged their shoulders at the fact that their desires were necessarily channeled toward the goals of capital, they also expressed excitement and pride in their ability to push themselves and prove themselves. Most strikingly, they both acknowledged that the work they might do if they chose, for example, to join a company like Goldman Sachs would not have much social impact or reflect their own personal interest, even as they reveled in the possibility of proving themselves within these areas. One student, Aaron, went so far as to tell me:

Working really hard and being stressed has been glorified in our culture. And it's kind of fun to feel that and be like at the lower rungs of this incredibly competitive, long-hours work environment, where people are paid a lot but they have to sort of grind for it. It's kind of like that combination of difficulty and perfection sort of drew me to it. Just wanting to have an interesting career where I had to use my intellect to make it work.

Aaron links stress with fun, making money with having an interesting career that uses his intellect, all of which reflects the tethering of neoliberal education to the needs of corporate finance, which, in turn, only facilitates a version of masculinity he does not state explicitly but which clearly is part of the "culture" that glorifies this form of stress.

Men and women who refuse this version of racialized masculinity are, inevitably, left to fend for themselves. Indeed, not a single young woman I spoke to mimicked such sentiments, and, instead, most felt ill at ease with the expectations of the competitive culture that Charlotte and Aaron describe above. They wondered why this was the only way to learn or aspire, and why their college experiences could not be more varied. Indeed, Charlotte does not merely see this as a problem just about herself. It is, instead, about the entire college community:

Within this school community, we reward those who are highly involved and still get good grades, the so-called "ideal Hamilton student." Amount of sleep becomes a competition. Number of executive positions held becomes a competition. Longest time spent in the library becomes a competition. Doing nothing after class on a Tuesday is an oddity on this campus, and students are committing themselves to things because they thought that's what they were supposed to do. I should know; I swam for a year in college because I thought it would look good on paper to continue with a sport I hadn't liked since I was nine. This busy bee mindset that exists on campus needs to change. We are going to work ourselves to a breaking point, and it won't prepare us for success in the real world. Yes, extra work can lead to extra money, but is that the point of being an adult?

The drive to "look good on paper" had caused Charlotte to do what she "was supposed to do" and work herself to a self-described "breaking point." In the end, what all of this can lead to is an absolute fear of doing anything at all; another way that students see the campus as a place of sickness rather than health. After telling me that she now really dislikes speaking in any classroom settings because of how fearful she is of being judged, Charlotte finally blurts out, "I just feel paralyzed by it. I never want to do anything wrong." The evocation of a feeling of paralysis might be the best way of articulating how mental unwellness gets wrapped into student college life. Rather than beginning and ending with the kinds of questions that have sparked her curiosity, Charlotte cannot even fathom asking questions anymore given her fear of failure and the toxic environment of competition she feels pressured to participate in every day.

And, in talking to other students, this breaking point was also associated with excess drinking, anxiety, depression, not wanting to leave their rooms for long periods of time, feelings of inadequacy, and as Adam, the student whose words began this chapter, described to me, suicidal ideation:

> I told some of my friends that the only time I didn't feel like taking my own life was when I was drunk.... Most of them thought it was a joke, but then, finally, one of them reported me to the counseling office. That's when I got sent home.

Conclusion

In this chapter I have tried to provide preliminary thoughts on the capitalist regime of knowledge-value that constrains how student populations can or cannot be curious. In turn, the constraints placed on student curiosity, based on the prerequisites of job success and economic mobility, have had significant and deleterious effects on the mental wellness of students on college campuses.

In future work on this subject, much further attention must be given to the institutional structures of the university that determine the kinds of majors, course requirements, and values that circulate on campuses. Perhaps more importantly, more attention must be given to intersectional systems of power: How do these institutional structures impact students differently based on their class, race, gender, sexuality, and/or religion? Indeed, in my preliminary research, the emotional experience of the neoliberal university was heavily gendered and racialized, and it is inevitable that women of color, for example, will experience the vagaries of the neoliberal university differently than their white counterparts, given their differences in position.

But what I would like to end by asking is: What would college and university life look like if student curiosity, in all of its complexity and possibility, were foregrounded and facilitated rather than always delimited and curtailed?

Indeed, one of the greatest insights derived from teaching a class on *curiosity* was that an explicit attention to curiosity (or the lack thereof) in everyday life opened up opportunities for students to develop a critical awareness that, in turn, allowed them to take a renewed ownership of their learning. What this also suggests is that some of the short-term solutions start with faculty. Students will generally be opaque to administrations and administrations are inevitably opaque to students. Administration cannot cater to students' individual needs, nor is its first obligation to students when it must cater to trustees and an entangled web of bureaucracy. Faculty, however, have direct relations with students: they can interact with them and advocate for a different way of thinking about university life. At the end of one long interview, Michael told me that he had found that "the best source for creating curiosity in life after college was professors."

Yet this is just another example of how the many unpaid labor burdens in the neoliberal university fall on faculty, who are already overworked and underappreciated. While research, teaching, and service are all part of the faculty mandate, the service and teaching components and the care that such student service entails are often overlooked in how faculty are assessed, how tenure files are read, and how faculty are compensated. As such, perhaps it may feel like an unfair request for those who are already faced with so much pressure in a system that is continuously producing their precarity.

At the same time, what faculty teach students may provide some potential benefits for everyone involved, faculty and students alike. As Moten and Harney remind, "It is teaching that brings us in," and it is in this space that we might begin to subvert the boredom, numbness, and passivity that comes with professionalization—grants, grades, and evaluations.[24] Specifically, what faculty need to learn with students is how to resist, to be a fugitive, to begin asking challenging questions that make us feel like we *can change the situations that we are in.* What I found most striking and sad is just how much students, and to a lesser extent faculty, felt like they were somehow completely without agency. Statements like, "We never question the status quo," "We aren't allowed to do anything," and "We don't know how to make things happen" were perhaps always intertwined with their loss of curiosity and feelings of anxiety, despair, and paralysis.

"The Campus Is Sick"   123

Indeed, the turning point for Adam during our time together was when he was able to take his feelings about the state of learning and mental health on Hamilton's campus, resist the administrative impulse to cordon off how and where he should voice his concerns, and turn it into action. He decided, after much contemplation, to contact the *New York Times* about his experiences and was shocked when a reporter from the *Times* contacted him and wanted to hear about his experiences. He was interviewed by the reporter, after which she wrote an exposé about the state of mental health on college campuses. In the end, his decidedly pessimistic view of college life had changed dramatically. Instead, as he embarked on life after college, his tone was marked by hope and a belief that, through persistent subversive action, his voice might be heard and things could change.

Without this kind of *hope* that change can occur and *the curiosity* to ask how we might change things—and here I am reminded of my discussions with this volume's coeditor Perry Zurn—students and faculty will remain embedded in this context of college unwellness.

Notes

1. Eugene Beresin, "The College Mental Health Crisis: Focus on Suicide," *Psychology Today,* February 27, 2017, https://www.psychologytoday.com/us/blog/inside-out-outside-in/201702/the-college-mental-health-crisis-focus-suicide.

2. Richard Handler, "Undergraduate Research in Veblen's Vision: Idle Curiosity, Bureaucratic Accountancy, and Pecuniary Emulation in Contemporary Higher Education," in *The Experience of Neoliberal Education*, ed. Bonnie Urciuoli (New York: Bergahn, 2018).

3. Arthur Kleinman's work in this area is quite helpful, especially as he outlines the basic dilemma faced by anthropologists of mental health. He writes that "the central theoretical problem for medicine . . . is the distinction between the normal and the pathological. . . . The simple reason for this is that social suffering and illness overlap, not entirely, but substantially. Economic depression and psychological depression and societal demoralization/anomie are systematically related. . . . Political economy creates suicide just as surely as genetics does. Global social disruptions contribute to substance abuse. Political and moral processes underpin the stigma of psychosis and cognitive disability just as they provide the structural basis for psychological and family trauma. Contrary to psychiatric epidemiologists' focus on one disease at a time, in the toxic and predatory environments of urban slums and shantytowns worldwide, depression, suicide, violence, PTSD, and substance abuse cluster together—the very terrain of social exclusion, health disparities, and social suffering." See Arthur Kleinman, "Medical Anthropology and Mental Health: Five Questions

for the Next Fifty Years," in *Medical Anthropology at the Intersections: Histories, Activisms, and Futures* (Durham, N.C.: Duke University Press, 2012), 118.

4. Nancy Schepher-Hughes writes, "Anthropology is a vocation based not necessarily on love, but rather on a deep curiosity that is open to many surprises, . . . Our job is to understand the way people think, the way they live in the world." See Ann Brice, "Celebrating 'Barefoot Anthropology'—Q&A with Nancy Schepher-Hughes," *Berkeley News,* April 28, 2017, http://news.berkeley.edu/2017/04/28/celebrating-bare foot-anthropology-nancy-scheper-hughes/.

5. Benedict Spinoza, *Spinoza: The Complete Works,* trans. Samuel Shirley et al. (Indianapolis: Hackett, 2002).

6. David Graeber, *Towards an Anthropological Theory of Value: The False Coin of Our Own Dreams* (New York: Palgrave, 2001), 20.

7. Paul Kockelman, "Value Is Life under an Interpretation," *Anthropological Theory* 10, nos. 1–2 (2010): 149–62, 149.

8. Anna Tsing, *Friction: An Ethnography of Global Connection* (Princeton, N.J.: Princeton University Press, 2005).

9. Michel Foucault, "Two Lectures," *Power/Knowledge: Selected Interviews and Other Writings, 1972–1977* (New York: Pantheon, 1980), 102.

10. Raymond Williams, *Marxism and Literature* (Oxford: Oxford University Press, 1977).

11. Sara Ahmed, *The Cultural Politics of Emotion* (New York: Routledge, 2004).

12. Harney and Moten write, "Professionalization cannot take over the American university—it is the critical approach of the university, its Universitas. And indeed, it appears now that this state with its peculiar violent hegemony must deny what Foucault called in his 1975–76 lectures the race war. . . . And there are other spaces situated between the Universitas and the undercommons, spaces that are characterized precisely by not having space. Thus the fire aimed at black studies . . . and the proliferation of Centers without affiliation to the memory of the conquest, to its living guardianship, to the protection of its honor, to the nights of labor, in the undercommons." Stefano Harney and Fred Moten, *The Undercommons: Fugitive Planning and Black Study* (New York: Minor Compositions, 2013), 41–42.

13. Dana Cloud, "From Austerity to Attacks on Scholars," *Inside Higher Ed,* May 3, 2018, https://www.insidehighered.com/views/2018/05/03/neoliberal-academy-age -trump.

14. Cloud.

15. Peter Demerath, *Producing Success: The Culture of Personal Advancement in an American High School* (Chicago: University of Chicago Press, 2009).

16. Katie Smith Milway and Alex Goldmark, "Four Ways to Cultivate a Culture of Curiosity," *Harvard Business Review,* September 18, 2013, https://hbr.org/2013/09/four-ways-to-cultivate-a-culture-of-curiosity.

17. Arjun Appadurai, "Putting Hierarchy in Its Place," *Cultural Anthropology* 3, no. 1 (1988): 36–49.

18. University of Pennsylvania, "About," accessed June 23, 2018, https://www.upenn.edu/about.

19. University of Pennsylvania, "Introduction to Penn," accessed 23, 2018, https://www.upenn.edu/about/welcome.

20. Helga Nowotny, *Insatiable Curiosity: Innovation in a Fragile Future,* trans. Mitch Cohen (Cambridge, Mass.: MIT Press, 2008).

21. Hamilton College, home page, accessed May 1, 2018, www.hamilton.edu. Linked to https://www.youtube.com/watch?v=pxKpIxfZIAY.

22. Michael's sentiments register with the work of Paulo Freire, who writes that educators are "resigned fatalistically to neoliberal pragmatism . . . while considering that [they are] still 'progressive' pedagogically and politically." Freire, *Pedagogy of Freedom* (Lanham, Md.: Rowman and Littlefield, 1998), 20. I am struck by Freire's attention to the emotional register of capitalist pragmatism, in his characterization of capitalist pragmatism as a kind of *resignation* and *fatalism* that undermines any progressive ideals of those who participate in the project. But what I found fascinating in this context is that fatal pragmatism is not just an issue facing educators but also students as well.

23. Handler, "Undergraduate Research in Veblen's Vision."

24. Harney and Moten, *The Undercommons,* 27.

PART III

Reimagining How We Relate

8

Autism, Neurodiversity, and Curiosity

Kristina T. Johnson

What we observe is not nature itself, but nature exposed to our method of questioning.

—Werner Heisenberg

One morning in early April, on a beautiful Boston day, I watched as a little boy stopped next to an old brick wall outside the local dry cleaner. Most of the bricks were a rusty red, but a few were a variegated black, and one black brick seemed to capture his attention in particular. He tapped it and ran his finger across it, tilting his head and swaying, seeming to contemplate it for a few minutes before resuming his walk to the park.

What about that brick had made him stop? Was he curious about why the brick was black among all its red neighbors? Had he tapped it to determine if black bricks felt different than other bricks, or had he just been randomly stroking bricks and happened to stop at that one? Maybe it was purely visual: he was intrigued by the high contrast of the black on red and paused a moment to enjoy the view. Or perhaps it was nothing at all; he had just stopped to take a break.

I shared several of these thoughts with the boy while we stood by the wall, pointing out my observations and remarking on the wall's texture and composition. But he gave no observable indication that he had heard me, understood me, or cared what I had said. He did not look at me, gesture for my attention, or share his thought process. I was but an outside observer to his rich inner world.

The little boy, Gabriel, has autism, and he happens to be my son. He also has a rare genetic disorder that inhibits motor planning, including the most sophisticated motor planning that humans perform—speech. While it is not uncommon for autistic individuals to have speech and communication challenges, individuals with this genetic disorder never master the motor planning necessary to speak even single words, and, to date, Gabriel is the first person missing the main gene of this disorder to walk independently. He has profound cognitive delays—the gene he's missing usually helps strengthen the connections between brain cells when something is learned—and what is effortless for most infants is a Herculean feat for him.

Still, does the fact that he can never tell me that he is curious or move in ways typically associated with curiosity imply that he is not curious? Of course not. But scientifically, how can we measure his curiosity? How can we characterize it, probe it, or understand its dimensions and dynamics in the ways that science offers neurotypical individuals?[1] Understanding Gabriel's curiosity—and that of every other child who deviates from the norm—requires both asking new questions and finding new ways of asking questions so that we share in the exceptional intricacy and diversity of their worlds.

Neurodiverse Curiosity Studies

For centuries scientists have been captivated by curiosity, the motivated exploratory behavior that seems to underlie human development. Nineteenth-century philosopher and psychologist William James named curiosity immediately following fear and love in his list of native reactions comprising the "impulses and instincts of childhood."[2] In the early twentieth century, Jean Piaget observed infants exploring objects from the earliest age, discovering that their actions produced effects.[3] In the 1950s and '60s, Daniel Berlyne sparked a new era of inquiry into the causation of curiosity, positing a neurophysiological mechanism for this behavior. He suggested that uncertainty in the environment induced a state of arousal, prompting exploration to reduce this uncertainty.[4] Still others have theorized that curiosity originates from an information gap between what one knows and what one wants to know,[5] an incongruity between expected and unexpected outcomes,[6] or simply an innate drive, propelling organisms to explore and work with no obvious reward.[7] And while no single unified definition or theory of curiosity has emerged,[8] almost every approach to the study of curiosity has had a common thread: they have all focused on typical development. Individuals who diverged strongly from the mean have been given their own studies, but usually only to identify the ways in which they differed from the "typical" population.[9]

For example, in one of the earliest studies of curiosity and autism,[10] researchers found that autistic individuals (N = 5, ages 4–7) took four times longer, on average, to approach a foot-wide red metal box with a lever on top than a group of typically developing 3–5 year olds.[11] The researchers also found that the autistic children spent less time exploring the box once they approached it, and that they quickly became uninterested in the box and its lever—much sooner than the "typically developing" group of participants. Autistic children exhibited diminished interest in the red box and, in doing so, their exploratory activity was deemed deficient.

Yet, in the middle of the paper, the authors mention that these children showed more than a hundredfold increase in lever interaction in the two directions that produced sounds, triggering a bell or a buzzer, suggesting that they were significantly more motivated by the sounds than anything else about the box. Since most of the autistic children had been initially referred to the doctor for "probable deafness," a common referral in young autistic individuals because of their lack of response to language,[12] the authors note this finding as "interesting" but give it little further discussion.

Almost fifty years later, we recognize these findings as more than interesting; they are indicative of the need to reexamine the ways in which we study individuals with autism and other developmental differences. Even accounting for the small sample size, the participants were clearly attracted to the sounds and sought more input from the bell and the buzzer than anything else about the experimental setup. While this does indeed differ from canonical exploratory behavior in neurotypical children, the lack of exploration is not the conclusion. Rather, their novel and intense exploration of unique phenomena forms the basis for a new line of inquiry.

What else would these individuals have explored if there had been a greater number and variety of auditory stimuli? Would chords or short ditties have had the same effect? Since many autistic children, including the children in the study, show decreased attention to human voice, how does their exploratory behavior change when the response is a spoken word versus a sung one? Or songs with lyrics compared to instrumental pieces?

These more nuanced lines of inquiry can suggest crucial study variables, allowing a systematic examination of the effects of certain stimuli for each child. By first establishing the way in which an individual excels in exploring, we can construct a baseline of activity and behavior for that child founded upon their strengths. We can characterize the intensity, duration, and diversity of their exploration and curiosity, as well as the features of the information or stimuli. We can also measure peripheral responses, such as their affect, interactions, and physiology. Then we can empirically investigate the parameters that alter the individual's exploration.

For example, how does the type of stimuli or the presentation of the stimuli alter the exploration? Berlyne used visually intricate patterns to determine the optimal complexity that engaged one's attention for the greatest amount of time in order to map the properties of curiosity stimuli.[13] However, studies have indicated that autistic individuals tend to explore images that they find personally interesting for longer and in a more detail-oriented manner than other images.[14] How, then, might visual attention be altered when the stimulus is not a pattern but rather an increasingly complex image of a child's favorite character or topic? If attention, as measured by gaze persistence, is plotted as a function of complexity, does it change over time for that child? Do variations in auditory complexity—for example, slight alterations of a favorite song—follow a similar curve to their visual counterparts?

While there is no shortage of parameters and variables one can explore, the intent is not to make the system endlessly more complex. Rather, our goal is to isolate the key variables that characterize an individual's natural curiosity. Once established, we can form and test hypotheses to probe this curiosity and compare data across individuals with similar characterizations. These individuals may not be grouped by traditional divisions, such as age or diagnoses, but they may display similar manifestations of curiosity. Then, within individuals or within groups, we can systematically investigate how small changes of certain parameters alter the manifestation of curiosity. Ultimately, this methodological, individualized process can produce a framework to inform the field of neurodiverse curiosity studies.

A Note on Language

While the CDC recommends using "person-first" language when referring to individuals with various diagnoses or distinguishing traits (e.g., "person with autism," "individual with a disability") in an effort to ensure that the individual is not defined by the diagnosis, label, or trait, many persons and groups prefer "identity-first" language, such as "autistic person" or "disabled individual."[15] Similar to many members of the Deaf community, these individuals feel that the features that motivated the diagnosis or labels are inherently tied to their identities.[16] Recognizing that identity is deeply personal, both expressions will be utilized interchangeably throughout this work.

In addition, this paper will attempt to address both autism and intellectual disability (ID), understanding that each of these terms describes a spectrum and that they are not mutually inclusive. Autism spectrum disorders (ASDs) can and do exist without accompanying ID, and ID can be completely detached from autistic behaviors or ASD diagnoses. However, both groups have been marginalized within studies of curiosity, and the research methods that augment the studies of one may also bolster studies of the other. And in many of the severest forms of either label, these diagnoses exist together, and, thus, one must account for the superposition of these spectra as well.

Finally, I acknowledge that all of the words and phrases employed here today are subject to the "euphemism treadmill," whereby words slowly evolve in meaning to become offensive, even if they were originally introduced to replace an offensive word.[17] Nevertheless, the intention of this work is accessibility in the broadest sense, and I look forward to improved inclusive lexical semantics in future work.

Case Studies

To further elucidate this inclusive framework, I present three individual profiles. (Names have been changed.) These case studies have been chosen not as a complete, representative sample but rather as a foundation upon which other neurodiverse studies of curiosity can build. The profiles were acquired through a combination of parent report and personal observation and focus primarily on preadolescent children; however, a broad range of language abilities and developmental stages have been included with the hope that many of the principles presented here can be extrapolated to other persons and populations.

Within each profile I share an overview of the individual's development to provide context and highlight the breadth of neurodiversity, especially across the autism spectrum. More important, I note ways that we could build the scientific method around their strengths, often employing technology to motivate new ways of asking questions and understanding the answers.

134   Kristina T. Johnson

Mark, Age Ten

Mark is a ten-and-a-half-year-old boy with a diagnosis of ASD. He also has a learning disability and has been referred for concerns regarding attention-deficit/hyperactivity disorder (ADHD), but his parents have not sought a diagnosis for the latter.

At two years of age, Mark had only a few functional spoken words. By age four, his language had dramatically improved to include sentences. He could engage in two-way conversations for a few minutes when motivated; however, his day-to-day use of language was still consistent with the typical early to mid-two-year-old level. At ten and a half, he converses at a similar rate and length to his peers, though his topics tend to focus heavily on things that interest him, such as dinosaurs and dragons.

His parents describe him as "very curious," "analytical," and "metacognitive"; he is always trying to ascertain how he thinks and operates. He loves to ask questions, including "why" questions, a hallmark of traditional curiosity questions.[18] Mark also enjoys experimenting with material properties and the effects of additives like hot water and soap. For example, he will take toy dinosaurs made of different types of material, including foam, rubber, and hard plastic, into the bathroom and will systematically add different amounts of water (e.g., little or lots) at different temperatures (e.g., hot, warm, or cold) with various additives (e.g., soap or shampoo). These experiments are self-driven and often performed surreptitiously, under the perception that his parents are unaware of his actions.

Although it may seem like Mark would perform admirably in typical studies of curiosity, asking him to play in this way or prompting him with other materials or activities does not necessarily result in similar exploration. In a classic study by Kreitler, Zigler, and Kreitler,[19] children were presented with familiar everyday objects, such as "medium-sized toys of a car, an iron, a telephone, and a piano." The researchers then counted the number of responses the child used to describe the items, as well as the number of "inspective" manipulations (i.e., visually inspecting the toy), "customary" manipulations (e.g., playing the piano, answering the pretend phone), and "exploratory" manipulations (e.g., trying to take the toy apart or determine how it operates). These variables were combined with others to discern different types of curiosity.

Indeed, Mark has rarely shown interest in typical everyday objects. In fact, Mark's parents reported not having to childproof the house in the way

Autism, Neurodiversity, and Curiosity 135

that most parents must because he never approached the knobs on the stove or other items that typically draw children's attention. Even though Kreitler and colleagues were one of the first groups to acknowledge that curiosity is "neither unitary nor homogenous" and encouraged evaluating a wide range of curiosity types before characterizing a child as "curious or noncurious," their proposed curiosity measures based on typical development would almost certainly capture Mark's weaknesses but not his strengths. He would likely be labeled "not curious."

In what ways could we capture his strengths? How can we characterize his curiosity in a way that is both personalized and rigorous? Like many autistic individuals, Mark exhibits strong specific interests in certain topics or objects that persist longer and with greater intensity than those of nonautistic individuals.[20] For example, for the last five years, Mark has been particularly enthralled by dinosaurs and dragons. Mark's self-stated goal in life is to become the "first hybrid human-dinosaur," and he independently uses the internet and other resources to learn about anatomy and genetics with the goal of altering his DNA to give himself wings to fly like a dragon.

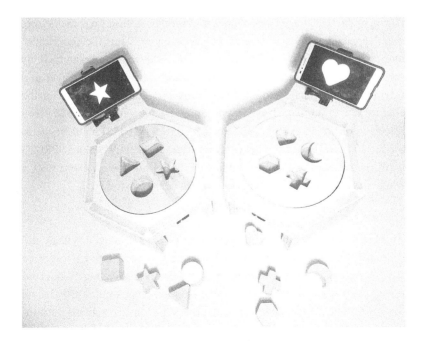

Figure 8.1. SPRING, a customizable learning platform.

136 Kristina T. Johnson

These devout interests, or "affinities," can be leveraged to motivate or evoke exploration and inquiry in ways that might otherwise remain hidden,[21] as in the case of the bathroom dinosaur science experiments. Affinities also provide a unique opportunity to investigate how different reinforcement mechanisms alter a child's exploratory behavior. For example, we have developed a research platform called SPRING that enables customization in the activity, the development level of the activity, and the reinforcement provided by the system (Figure 8.1).[22] It is similar in style to Banta's curiosity box, but wholly customizable and programmable.[23] The central module, shown as shape sorters in Figure 8.1, can be removed and replaced with different activities to match the developmental skills and interests of the child. Sensors within SPRING passively record user activity, minimizing the effects of examiner presence or intervention while enabling quantitative objective data collection.

By modifying the parameters of SPRING, one can systematically examine a child's exploration as a function of various reinforcement parameters or levels of ambiguity. For instance, since Mark loves dragons, SPRING could be programmed such that every time Mark inserts a square followed by two circles, his favorite dragon video appears on the device. Inserting other shapes might produce sounds and lights, but no dragons. Thus the significance of dragons as a variable in his exploratory behavior might be examined. By varying the reinforcement, including no reinforcement, the intrinsic and extrinsic motivational factors behind his exploration and problem solving could also be appraised.[24] Similarly, prompts could be shown on the SPRING screen, as displayed in Figure 8.1, or the screen could be left blank to examine his exploration and problem solving without assistance. Since SPRING is highly customizable, it and similar personalizable devices can unlock a whole domain of individualized data-driven curiosity studies.

Gabriel, Age Seven

As discussed earlier, Gabriel struggles with motor planning, language, and general learning. While expressive language is expected to be a lifelong struggle, receptive language has also been markedly challenging. Gabriel did not respond in any discernible way to spoken language until shortly before his fifth birthday, and then it was only to the word "car," referencing the family car, where a few of his favorite toys were kept. Between ages six and seven, he showed considerable growth, with occasional clear recognition of words like "dinner," "cow" (for a favorite dancing cow toy), and "watch" (as in, "watch a movie"); however, other words, including his name, continue to produce no overt response.

Undoubtedly, attempts to use language to discern the mechanics and motivations of Gabriel's mind will fall short. Even with alternative means of communication like an augmentative assistive communication (AAC) device, sign language, gestures, picture cards, and other cues, his vocabulary is limited to a few dozen words. And while communication is a major hurdle, it is not the only one. Standardized assessments consistently rate him either in the most severe categories, or such assessments cannot be used because he cannot complete them in the way they were intended. He has been recruited for over a dozen scientific studies, usually ones advertised specifically for autism, but he has not met the inclusion criteria for any of them. His lack of language, cognitive delays, and motor challenges cement his position outside the community of scientific inquiry.

Yet it is not Gabriel's responsibility to evolve to fit the mold of science. It is our duty as scientists to develop new ways to understand Gabriel. We need a new research framework that captures meaningful data on how he acts and, maybe someday, on how he thinks. We must ask new questions while jointly creating new ways to answer those questions. For example, how does *movement* of the stimulus vary the perceived complexity of the stimulus? What is the role of agency in exploration? How does personal interest in the topic or object alter curiosity behaviors?

Gabriel explores his environment primarily through sensorimotor actions, including stroking materials to explore textures, spinning items to explore visual dynamics, or tapping objects to surfaces to explore sounds. He finds visually engaging experiences, such as shadows, waterfalls, and dynamic light displays like scrolling LED tickers captivating. Like many autistic individuals, he seems to possess heightened sensory awareness. Some find this hypersensitivity aversive, but Gabriel seeks it out, suggesting a high threshold for optimal sensory input.

But while his sensory seeking is pervasive, it is also specific. A few years ago, a wide balance beam was built for Gabriel that lit up directly in front of his foot as he stepped on it, designed to provide a more enticing environment for him to practice stabilizing and walking. The colored lights were originally programmed to flash three times with each step, and, although Gabriel generally loves lights, he showed little interest. However, when the lights were changed to chase one another down the LED strip, similar to marquee lights, he eagerly approached the beam, willingly practicing challenging skills in order to activate the lights. Such an experience is reminiscent of the curiosity study with the autistic children manipulating the lever, except here we find that not only does the type of stimuli matter (e.g., lights, sounds, and textures) but the dynamics (e.g., how it moves, how it changes) affect the course of action as well. Therefore, within the realm of neurodiverse curiosity studies, and perhaps within all curiosity studies, we must consider what novel features, such as the dynamics of the stimuli, specifically characterize an individual's curiosity.

Moreover, it is not only what features or variables characterize a person's curiosity, but also how that curiosity evolves. Recently, Gabriel discovered that a pillow covered in sequins reflects sunlight from a window, covering the walls in golden sparkles of light (Figure 8.2). Twisting the pillow altered the design, intensity, and location of sparkles on the wall. Upon discovery, he spent more than thirty minutes exploring the various patterns of light, his rapt attention far exceeding his usual concentration on a single task or activity. He returned to the pillow and the window for further exploration on subsequent days. Eventually, he began playing with cars and stuffed animals—toys that had never independently held his interest—on top of the pillow (and on top of the pillow only), seemingly motivated to continue exploring the reflection of light in multiple constructs. His curiosity had a distinctive temporal evolution, growing and changing with time.

Even so, developmental assessments would suggest that this exploration is simply a manifestation of his overt developmental age. But is it infantile, or is it artistic? If Gabriel were able to describe his experience in a way that could be understood and shared, we would almost certainly ascribe it to the latter. With language, Gabriel might share the beauty he sees when the reflections cascade across the wall or wonder aloud why sunlight creates the patterns of light while the living room light does not. Without language, it is easy to assume that his actions are merely basal sensory exploration. How could we know differently?

We need new metrics. Berlyne clearly delineates between "perceptual" (stimulus-based) and "epistemic" (knowledge-based) curiosity.[25] The former is the major driver in the exploration of novel stimuli, one shared by animals, infants, and adults alike. In that case, however, the physiological arousal induced by the novelty of the stimuli is expected to decrease after repeated

Figure 8.2. Gabriel manipulates his sparkle pillow to reflect light.

exposure, which, in turn, reduces interest in the stimuli.[26] Yet Gabriel exhibited no such arousal reduction nor a diminishing interest over time. His interest appeared to *grow* with time, naturally scaffolding and expanding his exploration to different "sparkle" environments and interactions with other toys, suggesting something distinctive from the classical definitions of both perceptual and epistemic curiosity.

While researchers acknowledge that many variants of curiosity have yet to be fully defined, they still rely on measures like questionnaires and prescribed laboratory studies to test their theories.[27] But Gabriel cannot yet explain the motivations for his actions with the sparkle pillow using words, nor can he share his potentially profound sensory experiences in a way that can be cataloged or measured. No clinical study of curiosity would capture, or even replicate, this experience, as it appeared to occur almost through happenstance. How can we test these theories of curiosity for neurodiverse children?

Wearable physiological sensors—for example, watches, glasses, headbands, badges, and clothing that can detect or infer the wearer's physiological signals without involving wires and constrained environments—may enable a modern approach to tackling these questions and theories. These sensors can track the body's sympathetic nervous system arousal through electrodermal activity (EDA; formerly galvanic skin response).[28] They can also monitor heart rate, heart rate variability, skin temperature, posture, and respiration rate.[29] In fact, emerging systems do not even require the use of a wearable device; they can passively survey a person's physiology through standard cameras, combining light and color magnification with machine-learning analysis techniques.[30] With these tools, we can capture and characterize Gabriel's arousal systematically, and we can do so in a naturalistic environment. We can plot his arousal as a function of activity and behavior and monitor it over time. Is his physiological arousal a function of his curiosity, or is his curiosity a function of his arousal? Does his EDA evolve as his play extends beyond sparkles on the wall to include the reflections on trucks and books that he holds above the pillow? If spikes in arousal initially precede his exploratory behavior, how does this relationship change as his play expands?

Gabriel also has a penchant for music. Although his motor delays inhibit his ability to create sophisticated sounds without assistance, he shows heightened awareness and sensitivity to music over other auditory input. Even as a young toddler, he would choose, through the use of picture cards, to watch video recordings of piano concertos and symphonies, including complex compositions by Rachmaninoff and Dvorak, over animated movie clips or other "age-appropriate" offerings. Years later, he freely and extensively explores the different demo tracks on a digital keyboard, using the programming buttons to modify the tempo, rhythm, and dynamics. But the keyboard is complex. It took years of exposure for him to manually operate the multi-step tempo and track buttons, and he still lacks agency to deliberately and accurately select demo tracks. He clearly prefers certain tracks, however, because he will guide a friend or family member over to the keyboard and will continue requesting new music until landing on his favorite song. His lack of agency undeniably impedes his expression of musical curiosity.

Would a control panel with simpler, one-step buttons enable a more extensive, and perhaps more genuine, manifestation of his curiosity? Such a panel would have the added bonus of being able to track button presses and other actions, providing an objective log of his musical exploration over time. Could the differing exploration between the two systems—the complex keyboard and the simpler control panel—measure curiosity as a

Autism, Neurodiversity, and Curiosity 141

function of agency? Multiple panels could be built with relative ease, each one increasing slightly in complexity or capabilities by offering more songs or features. Does Gabriel always prefer the simplest access to music, suggesting that it is more about sensory feedback than exploration, or does his interest seem to expand when more options are presented? As with previous studies that examine the optimal levels of complexity, what is the threshold after which exploration declines?[31] Similarly, what is the relationship between physical exertion and curiosity? If the buttons are spaced farther apart, are they explored with the same intensity or frequency? Such measures would be valuable not only to other children with special needs but also to any educational or community setting serving a wide range of children and abilities.

Becca, Age 6

Becca is a six-and-a-half-year-old autistic girl, described by her mother as "happy," a "free spirit," and the "most confident person I know!" She dives into experiences without restraint and cares little for social etiquette. Becca will unabashedly arrive at school wearing costumes or outfits inspired by her favorite television characters, regularly choosing clothing based on its character-appeal and style over practicality. It is difficult to talk her out of an outfit with long sleeves and a sweater, even on a hot summer day, hinting that she can be equal parts creative and rigid in her actions and expressions.

Becca is a prolific artist, and she has reportedly never paused for even an instant before taking a marker to a piece of paper and beginning to draw. She can fill the pages of entire sketchbooks in rapid succession, never hesitating between one drawing and the next. She has no shortage of ideas, and always seems to know exactly what she wants. And while Becca's confidence and sense of self are marked assets, she also does not feel motivated to do things that do not interest her, which can make academic work and other obligations difficult. For example, Becca will often spend recess exploring leaves and trees and making tiny piles of wood chips. Asking her to leave recess to do an activity of someone else's choosing can prove challenging. Likewise, assessments and studies that require her to complete predetermined activities, including curiosity studies that examine her "spontaneous exploration" of a standardized selection of toys, are likely to be met with resistance and may elicit a performance not indicative of her true capabilities.[32]

Nevertheless, she exhibits undeniable exploratory behavior. Although she is not verbally curious like Mark, Becca will roam around her grandparents' large yard, climbing rocks, looking at leaves, and bringing grass to her cheek to experience its texture and scent. She experiences the world in a decidedly physical way and can spend hours engaged in what appears to be a very compelling and reinforcing internal world. Some days she will sit and talk to herself (not always in words that others might understand), often laughing aloud at something she is thinking about.

This type of curiosity may be difficult to capture in a laboratory setting, and the few studies that have attempted to do so in the natural environments have relied on recorded narrations of behavior,[33] which is time consuming to transcribe, quantify, and scale. Alternatively, multimodal data streams from video, audio, and wearable sensors enable rich new sources to objectively analyze naturalistic behavior and play.[34] Combining off-the-shelf cameras and open-source data-processing tools, it is possible to track body pose,[35] interactions, and gestures,[36] as well as facial expressions[37] and affect,[38] without the use of specialized equipment or clinical settings. If tolerated, wearable eye-tracking glasses can also help monitor gaze and attention,[39] differentiating the minute examination of a pile of wood chips from the inspection of ants marching home after a long day's work. Machine learning and artificial intelligence enables statistical analysis of these records, including extensive datasets over days and weeks, allowing us to build computational models of behavior and curiosity. These models can help form a baseline of curiosity activities and emotions for individuals like Becca. We then can hypothesize how small changes might affect her curiosity in large ways, taking care to join her world instead of pigeonholing her into ours.

Although Becca can and does occasionally speak, her language remains limited, and approximately 90 percent of her conversations are "scripted" from favorite television characters and scenes. While some of this scripting is appropriate to the situation at hand, observers who are unfamiliar with her nuanced references may not understand the context and may interpret her communication as gibberish or "nonfunctional." Abstract language remains difficult for her, and she does not ask or answer "why" questions. Yet she has entire television episodes memorized.

She is motivated by these television shows and seeks out opportunities to watch them, think about them, or draw pictures of them. As with many autistic affinities, the relationship she has with the shows and their characters can provide insight into her internal thought processes. For example, almost every picture she draws is a scene or a riff off a scene from an episode of a show. Likewise, if she repeats a line from a favorite episode and a parent or friend says the next line, her eyes will light up and she will smile gleefully as if to say, "Yes! You get it!" It is like a secret handshake, building trust and camaraderie, unlocking the passageway to her precious thoughts and feelings. The songs and plots from these shows can also help with transitions between activities, social situations, and difficult tasks, like acknowledging the need to go to the bathroom when in the middle of a favorite game. They seem to help organize her world, like a Rolodex of situations she can call upon to help process and relate to the emotions and experiences around her.

But these shows and characters may be more than just a conduit to her lush inner world. Becca's nuanced relationship with them suggests that she is conceptualizing information and making connections far beyond what her words or general actions may indicate. She may be exploring whole theoretical worlds in her head that can only be perceived if one joins her world and explores with her.

So how could we build neurodiverse curiosity studies for Becca? How is her curiosity expressed in the kingdom of her characters? If her characters ask "why" or "I wonder" questions, how does that influence the wonder she expresses through any modality—actions, scripting, or spontaneous speech? What if puppets of her characters explore her real world with inquisitive attitudes and actions? Does she join in? Does she imitate them or learn from them? How do small changes to the ways these characters explore affect how Becca incorporates their words or behaviors into her own life? Even with her favorite shows, she tends to relate more strongly to one character than the rest—for example, Prince Wednesday from *Daniel Tiger* or Gekko from *PJ Masks*. How does her assimilation of the information change when Prince Wednesday demonstrates curiosity behaviors versus the default protagonist Daniel Tiger? What is the effect of using words or songs versus only actions? These results may generalize to broader curiosity studies, especially in the context of curiosity and technology,[40] but until we understand the most fundamental drivers of these exceptional individuals, we will never know.

This chapter proposed a strengths-based research framework for neurodiverse curiosity studies. Through three distinct case studies, we explored how individual manifestations of curiosity may depend on interests, environment, and skills, and we noted how typical approaches to the study of curiosity may fail for autistic and neurodiverse children. We then described

144 Kristina T. Johnson

how novel methods and engineering solutions could personalize the approach to elicit and measure curiosity and examined how small parametric changes could significantly affect exploratory behavior outcomes. With these examples and techniques, we invite researchers to form and test new hypotheses, probing how curiosity evolves over time, how it is motivated by personal interests, and how it can be expressed both with and without language. We look eagerly to future studies that expand our understanding of curiosity in all individuals.

Notes

This work was supported by the MIT Media Lab Consortium and Learning Initiative. Special thanks to Perry Zurn and Arjun Shankar for inspiration and thoughtful feedback, and to the individuals and families represented by the case studies.

1. George Loewenstein, "The Psychology of Curiosity: A Review and Reinterpretation," *Psychological Bulletin* 116, no. 1 (1994): 75.

2. William James, *Talks to Teachers on Psychology and to Students on Some of Life's Ideals,* vol. 12 (1899; Cambridge, Mass.: Harvard University Press, 1983).

3. Jean Piaget and Margaret Cook, *The Origins of Intelligence in Children*, vol. 8 (New York: International Universities Press, 1952).

4. Daniel E. Berlyne, "A Theory of Human Curiosity," *British Journal of Psychology* 45, no. 3 (1954): 180–91; Daniel E. Berlyne, *Conflict, Arousal, and Curiosity* (New York: McGraw-Hill, 1960).

5. Loewenstein, "The Psychology of Curiosity."

6. William R. Charlesworth, "Instigation and Maintenance of Curiosity Behavior as a Function of Surprise versus Novel and Familiar Stimuli," *Child Development* (1964): 1169–86.

7. Harry F. Harlow, Margaret K. Harlow, and Donald R. Meyer, "Learning Motivated by a Manipulation Drive," *Journal of Experimental Psychology* 40, no. 2 (1950): 228.

8. Celeste Kidd and Benjamin Y. Hayden, "The Psychology and Neuroscience of Curiosity," *Neuron* 88, no. 3 (2015): 449–60.

9. Susan Harter and Edward Zigler, "The Assessment of Effectance Motivation in Normal and Retarded Children," *Developmental Psychology* 10, no. 2 (1974): 169.

10. Corinne Hutt, "Exploration, Arousal and Autism," *Psychologische Forschung* 33, no. 1 (1969): 1–8.

11. Corinne Hutt, "Temporal Effects on Response Decrement and Stimulus Satiation in Exploration," *British Journal of Psychology* 58, nos. 3–4 (1967): 365–73.

12. Leo Kanner, "Autistic Disturbances of Affective Contact," *Nervous Child* 2, no. 3 (1943): 217–50.

13. Daniel E. Berlyne, "Curiosity and Exploration," *Science* 153, no. 3731 (1966): 25–33.

14. Noah J. Sasson et al., "Children with Autism Demonstrate Circumscribed Attention during Passive Viewing of Complex Social and Nonsocial Picture Arrays," *Autism Research* 1, no. 1 (2008): 31–42.

15. Center for Disease Control, Communicating with and about People with Disabilities, https://www.cdc.gov/ncbddd/disabilityandhealth/pdf/disabilityposter_photos.pdf.

16. Lydia Brown, "Identity-First Language," ASAN, 2011, http://autisticadvocacy.org/about-asan/identity-first-language; Doman Lum, *Culturally Competent Practice: A Framework for Understanding*, 4th ed. (Belmont, Calif.: Cengage Learning, 2010).

17. Steven Pinker, "The Game of the Name," *New York Times*, April 3, 1994.

18. David W. Hung, "Generalization of 'Curiosity' Questioning Behavior in Autistic Children," *Journal of Behavior Therapy and Experimental Psychiatry* 8, no. 3 (1977): 237–45; Frederick F. Schmitt and Reza Lahroodi, "The Epistemic Value of Curiosity," *Educational Theory* 58, no. 2 (2008): 125–48.

19. Schulamith Kreitler, Edward Zigler, and Hans Kreitler, "The Nature of Curiosity in Children," *Journal of School Psychology* 13, no. 3 (1975): 185–200.

20. American Psychiatric Association, *Diagnostic and Statistical Manual of Mental Disorders: DSM-5*, 5th ed. (Washington, DC: American Psychiatric Publishing, 2013).

21. Ron Suskind, *Life, Animated: A Story of Sidekicks, Heroes, and Autism* (New York: Kingswell, 2014).

22. Kristina T. Johnson and Rosalind W. Picard, "SPRING: Customizable, Motivation-Driven Technology for Children with Autism or Neurodevelopmental Differences," in *Proceedings of the 2017 Conference on Interaction Design and Children* (2017), 149–58.

23. Richard Arend, Frederick L. Gove, and L. Alan Sroufe, "Continuity of Individual Adaptation from Infancy to Kindergarten: A Predictive Study of Ego-Resiliency and Curiosity in Preschoolers," *Child Development* 50, no. 4 (1979): 950–59.

24. Richard M. Ryan and Edward L. Deci, "Intrinsic and Extrinsic Motivations: Classic Definitions and New Directions," *Contemporary Educational Psychology* 25, no 1 (2000): 54–67.

25. Berlyne, "A Theory of Human Curiosity."

26. Berlyne, *Conflict, Arousal, and Curiosity*.

27. Jaime Jirout and David Klahr, "Children's Scientific Curiosity: In Search of an Operational Definition of an Elusive Concept," *Developmental Review* 32, no. 2 (2012): 125–60.

28. Ming-Zher Poh, Nicholas C. Swenson, and Rosalind W. Picard, "A Wearable Sensor for Unobtrusive, Long-Term Assessment of Electrodermal Activity," *IEEE Transactions on Biomedical Engineering* 57, no. 5 (2010): 1243–52.

29. Subhas Chandra Mukhopadhyay, "Wearable Sensors for Human Activity Monitoring: A Review," *IEEE Sensors* 15, no. 3 (2015): 1321–30; Javier Hernandez et al., "Bioglass: Physiological Parameter Estimation Using a Head-Mounted Wearable Device," in *The 4th International Conference on Wireless Mobile Communication and Healthcare (Mobihealth)* (2014), 55–58.

30. Ming-Zher Poh, Daniel J. McDuff, and Rosalind W. Picard, "Non-Contact, Automated Cardiac Pulse Measurements Using Video Imaging and Blind Source Separation," *Optics Express* 18, no. 10 (2010): 10762–74.

31. Harvey N. Switzky, H. Carl Haywood, and Robert Isett, "Exploration, Curiosity, and Play in Young Children: Effects of Stimulus Complexity," *Developmental Psychology* 10, no. 3 (1974): 321.

32. Paul McReynolds, Mary Acker, and Caryl Pietila, "Relation of Object Curiosity to Psychological Adjustment in Children," *Child Development* 32 (1961): 393–400.

33. Patricia Minuchin, "Correlates of Curiosity and Exploratory Behavior in Preschool Disadvantaged Children," *Child Development* 42 (1971): 939–50.

34. James M. Rehg et al., "Behavioral Imaging and Autism," *IEEE Pervasive Computing* 2 (2014): 84–87.

35. Zhe Cao et al., "Realtime Multi-Person 2D Pose Estimation Using Part Affinity Fields," in *Proceedings of the IEEE Conference on Computer Vision and Pattern Recognition (CVPR)* (2017), 7291–99.

36. Siddharth S. Rautaray and Anupam Agrawal, "Vision Based Hand Gesture Recognition for Human Computer Interaction: A Survey," *Artificial Intelligence Review* 43, no. 1 (2015): 1–54.

37. Tadas Baltrusaitis, Peter Robinson, and Louis-Philippe Morency, "OpenFace: An Open Source Facial Behavior Analysis Toolkit," in *IEEE Winter Conference on Applications of Computer Vision (WACV)* (2016), 1–10.

38. Daniel McDuff et al., "AFFDEX SDK: A Cross-Platform Real-Time Multi-Face Expression Recognition Toolkit," in *Proceedings of the 2016 CHI Conference Extended Abstracts on Human Factors in Computing Systems* (2016), 3723–26.

39. Jacqueline Gottlieb et al., "Information-Seeking, Curiosity, and Attention: Computational and Neural Mechanisms," *Trends in Cognitive Sciences* 17, no. 11 (2013): 585–93.

40. Marilyn P. Arnone et al., "Curiosity, Interest and Engagement in Technology-Pervasive Learning Environments: A New Research Agenda," *Educational Technology Research and Development* 59, no. 2 (2011): 181–98.

9

Obstacles to Curiosity and Concern

Exploring the Racist Imagination

Narendra Keval

Curiosity, like all thinking, is relational in nature; that is to say, it involves an intimacy with an imagined or real *other*. This means that curiosity requires a capacity to tolerate the anxieties of not knowing the other in advance but through a process of discovery. When we are curious about someone or something, we embark on a journey that moves us in our imagination from the safety and familiarity of knowing—our "psychic home" offering us relative certainty—toward the experience of unknowing and not knowing. Playing with our curiosity, which involves this risk of wandering in our imagination to unknown vistas, including those far away from the self as it is presently known, can stir up profound anxieties that have the potential for our undoing, threatening our continuity of being.[1] Much of our clinical endeavors focuses on discerning the imagined dangers of this curious intimacy and, in my case, the dangers associated with racial and ethnic others.

While the *Oxford English Dictionary* defines curiosity as "a strong desire to learn or know something," psychoanalysis frames this desire with an ambivalence, particularly with the emotional perils of knowing about self and other—especially in the context of ethnic or racial others. Understanding this conflict between self-discovery and deception goes to the very heart of our clinical work, preoccupied as it is with the anxieties and quality of thinking in particular states of mind that obstruct curiosity and concern about ourselves in relation to others in the world. This is perhaps reflected in the proverb "curiosity killed the cat,"[2] used to warn of the dangers of unnecessary investigation and exploration. The question of *what* or *who* will be discovered and killed in the desire to know centers on imaginary threats that include the potential annihilation of self from a true or genuine engagement with the *other* who symbolizes the threat of our undoing, a threat emanating from within. It conveys what is at stake: the psychological survival of self and the different ways in which a solution is sought to attend to these urgent anxieties.

This chapter will focus on understanding how retreating into a racist imagination is one attempt to resolve these anxieties by trying to bolt down certainty, which shifts the focus from an inner threat to an outer one, creating monsters of our imagination that are grafted onto the ethnic characteristics of others. More specifically, racist phantasies offer to allay these anxieties by simplifying the world into dyadic relations of "us/them," "good/bad," which become ever more ossified as boundaries that cannot be questioned and must be fixed and certain. In so doing, these racist constructions bring temporary relief to what is felt to be internally unbearable by preventing the emergence of curiosity and concern, thereby distorting reality and misrepresenting racial and ethnic others in ways that rob or silence their humanity.

Both recent media discussions and clinical case studies are used here to illuminate the central thesis that racism is a destructive state of mind that exploits others to manage emotional vulnerabilities. This is achieved by creating a false narrative to obstruct any curiosity and compassion or concern that might expose our anxiety. These psychosocial and political defenses involve a configuration of omnipotence, sense of superiority, intolerance, arrogance, cruelty, and coercion. They also involve formidable elements of disguise and trickery that aim to "fix" misrepresentations of reality that make them difficult to engage with and understand.

Given the political, social, and cultural upheavals in recent times that have given rise to xenophobia and an astonishing increase in race hate crimes, racist states of mind are all the more urgent to understand. In the first section I sketch out some of my thinking on these murderous, tragic, and misguided attempts that seek out a sense of identity and security at any cost, by looking at recent events such as the migration crises in Europe, Brexit (the United Kingdom's decision to leave the European Union), and the unprecedented turmoil in American politics created by the campaign of President Donald Trump. The second section briefly describes the experience of working with a patient's racism in the consulting room and how this more nuanced understanding can contribute to our thinking about race in our society.

Positioning Race, Curiosity, and Concern

In psychoanalysis, the acquisition of knowledge has a special significance because our capacity to comprehend reality is thought to be intimately connected to the trajectories of our emotional development. Curiosity and concern are processes that are understood here to be intertwined, so that the qualities related to inquisitive thinking—such as exploration, investigation, and learning—are bound up with a gradual capacity for empathy toward the object that has aroused the desire to know. In other words, curiosity and concern shape one another to bring about an expansion of awareness and potential for exploration of self and others that recognizes a common humanity.

These processes take place in the context of a developmental progression from a two-person to a three-person relationship as the basis of comprehending and relating to a diverse and complex social world. Besides the self, there is one "other," a first other: the maternal body and presence. This is initially experienced as an idealized place free of imaginary intrusions, our first geographical and psychical home,[3] rooted in infantile experience and a ruthless self-centeredness that knows no recognition of separate others. However, a capacity for a sense of guilt and concern that mobilizes reparative impulses can be facilitated, in which the "individual cares, or minds, and both feels and accepts responsibility"[4] toward others, expanding and enriching the capacity for a sense of exploration, playfulness, and creativity.

The paternal dimension serves as a second "other," creating a triangular, or Oedipal, structure that Freud referred to as the "primal scene."[5] McDougall conceptualized the scene in terms of the child's "total store of unconscious knowledge and personal mythology concerning the human sexual relation, particularly that of his parents."[6] While sexuality is central to the primal scene, much more is being worked out here through the child's curiosity and imaginative reconstruction of the interaction and relationship between the parents.[7] Whether the parental couple in the primal scene come together in a lively and pleasurable or destructive way is thought to have a profound effect on the capacity for thinking. Since thinking necessitates making links or connections, it also forms the prototype for the development of creativity as symbolized by how members of the parental couple are linked together in the mind.[8] A capacity to link thoughts, to think, and to create meaning is therefore shaped by the way the parents in the triangular situation are perceived and used.

In this way, the developmental tasks of recognition that take the trajectory from a dyad to a triad determine the way mental space is structured, increasing the capacity to comprehend and relate to the complexities of reality. The development of curiosity and concern requires the recognition of others as fellow human beings separate from oneself in a shared social space, where there is a possibility of mutual empathy or concern and accommodation. This is in sharp contrast to a mode of functioning that mobilizes splitting and projective mechanisms to obstruct that recognition,[9] leading to the collapse of a triangulated space. The particular appeal of racist narratives is the allure of simplicity through their power to call upon a regressive phantasy of return to a dyadic space as a response to the unstoppable march of modernity and its inherent uncertainties. This is evident in how external geographical spaces and boundaries that arouse such primitive passions on the international stage[10] are often gendered into notions of Mother Earth that are linked to myths of return to an imaginary homeland, promising a sense of security and belonging.

The structure of racial phantasies reflects an intense preoccupation with the other in its ethnic or racial form and, like all primal scene phantasies, they organize one's relation to the other through encounters with difference.[11] Such phantasies are concerned with fundamental questions about the relationship between self and other, or questions about one's origin.[12] Phantasies of race are also relational,[13] determining the extent to which connections between thoughts can be tolerated and allowed to come together to engage in a productive relationship. Here we are concerned with contrasting objects, their ideational representations, and the extent to which these can be allowed to interact with each other in the service of reflective thinking as well as a capacity to manage contradiction and complexity without being attacked.[14] This opens up a distinction that I suggest needs to be made between the use of *racial* and *racist* phantasies, whose functions are different: the former notices the ethnic characteristics of others and is motivated by a curiosity that aims to explore the self in relation to others within a triangular structure. By contrast, *racist* phantasies involve a regressive pull that demands absolute certainty and aims to thwart and damage others, closing down possibilities for intimacy with and learning from others.

Obstacles to Curiosity and Concern 151

The development of curiosity and concern in this formulation extends the trajectory of recognition from the notion of self/other within a dyad to a third other, thereby creating a triangulated space and laying the emotional foundations of a diverse mental and social world of mutuality.

Body, Psyche, and Nation:
The Collapse of Curiosity and Concern

Mira Nair's film *The Reluctant Fundamentalist* gives a powerful sequence of events in which action and reaction escalate in a frightening way, illustrating how effortlessly the dyadic cycle of terror and terrorism can feed itself perpetually.[15] In its unfolding, the story reflects a collapse of triangulation that obliterates any semblance of curiosity and concern that might potentially make room for some degree of mutual accommodation. We see a young Pakistani man, Chengez Khan, working in the world of corporate America, enjoying his identity as an American citizen. All this comes to a dramatic crash after the 9/11 terrorist assault on the Twin Towers. The audience is led through a chain of events that connect the burning of the Twin Towers with this young man walking through the airport with his colleagues, all suited and booted, just as he had done many times before. Only this time, he is stopped and led away by FBI officials, who first question him as to whether he is a foreign or American national.

From this point onward, we are led to believe that an apparently normal world of protocol is taking place in the face of suspicion but, in actual fact, a parallel world is taking shape. A paranoid, racist construction has taken grip, ambushing and obstructing the capacity for inquiry and concern under the guise of reason. We see the young man taken into a room and from there onward he is spoken to in a tone that already assumes his brown skin and country of origin make him a potential terrorist, a narrative that will become difficult to prove otherwise.

The film captures the chilling manner in which a racist mindset can infect and grip ordinary citizens, interpreting behavior in such a way as to confirm an inner template. This is a type of knowing in advance of experiencing the other. In the airport room, he is instructed to remove his clothes as the official puts on his plastic gloves, standing behind him, leaving little doubt in the imagination as to the menace that is about to strike. His hair and body are searched in a manner that suggests he is being treated like an animal. He is then instructed to remove his underwear and spread his legs, as he undergoes a further humiliating examination. He is then told to put his clothes back on and, as he does, the shock is palpably present on the reflection of his face in the window against a backdrop of the Twin Towers. The whole thing has taken place in a matter of minutes. He is not only shaken to the core but powerless in the face of what has just happened to him. The careful juxtaposition of imagery in the film conveys a silence in him borne of rage, burning from the inside like the Twin Towers. What has receded into the background is the official in uniform who has conducted the examination with military precision. He steps back without any overt emotion on his face, a silent casualty of the assault in which he has become a participant in an act of naked terror.

The narrative sequence tells us something important about the reenactment (repetition of an emotional dynamic) that has taken place, a mental split or partition between ordinary feelings of concern and a murderous rage one imagines in the terrorists' state of mind while they sat in the plane's cockpit, directing it toward the two towers. The violation of the two towers is mirrored in the physical assault of the young man at the hands of the official. We see the victim's demeanor change in an instant. He is not the person he was moments ago, when he was going about his daily life: deep in his soul, something fundamental has changed. The film highlights the particularly disturbing way in which the young man was forced to experience feelings of shock, powerlessness, and humiliation as his inner world is ripped apart through an assault on his physical and psychic skin, throwing his sense of self into profound terror, just as we imagine victims of terrorist massacres feel, giving us an indication as to the motivations of the perpetrators. These murderous acts and their unconscious enactment are designed to provoke a range of powerful feelings and reactions in both victim and witness, intending to destroy the capacity to think and reflect.[16]

I suggest that these types of concrete or physical enactments (action-reaction replaces considered thought) pervade racist narratives that aim to provide immediate certainty and relief by splitting the world into crude boundary markers such as us/them, dangerous/safe, good/bad, righteous/evil, and so on. These splits often follow sociopolitical lines of cleavage that include ethnicity, class, gender, sexuality, or disability, projecting across the divide unwanted or intolerable thoughts and feelings into others. Once the process is complete, it aims to restore a perception of emotional safety that

Obstacles to Curiosity and Concern 153

was felt to be under threat. Those on the receiving end are straitjacketed or squeezed into an identity not of their making, belying a crudity with which this emotional and institutional process can operate. This is echoed in the comments made in another sequence of the film when Chengez enters a café: "*Any* beard or turban is a target." In other words, in this reactionary, binary space, there is no room for becoming curious about the impact of one's actions on others.

It reminded me of the immediate aftermath of the terrorist attacks in London on July 7, 2005. At this time, a panicked, terror-stricken way of thinking about others who are ethnically different from white Anglo-British citizens had a tendency to get lodged in the private and public imagination. The deadly combination of both real and imagined threats stirred up quite unbearable anxieties at a personal, national, and global level that potentially compromised the capacity to remain in a reflective mental space. I recall my increased vigilance on the London underground tube in the immediate aftermath of the attacks, where I had unwittingly assumed the mindset in which everybody was a potential suspect. In this atmosphere, the capacity to think humanely of fellow citizens is hijacked by a state of mind that is quick to expel and lodge the anxiety outside the self rather than process it. The shooting of an innocent Brazilian man, Jean Charles de Silva e de Menezes, by counterterrorism police at the Stockwell underground tube station in London may have been a further tragic outcome of a racist mindset and the tendency to panic that it engenders.

The evacuation of, rather than the engagement with, anxiety about strangers is a remarkably recurring theme in identity politics. Racist populist movements use phantasies that dehumanize others in terms of diseases, insects, or vermin, which are felt to threaten and destroy the national body politic. This language also suggests that others are parasites, invading and robbing the body of the nation with their needs and desires, which in turn produces paranoid anxieties about economic and emotional resources being depleted or robbed by foreigners. It conveys a preoccupation that dangerously equates the body of the ethnic other with psyche and nationhood.[17]

Building walls has mined the divisions of people into "us" and "them" to be exploited for political purposes, where "foreign bodies" are expunged to the other side of the wall[18] (cleansing the body and psyche of an imagined contamination by foreigners that is experienced viscerally). This type of splitting and ethnic cleansing, however, has a further aim: to create a heightened

154   Narendra Keval

sense of moral superiority over others that disguises a nexus of hate and disinformation that misrepresents reality. Trump's campaign, for example, used racist phantasies to create a climate of anxiety and fear that extended to attacks on women, disabled people, LGBT people, Jews, African Americans, immigrants (especially Latinos, and those perceived to be "foreigners"). His policy of "extreme vetting" advocated "a total and complete shutdown of Muslims entering the United States until our country's representatives can figure out what the hell is going on. We have no choice . . . we have no choice."[19]

Trump's narrative has unraveled a compelling and captivating unconscious phantasy. Nationhood has become concretely equated[20] with an idealized notion of the white female body that needs to be cleansed and protected from foreign rapists, apparently giving political license to build an unconscious phantasy, a grand chastity belt to make it "an impenetrable, physical, tall, powerful, beautiful southern border wall."[21] The flipside of this idealization is evident in his degrading views about women; he was caught on audiotape saying he could do anything he liked, "grabbing women by the p***y."[22] Fear and contempt of women was evident in his insinuating comments toward a female Fox News journalist during the CNN first Republican presidential debate, when he attributed her "hostile questioning" to menstruation.[23] It was a further elaboration of a phantasy of another contaminant: the biological fact of blood within the body, suggesting a familiar component in the racist phantasy based on a dangerous equation between psyche, nation, and the procreative capacities of the maternal body, whose anxieties and threats are also projected onto ethnic others.

Corrupting Curiosity and Concern:
Racist Phantasies of Cleansing and Restoration

These anxieties and threats were managed through narratives of "purity" and "homogeneity" in the Trump presidential campaign to exploit sections of the dispossessed American population, what some have called a "forgotten people" who have been living in heartbreaking social and economic landscapes. This section of the population has suffered years of hopelessness and desolation from poverty, hit hard by forces of globalization that have affected local industries, and feel they are living in an increasingly fractured and disunited country. Along a section of Route 45 is Washington County, Alabama, one of America's poorest states, where a quarter of the people live

Obstacles to Curiosity and Concern   155

in poverty; unemployed and unimpressed, one resident commented about his dilapidated town: "Bad roads, bad bridges, *they* don't look out for us." In Marion County, the poorest in West Virginia (and one of many relying on the coal and steel industry), four times as many babies are born with a drug addiction than the national average. One resident commented, "It brings tears to my eyes, no way out, there is nowhere for them to go, there are no jobs, if *they* took coal mining away, we're done." In eastern Kentucky, where more than a third of the people live in poverty, similar comments emerge: "*They* made us feel we are unimportant, *they* took the farming away, *they* took the tobacco away, took the coal mines away, basically *they* took everybody away."

Similar narratives have emerged in the British context, where one report described the cathedral city of Peterborough as under siege, with migration being held responsible for putting pressure on public services and local resentment about the *changing character* of the ancient English settlement. In one popular street, a traditional English baker's shop finally closed after 136 years. The blame is placed firmly at the door of the new Polish delicatessen two doors down. One resident commented, "three generations that ran this shop for over 100 years, it's gone too far, the country's gone too far, this country is never going to be the same again. We can only hope that we can put a stop to it." A Sheffield resident commented, "We've lost the steelworks, coal, everything is gone, everything is going."

In racist discourse, social grievances (e.g., antiestablishment feeling, alienation, unemployment, loss of local industry and community, immigration) often become the battlegrounds, but what is at stake is the sense of self. One report in the aftermath of the Brexit result showed a woman raising her fists in triumph saying, "Just glad we are going to be out. This is *our* England, *our* England," while another reported a sobbing, grief-stricken elderly man saying, "I have got my country back, what I've got I want to keep." It conveyed a deep wound in his sense of self and identity that he believed could be healed through reclaiming an idealized object called "our country," which would right a perceived wrong.

What is hidden beneath these moral panics are allusions to profound feelings of loss and a longing for "what once was and is no longer."[24] Elsewhere I have suggested that "racist events wherever we encounter them reflect a 'racist scene,' a variant of the phantasy of the primal scene . . . which is saturated with different layers of meanings."[25] This involves a narrative of an imaginary lost love whose structure contains elements of symbolic loss, bewilderment about psychic/social change, uncertainty, a sense of powerlessness and betrayal, coupled with feelings of shame and humiliation. This toxic amalgam can serve to bind the emotional turmoil into melancholic responses[26] and be used to replace the pain of mourning by fueling the satisfactions of a grievance and vengeful feelings that are opposed to any notion of a shared social space.

One of the deeper sources of lament in racism is a complex and potentially toxic melding of narcissistic injuries derived from both the personal and sociopolitical realms of experience. Political rhetoric often uses this area of human vulnerability as a feeding ground for racist phantasies to create a world of "alternative facts" that ultimately distorts the recognition of others as fellow human beings. The Brexit campaign used giant posters of migrants in long queues (an image likened to Nazi propaganda during the last world war)[27] to imply floods of foreigners were invading Britain because it remained in the European Union. In this way meaning was corrupted by depicting the arrival or presence of the stranger or foreigner as a symbolic loss representing a loved person such as community, country, or nation imbued with the central feeling of being robbed or depleted, thus leaving a profound sense of powerlessness. The notion of getting a country back implies it was a phantasmatic object taken or stolen, an object to which one remains entitled. This grievance is further fueled by an outrage that a nation-state, authority, or establishment ("they") had allowed this to happen in the first place. In this sense, a perceived influx of strangers, who are permitted to contaminate an idealized relationship and physical landscape, is felt to be a betrayal.

These psychological injuries and their multilayered losses are rarely forgotten or forgiven because the feeling of being robbed or depleted, shamed and humiliated, is felt to be unbearable. Instead of acknowledging this loss, mourning and accommodating the other, bitterness, grievance, and a sense of entitlement predominate. A pitched battle ensues with a phantasy couple, as represented by an authority such as a government using the fertile soil of social battlegrounds to exact vengeful feelings in a "tit-for-tat" manner. Fallen under the spell of what some see as a brilliant demagogue, one veteran factory worker commented, "We've been ignored and ignored and ignored, been waiting for years for someone like Trump to come up." That this hurt translated into a toxic grudge using the ballot box as an anger management tool is evident in the effortless slide from a poverty of circumstance to a poverty of thinking, manifest in the degradation of language connected to a degradation of virtues.

Racist phantasies in this context were served up to offer those most vulnerable and aggrieved, with an idea of decontaminating an imagined utopia of ethnic others through cleansing and evacuation, creating a reimagined community to soothe the hurts of narcissistic injuries. They attempt to restore the individual or community to a former state of completeness, but it is a delusional idea promising a return to a mythical homeland as a solution to profound anxiety.

Both the Brexit and Trump campaigns repackaged some of the oldest prejudices in the service of vengeful feelings that were percolating, decades in the making. Both campaigns used racist phantasies to give free rein to a type of murderousness that corrupts legitimate protest and desire for change through the democratic process into destructive mayhem. Listening to some of the stories of those most affected, living and working in the "rust belt" of America, suggests that the racist narrative tapped into a punctured potency of the dispossessed. Perhaps the anger and bitterness toward the establishment was for their perceived cuddling up to the "forces of globalization," sharing the same bed with strangers, foreign economic powers that put pressure on thriving local industries to enlist cheaper labor abroad, leading to domestic job losses, homelessness, hopelessness, and despair.

The politicization of a border wall in the most southern region of the sexual body politic, to keep foreign intruders out, urges us to consider a phantasy that wishes to reassert white male potency in an impotent-making world of seismic economic shifts involving foreign players. The imprint of these forces on the physical landscape of "middle America" reflects an inner world of desolation and deadness arising from a profound loss. Bakersfield, an oil town once built on the riches of the land, is now a ghost town, perhaps holding a mirror of what had once been idealized in the American body politic but is no longer. Trump's calculated move echoes this in a simple and alluring way, through an assertion that the American dream is dead, but it will be brought back to life by making America great again.

Race in the Consulting Room: Curiosity under Fire

This section sketches out my thinking on clinical work with a patient who, at certain moments of our encounter, retreated into his racist imagination to manage anxieties about his emotional safety with me. His wish for absolute certainty in his engagement with me conveys the underlying terrors of letting his mind wander in a way that does not prejudge me but allows a sense of curiosity to evolve through our encounter. The intention here is to describe the type of dynamics that can emerge in some patients' need for absolute certainty, dynamics that might in turn serve as an analogue of wider social and political stresses that can harvest nascent racism to manage anxieties about change and loss of control.

Case Vignette

An Italian man[28] I saw for an initial consultation left quite an impression on me, such that, many years later, I continue to think about our experience together and the insight it offered into being with a patient whose only means of communicating just how frightening it was to be himself was to try to frighten, intimidate, and humiliate others.

He entered my consulting room, looking confident but suspicious as he placed his coat over mine on the door, sat down, stroked his chin, and looked at me patronizingly. I had planned to see him briefly to discuss a treatment vacancy with him, but it was not long before he started to go into a tirade about how he "was not going to be messed about." How experienced was I? Was I going to be like his previous therapist who ended his treatment abruptly? He was certainly not going to put up with that nonsense with me. I had a feeling from this opening gambit that my being Asian had rattled him, as he had managed to create an abrasive and volatile atmosphere within seconds of meeting with me.

His insistence that there was only one version of events to comprehend (i.e., his) was irritating me enough to make me want to kick him out of the room. This atmosphere and my initial response to it became an important source of understanding about how this man was inviting a potential reenactment of a wish to evacuate ("kick out") rather than engage and understand what was driving his urgent need to establish a sense of security about his treatment. This inner state was difficult to reach and understand by his insistence that only his viewpoint was valid, preventing an exploration where he and I could think *together,* in a spirit of curiosity, about his traumatic experience with a previous therapist.

I acknowledged his sense of urgency but needed him to tell me about his previous treatment and how the ending came to be so abrupt. I was under the impression that his cessation of treatment had been planned, but he was clearly disgruntled. As he spoke, he seemed more preoccupied with the fact of ending itself, unwilling to convey anything about his experience of the

Obstacles to Curiosity and Concern   159

therapy. His distress turned into omnipotent control and demand to put things right.

He became irritated, demanding that I stop pussyfooting around (i.e., exploring) and offer him a treatment that would end only when *he* decided to leave. He said he had heard all the therapy "lingo" before, so I should not try any of that with him either. It stopped me in my tracks, unable to think for a few moments and feeling as though he was demanding total control over whether I could even think my own thoughts! I could see that this form of abrasive engagement made him feel triumphant, something that was familiar to all who had come into contact with him, including previous therapists. However, the inner place of desperation from which much of this provocative behavior came seemed elusive.

When I was better able to gather my thoughts, I commented on his wish to test whether I could manage his abrasive behavior enough to help him. He replied, somewhat mockingly, that it was a shrewd observation. In his agitated state, any attempt to empathize with his anxieties received a fleeting recognition that was quickly perceived as an attempt to make him feel even more vulnerable with me, increasing his anxieties and attempts to control me. Naming his anxiety, and frank terror of being with me, could easily feel humiliating and inflame his sense of injury, hence his desperate attempts to establish control by any means necessary. This escalated in the session to the point where he began making derogatory comments about my cultural background and telling me the consulting room was "wreaking" before dismissing me as incompetent.

Two throwaway remarks were telling. First, he demanded that only he should decide the ending date of any treatment that was offered. Second, he said he hated the silence in the room when I was thinking. This need to establish control and dictate my behavior seemed to be a way of communicating his psychic terrors of being suddenly left without anything to hold him emotionally, rupturing his sense of continuity. It threw him into a paranoid state that demanded absolute control of others. Among other things, his wish to stop me thinking was perhaps aimed to create an experience inside my mind where I was temporarily unhinged in my thinking and unable to connect my thoughts. In other words, a relational disaster of losing control that he experienced was now being played out in my mind with my thoughts.

His use of racist thinking offered him temporary refuge from possibly spiraling into a more severe breakdown, by becoming superior, dictating the terms of our engagement where he wanted absolute control. As these attempts failed him, he escalated his maneuvers by trying to wound me. In this way he could disavow his own feelings of humiliation, of floundering in a mental and emotional mess that now took on racist overtones. It is of course telling that, in his attempts to inflict attacks on my personal and cultural identity, he was trying to tear, in me, the very thing that was at stake: the fabric of a sense of self.

Despite his contempt for me, his desperation was vital but difficult to reach when he was determined to throw everything at me to see if he and I could survive and continue thinking. This is difficult to do when the very act of thinking itself becomes the object of attack. In this state there is no space for curiosity to emerge, as other viewpoints and feelings are felt to be intolerable. There is a marked absence of any breathing or thinking space to both observe and be observed[29] within a triangular space that might enable the taking of different positions and creating the possibilities for empathy and concern. Instead, the urgency of psychic survival means that refuge is sought in control through a particular kind of coupling that acts like a gang with an attitude of superiority that is played out with the analyst in the "live theater" of the consulting room. Here the difficulty is to remain emotionally open enough to be able to continue being "curious under fire," when so much anxiety is being discharged, and all under the patient's watchful eyes. It requires us to allow ourselves to let our imagination breathe, aiming to recognize, understand, and empathize with and be altered by that which the patient must not inflict but convey. Then a different space, even if only momentary, may emerge to allow some exploration.

A more malignant atmosphere, however, can put both patient and analyst under strong pressure to evacuate anxiety and therefore risk unhelpful enactments that strive for absolute certainty. We can inadvertently become intolerant of intolerance in our patients by unwittingly putting an "analytic coat" over them, just as this patient placed his coat over mine, trying to engulf, control, and dominate rather than collaborate with me.

Triangulation versus Strangulation of Political Life: Keeping Curiosity and Concern Alive

As you can gather, my attempts to reach this patient were often experienced like a red rag to a bull, intensifying his contempt. When the atmosphere in the room is so noxious, there is little room for a third or triangulated position that involves a different viewpoint or a new perspective, as this would be experienced as "stepping out of line": the analyst having an independent mind that is beyond the reach of the patient's wish for control. In some circumstances, it is possible to free up this paralysis of thought by describing the atmosphere to the patient in a manner that does not feel too intrusive and wounding, placing the observation in a third space for both parties to observe, think about, and comment upon.

Some of these therapeutic situations have a certain resonance with the way political discourse has emerged in recent times, using race to corrupt, bully, or terrorize and stop meaningful dialogue. The attack on the potency of others throws light on how racism organizes itself both internally and externally by keeping people straitjacketed into prescribed roles so that the racist dictum is kept in force: "know your place" and do not step out of line. Thuggery, both overt and covert, is always present to one degree or another and can be enacted by some of the very institutions that supposedly support reason and humanity. The building of walls, for example, to manage the migrant crises in Europe, leaves open to question the extent to which these are aimed to keep racist projections in place. The wall will ensure that migrants are kept at a distance in squalid conditions, keeping them in permanent dependency and powerlessness. Keeping them out of sight and out of mind behind the walls bolsters the delusion that it is the migrants themselves who are responsible for their deprived conditions and squalor. It also ensures that those on the inside "know their place," bolstering a moral superiority.

The imagery of a wall or fortress conveys not only the difficulties of penetrating a demeanor that is prickly and quick to react and evacuate anxiety but also a mental armature that conceals the cunning tactics used to subvert reality and corrupt meaning. Another patient once employed an image of hiding from her vulnerability in an army bunker—terrors she could fend off delightedly by believing she could command and control everything, including my attempts to reach her. Here, terrorist tactics are often utilized not only to assassinate the analyst's concern but the patient's collaboration in the therapeutic process,[30] which potentially threatens to expose his or her vulnerability by creating a world of "alternative facts," including racist thinking.

The vocabulary of "fake news" and "alternative facts" in recent political discourse depicts a longing for a return to an idealized body politic in the form of a pure and uncontaminated nation-state free from imaginary intrusions of so-called foreigners. But there is nothing to return to; it is a myth. Nevertheless, it is most compelling to those who are vulnerable in society, who amid economic and emotional deprivation look for a way out through a solution that claims to offer an immediate sense of location, meaning, and security. This solution evacuates their anxiety through a literal cleansing of others, which can lead to a collapse of any curiosity and concern toward others.

One of the dangers in our current political climate is the crushing of curiosity and compassion toward others, who become the carriers of vulnerability. In the consulting room, my patient tried to do this by attempting to get me to experience feelings of vulnerability and inferiority through his manner of relating, in turn seeking to establish a sense of security through his superiority over me. It was not surprising that attempts to think with him and challenge some of the safety of his racist defenses were met with rage, as he was assessing my capacity to be both *affected* by him and retain my authority, role, and *moral compass* in continuing to think with him. In other words, despite all his bluster and noxious ways, here was a patient who had taken the risk of bringing himself to see me in the hope, however faint, that he could be emotionally reached and helped, despite the obstacles he put up.

We have witnessed in recent times a grave danger of reactionary rhetoric that reflects some of the flagrant displays of sadism and loss of moral compass by terrorist organizations. These, like racism, aim to ensure that triangulated mental and social spaces, where curiosity and concern can thrive, collapse into dangerous, regressive, and totalitarian spaces. This is already evident, given the alarming attacks on the free press and intimidation of any opposition or alternative points of view. The executive order of "extreme vetting" from President Trump's administration, banning refugees and immigrants from Muslim-majority countries from entering the United States, induced chaos, persecution, and terror in the victims. At Washington-Dulles airport, a five-year-old Iranian boy was perceived to be a threat to national security.[31] The current deportations taking place of Mexican "illegal" migrants, who have lived and thrived with their families in the United States for many years, involves parents being separated from their children on a mass scale.[32]

I suggest that an imposition of this mayhem on families may well reflect the chaotic or fragmented state of the current administration, which lacks

Obstacles to Curiosity and Concern   163

any internal coherence in statements or policy. Grand gestures of building walls may come out of desperation to split the world into "good" and "bad" or demarcate an "axis of evil"[33] to justify moral superiority—a superiority that comes at the cost of human misery and prevents any acknowledgment of responsibility for the damage wreaked on others. Notice the effortless way in which the shadow of unreason disguises itself as reason in the following statement made by Rex Tillerson, former secretary of state, after Trump's first executive order for the travel ban failed and a second ban was pursued:

> To our allies and partners around the world, please understand that this order is part of our ongoing efforts to eliminate *vulnerabilities* (my emphasis added) that radical Islam can and will exploit for destructive ends.[34]

The grotesque deformation of politics in recent times sees a growing trend of authoritarian leaders who are using nationalist sentiments and the racist impulse to call upon unconscious phantasies of an idealized time, laying claim to a sense of belonging and certainty, pure and uncontaminated by the real complexities of life. However, these emotionally tempting solutions reflect the terrors of thinking about who or what may be discovered in engaging meaningfully with others, recognizing them as fellow human beings. Indeed, curiosity and empathy or concern requires a willingness to relinquish phantasies of omnipotence and superiority, a trajectory that demands moving from a two- to three-dimensional thinking that reflects psychic complexity, diversity, and our common humanity. Central to these discoveries is a capacity to bear loss, to mourn, and to accommodate others in a shared social space that is not without tension, conflict, and contradictions. It is a lifelong struggle to learn and comprehend the complexity and limitations of this ordinary human reality, a development that necessarily brings about a quality and depth of thinking and feeling.

Unfortunately, our current political discourse about the *other* reflects a dangerous confluence between a malignant narrative of an idealized nation-state that demands cleansing, purification, and reunion and a utopian phantasy of the suicidal terrorist who dreams of oblivion as a place in heaven, free of unwelcome intrusions and the frustrations of life. One of the most challenging tasks of our times is to cultivate spaces for curiosity to thrive in a way that recognizes differences and similarities between us, thereby allowing for human vulnerability to be tolerated without seeking to attack others.

164 Narendra Keval

This would mean "decoupling" narcissistic injury from inflammatory wishes served up by racist phantasies claiming to evacuate mental pain. Our willingness to be potent and humane witnesses, continuing to exercise the capacity to think, remain curious "under fire," and expose lies or "false narratives" that attack a sense of concern toward others, is ultimately the ongoing hope for the future.

Notes

1. D. W. Winnicott, "The Theory of the Parent-Infant Relationship," *International Journal of Psychoanalysis* 41 (1960): 585–95.

2. Benjamin Johnson, *Every Man in His Humour* (1598), www.fullbooks.com/Every-man-In-His-Humour1.html.

3. Sigmund Freud, *Civilisation and Its Discontents*, in *The Standard Edition of the Complete Psychological Works of Sigmund Freud,* vol. 21 (London: Hogarth, 1930), 57–146.

4. D. W. Winnicott, "The Development of the Capacity of Concern," *Bulletin of the Menninger Clinic* 27 (1963): 167–76.

5. Sigmund Freud, "From the History of an Infantile Neurosis," in *The Standard Edition of the Complete Psychological Works of Sigmund Freud,* vol. 17 (London: Hogarth, 1918), 3–123.

6. Joyce McDougall, *Plea for a Measure of Abnormality* (New York: International Universities Press, 1980), 56.

7. Lewis Aron, "The Internalized Primal Scene," *Psychoanalytic Dialogues* 5 (1995): 195–237.

8. W. R. Bion, "A Theory of Thinking," *International Journal of Psychoanalysis* 43 (1962): 306–10; Donald Meltzer, *Sexual States of Mind* (Perthshire, Scotland: Clunie, 1973).

9. Melanie Klein, "Notes on Some Schizoid Mechanisms," *International Journal of Psychoanalysis* 27 (1946): 99–110.

10. Edward Said, *Freud and the Non-European* (London: Verso in association with the Freud Museum, 2003).

11. Luz Calvo, "Racial Fantasies and the Primal Scene of Miscegenation," *International Journal of Psychoanalysis* 89, no. 1 (2008): 55–70.

12. Jean Laplanche and Jean-Bertrand Pontalis, *The Language of Psychoanalysis* (New York: W. W. Norton, 1974).

13. Narendra Keval, *Racist States of Mind: Understanding the Perversion of Curiosity and Concern* (London: Karnac Books, 2016).

14. Michael Feldman, "The Oedipus Complex: Manifestations in the Inner World and the Therapeutic Situation," in *The Oedipus Complex Today,* ed. John Steiner (London: Karnac, 1989).

15. Mira Nair, dir., *The Reluctant Fundamentalist* (Cine Mosaic, 2007), based on the novel of the same name by Mohsin Hamid.

16. John Alderdice, "Introduction," in *Terrorism and War, Unconscious Dynamics of Political Violence,* ed. Coline Covington et al. (New York: Karnac Books, 2002), 1–18.

17. Phil Cohen, *Home Rules: Some Reflections on Race and Nationalism in Everyday Life,* The New Ethnicities Unit (London: University of East London, 1993); Steve Reicher and Nick Hopkins, *Self and Nation* (London: Sage, 2001).

18. Lene Auestad, "The Social Unconscious and the Herd," *New Associations* 20 (Spring 2016).

19. Doug Saunders, "Trump's True Believers: How He's Gone Farther Than Europe's Far Right, and Who Got Him Here," *Globe and Mail,* January 5, 2017, https://www.theglobeandmail.com/news/world/how-trump-has-gone-farther-than-europes-far-right-and-who-got-himthere/article27713704/.

20. Hanna Segal, "Notes on Symbol Formation," *International Journal of Psychoanalysis* 38 (1957): 391–97.

21. BBC, "Donald Trump's Mexico Wall: Who Is Going to Pay for It?" *BBC News,* February 6, 2017, https://www.bbc.com/news/world-us-canada-37243269.

22. Rachael Revesz, "Full Transcript: Donald Trump's Lewd Remarks about Women in *Days of Our Lives* set in 2005," *Independent,* October 7, 2016, https://www.independent.co.uk/news/world/americas/read-donald-trumps-lewd-remarks-about-women-on-days-of-our-lives-set-2005-groping-star-a7351381.html.

23. BBC, "Donald Trump Axed from Event over Megyn Kelly Blood Comment," *BBC News,* August 8, 2015, http://www.bbc.co.uk/news/world-us-canada-33833516.

24. Keval, *Racist States of Mind.*

25. Keval, *Racist States of Mind.*

26. Sigmund Freud, "Mourning and Melancholia," in *The Standard Edition of the Complete Psychological Works of Sigmund Freud,* vol. 14 (London: Hogarth, 1917), 243–58; David Gadd, "Racial Hatred and Unmourned Loss," *Sociological Research Online* 15, no. 3 (2010): 1–20; Paul Gilroy, *Postcolonial Melancholia* (New York: Columbia University Press, 2006).

27. Stephen Hopkins, "Nigel Farage's Brexit Poster Is Being Likened to 'Nazi Propaganda,' Compared to Auschwitz Documentary Scene: A 'Prominent White-Skinned Man Also Removed from Image,'" *HuffPost,* June 22, 2016, https://www.huffingtonpost.co.uk/entry/nigel-farages-eu-has-failed-us-all-poster-slammed-as-disgusting-by-nicola-sturgeon_uk_576288c0e4b08b9e3abdc483.

28. Some details have been altered to protect this patient's identity.

29. Ronald Britton, "The Missing Link: Parental Sexuality in the Oedipus Complex," in *The Oedipus Complex Today,* ed. John Steiner (London: Karnac, 1989).

30. Salman Akhtar, "The Psychodynamic Dimension of Terrorism," in *Terrorism and War: Unconscious Dynamics of Political Violence,* ed. Coline Covington et al. (London: Karnac, 2002).

31. Rachel Roberts, "White House Claims Five-Year-Old Boy Detained in US Airport for Hours Could Have Posed a Security Threat," *Independent,* January 31, 2017,

https://www.independent.co.uk/news/world/americas/white-house-five-year-old-boy-detained-dulles-international-airport-hours-sean-spicer-pose-security-a7554521.html.

32. Hilary Andersson, "Trump's Fortress America," *Panorama Investigation,* BBC Productions (2017), http://bbc.co.uk/panorama.

33. George W. Bush, "State of the Union Address," *Washington Post,* January 29, 2002.

34. Sabrina Siddiqui, Lauren Gambino, and Oliver Laughland, "Trump Travel Ban: New Order Targeting Six Muslim Countries Signed," *Guardian,* March 6, 2017, https//:www.theguardian.com/us-news/2017/mar/06/new-trump-travel-ban-muslim-majority-countries-refugees.

10

Curious Entanglements

Opacity and Ethical Relation in Latina/o Aesthetics

Christina León

Scenes of Curiosity in the Classroom

Let me begin with a scene of pedagogy that continually motivates my work, both as a professor and as a scholar, in order to consider modes of curiosity in relation to the position of Latina/os and *latinidad* in an age of growing demographic awareness. Like many Latina professors hired under the aegis of Latino studies, I am implicitly charged with the pedagogical task of teaching students about latinidad often within the limits of a term. As a scholar of not only latinidad but also literature and performance, I remain skeptical that teaching novels or art can, in fact, divulge totalizing information about heterogeneous and ever-fluctuating peoples, even if our departments are branded as the new empathy trainers of the twenty-first century. With this in mind, I have fretted over a course assigned to me in my first year on the tenure track: "Literature of American Minorities." Chiefly, I was concerned about an unintentional Epcot effect wherein I took students on a salacious tour that rimmed the fringes of the U.S. literary canon—one in which writers of color, queer writers, and marginalized voices became peripheral curiosities. Yet this very ethicopolitical challenge transformed the course into the lower-division class that I enjoy teaching and have learned from constantly.

As with many student-centered pedagogues, I do a survey on the first day of my courses in order to know my students beyond a matching of face to name (and later to performance). My students, who often take the class for a Gen Ed requirement (in this case, "Difference, Power, and Discrimination"), overwhelmingly answer the question in kind with the baccalaureate core itself—that is, they come to the classroom to know about "different people and cultures." I remind them that they are in a literature classroom and ask them how they expect literary works to achieve such high-minded goals. I find, though, that they are really quite curious. And, like any pedagogue worth her salt, I don't want to squash this curiosity. Nonetheless, I am suspicious of the implicit assumption that one class based upon literature could teach the truth about myriad peoples. So I reroute this curiosity as an open one, as an ethical one. Rather than teaching them about people via fiction, I try to show how fiction (and aesthetics more broadly) might be an occasion to learn how to encounter difference without deadening it into broad generalizations. This class and its charge brought me to consider how an aesthetic form might be a way in which to communicate both singular experience and sociopolitical context without providing empirical evidence of demographics. These pedagogical scenes bring me back to my research in fundamentally important ways.

Curiosity, Opacity, and Latinidades

Some of what follows has been the theoretical foundation for my current book manuscript, "Radiant Opacity: Material, Ethical, and Aesthetic Relations in Latindad," which considers the place of literature and aesthetics in regard to ethicopolitical engagements with difference.[1] Here I linger on the question of curiosity and how curiosity relates differently across bodies and disciplines. How might we develop an ethical approach to cultivating a curious aesthetic intervention rather than casting certain marked bodies and cultural productions as mere curiosities—ones that can be dealt with in a week or tribute month? I dwell specifically in the space of minoritarian aesthetics broadly conceived, and Latina/o aesthetics more narrowly, in order to consider the pedagogical and scholarly tasks of teaching that traffic in difference. While subaltern knowledge production and canon-building gestures marked the terrain of the late twentieth century with epistemic imperatives, I turn to how aesthetics and curiosity commingle in the sensorium—how the place of the senses, instead of discrete knowledge, might be one way to sustain an ethical form of curiosity and, hence, readerly encounter and relation.

This essay also adds to ongoing conversations in Latina/o studies by proposing opacity, vis-à-vis the Martinican thinker Édouard Glissant, as a form of ethical relation to latinidad that would not need to anticipate or fully know Latina/o alterity. Such an emphasis on opacity might spawn a form of curious engagement with aesthetics, ethics, and politics, without emphasizing the identificatory trappings of weak multiculturalism that, in form, colludes with waves of recent U.S. legislation demanding legal documentation and encouraging racial profiling. Instead, I theorize opacity as a visual concept that disrupts logics of visibility and concentrates on the textures of relation rather than producing demographic knowledge. Importantly, opacity allows us to stay in ethical relation to alterity without having to sediment difference into a domesticated realm that mimics the limiting language and logic of rights. Opacity, then, functions as a way to remain openly and ethically curious as a form of engagement with Latina/o aesthetic production, or any minoritarian aesthetic production. I am sparked by Tyson Lewis's statement that approximates my own pedagogical and scholarly concerns. As Lewis states, "Curiosity perpetually stumbles into the void at the heart of the order of things and thus suspends our ability to name/identify such and such according to prescribed criteria—it effectively disconnects objects and beliefs by tripping over a detail, remnant."[2] My aim is to consider Latina/o studies vis-à-vis a stumbling in relation to aesthetic opacity, rather than the mastery demanded of area/identitarian studies, to either (1) tell us about all of the wrong that has been done or (2) pave the way for an unfettered, smooth transition to a liberatory future.

Theorists of Latina/o studies have lucidly shown that demographic homogenization through media and the call to rally under visibility and unity has brought some significant gains in the political realm, but such calls also foreclose nuanced engagements with the multiplicity and dissonances within Latina/o lives and cultural production. Viewed from the vantage points of literary and performance studies, such politics of representation evoke a form of curiosity that, one might argue, is not radically curious—but is instead anticipatory of a priori notions of latinidad, whether through culturally tourable novels or media depictions of Latina/os as religious, family oriented, and culturally aligned. Consider that a form of curiosity spawned by weak multiculturalism colludes with historical work on curiosity—tracing it to travel literature. Nigel Leask writes of such travel literature as an aesthetics of curiosity in the late eighteenth and early nineteenth centuries, adding, "Curiosity was of course by no means limited to travel. . . . The term has a long and ambivalent history in European culture as the disposition of mind which desires knowledge of the world, but one which easily oversteps the boundaries set by God in a Faustian show of intellectual pride."[3] Instead of craving a trip into exotic lands and cultures, how might we foster a mode of curiosity that stays curiously open—rather than demanding static and sociological knowledge from aesthetic modes?

In what follows, I stumble into the tangle of questions that crop up when thinking about curiosity in relation to latinidad, dwelling specifically on the contours of our visual cultures and how they meet with a pan-ethnic category that is often rendered through the lens of demography. I show how forms of representation that purport to be transparent actually curtail ethicopolitical engagements with the difference of latinidad. Following this dilemma, I chart out how opacity might be an ethical, attendant term for thinking through the curious relations that encase minoritarian aesthetics broadly, and latinidad in particular. In order to consider this theoretical premise within a particular figure caught between the representations endemic to visual culture and the ethics of encounter, I consider how questions of curiosity might be understood through the face. I trace different figurations of face or faces in latinidad, showing how they've been used as both a marker of demography *and* as a form of aesthetic opacity. Finally, I reflect upon how these two poles of curiosity, the colonial urge to master difference and a more radically open curiosity, are necessarily entangled, both etymologically and materially. Rather than sanitizing or idealizing curiosity, the work that follows suggests that in order to do justice to cultivating an ethical approach to curiosity, we must be vigilant about the violences that have been waged under its epistemological promise. As a concomitant term to curiosity, this essay contends that opacity might proffer a way to keep asking ourselves how we curiously engage with the face of another without forcing it into static, flattened notions of difference.

Latinidad and the Problem of Transparency

The category of Latina/o in the United States, while fairly recent in usage, has sedimented into a kind of settled amnesia—wherein myriad faces unite under one front. Cristina Beltrán's trenchant work in *The Trouble with Unity* poses the unity and demographic creation of a Latina/o sector as a convenient and oversimplified homogenization of an otherwise diverse, fragmented, and contestatory set of subjects.[4] She shows how the amalgamation that is latinidad poses itself as a sleeping giant, a leviathan, that cuts both ways: on the one hand, Latina/o elites have used the overarching term to guarantee some semblance of rights and political purchase; on the other hand, conservative fear mongering has used the term to amalgamate a threat and wash over inherent differences. In short, both attempts at using the term politically invoke a giant, a giant that never seems to have gigantic agential access. Very real political urgencies often produce a temporal structure that urges shorthand categories—ones that I think can be very necessary when considered as a catachresis that names need rather than stagnant truths.[5] Yet the time of ethics—of ongoing relations of reading, desire, and encounter—can sometimes lag, or stumble, behind the demands of politics, especially those that seek to represent and read without much attention to nuance, ambivalence, or singularity. So perhaps Beltrán's notion that calling someone Latino "is an exercise in opacity"[6] resonates as more than just a political practice; it ought also to be considered ethically.

One of the major representative burdens outlined by contemporary Latina/o scholars is the interpellative demand for minoritarian subjects to be either transparent signifiers of culture or evidence of some demographic generalization. In *Dead Subjects: Toward a Politics of Loss in Latino Studies,* Antonio Viego links forms of ego psychologization to an assimilative project that promises Latina/os the wholeness and agentiality that he claims has dominated activism and academic writing on latinidad.[7] The danger is that some subjects are afforded nuance while others (specifically ones that are marked *as* Others) are objectified in this lie of wholeness—made to be what he calls "dead signifiers." By being called upon to present themselves as whole and transparent, ethnic-racialized subjects do not gain more agency—though that seems to be the promise behind such interpellative gestures. Demands for transparency reduce and deaden. He writes: "There must be much less pretension to understanding in this regard, since ethnic-racialized subjectivity has suffered from too much understanding. This is not to say that ethnic-racialized subjectivity and experience has been understood, but rather to say that the project of understanding is imagined as completely within reach."[8] The desire for too much wholeness and too much knowledge becomes a kind of burden for very specific subjects, bodies, and objects, and such a burden is bound up with a demand for transparency.

Opacity as a Curious, Ethical Attendant Term

If, as Viego claims, transparency is a particular burden of representation or violence for those under the sign of latinidad (and, no doubt, many other marked demographics), then reading with and for opacity may represent another valence, an ethical valence, through which to consider the question of differences in relation to one another. Opacity, for me, escapes the allure of an elusive negativity and the dualistic thinking it can often invoke. Likewise, I do not understand all transparency as necessarily nonresistant—transparency and visibility can often lead to more democratic and accountable forms of politics. My insistence upon opacity is not an excuse to feign ignorance in the face of injustice but instead a call to sustained reading, relationality, and encounters. Certain kinds of visibilities very much carry their own violences, and a lack of transparency can be an effective and necessary mode of resistance to reduction. Opacity materializes as a resistance, an indeterminability, or a recognition of the limits of our gaze, knowledge, or interpretation—the kind of stumbling that marks the terrain of curiosity. In what follows, I chart a constellation of thought to lay out the ethical stakes of opacity and relationality that would resist the demands for transparency.

Thinking about and through the Caribbean at a time when political discourse was flooded with the promise of rights and programmatic politics, Francophone Martinican writer and thinker Éduoard Glissant considers the place of literature, and more specifically poetics, to be a realm within which sustained reading and encounters take place if we can hold on to relational difference without reducing it to transparency. Poetics becomes the place where, Glissant claims, "We clamor for the right to opacity for everyone."[9] In *Poetics of Relation,* Glissant puts forward this "right" to precisely undermine a *discourse of rights* that needs to fully *know* those that it seeks to protect. Moreover, it is not an "I," but a relational we, that clamors. "We clamor for the right to opacity for everyone *[Nous réclamons pour tous le droit à l'opacité]*."[10] The translation of the verb *réclamons* as "to clamor" brings with it some felicitous figurations: the notion of a disparate mass that does not harmonize, the cacophony of a "we" that calls and demands, and the struggle inherent in this almost impossible demand. The word *droit*—translated as "right" with clear connotations of legitimacy/law, also carries that which is not bent—an unyieldingness, an urgent and always already ethical call for opacity. Glissant notes that "the theory of difference is invaluable. . . . But difference itself can still contrive to reduce things to the Transparent."[11] Opacity, for Glissant, is that which allows relationality to take place. He writes, "Opacities can coexist and converge, weaving fabrics. To understand these one must focus on the texture of the weave and not on the nature of its components."[12] Such a weave of opacity emphasizes the textures of relation rather than the classification of the thread. Hence the sensorial experience of relation and difference is emphasized through an opacity that resists transparent notions of ontological parsing.

Similarly emphasizing the ethical charge of opacity and relationality, Judith Butler's *Giving an Account of Oneself* considers the question of how we tell stories about ourselves and how we demand them of others.[13] Butler postulates that the very incompleteness of one's account of oneself, and the relational structure of that account through address, conjures up an ethics within which the subject's primal opacity and radical relationality figure necessarily. Rather than a firm epistemological ground, it is a limit of knowing that places one in the realm of ethics. Such an ethics hinges upon the unknowingness that subtends relationality, encounter, and reading. Moreover, our radical relationality is necessarily enmeshed in the fact that we are opaque to ourselves (as we are to others). Such an ethical frame, that we are always given over to a relationality that marks an interdependence, moves Butler in her more recent work to map the relational as concomitantly the terrain of the aesthetic.[14] Aesthetic encounters necessitate relationality—they are primarily sensorial, given over to impression, without ever quite having a firm grasp on that which we sense. We stumble. In this constellation, Butler links aesthetics and ethics through the relational and the sensorial— two registers that confound, complicate, and nuance claims to veracity. Butler's notions of opacity and relationality, as they pertain to autobiography and narrative specifically, help us to consider how Latina/o subjects are often called upon to "give an account" of themselves transparently through the demand for culturally tourable novels that explain the intense *sabor* of island food or, perhaps more materially and urgently, through increasing laws that demand identifying papers (which often require identification that bears a face) to account for the very existence of Latina/os in the United States. Put another way, the burden of representation commingles with the ruse of visibility in very specific ways for latinidad.

Face Value

It is in this terrain of visibility and representation that I would now like to consider the question of the face, or many faces, in relation to curiosity. Here, I think, we can find that the question of curiosity and how one may either occasion curious looks or look curiously at another might be held in productive tension regarding the face-to-face encounter, an encounter that those marked by difference have had to learn to navigate—one wherein the political and ethical interweave. The face beholds another and can be held by the face of an Other, but so too is the face where searching eyes seek answers. Faces, too, often become the aesthetic representation of demographic awareness—for either conservative or progressive political means. As a rising demographic in the United States, latinidad is often rendered as an amalgamation of faces that either amass or invade. But faces often do not reveal much in relation to large generalizations—instead, the face-to-face can be a site of recognition, desire, undoing, objectification, and affective traffic. Before a mouth opens to utter a word, faces can communicate quite a lot—but that lot would not be in the register of the knowable or veracity. Rendered static, or statistic, the face becomes an occasion to reduce one to a deadened subject. In what follows, I chart curious looks that impress upon faces—signaling a difference between a curiosity that can respect the right to opacity and one that, with hubris, violently seeks transparency when looking into the face of another.

Latina/os are often judged visually, through xenophobia, through fears of immigration, and, more liberally, for things like diversity work. Indeed, it should come as no surprise that the much-anticipated *Norton Anthology of Latino Literature* became the only anthology in Norton's series to feature, on its cover, a panoply of faces in various shades of brown. The Latina/o face is more often the face of demography—the face of diversity—the face that we must face if we aim to do justice to shifting populations. And yet I would argue that the face, taken at face value, precisely demurs serious ethical, political, and, namely, aesthetic consideration. Such demographically minded forms of representation offer a face instead of a question, a face that renders representation as strictly and simply referential to a people. Doris Sommer invokes worry and caution in relation to minoritarian literature, focusing on moments within the texts that perform a kind of refusal to mastery or easy intimacy: "Worry should be part of the work, if we learn to read the distance written into some ethnically marked literature. A variety of rhetorical moves can hold a reader at arm's length or joke at their pretense of mastery, in order to propose something different than knowledge."[15] It may seem strange to propose something different than knowledge, when much of the insurgent and foundational scholarly work in area studies touted alternative, postcolonial, and decolonial knowledges. Yet the insistence upon knowledge and epistemic certainty places a burden on minoritarian cultural production—the burden of representation.

In this vein, Doris Sommer asks us to worry, and worry we should. We all know far too well that in the age of the corporate university, diversity as a branding technique works less for difference and more to sanitize the face of the university—precisely by featuring faces of color. In "The Language of Diversity," a chapter in her book *On Being Included: Racism and Diversity in Institutional Life*, Sara Ahmed shows that the work of diversity is often achieved by the mere institutional speech act of claiming diversity. She writes, "My interviews with diversity workers taught me about the relationship between words and bodies, how certain words stick to certain bodies, such that bodies can in turn become stuck."[16] My contention here is that representations of latinidad often use the figure of the face as a synecdoche for a demographic that could never be codified by a series of such figures. Latina/os seem to be precisely stuck with the face as the only form of representation.

Face or a disfigured face, according to Paul de Man, is the trope of autobiography, no simple genre and one that happens to be the hermeneutic assigned to most Latina/o cultural production—from poetry to novels to performance. De Man links the writing of life to death and the giving of face to defacement.[17] In order to communicate this dual function of autobiography, de Man chooses the trope of prosopopoeia—that figure of speech within which an absent, dead, or fictional person is speaking. Prosopopoeia, which de Man describes as both a headstone and as writing from beyond the grave, means that while autobiography gives us a face of a life, that face also carries its own disfiguration—or, we might say, aesthetic morphing. In the interplay between face and defacement, a static notion of a demographically marked and anticipatable face is a radical reduction. When we take the face at face value, we afford no form or formal engagement with face. Or, to think with Levinas, we do not proceed with the face-to-face as the encounter, par excellence, of ethics. Instead, taking latinidad as only a panoply of faces renders them, as Antonio Viego would call them, dead signifiers.

Faces, too, tend to be privileged as sites of affect—as the place of communication not just with tongue and mouth, linguistically. A face can also be the bodily site upon which emotional registers play out, perhaps articulating in a different register than what language offers. In *Feeling in Theory*, Rei Terada points to the face and engages precisely with de Man's work on prosopopoeia: "The figure that bestows face, reflects his [de Man's] pre-occupation with the shaping of information and of the emotionality of information processing."[18] Such information, de Man and Terada remind us, is delivered not without a certain kind of pathos. And in the information age, numbers, polls, and statistics are the name of the game. As such, faces frozen or taken at face value are often in a curious position vis-à-vis how we receive statistical values.

There is an aesthetic and affective import to the face in this age, which, Michel Foucault would remind us, is in the business of managing life through biopolitics. The difficulty or ethical dilemma we face, then, as curious subjects in the age of biopolitics (and, to be sure, necropolitics) is that information is not the epistemological telos—it is, more often than not, a signifier in a chain of signifiers that hide their relativity and, hence, their value. If we approach an ethical and political problem, that of difference, with the goal of epistemological certitude, and if we do so with the flimsy data of information—taken at face value—we deaden alterity. Perhaps the face is best read for affect, for opacity, and for things other than knowledge. Silvan Tomkins's illuminating work on affect in the cybernetic fold privi-leges the face as one of the primary sites of affect. And Rei Terada chimes in with this very sentiment: "The face is to visibility what the voice is to audi-bility: of all physical surfaces, it has the greatest reputation for expressivity, an alleged ability to externalize invisible emotions in a virtually unmediated way."[19] This expressivity of the face does not divulge knowledge as such or information. Rather than epistemology, the face is a site of relation, affect, and encounter. Pathos and ethos rhetorically reign in this corporeal site, while logos recedes.

In the face of another, we are often curious—searching eyes, reading mouth gestures, and noting when to look directly and when to look away. These encounters are deeply felt as relational, and this may be one reason that Levinas privileged it as the site of ethics. The curiosity inspired by the face of another, though, may very much carry what philosophers in Fou-cauldian studies have called the "violence of curiosity." Lauren Guilmette signals this violence of curiosity as the affective frame of modern biopolitics.[20] Indeed, if one has any doubt about what it might mean to feel the impact of the violence of curiosity, just ask a trans or genderqueer person whose body, face, and person are constantly under scrutiny to figure them out—to pin-point alterity. The same would go for ethnically marked folks whose color and phenotypes warrant unusual stares and long guessing games. Disability studies too, with the seminal work of thinkers such as Rosemarie Garland-Thomson,[21] has long taught us about the effects of curious stares in relation to corporeal difference. Taking this focus on the violence of curiosity as an affective frame, especially as it is in relation to sex and biopolitics, I would add that critical race and postcolonial scholars have always focused on the colonial, racist logics that produce the ethnically or racially marked Other under strict categories that often discipline and scrutinize, under the aegis of managing life. Biopolitical imperatives often use curiosity about alterity as a way to produce knowledge about the problem of reproduction at the intersections of race, ethnicity, and sex. In these scenes where strange terms like "anchor babies" commingle with the precarious futures of dreamers with the fate of DACA (Deferred Action for Childhood Arrivals), there is often an imperative to know the problem, to pin down numbers and bodies, and to rely far too heavily upon the biopolitical imperative behind demographics.

But it also seems that the violence of curiosity is caught up in what feminist scholars have often called the gaze or scopophilia—taking pleasure in consuming difference optically. And here we are reminded that while Foucault was writing genealogies of biopolitics, he also claimed that "visibility is a trap."[22] Yet, much as one would like, we do not have much of a choice about being in a visual culture, and prelapsarian wishes that fetishize lettered cultures carry their own violences. Instead, opacity might proffer a particularly entangled way of thinking with and around the difficulties of visual culture.[23] So then a guiding question might be: How do we curiously engage with the face without forcing it into false transparency or flattened difference?

One face that bears the marker of latinidad and speaks beyond the grave is that of Ana Mendieta. The iconic Cuban American feminist artist is best known for using her body markedly and centrally in the majority of her oeuvre. From her earth body works to the *silueta* series, Mendieta used her body as both the frame and source material of her work. While known for using her body as a scale, a scale that critics often commented on as being both small and explosive, Mendieta also made early performance pieces using her face. These photographs were part of a series entitled *Untitled (Glass on Body Imprints—Face),* wherein she placed a plate of plexiglass against various parts of her body—pressing it almost like a second lens that highlights the camera's lens—noting the materiality and impact of being seen or being visible. In this series, this impact is notable as something that flattens and, through that flattening, morphs and transfigures.

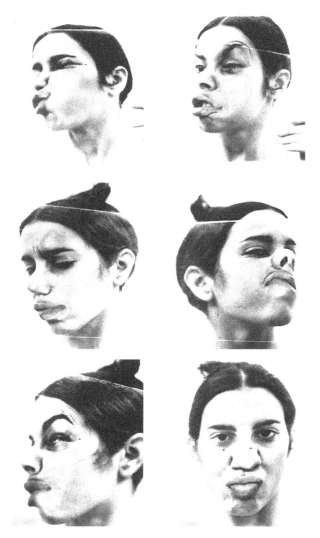

Figure 10.1. Ana Mendieta, *Untitled (Glass on Body Imprints),* 1972. Unique suite of thirteen lifetime black-and-white photographs, 10 × 8 inches each. Collection Princeton University Art Museum, Princeton, New Jersey. Copyright the Estate of Ana Mendieta Collection, LLC. Courtesy of Galerie Lelong & Co.

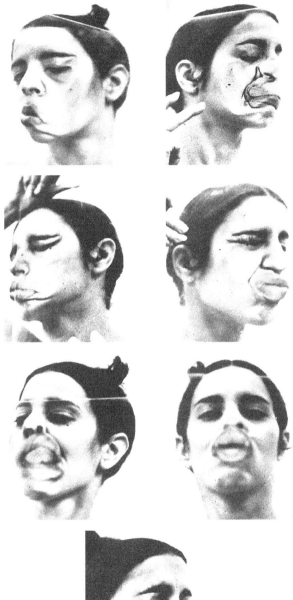

180 Christina León

These early works were notably performed and documented during her work at Iowa University, where she earned her MFA. Mendieta landed in Iowa not by choice but through Operation Peter Pan. This operation was CIA sponsored, a series of exoduses that to date marks the largest number of unaccompanied minors in mass exodus: fourteen thousand in total between 1960 and 1962. The operation preyed on the fears of Cubans on the island, fears stoked and fanned by both the CIA and the Catholic Church, that the Cuban government would enforce Patria Potestad law—their children would no longer be theirs to raise in accordance with their familial values versus the state's values. As a result of these fears, Ana Mendieta and her sister made the lonely trek from Havana to Miami and then were assigned to an orphanage in Dubuque, Iowa. There Mendieta began her search for belonging, often turning to the elements of the earth to make her early land art that would come to bear her materialist signature.

While Mendieta's family had both racial and class privilege in Cuba, the ninety-mile stretch between her homeland and the United States functioned as a translation abyss in regard not just to language but also to race, ethnicity, and culture. Upon arriving in the United States, she went from being considered white in Cuba to brown in her new, strange home. Moreover, the assaults she experienced, both verbal and, later, physical, were most certainly at the violent intersections of racism and sexism. No wonder, then, that her face told a story so many in Iowa did not want to read. Instead of facing alterity, they slandered her with racial epithets and sexist slurs—usually a toxic mixture of both. With this context in mind, we can see that she endured not a radical, ethical curiosity, one wherein an unfamiliar face becomes an occasion to extend relational gestures. The siphoning of her person into insults that relied upon misogynist and racist stereotypes made her into a "dead signifier." But rather than resigning herself to such stultification, she defiantly used her face as both canvas and performance—rendering it grotesque, inquisitive, morphed, and translated. Her portraits show us that what seems like a transparent lens, perhaps the gaze of curiosity, can turn hard and make impact. Each snapshot, fascinatingly, shows a slightly different affect or expression. Yet, as photographs, these pieces are perhaps most eerie because they are frozen. We see the effect of force on a face, the flattening gestures that violent gazes can produce, and we are held in thrall because we want the face to return back to "normal"—that is to say, expressive and gestural. These portraits imbue her face with the uncanny, the unhomely or unfamiliar, and show that what we deem to be foreign to place and face is part of the same relational matrix that envelopes us. Mendieta's photos, if they are autobiographical and if they do respond to the sociopolitical context in which she found herself, play more with the defacing effects of curious, but lecherous, gazes. A lecherous gaze of curiosity, then, willfully disavows nuance and opacity to the subject it faces—taking a marker of difference and using that codified difference to enforce a gaze that feigns transparency but has the material consequence of flattening and freezing through its optics. Such defiance against static renderings and such interest in deformation, disintegration, and the fleeting moment would mark Mendieta's career up until her early, untimely death. Perhaps this ability to both capture moments and portray their flight is one way in which Mendieta fought back against the stereotypes that thought they knew her as part of a new hoard of invaders. Perhaps she battled with their hubristic notion that her person was transparently knowable by waging her own aesthetic opacity, rendering herself as fleeting as a facial gesture and as hard to pin down as a grain of sand being pulled back into the ocean.

Entangled Curiosities

Because curiosity can morph like a face, I hesitate to proffer a definition of curiosity here and, rather, defer to both the way it has been used and its multivalent effects. A turn to the etymology of the word can be telling. Curiosity in its modern usage comes from the middle of the fourteenth century, when it meant "eager to know," often in a negative sense. It derives from the Old French *curios,* which meant solicitous, anxious, inquisitive, odd, and strange. This root, however, is quite entangled with the Latin *curiosus,* which means, on the one hand, careful and diligent and, on the other hand, eager and meddlesome. The word's tangled roots are akin, fascinatingly, to *cura,* which would connote cure and care. In the 1800s curiosity was often a euphemism or code for the pornographic. It is precisely in this entangled weave of both linguistic and also very material histories that we see the dilemma of curiosity, especially as it pertains to those marked by difference. But I would wage that instead of trying to sanitize the term, to wash it of its colonial past, such roots must break and become errant. Here, in this tangled weave, it becomes essential that we engage with both the political *and* the ethical—two registers that may benefit from further entanglement.

Politics seeks to know those whom it speaks for, while ethics keeps us humble in the face of another, knowing that that face holds a resistant opacity. This process of fostering an ethical curiosity means immersing ourselves in this rhizomatic history in order to begin to do justice to difference—honing a curiosity in our students that remains accountable to the violence of curiosity. Perhaps, then, opacity might be an attendant term, one that hastens us to be humble in the pursuits of knowledge, to keep relation and reading open and to infuse our imaginaries with the unknown—not to domesticate or know, but to keep learning.

In such a messy weave of etymology, it seems prudent to come back to Glissant, who preferred to traffic in the tangles of rhizomes rather than the linear logic of roots. In a provocatively titled chapter, "Ethics of Entanglement," John Drabinski seeks to think about the abyssal, catastrophic origins of ethics and relation by putting into conversation Levinas and Glissant.[24] The entanglement, here, is the irreducibility of relationality. What does this mean for curiosity? Let's take a step back to think about knowledge claims and the temptation of the biopolitical lure of information in the form of statistics, narratives, anecdotes, and numbers. What sort of knowledge is produced through these various means? They are, to be sure, incompatible in many ways with the aesthetic insofar as they pinpoint, manage, and try to grasp life. Such a seizure or grasp is the very thing Glissant seeks to undo with his notion of opacity, that right to which we clamor for all. In reflecting upon *Poetics of Relation,* Drabinski writes: "Seizing and grasping figure in the act of knowledge of what is and has long been political and cultural practice under colonialism. But there is also the composition of knowing and contact *outside* that totalitarian economy, a sense of relation that keeps the opacity of the Other safe without insisting upon simple separation."[25] Simple separation, of course, would be the privilege of unknowing—the kind of austerity and purity assigned to others for whom folks with privilege cannot speak and, hence, do not consider. That kind of fetishized alterity ultimately washes the hands of those who are not marked in such a way. Instead, we follow Drabinski, who follows Glissant: "Opacity, contact, *then* composition. The composition of knowing in a composite cultural context crafts meaning in the imaginary—that precarious aesthetic sphere of knowing and being that structures a relation to the world—out of fragments of the past and present that bear no atavistic relation to rooted memory and history."[26] The emphasis on the imaginary is part of the world-making that comes from the abyssal histories from which relation emerges. The imaginary is the poetic vision of the open boat, the ability to foreground relation over seizure, and the urgent call to take stock of messy, often fissured, pasts. Such a relationship asks for the poetic vision of imagination over the colonial project of knowing, instead emphasizing chaos, echo, and totality—the three forms of worlding Glissant theorizes. The imaginary requires that we not only rest on firm knowledge claims but also give ourselves over to aesthetic relation, to the impressionability of the senses. This enfolds us in relation, making the subject and object split of both impression and imagination hard to discern. I would wager that this is when reading truly begins.

The issue of entanglement urges us to recall the problem of curiosity in the classroom and how to foster reading practices that respect the singularity of difference. Curiosity can be used as a means to further ethical relations, readerly and otherwise. It can, as we have seen, be used as a catalyst for more colonial knowledge projects. It is inescapable that these two facets of curiosity are linked, entangled, and embody the enmeshment of political and ethical urgencies. On the one hand, we need subaltern knowledge and voices. On the other, we learn little from them when we turn them into objects of mere curiosity—the collection of Orientalist tapestries and perfumes captured in Dorian Gray's house or the heads of game animals stuffed in Hemingway's den. Politics demands representation, and ethics slows us down in the face of representation. It is these two, incongruent temporalities that make teaching minoritarian aesthetics at once incredibly important and difficult.

Acknowledging the difficulty of such a task, I ask students to engage with the sociopolitical context of a piece while also attending to the nuances of the aesthetic choice, with careful attention to form and with the same eye they would give to supposed canonical writers. Teaching students to read for opacity in the classroom does not mean encouraging all things obfuscating, nor does it open the floodgates to purple prose.[27] Instead, it reminds them that the task of reading may not always be "to get it"—or, as Glissant would say, "to seize it." Our work in the literary classroom, as well as many humanities- and social justice–based classrooms, may not be primarily about accruing knowledge linearly, in a way that adds up to mastery. It may, instead, require that students learn to sit with the discomfort of unknowing, to be in relation to a complexity that is always unfolding and never complete. The pedagogical payoff here is that teaching students to sit with and learn

184   Christina León

from opacity—to stay in relation without fully knowing—asks them to be humble, to be students. What leaves the classroom, as they begin to learn that I do not require mastery, is the profound anxiety that surrounds all that they do not yet know, all that they fear others know. What rushes in, in the form of careful, conversational, and close engagement with texts, art, theory, and histories, is a cacophony of voices responding to aesthetics from minorities. Reading curiously for opacity may be a scholarly practice of humility that students, interpellated as consumers and churned out as workers, seldom get afforded in their lives. While it seems rather risky to teach with an attunement to opacity in the classroom, I find that if students can trust themselves enough to let go of the pretense of mastery, they relax into the terrain of thought and aesthetics that traffics less in easy answers and more in the curious quagmire that surrounds us all. If students, then, are allowed to be students, allowed to not know every identitarian category or minority difference before discussion or before sustained encounters, then the work of reading can begin and the work of imagination can begin. If we learn to teach with an attention to opacity, to the moments in a text, history, work of art, or performance that push us out, that draw our attention to the sensorial (and not just the empirical), that, to be sure, entangle us in relation, perhaps then we have begun to do justice to our pedagogical task.

It is in entanglement and relation that curiosity would be best sustained—paying heed to the "texture of the weave" and not just using curiosity as a way to more fully discover, and conquer, the unknown. By emphasizing that any work on curiosity must stay vigilant about the violences waged in its name, I do not mean to discard the project of curiosity. Rather, making curiosity more accountable to its pursuits and more invested in ongoing relation, we might foster an ethical approach to curiosity. In its distillations as an affective and ethical mode that does promote learning, we might ask our students to interact with texts in ways that keep us asking more and more questions, rather than statically finding answers. The aesthetic, when emphasized in relation to minority positions and politics, might be one place to curiously cultivate questions rather than seek static, demographically minded answers.

I want to insist on a humble, yet overlooked, form of curious engagement with latinidad—one that attends to curiosity not as a strong colonial gaze but the kind of engagement that looks for surprise, for detail, for form, for aesthetics—and, perhaps, an aesthetic education of radical and ethical curiosity. Gayatri Chakravorty Spivak highlights the aesthetic realm as a space within which to continue to consider opacity—something akin to the irreducibility of singularity and the contingent. She writes:

> The most pernicious presupposition today is that globalization has happily happened in every aspect of our lives. Globalization can never happen to the sensory equipment of the experiencing being except insofar as it always was implicit in its vanishing outlines. Only an aesthetic education can continue to prepare us for this, thinking an uneven and only apparently accessible contemporaneity that can no longer be interpreted by such nice polarities as modernity/tradition, colonial/postcolonial. Everything begins there, in that space that allows us to survive in the singular and the unverifiable, surrounded by the lethal and lugubrious consolations of rational choice.[28]

In Spivak's work I find resonance with the spirit of Eve Sedgwick's late work that emphasized relational and reparative modes of art and reading. Such energies move us away from ideological critique in order to devote less in scholarly attention to paranoid critique and strong theory that seeks to explain the globe through the anticipatory hermeneutics of capitalism and neoliberalism.[29] By introducing opacity into the promising work of curiosity, I hope to conjure an attendant term that keeps the space of curious relation open, entangled in the pleasures afforded by tending to, rather than glossing over, the moments where difference does not fully reveal itself. It seems to me that opacity can function here as an ethical imperative in relation to curiosity—one that keeps curiosity open instead of curating a curio of difference—a boutique of carefully placed and easily dismissed curiosities. As such, we have much to learn about latinidad as it continues to unfold in the theater of our political world, our classrooms, our readings, and our everyday, textured sensorium.

Notes

1. My current manuscript is grappling with the lack of ethical work on latinidad. As such, I will, at times, separate the ethical and the political in this essay. I do so not in order to separate their work as concepts, but to show how certain constricted notions of politics have kept ethical questions at bay in Latina/o studies.

2. Tyson E. Lewis, *The Aesthetics of Education: Theatre, Curiosity, and Politics in the Work of Jacques Rancière and Paulo Freire* (London: Bloomsbury, 2012), 102.

3. Nigel Leask, *Curiosity and the Aesthetics of Travel Writing, 1770–1840: 'From an Antique Land'* (Oxford: Oxford University Press, 2002), 23.

4. Cristina Beltrán, *The Trouble with Unity: Latino Politics and the Creation of Identity* (Oxford: Oxford University Press, 2010).

5. Gayatri Spivak, throughout her career, has given us a few ways to think more creatively about terms often associated with identity. In her work, she has lauded the term *strategic essentialism* only to find it woefully misread. Hence, I look back to her essay "Can the Subaltern Speak?" where Spivak's engagement with Derrida showcases that one of his motivating theoretical nuances was to think about catachresis—the abuse of metaphor—as an originary figure. If, at the supposed origin, we find not a solid root but yet another figure of metaphoricity broken, then we have no essential kernel of truth and no directive telos of identity.

6. Beltrán, *The Trouble with Unity*, 6.

7. Antonio Viego, *Dead Subjects: Toward a Politics of Loss in Latino Studies* (Durham, N.C.: Duke University Press, 2007).

8. Viego, 67.

9. Édouard Glissant, *Poetics of Relation* (Ann Arbor: University of Michigan Press, 2009), 194.

10. Glissant, 194.

11. Glissant, 189.

12. Glissant, 190.

13. Judith Butler, *Giving an Account of Oneself* (New York: Fordham University Press, 2005).

14. In *Senses of the Subject* (New York: Fordham University Press, 2015), Butler writes: "What follows is a form of relationality that we might call 'ethical': a certain demand or obligation impinges upon me, and the response relies on my capacity to affirm this having been acted on, formed into one who can respond to this or that call. Aesthetic relationality also follows: something impresses itself upon me, and I develop impressions that cannot be fully separated from what acts on me" (11).

15. Doris Sommer, *Proceed with Caution, when Engaged by Minority Writing in the Americas* (Cambridge, Mass.: Harvard University Press, 1999), xi.

16. Sara Ahmed, *On Being Included: Racism and Diversity in Institutional Life* (Durham, N.C.: Duke University Press, 2012), 62.

17. Paul de Man, *The Rhetoric of Romanticism* (New York: Columbia University Press, 1984), 62. Cf. "Prosopopoeia is the trope of autobiography, by which one's name . . . is made as intelligible and memorable as a face. Our topic deals with the giving and taking away of faces, with face and deface, *figure*, figuration and disfiguration" (76).

18. Rei Terada, *Feeling in Theory* (Cambridge, Mass.: Harvard University Press, 2001), 52.

19. Terada, 53.

20. Lauren Guilmette, "The Violence of Curiosity: Butler's Foucault, Foucault's Herculine, and the Will-to-Know," *philoSOPHIA* 7, no. 7 (2017): 1–22.

21. See, for example, Rosemarie Garland-Thomson, *Staring: How We Look* (Oxford: Oxford University Press, 2009).

Curious Entanglements 187

22. Michel Foucault, *Discipline and Punish: The Birth of the Prison* (New York: Vintage Books, 1995), 200.

23. In her recent monograph, *Entanglements, or Thinking about Transmedial Capture* (Durham, N.C.: Duke University Press, 2012), Rey Chow makes the excellent point: "As Foucault demonstrates in works such as *The Archeology of Knowledge* and *The Order of Things,* with the progressively widening chasm between words and things, visibility can no longer be treated as the secure opposite of what is hidden, or as the simple unveiling of data that can be accessed similarly in (or that share a resemblance with) words. Rather, visibility is now caught up in the shifting relations of political sovereignty and in the discontinuities among different representational regimes" (153).

24. John E. Drabinski, "Ethics of Entanglement," in *Levinas and the Postcolonial: Race, Nation, Other* (Edinburgh: Edinburgh University Press, 2013), 129–64.

25. Drabinski, 152.

26. Drabinski, 152.

27. Here it seems worth noting that opacity is often charged with elitism, while clarity is charged with accessibility. I do not think these two aspects of writing or reading are at all disentangled. What may be clear to one person, whether by language or experience, may be radically opaque to another. For more on this problem of clarity and opacity in relation to feminism, see Aída Hurtado and Cynthia M. Paccacerqua, "Not All Clarities Are Created Equal: The Politics of 'Opaqueness,'" *Hypatia* 30, no. 3 (2015): 620–27.

28. Gayatri Chakravorty Spivak, *An Aesthetic Education in the Era of Globalization* (Cambridge, Mass.: Harvard University Press, 2012), 4.

29. See Eve Sedgwick's essay "Paranoid Reading and Reparative Reading, or You're So Paranoid You Probably Think This Essay Is about You," in *Touching Feeling* (Durham, N.C.: Duke University Press, 2002), 124–55.

11

Transsexuality, the Curio, and the Transgender Tipping Point

Amy Marvin

Or, you know. In my Sybil Vane.
I made great plans to be bratty all week
but at least a divorcée in a whatever
apartment where I have already let
the coffee burn for myself to clean
after a change of mask and costume,
a salon confessional, a CfP. There'd have been
gloves and buttons involved
piles of shirts to come on
spontaneous or world-historical underboob
no teaching and minimal committee work
I mean it like a flood alert.
A paragon, like
I'd fuck me.
—"Self-portrait as a Karen," by Kay Gabriel, from *Elegy Department Spring*

Curiosity and the Transgender Tipping Point

Trans subjects, and I employ the term "subjects" with a purposeful bivalence to signify both "topics of concern" and "individuals of concern," have received renewed attention and visibility during these tumultuous 2010s. At the level of mass cultural curiosity, the notion that trans people could be sympathetic or even to some extent respectable, already indicated by the move from media venues such as Jerry Springer to the less carnivalesque platform of Oprah in the 2000s, was solidified through the phenomenon of the "Transgender Tipping Point" via *Time Magazine* in 2014[1] and the spectacle of Caitlyn Jenner's transition in 2015.[2]

Both media events were framed with a similar narrative: first, that "trans" was a phenomenon not receiving due attention until recently; second, that "trans" presented a set of up-and-coming social issues and possibilities for progress as a cutting-edge social movement; third, that visibility, media, and specific (nameable and photographable) voices are its vanguard; and fourth, that this movement faces a threat from entrenched gender norms and institutions, including specific resistance from traditional or conservative views and policies and perhaps a number of skeptical feminists. The general message relayed to the public by mass culture is that "trans" is located at the cutting-edge of concern across multiple fronts, finally arriving and coming into its own as a movement, and capable of great progress through renewed sympathetic public curiosity.

Public curiosity often frames visibility as a positive force, but visibility for trans people is frequently ambivalent. In Talia Bettcher's "Evil Deceivers and Make-Believers," she emphasizes that visibility for trans people is accompanied by negations of gender/sex credibility or even heightened violence.[3] Viviane Namaste also emphasizes that the production of trans visibility according to gender in the abstract can render the needs of specific populations of trans people invisible, including trans refugees, migrants, sex workers, drug users, poor trans people, and homeless trans people.[4] It is thus important not to ascribe public curiosity to any clear good for trans people, since structurally the visibility of trans populations may be accompanied by heavy politicization, exclusion, and violence, frequently at the intersections of misogyny, racism, xenophobia, economic inequality, and the disenfranchisement of sex workers in society.

While a mass cultural awareness and curiosity about trans people has marked some institutional changes, such as a tenuous lifting of some restrictions for passport gender marker changes in the United States and increased institutional support for gender-neutral bathrooms, violence (both physical and economic) continues to be directed toward vulnerable trans populations such as economically disenfranchised trans women of color, trans women sex workers, and trans people with precarious housing situations. For example, being careful to note the decontextualization and appropriation of violently murdered transfeminine people of color,[5] the increased visibility and policy changes of the 2010s did not prevent the disproportionate levels of violence and murder against specific trans populations (mostly trans women and transfeminine people from South America and, in the United States, black trans women) in 2017.[6]

Increased mass curiosity about trans people may thus address issues for specific populations of trans people, such as codifying proper name, pronoun, and terminology recognition as well as legal, more inclusive bathroom access in certain workspaces and public spaces, but this may only benefit trans people who have not already been shut out of them. The kind of trans activism that achieves attention and visibility risks disproportionately benefiting specific populations of white middle-class or affluent trans professionals and college students, or others who can match what Dan Irving calls "the mediation of transsexuality through capitalist productive relations,"[7] as the hand of activism as visibility passes by populations of trans people considered outside the graces of economic and societal use. Though the current moment of visibility, attention, and a seemingly more friendly curiosity may seem like progress, I approach it with healthy suspicion.

Beyond the tenuous causal link between attention, visibility, curiosity, and trans amelioration, let alone trans amelioration across differences, heightened attention and visibility can bring unwanted or even dangerous results. The ocular lens of the transgender tipping point may bring attention to trans people in ways that are reductive and exploitative, and already the increasing degree to which conservative platforms have explicitly listed policies against trans people marks a backlash against the media's call for attention and acceptance. The Kansas Republican Party, for example, in February 2018, voted for an explicit platform to "oppose all efforts to validate transgender identity" at the state level.[8]

In this essay I consider the grounds of my suspicion about post-transgender tipping point curiosity, especially when public interest in trans subjects seems to originate from an unprecedented place of acceptance. Specifically, I focus on a product I call "the curio" and a process of production I call "curiotization." First, I unpack the curio as an object that is alienated from its context, history, and world, and through this removal becomes intensified as a site of curiosity. I then describe curiotization as the process through which people or groups of people become intensified subjects of curiosity. After tracing an implicit concern about curiosity in existing trans studies,

Transsexuality and the Transgender Tipping Point   191

I read the song "Walk on the Wild Side," alongside María Lugones's discussion of world traveling, as an example of curiotization. After this I turn to contemporary examples of curiotization in mass media journalism about trans women breastfeeding and the framework of the transgender tipping point. I conclude that one way that cultural production can attempt to avoid curiotization is through more complex, particular, contextual, and historicized engagements with trans subjects.

The Curio

Having grown up frequenting museums and spending much time with eclectic people in their homes, the first thing I think of when I hear the word "curio" is an object set before me to engage my attention or even fascination. A sapphire-encrusted beetle pinned behind a display cabinet, a grinning mask beset by daggers hanging on the wall, a circuited metal bird surrounded by a cube of glass, a human skull resting on a coffee table; each of these might draw me in as magnets of my curiosity, calling me to ask, inquire, converse, or give silent attention. Such curiosity may be open to surprise and wonder, and the manner of presentation does not necessarily bring me to controlled, disciplined, academic consideration as in the case of what Perry Zurn calls "serious curiosity" (See Zurn, this volume). Indeed, eclectic objects presented before me seem more likely to elicit the curiosity that Zurn refers to as "frivolous," since I am likely to have no continuing stake in giving attention and discussion to the odd mummified rabbit paw or moose-antlered tiara gracing your study. However, a carefully crafted conversation, story, or museum exhibit can more finely hone my curiosity about objects beyond a frivolous engagement by providing further narrative and context, and perhaps even carry over my curiosity to more sustained forms of interest. The curio is thus initially an object that elicits variable attention productive of multivalent curiosities, but tending toward a frivolous or at least noncommittal mode.

It is also useful to note that, along with the potential for a frivolous curiosity, the curio itself is often presented through an alienation from living context, history, and world. One easy mistake might be to call any decoration that could lead to a conversation a curio, perhaps a book placed on the coffee table featuring possums wearing various adorable hats, or a reference to more immediate mass culture, say, if I were to have a replica of Wonder

Woman's shield hanging in my office. Another mistake might be to equate the curio with a form of kitsch or ironic or absurd décor. For example, I currently have an obnoxious red painting of a rooster hanging in my living room that I purchased for five dollars at a yard sale just because people find it absurd or dreadful or amusing. The curio, on the other hand, is removed from its time and space and world, but its dislocation is precisely that which elicits the onlooker's curiosity. It is also possible that what is not a curio for me, like the rooster painting, could very well be a curio for you, and vice versa.

This is one reason why the phenomenon of the curio often participates in the exoticization and appropriation of colonialism and Orientalism.[9] A white person vacations in New Orleans and purchases a "voodoo doll" for their shelf, alienated from its cultural context but nonetheless eliciting curiosity from houseguests. A museum displays hieroglyphic tablets that have been stolen from non-Western cultures through colonialist excavation, beset by a neat stand with a placard. Placed adjacent to a mummified cat, once a living person's revered companion, both displays might be arranged to create a helpful walkway for museum visitors for the convenience of their curiosity. Trans poet and minister Elena Rose connected this form of exoticization via collection with trans dehumanization in her 2006 poem "On Cartography and Dissection," writing:

> And there it is: you're illuminated in a manuscript, a centaur, a Celestial, an Eskimo, a manticore, an autogynephiliac. You're made of stories, and your own voice is generally drowned out by them. You're a Monster, and it ain't your Here to Be in any more. You're the one brown kid in someone else's town. You're the transsexual etherized upon the table. Monsters aren't in their own stories; they're in someone else's, some Center's, some subject's object.[10]

The curio, whether object or human, evokes its life, time, and place only through its extraction into the collectors' world.

Another important clarification is that the curio does not need to be alienated from the past; it can also draw an onlooker's curiosity when pulled from a present or future world. Consider, for example, the Mütter Museum in Philadelphia, which displays medical oddities in the form of surgical utensils, preserved body parts, bones, and entire remains. Exhibits include the *Soap Lady,* an entire body preserved through body fat decomposing into

Transsexuality and the Transgender Tipping Point 193

a waxy substance, as well as cutting-edge medical devices used for spinal surgery. The Mütter Museum is in this way not so different from traveling Body Worlds exhibits, which display human and nonhuman bodies preserved through the process of plastination.[11]

While the bodies housed in the Mütter Museum or Body Worlds do harken back to the past in the form of the history of medicine and the history of these particular bodies, their alienation from life also produces fascination about human bodies and their many possible variations and transformations in the present. Despite evoking this fascination, however, they are not set up with much interest to the world of the person preserved. Relatedly, the creators of the Body Worlds exhibits, Angelina Whalley and Gunther von Hagens, state, "Body Worlds exhibitions were conceived to educate the public about the inner workings of the human body and to show the effects of healthy and unhealthy lifestyles."[12] These exhibits may evoke what Zurn calls "morbid curiosity," which fetishizes pain and involves "an empty gaze, intent on seeing yet without any interest in understanding."[13] They may also admit to a more complex curiosity about human embodiment and health in the present, though it would be wise to inquire further into the meaning of "unhealthy lifestyles."

In addition to curios pulled from the present, we might consider curios that call forth an as-yet unrealized future. One example is the futuristic curios housed at Epcot, or Experimental Prototype Community of Tomorrow, in the Walt Disney World theme park. Walt Disney described Epcot as "a community of tomorrow that will never be completed but will always be introducing and testing and demonstrating new materials and systems."[14] Accordingly, Epcot has a section called Future World, which focuses on these new technologies. One popular Disney tourism website advertises, "Through a combination of hands-on activities and fantastic attractions, you'll find exhibits that focus on ocean life, the land and our environment, imagination, health, energy, communication, space exploration, and transportation."[15] With its futuristic aesthetic, the park is designed to showcase both current and future technology, often in the form of interactive displays for children. The objects hail from the future and often the cutting-edge of the present, and sometimes an imagined future projected from our past. However, their removal from the context of their actual development and future possibilities marks them as curios, drawing attention to the future from which they are pulled only through their alienation into the theme park's manicured present.

Though the curio is alienated from its living context, the remnants of its world and history imbue the object with its curious character. It is marked as out of place and out of time, and through this rupture draws curiosity into its orbit. This curiosity may tend toward the frivolous but may also admit to serious consideration, inspire cultural production, or serve as a curiosity that expands beyond the object toward broader horizons. Going beyond the curios of Future World, Disney captures and markets a more explicit transition from curio to broader curiosity in *The Little Mermaid*: "I've got gadgets and gizmos a-plenty / I've got whozits and whatzits galore / You want thingamabobs? I've got twenty! / But who cares? No big deal, I want more."[16] The curiosity that the curio attracts may be multivalent and open to new horizons even as it continues to depend on an alienated and easily reduced object.

Trans Curiotization

Now that I have discussed presentations of both objects and the preserved dead as curios, I will focus on curiotization. Curiotization is the process of transfiguration into a curio that is focused on groups of people, and often living ones at that. Returning directly to the subject of curiosity about trans people, much of trans studies literature discusses the ways that trans people (and historically transsexuals) have been objectified by nontrans media and researchers. As a note of clarification before I launch into this discussion, I often focus on transsexuality due to the historical precision of the term in relation to the particular curiotizing processes I am discussing. However, I generally understand "trans" to be a messy pluralism of gender nonconformity but also gender conformity, changes of sex, similar politicization of bodies, and so forth, converging in complicated ways across time and space. First, I will emphasize that trans studies has long been invested in the relationship between trans people and curiosity. Second, I will show how considering curiotization is specifically useful for the post–"transgender tipping point" moment.

In her book *Whipping Girl,* Julia Serano argues that media and academics have often focused on transsexual women's bodies as an objectified means to an entertaining or theoretically useful end. Serano traces one aspect of this practice to media, which objectifies transsexual women (and often transsexual men) by drawing out the audience's fascination with body transformation, surgery, and femininity.[17] On the other side of this coin is what Serano calls "ungendering," through which academics cite transsexual bodies as theoretical devices for showcasing the subversion, deconstruction, and inconsistencies of gender and sex without taking into account the lived experience of transsexual people.[18]

Serano is primarily concerned about the erasure of lived experience, writing, "By reducing us to the status of objects of inquiry, cissexuals free themselves of the inconvenience of having to consider us living, breathing beings."[19] This concern also relates to the processes through which trans people are transformed into objects of curiosity. For example, one aspect of media portrayals that Serano discusses is the uneven attention given to medical transition as a dramatic and "artificial" transformation, in contrast to other medical procedures and changes in appearance.[20] Additionally, when Serano discusses academic critiques of trans people, she is interested in the ways critics approach the subject without due care. Serano cites Bernice Hausman as manifesting anti-trans academic curiosity par excellence. Hausman in her 1995 book *Changing Sex* writes:

> No matter how much I applied myself to the task [of my dissertation], most of my thoughts on the issue seemed uninspired, boring, even obvious. . . . I inadvertently found texts that dealt with transsexualism. Now that was really fascinating. For about six months I read anything and everything I could find about crossdressing and sex change. I attended a national conference for transvestites and transsexuals. . . . The possibilities for understanding the construction of "gender" through an analysis of transsexualism seemed enormous and there wasn't a lot of critical material out there.[21]

Though Serano is concerned about objectification and the erasure of lived experience, this also involves an interest in the processes through which trans people are produced as a focus of the attention and visibility of curiosity, and the ways in which this mode of curiosity transforms transsexual subjects in media and academic knowledge production. Serano's concerns, along with Viviane Namaste's focus on the erasure of transsexual women's lives by doctors, academics, and institutions,[22] and Jamison Green's experience of being seen "as a frog" while answering questions on university panels about his life

196   Amy Marvin

as a transsexual man,[23] strike me as concerns with becoming the subject of curiosity.

A focus on the process of curiotization, and the transfiguration of trans people into curios, is useful because it highlights the effects of curiosity in shepherding the process of objectifying, ungendering, and annihilating lived experience that Serano and other writers discuss when reflecting on non-trans cultural production about trans people. While it is important to directly discuss this objectification and the erasure of lived experience, I find it interesting to also focus on the modes of curious attraction through which non-trans people are brought into our orbit, and I suggest that curiosity affects personal interactions with and cultural productions about us. One might be tempted to call trans people tools of the media or thesis puppets, signifying the purposeful reduction of trans people into a mere means for various entertainment or academic ends, but this frames non-trans people as too diabolically cognizant of the effects of their curiosity, attention, and fascination with trans people. Rather, I want to suggest that the frequent curio status of trans people often attracts non-trans people to us in ways they may not understand, even as the results of their curiosity are convenient for cultural production, careers, and/or pursuing their desires for us.

Another reason to focus on curiosity is because earlier critiques of dehumanization and objectification in trans studies may be limited when considering heightened interest in this post–tipping point moment if they do not foreground the ways in which different groups of trans people are subjected to curiosity in different ways over time. If the "transgender tipping point" does indeed mark a new moment for trans people, it may also bring a new form of curiotization based on new paradigms of acceptance and resulting contestations of trans lives.

A form of curiotization I find useful to highlight in the context of trans acceptance is an older one from trans history, but it stands out as useful for understanding the complexities of trans people functioning as curios. Consider the following lyrics: "Holly came from Miami F L A / Hitchhiked her way across the U S A / Plucked her eyebrows on the way / Shaved her legs and then he was a she."[24] You may recognize these lyrics from Lou Reed's 1972 song "Walk on the Wild Side." This song is not dissimilar from others such as "Lola" (1970) by the Kinks and the less redeemable "Dude Looks Like a Lady," released by Aerosmith in 1987. Lou Reed was a key member of the Velvet Underground, a band that, like Andy Warhol, is famous for inhabiting the "underground" of New York City. In this context, their cultural production was largely based on using their experience seeking and hanging out with the dispossessed and outcasts of New York as a fount for their music. Defending the song from charges of transphobia, Reed's friend and backup singer Jenni Muldaur asserted:

> Lou was open about his complete acceptance of all creatures of the night. . . . That's what that song's about. Everyone doing their thing, taking a walk on the wild side. I can't imagine how anyone could conceive of that [being transphobic]. The album was called *Transformer*. What do they think it's about?[25]

This defense of the song is also a clue toward its role in curiotization, and this specific mode of curiotization is helpful for understanding the post-transgender tipping point curiosity.

To better understand curiotization in this context, I turn to María Lugones's essay "Playfulness, 'World'-Travelling, and Loving Perception." In her essay Lugones defines a "world" as "inhabited at present by some flesh and blood people," which is inclusive of the dead. "Worlds" are multiple, and some "worlds" may take the form of a "dominant culture's description and construction of life, including a construction of their relationships of production, of gender, race, etc.," as well as nondominant constructions.[26] Lugones is thus emphasizing that people can take differing and multiple situated perspectives, and also that people can be differently constructed and perceived across these "worlds" even as they might travel between them.

In this context Lugones discusses arrogant perception and loving perception, building upon the work of Marilyn Frye. Lugones grounds her description of arrogant perception in a reflection on her relationship with her mother, writing, "I could not identify with her, I could not see myself in her, I could not welcome her world."[27] In contrast, Lugones emphasizes that a loving perception does not involve such an isolated, independent comportment toward another. Continuing her reflection, she writes, "Loving my mother also required that I see with my mother's eyes, that I go into my mother's world, that I see both of us as we are constructed in her world, that I witness her own sense of herself from within her world."[28] Arrogant perception in its independence cannot fathom the other's world, while loving perception considers their world on its own terms, centering not only this difference but also connections across difference.

198   Amy Marvin

I understand curiotization to be a failure of attempted world traveling that is in some ways distinct from Marilyn Frye's definition of arrogance upon which Lugones builds,[29] but it shares an inability to reach the other. With objects, I described their removal from time and place and world, a removal that generates a particular form of curiosity. With people, I will home in on the meaning and process of this removal in more detail.

Let's return to "Walk on the Wild Side." The song provides a framed snapshot of gay and trans life in New York City during the early 1970s, and in this way marks a time and place. The phrase "Walk on the Wild Side," too, evokes an attention to and fascination with the characters in the song, drawing in curiosity about their "underground" status as "creatures of the night," in Muldaur's words. In this way, we might even interpret the song as an attempt at loving perception, and indeed Lou Reed, like David Bowie, was one of very few men even to this day who will admit to loving and being loved by trans women. But in presenting the characters as sources of fascination, the song also strips away their living context. We are pulled in to wonder about their world, but not in order to actually see ourselves from the vantage points of that world, or really understand it in careful, particular, and historical complexity. "Walk on the Wild Side," like the "Future World" instruments at the Epcot center, presents its characters as beacons of interest in their little "underworld" but never adds texture to this world. In this way, curiotization represents the transformation of a person or group of people into subjects of curiosity but at the risk of dissolving their living context and history. The curiotizing subjects flirt with loving perception while peering through a fascinated but walled-off looking glass similar to arrogant perception.

The reason why I find this process of curiotizing through cultural production interesting to look at, in addition to earlier critiques of objectification and erasure such as those found in the work of Serano and many others, is that the current and post-"transgender tipping point" moment constructs itself as extending sympathy, understanding, and respectfulness toward trans people in a way that is likely to change the modes of curiosity directed toward trans subjects. In this context, I find it useful to consider how the combination of increased attention and visibility along with curious goodwill may lead to failed understandings through the alienation from living context, history, and world represented by the curio.

Curiotization and Tipping Points

The fact that "Walk on the Wild Side" is a song, and thus necessarily curtailed, may lead to some sympathy for the limitations of its medium. Considering more recent moments of curiotization in the post–tipping point era is thus useful for elaborating contemporary nuances. To do this I will take up an example of mass media journalism curiotizing trans women breastfeeding before I move to the larger mass culture curiotization produced by the transgender tipping point.

In the post–tipping point moment, journalists often portray "trans" as a cutting-edge topic. Though anti-trans journalism persists during "trans moments," often in a dialectic with assertions of progress, many journalists in the 2010s aim for more sympathetic coverage. Despite increasing neutral or positive coverage of trans issues, non-trans journalists still frequently cover trans subjects through a process of curiotization. For example, in February 2018 news broke internationally about a trans woman who breastfed her baby under clinical supervision. The news was based on a report published in the journal *Transgender Health* a month before by Tamar Reisman and Zil Goldstein, who wrote of a clinic treatment, "We believe that this is the first formal report in the medical literature of induced lactation in a transgender woman."[30] While this was by far not the first instance of trans women breastfeeding (including with medical supervision), let alone lactating in general, the authors made sure to clarify this was the first published formal report.

Newspaper articles, however, took the notion of a "first formal report" and distorted it beyond reality to assert that this was the first time that a trans woman had ever breastfed, some cases even going so far as to suggest that trans women had never lactated prior to this moment. The UK's *Daily Mail* was one of the first newspapers to report the story, with the headline "Transgender Woman Becomes First in the World to Breastfeed for Six Weeks after DIY Hormone Therapy and Breast Pumping."[31] Other newspapers followed suit with similarly distorted titles: "Transgender Woman Becomes First in World to Breastfeed Baby" from London's *Evening Standard,*[32] "In First, Transgender Woman Able to Breastfeed" from India's English-language *Deccan Chronicle,*[33] and "Transgender Woman Becomes First to Breastfeed Baby" in the *New York Post.*[34]

It is important to note that most news articles on the subject were presented in a neutral or even positive light, centering the (unidentified) thirty-year-old trans woman as a woman, referring to her with correct pronouns, and describing her experience as that of a mother wanting to care for her child. Thus it might be tempting to critique the news headlines and stories on the grounds of bad journalism in the mode of inaccuracy rather than transphobia. However, several elements conspire in this context to produce curiotization, even as they frame a trans woman breastfeeding as an advancement or progress.

First, the headlines present the preservative care of a trans woman breastfeeding as if it emerged ex nihilo through some novel development in medical technologies. While the *New York Times* featured the more nuanced headline "Transgender Woman Breast-Feeds Baby after Hospital Induces Lactation," it still frames this as a novel or futuristic moment, arguing, "If confirmed in wider studies, the regimen could represent a next major stage in transgender parenthood."[35] The articles largely do not include conversations or comments from trans women beyond the published essay, which has a trans woman coauthor but does not discuss trans women beyond the specific case.

If journalists had spoken with more trans women, they may have learned that trans women have already breastfed with and without the supervision of doctors and that lactation in trans women, while not common, is certainly not an unprecedented or even novel event. By sensationalizing the publication about trans women breastfeeding as its first novel occurrence, as if it were a sudden feat of future tech, the authors displace trans women's bodies and their capabilities from trans women as an embodied community of knowers. While this distortion may rouse the curiosity of non-trans readers who do not know any better, the journals are using their narrative frame of trans progress to court public curiosity by paving over knowledge and experiences shared among trans women that have not yet entered mass media print.

The journalist narrative of a trans woman breastfeeding as a novel medical development also curiotizes trans women's bodies as a product of futuristic science. In an article on breastfeeding as a trans woman, written for Seattle's *The Stranger* in June 2017, Dana Fried commented on the framing of trans women's breasts as unreal or artifice, writing:

> There's a weird but surprisingly common notion that trans women's breasts aren't "real." When I told people about my plan to breastfeed, the most common

reaction from both laypeople and medical professionals was "Wait, you can do that?" But had I not mammary glands? If you filled me with prolactin, would I not leak?[36]

Fried rightly points out that, in addition to the objectification of trans women's bodies discussed by Serano, our bodies are also often reduced to hypermedicalized and artificialized curios. Instead of acknowledging the continuum of hormones shared across men's, women's, and nonbinary bodies, as well as the shared hormonal situation across cis and trans bodies, the journalists choose to instead alienate trans women's bodies as especially constructed and futuristic. Like the constructed binary between men and women, "cis" and "trans" exists as more of a continuum than any barriered split, but this actuality is occluded through contemporary mass media curiotization. This is the displacement through which public curiosity about trans women breastfeeding is produced.

The displacement of trans experience in the name of curiotization is also carried out in mass culture through the specularization of history encouraged by the "transgender tipping point" narrative. The declaration of the mid-2010s as a transgender tipping point fixates the consideration of trans history upon the present as a moment of progress while equating trans progress with mass cultural visibility. This framework also dismisses other moments in trans history, including earlier moments of trans visibility in mass culture, as mere stages along the path to the present.

If we consider other moments of mass culture trans curiotization, including the cultural moment that gave rise to "Walk on the Wild Side" in the '70s and the attention given to Christine Jorgensen as a famous transsexual in the '50s, it is important to consider how these moments of visibility phase in and out. As Riley Snorton argues, these moments and their history are also specularized based on whiteness, with black trans people forced into the underside of representation to concretize white trans figures such as Jorgensen.[37] Given these moments of attention, one might worry that the "tipping" implied in the transgender tipping point is but a seesaw, arcing between erasure and skewed mass cultural visibility, while distorting prior histories for the sake of fascination and a sense of curious forward movement. Given the continued failure of schools to educate students about trans lives and trans history, it thus may be unsurprising if mass cultural trans awareness turns out to involve a goldfish memory optics in which trans subjects are intensified, distorted, and forgotten according to non-trans whims.

Considering the politics of curiosity also helps explain why anti-curiotizing yet curious people who write on trans subjects may benefit greatly from having particular trans friends whom they care about (albeit not in a reductive or creepy way), as well as having a more nuanced and informed sense of trans histories and cultures. This can make it easier for trans subjects to escape from glass cabinets and exist in living, breathing worlds.

A "World-Historical" Epilogue

To further specify what I mean by this, I am interested in not only the expansion of "trans" in media and scholarship to include a lived and historical sense but also an acknowledgment of "trans" as "world-historical." In one sense I do very much want to evoke G. W. F. Hegel here, but only in a slightly cheeky, noncommittal, and nongrandiose way. The historical contingency and complex history of "trans" across invertedness, transvestism, transsexuality, transgenderism, and now transness have often been evoked to critique or trivialize trans identity and throw into suspicion its mark upon the world.[38] However, I want to suggest that this history also signals the concrete impact "trans" has had on world history, including contemporary history.

In "Tracing this Body: Transsexuality, Pharmaceuticals, and Capitalism," Michelle O'Brien situates the ability of trans people to access medicine within larger contexts of historical transnational capitalism including pharmaceutical companies, trade agreements, and the U.S. global War on Drugs. Whereas Hausman might have used these conditions to emphasize the contingency or problematic constructedness of transsexuality, O'Brien instead takes a cyborg material feminist turn linking her complicity with biomedicine and transnational capitalism to the potential for resisting these systems. O'Brien writes:

> We are all in the midst of structures of tremendous violence, oppression, and exploitation. There is no easy escape or pure distance from them. Our ability to resist, in this world, at this time, is deeply inseparable from our ongoing connection to these very systems. But resist we do. Every day, in so many ways, we are struggling towards a new world of liberation, healing, and respect.[39]

O'Brien thus takes up the cyborg's mantle of subversion through impure enmeshment within world material flows.

While I am sympathetic to O'Brien's material reclamation of transsexuality as potential subversion within problematic world/historical material flows, which of course harkens back to '90s trans studies and the influence of not only Donna Haraway but also Gloria Anzaldúa, Sandy Stone, and Susan Stryker upon its theoretical architecture, I also want to reverse-engineer O'Brien's empowering lament into a wider enmeshment of "trans" with world history.

Contrary to what I referred to as the goldfish memory optics offered by the transgender tipping point, wherein "trans" has suddenly achieved its moment seemingly ex nihilo, and trans people spring up like mushrooms without engagement with each other, I think the complicated material pathways emphasized by O'Brien point toward a larger investment of material history within "trans," as well as a larger investment of "trans" within material history. Like it or not, "trans" has made its mark, working in tension (or dare I say a historical dialectic) with other endocrinological developments and changes in sex such as the pharmaceutical development of hormone supplements and birth control as well as shifts in the landscape of culture and production, including the ongoing impact of feminist movements. If the curiotization of transsexuality and other trans identities consists of removing "trans" from its history and place, then a key move toward de-curiotizing might be to restore the place of "trans" and its rich and varied lived experiences within the histories of worlds.

Take, again, "Walk on the Wild Side." While the optics of the curio might turn its trans characters into decontextualized objects of fascination, the song refers to people like Candy Darling and Holly Woodlawn, who had rich inner and outer lives, as well as places within history (although I wish to caution that their worlds are not reducible to a mere "transness"). Many listeners may remain within a curiotizing orbit with Reed's song, but the lives and histories to which "Walk on the Wild Side" points may also lead more diligent listeners to their own de-curiotizing process by inspiring an interest in context and connection. This not only adds a richer topography to the song but also helps expose broader curiotizing moves such as the transgender tipping point's insistence upon the sudden "arrival" of "trans."

What I am suggesting here is not a haphazard ahistorical imposition of "trans" across different histories and cultures à la Leslie Feinberg's 1996

204 Amy Marvin

Transgender Warriors: Making History from Joan of Arc to Dennis Rodman,[40] but instead a more grounded reading of the plural, idiosyncratic, and changing identities that we may (rightly or wrongly) subsume under "trans" into specific historical pathways. This—combined with the other core, modest point found in much of trans studies that a focus on lived experience is crucial—strikes me as a useful start toward curiosity beyond the curio.

Notes

1. Katie Steinmetz, "The Transgender Tipping Point," *Time,* May 2014.
2. Buzz Bissinger, "Call Me Caitlyn," *Vanity Fair,* July 2015.
3. Talia Bettcher, "Evil Deceivers and Make-Believers: On Transphobic Violence and the Politics of Illusion," *Hypatia* 22, no. 3, 2017: 50.
4. Viviane Namaste, *Sex Change, Social Change: Reflections on Identity, Institutions, and Imperialism* (Toronto: Women's Press, 2005), 277–78.
5. See Viviane Namaste, "Undoing Theory: The 'Transgender Question' and the Epistemic Violence of Anglo-American Feminist Theory," *Hypatia* 24, no. 3 (2009): 11–32; Riley Snorton and Jin Haritaworn, "Trans Necropolitics: A Transnational Reflection on Violence, Death, and the Trans of Color Afterlife," in *Transgender Studies Reader 2,* ed. Susan Stryker and Aren Aizura (New York: Routledge, 2013), 66–76.
6. Maggie Astor, "Violence against Transgender People Is on the Rise, Advocates Say," *New York Times,* November 9, 2017.
7. Dan Irving, "Normalized Transgressions: Legitimizing the Transsexual Body as Productive," in Stryker and Aizura, *Transgender Studies Reader 2,* 16.
8. Jonathan Shorman and Hunter Woodall, "Kansas GOP Votes to 'Oppose All Efforts to Validate Transgender Identity,'" *Wichita Eagle,* February 18, 2018.
9. Edward Said, *Orientalism* (London: Routledge and Kegan Paul, 1978).
10. Elena Rose, "On Cartography and Dissection," *Taking Steps* (blog), September 9, 2006, http://takingsteps.blogspot.com/2006/09/on-cartography-and-dissection.html.
11. Simon Ruchti, "Corpse-Less: A Battle with Abjection," in *The Anatomy of Body Worlds: Critical Essays on the Plastinated Cadavers of Gunther von Hagens,* ed. T. Christine Jeperson, Alicita Rodriguez, and Joseph Starr (Jefferson, N.C.: McFarland, 2009), 189–201.
12. Body Worlds, "Philosophy," https://bodyworlds.com/about/philosophy/.
13. Perry Zurn, "Curiosity: An Affect of Resistance," presentation given at the philoSOPHIA Conference, Boca Raton, Florida, April 1, 2017.
14. Quoted in Jeremy King, "Looking Back: Walt Disney's Epcot Center, We've Just Begun to Dream (June 21, 1981)," *Tampa Bay Times,* January 12, 2018.

15. DIS, "Epcot-Future World," Werner Technologies (n.d.), https://www.wdwin fo.com/wdwinfo/guides/epcot/ep-futureworld.htm.

16. Alan Menken and Howard Ashman, vocalists, "Part of Your World," by Howard Ashman, recorded October 1989, track 6 on *The Little Mermaid: An Original Walt Disney Records Soundtrack,* Walt Disney.

17. Julia Serano, *Whipping Girl: A Transsexual Woman on Sexism and the Scapegoating of Femininity* (Emeryville, Calif.: Seal Press, 2007), 62.

18. Serano, 195–96.

19. Serano, 187.

20. Serano, 56–57.

21. Bernice Hausman, *Changing Sex: Transsexualism, Technology, and the Idea of Gender* (Durham, N.C.: Duke University Press, 1995), vii.

22. Viviane Namaste, *Invisible Lives: The Erasure of Transsexual and Transgendered People* (Chicago: University of Chicago Press, 2000), 3.

23. Jamison Green, "Look! No, Don't! The Visibility Dilemma for Transsexual Men," in *The Transgender Studies Reader*, ed. Susan Stryker and Stephen Whittle (New York: Routledge, 2006), 500.

24. Lou Reed, "Walk on the Wild Side," recorded August 1972, track 5 on *Transformer,* RCA Records.

25. Edward Helmore, "Lou Reed's Friends Dismiss Claim That Walk on the Wild Side is Transphobic," *Guardian,* May 20, 2017.

26. María Lugones, "Playfulness, 'World'-Travelling, and Loving Perception," in *Pilgrimages/Peregrinajes: Theorizing Coalition Against Multiple Oppressions* (Lanham, Md.: Rowman and Littlefield, 2003), 9–10.

27. Lugones, 6.

28. Lugones, 8.

29. Marilyn Frye, *The Politics of Reality: Essays in Feminist Theory* (Trumansburg, N.Y.: Crossing Press, 1983), 73–75.

30. Tamar Reisman and Zil Goldstein, "Case Report: Induced Lactation in a Transgender Woman," *Transgender Health* 3, no. 1 (2018): 25.

31. Mia De Graaf, "Transgender Woman Becomes First in the World to Breastfeed for Six Weeks After DIY Hormone Therapy and Breast Pumping," *Daily Mail,* February 13, 2018.

32. Patrick Grafton-Green, "Transgender Woman Becomes First in World to Breastfeed Baby," *Evening Standard,* February 14, 2018.

33. Anonymous, "In First, Transgender Woman Able to Breastfeed," *Deccan Chronicle,* February 14, 2018.

34. Lauren Tousignant, "Transgender Woman Becomes First to Breastfeed Baby," *New York Post,* February 14, 2018.

35. Ceylan Yeginsu, "Transgender Woman Breast-Feeds Baby after Hospital Induces Lactation," *New York Times,* February 15, 2018.

36. Dana Fried, "My First Time Breastfeeding My Daughter," *Stranger,* June 21, 2017.

37. Riley Snorton, *Black on Both Sides: A Racial History of Trans Identity* (Minneapolis: University of Minnesota Press, 2017), 174.

38. Hausman, *Changing Sex.*

39. Michelle O'Brien, "Tracing This Body: Transsexuality, Pharmaceuticals, and Capitalism," in Stryker and Aizura, *Transgender Studies Reader 2,* 64.

40. Leslie Feinberg, *Transgender Warriors: Making History from Joan of Arc to Dennis Rodman* (Boston: Beacon Press, 1996).

PART IV

Deconstructing the Status Quo

12

Peeping and Transgression

Curiosity and Collecting in English Literature

Barbara M. Benedict

"'Curiouser and curiouser!' cried Alice" in Wonderland as she encounters the grinning Cheshire cat, the baby-turned-pig, human playing cards, and her own telescoping neck that wriggles, serpentlike, into the trees.[1] These phenomena appear "curious" because they transgress nature by muddling categories: a cat that grins is both human and feline; a human baby turned porcine and a neck that becomes a snake are simultaneously two sorts of creature. At the same time, Alice is herself curious, repeatedly asking questions and investigating rabbit holes, hidden gardens, and strange foodstuffs. Lewis Carroll's *Alice in Wonderland* exemplifies the double nature of curiosity itself. As a subjective quality, it can denote inquiry, inquisitiveness, oddity, and strangeness: the scientist, the seeker, the detective, the peeper, and the pryer. It can be admirable or reprehensible: Pandora and Peeping Tom, Psyche and Sherlock Holmes, Faust and Frankenstein, Eve and Oedipus. As an aspect of strange things, it can signal rarity or revulsion. Curiosity is both the human passion for knowledge and the transgressive aspect of phenomena that provoke inquiry. Thus it has always provided rich fodder for writers and thinkers, and never more so than at the period when inquiry became a discipline all its own in the Age of Science and the Enlightenment: the mid-seventeenth to the early nineteenth centuries.

This essay surveys literature and culture from the late Renaissance to the twentieth century to trace the development of both the idea and the objects of curiosity. Throughout more than three hundred years, curiosity retains the moral and phenomenological ambiguity that inheres in ideas, people, and objects that stand outside the norm. As it shifts from denoting a quality of things to a trait of people, it weaves between drawing derision for

210 Barbara M. Benedict

perversity and prompting praise for discovery. The etymology of the word
helps to explain its double meaning. Originally, "curiosity" derived from
"*cura,*" the Medieval Latin name for "care." In the Middle Ages and into
the seventeenth century, the term denoted skillfulness, careful workman-
ship, and elaborate artistry, exemplified by the stone and wooden sculptures
artists carved for the church. These decorations possessed the same fastidi-
ous detail on the parts unseen by viewers as on the parts open to public view.
Curiosity consequently came to mean objects that exhibited such nicety and
that required attention both to execute and to observe.

However, later in the seventeenth century, two important events changed
the meaning and the connotations of both word and idea. The first was the
secular curiosity cabinet, or *Wunderkammern.* These could constitute display cabinets stacked with rarities of art or nature—carefully carved jewels,
miniature paintings, or elaborate clocks and instruments—or they could
be whole rooms festooned with exotic specimens from around the globe:
crocodiles, unicorn horns, shells, branches, rocks, Chinese shoes, relics, and
remains. These early museums were intended to induce both wonder—the
awestruck marveling at strangeness—and curiosity: the empirical investigation of phenomena.[2] Both natural and artful curiosities exhibited the kind of
skillful artistry that the term "curiosity" originally denoted, be this the skill
of the artisan himself or the skill of God in changing natural forms to make
things appear to be what they were not.

Early churches had displays of curiosities and fine ritual items to stimu-
late reverence in the faithful. These displays were mediated by the church
and only exhibited on rare occasions. In contrast, secular displays of objects
appeared in the private abodes of princes and elite gentry to exhibit their
wealth and taste, the power of the state or the individual, not the power of
God or the church. These men practiced what was termed "the habit of
curiosity"—that is, collecting—and did so for their own satisfaction. In this
way both displays and collectors began to seem irreligious, transgressive,
threatening. This is especially true because collecting shifted from being
an elite activity to a highly popular, middle-class, even working-class, recre-
ation. Small and huge accumulations of everything from pebbles to paintings began to appear everywhere in Britain, and societies of connoisseurs
and virtuosi sprang up, flooding the land with commodities, collectibles,
and material objects, and appropriating traditional relationships and social
valuations.

Mini-museums also appeared in universities, theaters of anatomy, and the repositories of scientific societies, and therein lies both the second change and the reason that curiosity garnered a pejorative implication as prurient, foolish, and self-indulgent. This change was the birth of science. In 1660 the new king Charles II established Britain's first scientific institution: the Royal Society for the Advancement of Learning. This society threw out earlier Aristotelian, inductive, simplifying systems of classification and threw itself into a new method of investigation of nature: empirical and repeated experimentation—that is, figuring out answers to age-old questions by touch, taste, sight, smell, and sound, and reflection upon them. A host of elite and middle-class gentleman dilettantes, clerics, explorers, travelers, and physicians rushed to join the new enterprise, all curious about questions that once the church alone had had the authority to answer: the nature of species; the formation of clouds; the processes of human reproduction; the components of earth, air, and fire; the movement of the planets—indeed, any of the mysteries that God had wisely hidden and that the Bible had warned man not to pry into. These men called themselves "natural philosophers," dedicated to the establishment of a comprehensive empirical "philosophy" or systematic map of nature itself.

Their curious investigations ranged from the sublime to the ridiculous, and contemporary writers had a hard time telling one from the other. The experiments that Robert Boyle performed, for example, included transfusing the blood of dogs, and while we recognize the enormous value of transfusion, to contemporary satirists it appeared pointless, cruel, and, worse, a violation of God's natural order. One such satirist, the playwright Thomas Shadwell, depicted Boyle, thinly veiled as the character Sir Nicholas Gimcrack (i.e., Toy or Plaything), claiming he has transfused the blood of a sheep into a man and harvested his wool for profit. Sir Nicholas is, as it turns out, lying and made no profit because, he explains loftily, he is a speculative or theoretical scientist and so never does anything "of use: Knowledge is my ultimate end."[3] No one questioned Isaac Newton's discoveries of gravity and in optics; indeed, he became president of the Royal Society in 1703. But when Robert Hooke, the first keeper of the Royal Society's repository of specimens, fell in love with the fashionable new scientific instrument, the microscope, and enthusiastically compiled a huge volume of finely etched drawings of things he had looked at through the device, some contemporaries ridiculed him for choosing to honor worthless things: a pencil tip, his own urine, a fly's eye, a flea. The satirist Samuel Butler, for example, mocked him in *The Elephant in the Moon* (c. 1676) by describing enthusiastic scientists looking excitedly at the moon through a telescope to see armies swarming on its surface and riding a huge elephant, only to discover that a mouse had been trapped in the telescopic tube, become bloated and putrid (hence the elephant), and so attracted gnats (hence the armies). Later in the century, the poet Peter Pindar depicted the then-president of the Royal Society, Sir Joseph Banks, as ridiculously empirical. Having boiled a flea and discovered that it turned pink, he concluded that fleas are really a sort of miniscule lobster.

To contemporary writers, topics of curious inquiry—antiquities, physical nature, the occult, sex—could reflect investigators' piety or skepticism, naïveté or impertinence. When the cleric and Royal Society member Joseph Glanville investigated, with strict, empirical methods, a vast volume of reports of witches, poltergeists, and ghosts, he determined that most were certainly true because he could hear knocking and booing and smell supernaturally unpleasant smells. While this proved his belief in the supernatural, it also prompted more satire of scientists' credulity and obsessiveness, and of empiricism's limitations. Jonathan Swift in *Gulliver's Travels* (1726), for example, devotes a quarter of the book to satirizing the Royal Society, disguised transparently as the Floating Island of Laputa, hovering way above the heads of mere mortals below. These scientists have one eye cast up to view the heavens and another turned inward for fetid self-examination, and are so absorbed in speculations that they need servants to bat them with an empty bladder gently on the ears when they ought to listen and on the mouth when they should reply. They are both objectively and subjectively curious.

Moreover, although these early scientists may have seemed silly to contemporaries, they did all deliberately refuse to accept conventional explanations or biblical myths, and thus they presented an autodidactic challenge to ideas society had long accepted. Boyle, indeed, called himself "the Skeptical Chemist," and despite Glanville's attempts to sanitize his empiricism by arguing that his investigations of the supernatural proved the reality of God, accusations of atheism persisted. After all, why would you need to prove God's existence unless you doubted it?

The result of this threat was that, throughout the century, curious men came to mean not men who inquired but rather men who were themselves fit subjects of inquiry: What made them tick? Why were they doing these foolish and irreligious things? What was wrong with them? The answer satirists came up with was that these curious men were, as Freud would say, compensating for a fundamental lack of masculinity. All their fiddling and peeping into sacred mysteries and their pointless accumulation of objects was a masturbatory diversion of sexual energies. They dabbled in natural philosophy because they could not perform naturally. Swift's natural philosophers, for example, stare at the skies while their wives sneak down to the land below for lower matters: sexual gratification.

However, it wasn't just men whose curiosity made them curiosities. In fact, women were even more often indicted for inappropriate prying, and since they were defined by their sex, their curiosity was represented as sexual. A series of "Curious Maid" poems in the 1720s portrayed women attempting to peer into their own genitals to discover what they possess that drives men mad with desire, and caricatures often show men peeping at naked women as curiosities—that is, phenomena stimulating inquiry. At the same time, women were upsetting gender norms by writing novels and periodicals, many of which interrogated unjust social mores, and thus entering the masculine cultural space. This was deemed at the time an impertinent stepping out of their God-given, subordinate roles. Hence, women's Pandora-like curiosity became identified with cultural ambition. One common reaction in eighteenth-century literature was to represent women not as investigators but as subjects of investigation. Since they were aping masculine roles, they were depicted as curious deformed kinds of men, men-but-not-men. Again, curiosity as inquiry mutates into curiosity as monstrosity: seeking to know or do more than God has given you shows an unnatural appetite to transgress natural, social, and moral laws.

The ubiquity of, and ambivalence toward, curiosity and collecting in the eighteenth century as literary topic and method is exemplified by the works of the most renowned contemporary poet, Alexander Pope (1688–1744). Pope lived in an age of fashionable collectors, collecting, and commercialism, and collectibles and many of the scientific enterprises of his time, including antiquarianism, interested him.[4] In his verse he refers to collectors like the antiquarian Thomas Hearne and the Keeper of Records Richard Topham; he addressed his fourth *Epistle* (1731/1735) to the distinguished collector Richard Boyle, third Earl of Burlington; and his early poem "To Mr. Addison, Occasioned by his Dialogues on Medals" (1713) meditates on his sometime friend Joseph Addison's numismatic collection.[5] His own villa contained dozens of

214   Barbara M. Benedict

prints and other collectibles, and late in his life, he succumbed to the lure of collecting *naturalia,* even receiving the gift of a stone from the preeminent collector Sir Hans Sloane, whose vast hoard became the British Museum.[6] Early on, Marjorie Hope Nicholson, among other critics, noted the affinity of Pope's grand enterprise to write a systematic philosophical treatise on ethics with the Royal Society's project.

The ambiguities of empiricism and collecting also concerned contemporary philosophers. The experimental philosophy of the Royal Society was founded on the practices of observation as a conscious, systematic procedure rather than a will-less and involuntary observation that could produce no verifiable, general knowledge. In his chapter "Of Perception" in *An Essay Concerning Human Understanding,* first published in 1689, John Locke argues that perception *"is the first simple idea of reflection,"* for "in bare naked perception, the mind is, for the most part, only passive; and what it perceives, it cannot avoid perceiving."[7] However, *"Perception is only when the mind receives the impression."*[8] Unorganized or uncollected perception keeps the creature in an animalistic state, but discerning, comparing, and compounding lead to knowledge.[9] Thus for Locke and the natural philosophers that followed him, knowledge constituted understanding the relationships between phenomena, and this knowledge could be achieved by systematic observation, sensation, and reason or reflection: by, in short, collecting information—by structuring curiosity—through sensual perception and organizing it by logic and memory.

Pope's four *Epistles to Several Persons* (1731–35), or *Moral Epistles,* embody such an enterprise but also reveal its methodological instability.[10] They constitute a collection of poems discussing wealth and character through portraits of contemporary types to illustrate a system of "practical Morality" that, as Pope asserts, spans "all the Circumstances, Orders, Professions, and Stations of human Life."[11] The poems present Pope's theory of the "ruling passion," a moral system mirroring the scientific enterprise to methodize nature. This attempt to reconcile the unique, individual "type" with the representative class itself reflects conflicting practices of collecting. Whereas Renaissance and seventeenth-century collectors were generally content to gather one, fine example of a natural phenomenon or species—a unicorn [narwhal] horn, a microscope, a rock imprinted with the shape of the crucified Christ, for example—and unique examples of high art, the virtuosi of the seventeenth and eighteenth centuries, like Sir Hans Sloane and Ralph

Thoresby, were moving away from wonder at the unique and toward accumulation: more is better. At the same time, marvelous objects like relics and curiosities still littered their museums.[12]

The rival concepts of collecting reflect conflicting ideas of knowledge. Pope argues in *Epistle I: To Richard Temple, Viscount Cobham* (1730–33; published 1734), that every specimen is worth observing and collecting because each is unique:

> There's some Peculiar in each leaf and grain,
> Some unmark'd fibre, or some varying vein;
> Shall only Man be taken in the gross?
> Grant but as many sorts of Mind as Moss.[13]

At the same time, Pope betrays the neoclassical fondness for types, classifications, categories, identifiable species of mankind. If every tuft of moss is unique, still it belongs with hundreds of others to the general class of moss. It is the poet's privilege to spy out the unique but the scientist's task to find the category. Pope's character sketches attempt both: to find the particular in the general and the general in the particular.[14] Indeed, his theory of the "Ruling Passions" maintains that the secret of reading a man's character lies in discovering his primary motivating vice, the general truth of his character. Although the theory itself was not new, Pope's treatment emphasizes the empirical procedures required to identify each man's ruling passion. As F. W. Bateson observes, "the basis of Pope's satire is *fact*."[15] The "Argument" in *To Cobham* recommends the empirical method of eyewitness observation, balanced by reading books or authorities, in order to gain "the *Knowledge* and *Characters* of *Men*."[16] In order to form "General maxims," observers must note both the common and the unique qualities of individuals. This procedure for classification echoes naturalists' endeavors to differentiate aberrations from species.

Pope persistently represents the reduction of people to commodities and curiosities. In *Epistle to Dr. Arbuthnot* (1731–34, published 1735), he famously portrays the effeminate courtier Lord Hervey, who had joined Pope's enemy Lady Mary Wortley Montague to attack him in print, as Sporus, a "Thing of silk," "a Butterfly," a "Bug with gilded wings, / This painted Child of Dirt that stinks and stings," a "Spaniel," "Puppet," and "Toad."[17] Sporus is a curiosity, transgressing genders, species, and elements, a work both of art and nature,

216 Barbara M. Benedict

a mammal, amphibian, and insect, an object and a person: "Amphibious Thing!" and "vile Antithesis."[18] He,

> Half Froth, half Venom, spits himself abroad,
> In Puns, or Politicks, or Tales, or Lyes,
> Or Spite, or Smut, or Rymes, or Blasphemies.[19]

The fragmentation of this litany of vicious emissions represents the multiple categories the ambiguous, amphibious Sporus spans: the rhetoric, like the description, employs conventions of naturalistic description to depict a creature made of categorical transgressions.

The ironic opposition of luxurious things to intellectual or spiritual values appears everywhere in Pope's verse, but perhaps most notably in the mock-epic *The Rape of the Lock* (1714). Here the protagonist Belinda sits at a dressing table bearing the spoils of the world, which her maidservant "culls with curious toil":[20]

> This Casket *India*'s glowing Gems unlocks,
> And all *Arabia* breathes from yonder Box.
> The Tortoise here and Elephant unite,
> Transform'd to *Combs,* the speckled and the white.[21]

Belinda's dressing table, beautiful as it (and she) is, becomes a curiosity cabinet of commodities devoted to her adornment. The jewels, perfumes, and exotic animals of the world are reduced to adornments and collectibles celebrating the superficial and the physical self. Collecting as method and subject thus enables Pope to explore the valorization of materiality over morality, consumption over contemplation, and accumulation over propriety as Britain moved into the modern age. In a curious coincidence, Pope was deformed from a childhood accident, small, thin, and hunch-backed, and a Catholic in a Protestant land. Hostile caricaturists often depicted him as an ape. Once again, the curious man became the curiosity.

Although Pope incorporates the inquiry, collecting, and objects in his poetry, the genre that exploits curiosity most thoroughly is the novel. As the name indicates, novels were from the start a genre dedicated to the new. Borrowing their format from early autobiographies, biographies, classical epics, travel tales, and picaresque fiction, eighteenth-century novels trot from episode to episode, accumulating a collection of adventures. Such genres exploit readers' curiosity about far-off lands and illicit or strange experiences, ostensibly redeemed from the charge of being pure entertainment by the ubiquitous authorial insistence that readers will apply moral lessons from the texts—protagonists' errors or achievements—to their own lives.

Novels typically exploit curiosity in two ways: they present oddities, or curiosities, to elicit surprise, humor, or horror, and also a problem or question that engages the reader's curiosity, and which the plot will resolve. The reader's curiosity thus remains key to the genre's function and effectiveness by prompting rethinking. Analyzing Charles Dickens's *The Old Curiosity Shop*, discussed below, Sarah Winter argues that "curiosity affords the impetus for the kind of questioning that readers . . . are taught to engage in as a means of overcoming habitual prejudices, including those they have acquired at school."[22] Just as a visitor to a curiosity cabinet must balance wondering at the uniqueness of each specimen and finding similarities or links between them, readers must hunt down plot clues, investigate characters' motives, and speculate on plot twists and endings in order to engage in the fiction. Asking why readers read novels through, rather than skipping to the end, the literary theorist Peter Brooks argues that reading is a process of recognizing repetitions in plot, theme, and imagery; these draw readers to desire their resolution in an ending that pulls them together.[23] Reading novels thus seems to work similarly to the thoughts created by brain networks (See Bassett, this volume): readers identify "facts," or pieces of information—be these a character's motivation, an event, or a description—that they seek to link with other pieces of information in the book. Readers thus forge networks of connections to explain the plot and further connect these to their own lives, "realizing" the fiction and bringing it to life.

Different subgenres of the novel portray and elicit curiosity differently. Early travel fiction, like Aphra Behn's hybrid *Oroonoko, or the Royal Slave* (1688), offers readers exotic scenes, romance, and satire, stimulating curiosity about foreignness, prohibited sexuality, and contemporary mores, all somewhat derogated subjects of inquiry in a turbulent society. Early eighteenth-century novels exploit readers' curiosity about contemporary issues. Daniel Defoe's *Robinson Crusoe* (1719) asks how a man could survive entirely alone on an island, and portrays Robinson experimenting with natural resources to build his own little kingdom. *Moll Flanders* (1722), Defoe's depiction of the underworld of London, supplies readers with a kind of how-to handbook

218   Barbara M. Benedict

to survive London's thieves, prostitutes, and poverty, while *A Journal of the Plague Year* (1722) investigates the causes of and responses to the bubonic plague in Restoration London. Later so-called it-narratives recounting the adventures of objects, like an atom or a coin, fuse curious objects and objects' curiosity to make humanoid things agents of social investigation. These and other eighteenth-century novels, like such early periodicals as *The Athenian Mercury* (1691–97), which was dedicated to answering readers' questions, both evoke and profit from readers' curiosity.

By the last decades of the eighteenth century, however, a postempirical wave of disillusion turned novelists away from the systematic investigation of the human species to a new thrill in the mysterious, irrational, and violent: areas derided by Enlightenment reason. Gothic novels—precursors of detective and mystery fiction—present the physical world as embedded in a supernatural world, where empiricism is transformed into the impalpable: inexplicable sounds, smells, sights, and touches, and formless feelings of dread besiege the heroine in a twilight world where nothing seems clear. Throughout, the heroine questions and investigates, opening doors to dark chambers and harrowing down ominous tunnels—but with frustratingly few and usually misleading results. The heroine of Ann Radcliffe's *The Mysteries of Udolpho* (1794), for example, must constantly test her reasoning against her sensory impressions. She thinks she sees and hears supernatural forces but she resists superstition. Her curiosity is dangerous, since it leads her into hazards; inadequate, because it does not provide answers; and yet redeeming, because it eventually leads her to the truth, an escape from tyranny and the recovery of her inheritance.

Romantic fictions, often ironically, characteristically depict the empirical urge for inquiry as a hazardous invasion of the natural, or the unnatural, social order. William Godwin illustrates the dangers of curiosity in *Things as They Are; or, The Adventures of Caleb Williams* (1796), in which the eponymous protagonist, a servant, possessed by all-consuming curiosity, discovers his master is a murderer. While his investigations reveal the injustices in the institutions of law and punishment in a class-bound society, his curiosity leads to terrible suffering, his own madness, and his master's death. By dramatizing the curious man's adventures against a wide backdrop of British life, Godwin suggests that asking questions can lead to the exposure of corruption and to political reform (See also Zurn, this volume). Mary Shelley's *Frankenstein* (1818) notably casts Dr. Victor Frankenstein's unnatural creation of a being from a collection of dead human parts as the arrogant result of a transgressive, scientific curiosity. This contrasts with the Creature's original innocent investigation of nature in the process of learning, before humans' rejection turns him murderous.

During the Victorian period, attitudes toward curiosity in literature tend to split sharply along the lines of gender. When curiosity appears as expansive inquiry, whether philosophical or geographical, it is practiced by men and generally wins praise and success—although, as Charles Darwin's *The Origin of Species* (1859) shows, it could easily appear transgressive. Indeed, some texts appear aimed at critiquing the expansionist urge. In Rudyard Kipling's *The Man Who Would Be King* (1888), for example, the two ambitious protagonists embark on adventurous travel purely for personal gain: the titular one ends up dead, and his loyal friend horribly crippled. When curiosity appears as social or personal inquiry, it appears in female characters and seems more proximate to passion than intellectual investigation. In Charles Dickens's *David Copperfield* (1849–50), for example, Miss Rosa Dartle unnervingly keeps interrogating David by questioning his every statement and concludes with, "I only ask for information";[24] "I ask because I always want to be informed, when I am ignorant;"[25] "I am not suspicious. I only ask a question. I don't state any opinion."[26] Suspicion attaches to questions that seem not to have a clear social purpose: "I only ask because I want to know" hints at a hidden motivation (See also Lewis, this volume). In Dickens's novel, the effect of this barrage of questions preceding the unconvincing denial of any ulterior motive other than "pure" curiosity is to make Miss Dartle's curiosity seem a subtle campaign to make David appear a fool. Miss Dartle, notably, bears a deep scar on her lip: once again, the disfiguring trait of female questioning appears as physical deformity.

Perhaps the most obvious example of the disruptive effect of female curiosity appears in the first textual example in this essay, Lewis Carroll's *Alice's Adventures in Wonderland* (1865), the most prominent but not the first book to harness children's natural curiosity. Historically, children's curiosity was often unwelcome; even today, such figures as Harriet the Spy reflect adult distrust of prying children (See also Engel, this volume). Alice exhibits two kinds of curiosity, both suspect: an irrepressible appetite and a learned speculation. As Nina Auerbach explains, "The pun on 'curious' defines Alice's fluctuating personality. Her eagerness to know and to be right, her compulsive recitation of her lessons . . . she is both the croquet game without rules

220 Barbara M. Benedict

and its violent arbiter."[27] Whereas Auerbach traces these impulses to the Victorian idea of girls as swinging between "extremes of original innocence and original sin," they also echo earlier categorizations of and ambivalence toward curiosity.[28] At the start of the book, Alice jumps down the rabbit hole after the white rabbit, "burning with curiosity."[29] Although the jump may seem ominous, perhaps a warning to overly curious children, Alice's passion for finding things out enfranchises her, enabling her to escape the lies and mystifications of Victorian rule-bound society. Some of her questions in fact mimic those of early scientists and nineteenth-century explorers. She asks, "I wonder how many miles I have fallen by this time?" and, estimating she must be near the earth's center, she attempts to calculate by navigational rule: "Let me see: that would be four thousand miles down, I think. . . . But then I wonder what Latitude or Longitude I've got to? . . . Is this New Zealand or Australia?"[30] In turn, by questioning the creatures—wondering why the Mouse's tale is sad, demanding the Caterpillar's identity, and so forth— she shakes the pieties of the self-important creatures around her. Likewise, by dismissively—or pretentiously—mouthing the questions legitimized by her schooling, she undermines the authority of masculinized inquiry.

Wonderland appears to Alice mad because its codes differ from those of Victorian England. In this way it resembles the exotic lands England had colonized, with unfamiliar times, with or without tea, games, words, and social codes. Carroll peoples Wonderland itself with curious creatures who unwittingly parody English types, suggesting colonialist satire of natives' imitation of Europeans, like Joseph Conrad's "improved specimen": the fireman trained to care for the ship's boiler, who resembles "a dog in a parody of breeches and a feather hat, walking on his hind legs" in *Heart of Darkness*.[31] The rabbit with a watch, white gloves, and a waistcoat; the child-turned-pig; the mock-turtle; the cat with a grin, and the grin that hangs alone in the air; talking animals; cards behaving like people (as in Pope's *Rape of the Lock*); and more are ontological transgressions, creatures and things that behave outside their categories. Auerbach interprets all these creatures, even "Fury" personified as a dog, as aspects of Alice's own personality; indeed, as the Cheshire Cat remarks, she is as mad as all of them.[32] Often Alice's "curiosity seems to lead her nowhere," so that "Alice's curiosity is . . . an act of insanity."[33] Alice and, indeed, the whole book, thus dramatize the chaotic potential of curiosity to question and denaturalize custom, mores, and nature itself. Importantly, this aspect pertains to the most aggressive deployment of curiosity of the period: imperial expansion. Daniel Bivona reads *Alice* as a prototype of the imperialist colonial, who attempts to compel Wonderland's creatures to obey the rules she knows.[34]

In contrast to Carroll's children's literature, Anthony Trollope's novel *Can You Forgive Her?* (1864–65) exploits the audience's curiosity by its suggestion that the sins of the titular "her," which are probably sexual, given the specificity of gender, lie within. This plot yokes the reader's curiosity to the aberrant, "curious" behavior of the protagonist, who jilts an ideal suitor for a ne'er-do-well, but is forgiven and finally weds the "right" man. Readers are invited to query their own moral standards by forgiving the heroine, or not. Trollope's novel alludes to a tradition of plays, both comic and tragic, which center on the question of how to judge the moral conduct of the heroine. By shrinking curiosity to specific questions about social mores, Trollope preserves the Victorian ethic of sexual repression and the domestic control of women. This comes to mark the melodramatic fiction of the late Victorian period, in which women's sexual appetite again appears as a transgressive curiosity that destroys them.

Other Victorian novels use the meaning of curiosity as collecting to anatomize the contemporary confusion of things and people, none more so than Charles Dickens's *The Old Curiosity Shop* (1840–41).[35] The book opens in a murky junk shop, crammed with useless, broken, or obsolete items, the debris of a chaotic and materialistic society:

> The place through which he made his way at leisure was one of those receptacles for old and curious things which seem to . . . hide their treasures from the public eye in jealousy and distrust. There were suits of mail standing like ghosts in armour, here and there; fantastic carvings brought from monkish cloisters; rusty weapons of various kinds; distorted figures in china, and wood, and iron, and ivory; tapestry, and strange furniture that might have been designed in dreams.[36]

The dustiness and inutility of the dreary contents of this curiosity cabinet serve to indict both England's murky, superstitious, and bellicose past, and the contemporary practice of discarding or ignoring it. Moreover, like the collections mocked in the previous two centuries, this collection exhibits mere accumulation rather than an aesthetic or scientific system. James Buzard remarks that this description is "an *inefficient* inventory" that "[lumps] possibly distinguishable items together" instead of demarcating them to "proliferate[] meaning."[37] The shop is tended by human versions of the contents. Grandfather Trent, the aged and gambling-addicted owner, is a reiteration of the antiquarian: "The haggard aspect: of the little old man was wonderfully suited to the place; he might have groped among old churches, and tombs, and deserted houses, and gathered all the spoils with his own hands. There was nothing in the whole collection but was in keeping with himself; nothing that looked older or more worn than he."[38] He is a collector—a curious man—turned into a curiosity amid "a universe of dead things" that symbolizes England's heartless capitalistic system, in which people are treated as objects and objects act maliciously.[39]

Many of the characters in the story appear as objects or quasihuman oddities. Little Nell Trent, the novel's doll-like heroine; waxworks, transformations of the human body into inert material; giants, who pull the body past its natural limits. However, it is the monstrous landlord Quilp who best epitomizes a human curiosity. A dwarf so hideous he scarcely appears human, he explodes unpredictably in malice or anger, and terrifies merely by his appearance:

> An elderly man of remarkably hard features and forbidding aspect, and so low in stature as to be quite a dwarf, though his head and face were large enough for the body of a giant. His black eyes were restless, sly, and cunning; his mouth and chin, bristly with the stubble of a coarse hard beard; and his complexion was one of that kind which never looks clean or wholesome. But what added most to the grotesque expression of his face, was a ghastly smile, which, appearing to have no connection with any mirthful or complacent feeling, constantly revealed the few, discoloured fangs that were yet scattered in his mouth, and gave him the aspect of a panting dog.[40]

His ludicrous dress—"a large, high-crowned hat," and dirty linen—and his "frowzy fringe" of hair suggest a werewolfish creature, dressed as a man in order to infiltrate society for nefarious ends.[41] His very name, which incorporates the French word for "who," *qui,* hints at his outlandish and uncategorizable nature, as do his habits. He eats not only his dinner but also the plate that holds it, and regards his wife with cannibalistic relish: "'Oh you nice creature!' [he said], smacking his lips as if . . . she were actually a sweetmeat."[42] Quilp's transgressiveness includes "crossing geographical and ideological boundaries" by trading on the black market as well as the official economy and "domesticating his counting house," thus eroding gender boundaries.[43] His dwarfish stature literally embodies not only his stunted morality but also his species marginality. Like the small-minded Lilliputians in Swift's *Gulliver's Travels*, he is a reductio ad absurdum of humanity, and thus both human and not.

The novelist Vladimir Nabokov remarked that curiosity is the purest form of insubordination. Thus, the urge to disobey rules, to push throughout boundaries, to transcend or fracture categories, marks curious people and things in British cultural and literary history. True, the identification of curious things, which elude categories, and curious people, who question established truths, gained momentum and cultural prominence in the Enlightenment from the seventeenth-century birth of science and the cheap printing press. Nevertheless, the wash-over between strange objects and pushy people spreads throughout British literature to the Victorian period—and beyond. Both the unclassifiable phenomena in curiosity cabinets and the inquiring people who insist on asking questions overstep boundaries, and by so doing hold both the promise of freedom and the threat of danger. Whether by satirizing or questioning God's existence, or the social order; by valuing foreign, "outlandish" lands and customs; by intruding into closed spheres, private, male, or elite; by experiments that confuse the useless and the useful, the beautiful and the ugly; by prurient scopophilia in place of useful work; or by the imperial appropriation of other countries and bodies, exercises of curiosity challenge and unsettle conventional hierarchies of value. Although the birth of science and the cheap printing press brought curiosity into the center of culture in the Enlightenment, subsequent British literary history shows that all genres in some way elicit or contain curiosity and curiosities. In the twentieth and twenty-first centuries, indeed, novelists structure curiosity most purely as detective and mystery fictions, in which readers must (or should) actively forge the connections between isolated fragments of information to make the network that leads to the solution. The immense popularity of these genres suggests that, albeit we live in an age of information, we yearn for the practice and activity of curiosity. Curiosity, be it ambition or transgression, denotes dissatisfaction with the way things are. It is the urge to look under the stone for the hidden truth.

Notes

1. Lewis Carroll, *The Annotated Alice: Alice's Adventures in Wonderland and Through the Looking Glass,* introduction and notes by Martin Gardner (New York: New American Library, 1960), 35.

2. Barbara M. Benedict, *Curiosity: A Cultural History of Early Modern Inquiry* (Chicago: University of Chicago Press, 2001), 4–5, passim; Arthur MacGregor, *Curiosity and Enlightenment: Collectors and Collections from the Sixteenth to the Nineteenth Century* (New Haven, Conn.: Yale University Press, 2007), 1–30.

3. Thomas Shadwell, *The Virtuoso* (London: Henry Herringman, 1676), act 2, 30.

4. Craig Ashley Hanson, *The English Virtuoso: Art, Medicine, and Antiquarianism in the Age of Empiricism* (Chicago: University of Chicago Press, 2009); Brian Cowan, "Open Elite: Virtuosity and the Peculiarities of English Connoisseurship," *Modern Intellectual History* 1, no. 2 (2004): 151–83.

5. See Pat Rogers, *Essays on Pope* (Cambridge: Cambridge University Press, 1993), 240–60; *Lord Burlington: Architecture, Art and Life,* ed. Toby Barnard and Jane Clark (London: Hambledon Press, 1995); Morris R. Brownell, "Introduction," *Alexander Pope's Villa: Views of Pope's Villa, Grotto and Garden: A Microcosm of English Landscape* (London: Greater London Council, 1980), 7–9.

6. Alexander Pope to Sir Hans Sloane, March, 30, 1742, in *The Correspondence of Alexander Pope,* ed. George Sherburn, vol. 4: 1736–1744 (Oxford: Clarendon Press, 1956), 391; see also Morris R. Brownwell, "Introduction" to John Serle, *A Plan of Mr. Pope's Garden* (University of California, Los Angeles: William Andrews Clark Memorial Library, 1982), iii–xv.

7. John Locke, *An Essay concerning Human Understanding,* abridged and edited, with an introduction and notes, by Kenneth P. Winkler (1689; Indianapolis: Hackett, 1996), book 2, chapter 9, 56, emphasis in original.

8. Locke, book 2, chapter 9, 56, emphasis original.

9. Locke, book 2, chapter 11, 63.

10. James Steintrager notes the contradictions in Locke's epistemological distinctions and the threat of the material in Pope's work in "The Temptation of Alexander Pope: Materialism and Sexual Fantasy in 'Eloisa to Abelard,'" in *Sex and Death in Eighteenth-Century Literature,* ed. Jolene Zigarovich (New York: Routledge, 2013), 127–46. See Jonathan Lamb, *Preserving the Self in the South Seas, 1680–1840* (Chicago: University of Chicago Press, 2001), 77–113.

11. Alexander Pope, "Advertisement," *Epistles to Several Persons,* reprinted in F. W. Bateson, introduction to Alexander Pope, *Epistles to Several Persons (Moral Essays),* ed. F. W. Bateson (1744; London: Methuen, 1951), xvii, xi–xx.

12. Lorraine Daston and Katherine Park, *Wonders and the Order of Nature, 1150–1750* (New York: Zone Books, 1998).

13. Pope, *Epistles to Several Persons,* pp. 16–17, lines 15–18.

14. Benjamin Boyce, *The Character-Sketches in Pope's Poems* (Durham, N.C.: Duke University Press, 1962), 8–23. Jacob Fuchs observes a similar dynamic in Pope's technique of forefronting the present in his Horatian imitations in order to illuminate the relationship between contemporary and ancient figures in *Reading Pope's "Imitations of Horace"* (Lewisburg, Pa.: Bucknell University Press, 1989), 19–20.

15. Bateston, introduction, xliii.

16. Bateston, 549.

17. Bateston, 305, 313, 317, 309–10, 319.

18. Bateston, 326, 324.

19. Bateston, 320–22.

20. Alexander Pope, *The Rape of the Lock, in Miscellaneous Poems and Translations by Several Hands* (London: Bernard Lintot, 1712), 131.

21. Pope, *Rape of the Lock,* canto 2, 133–34.

22. Sarah Winter, "Curiosity as Didacticism in *The Old Curiosity Shop*," *Novel: A Forum on Fiction* 34, no. 1 (Autumn, 2000): 52.

23. Peter Brooks, *Reading for the Plot: Design and Intention in Narrative* (New York: A. A. Knopf, 1984).

24. Charles Dickens, *David Copperfield* (Oxford: Oxford University Press, 1987), 293.

25. Dickens, 431.

26. Dickens, 432.

27. Nina Auerbach, "Alice in Wonderland: A Curious Child," *Victorian Studies* 17, no. 1 (September 1973): 33.

28. Carroll, *The Annotated Alice,* 44.

29. Carroll, 26.

30. Carroll, 27–28.

31. Joseph Conrad, *Heart of Darkness,* 2nd ed. (Boston: Bedford Books, 1996), 52; see Donald Rackin, *Alice's Adventures in Wonderland and Through the Looking-Glass: Nonsense, Sense, and Meaning* (New York: Twayne, 1991), 92.

32. Carroll, *The Annotated Alice,* 40, 38.

33. Rackin, *Alice's Adventures,* 14.

34. Daniel Bivona, "Alice the Child-Imperialist and the Games of Wonderland," *Nineteenth-Century Literature,* 41, no. 2 (September 1986): 143–71.

35. Bill Brown, "Thing Theory," *Critical Inquiry* 28, no. 1 (2001): 100.

36. Charles Dickens, *The Old Curiosity Shop* (Oxford: Oxford University Press, 1987), 4–5.

37. James Buzard, "Enumeration and Exhaustion: Taking Inventory in *The Old Curiosity Shop*," *Dickens Studies Annual,* 39 (2008): 21, 20.

38. Dickens, *The Old Curiosity Shop,* 5.

39. Michael Hollington, "The Voice of Objects in *The Old Curiosity Shop*," *Australasian Journal of Victorian Studies* 1 (2009), 7. See his translation of Theodor W. Adorno, "An Address on Charles Dickens's The Old Curiosity Shop" ("Rede über den

Raritätenlanden von Charles Dickens"), trans. Michael Hollington, *Dickens Quarterly* 6, no. 3 (1989): 96–101; Catherine Waters, *Commodity Culture in Dickens's Household Words: The Social Life of Goods* (Farnham, U.K.: Ashgate, 2008).

40. Dickens, *The Old Curiosity Shop,* 23.

41. Dickens, 23.

42. Dickens, 35.

43. Gareth Cordery, "Quilp, Commerce and Domesticity: Crossing Boundaries in *The Old Curiosity Shop,*" *Dickens Quarterly,* 26, no. 4 (December 2009): 210, 223.

13

Curiosity and Political Resistance

Perry Zurn

Curiosity manifests itself in multiple guises. There is a sort of frivolous curiosity that asks vacuous questions, questions of little—and certainly no lasting—import to anyone. This curiosity vainly pursues rapidly changing lines of questioning, sometimes out of boredom and other times out of sheer pleasure in the minute, the contingent, or the ephemeral. It is excessive, without root in existential need, social utility, or rational armature. It produces, by turns, a dizzying array of details and a banal buzzing to blanket the otherwise jagged architecture of daily life. Then there is an eminently serious curiosity, the sort promulgated by somber-lipped academics, corporate investigators, or criminal courts. It is controlled, it is disciplined. It works within institutional constraints and moves at a swift clip down well-trimmed pathways. It builds an ever more intricate system of knowledge, whether through an expanding scaffold of classifications or a network of correlates. This curiosity is patient, hard-nosed, and exacting.

But there is a third sort of curiosity that is neither terribly serious nor entirely unserious. This particular configuration of the curious impulse begins by fidgeting with the fissures of social mores and political strata, poking and prying in search of a new space to stand tall. It bravely barrels into the darkest recesses of suffering and pain, steels itself, and lays bare the true face of social inequality and social death. And it raises its head to the sky, imagines as-yet-inconceivable worlds of justice and of peace, still so easily dismissed as feverish fantasies or illogical hopes. This curiosity is politically resistant. This curiosity is from and for the margins. If the first sort of curiosity flourishes in media and technology, while the second settles into museums and bureaucracy, this last comes alive in the streets and poetry, in

228   Perry Zurn

shared meals and political protests. Nabokov once wrote, "Curiosity [. . .] is insubordination in its purest form."[1] Although not every form of curiosity is aptly characterized thus, curiosity's insubordinate potential has rarely received the attention it deserves. It is this curiosity that forms the focus of the present essay.

In what follows, the resistant potential of curiosity will be first framed by theories of political curiosity writ large and then explicated through three case studies: the Civil Rights Movement in the 1960's, prison resistance networks in the 1970's, and a more recent initiative for accessible restrooms. From these archives, an anatomy of politically resistant curiosity will be drawn.

Theories of Political Curiosity

Across the history of philosophy, curiosity has most often been understood as a question of ethics or epistemology. Many thinkers have debated whether curiosity is consistent with virtuous and/or scientific inquiry, while others have quarreled over precisely what sort of curiosity is most conducive to childhood learning and development. Philosophical studies of curiosity have therefore developed in dialogue primarily with the fields of theology, science, and education.[2] While important, these studies have left vastly undertheorized curiosity's role at the social and civic level. There are, however, untapped resources within the history of philosophy from which to draw a theory of resistant curiosity. Friedrich Nietzsche, Michel Foucault, and Jacques Derrida offer accounts of political struggle that include implicit characterizations of an insubordinate curiosity. Whether working against the structures of civilization and consciousness, sedimented power relations, or sovereignty, Nietzsche, Foucault, and Derrida describe a curiosity capable of an irreverent refusal and creative reconfiguration of the political landscape.

For Nietzsche, human consciousness is the product of civilization, with all the dissimulation, repression, and cruelty that it presupposes. Knowledge and morality—as the costars of consciousness—are born and bred in a scene of struggle. It is upon a landscape ravaged by this struggle that curiosity appears. Nietzsche grants that there is a kind of curiosity that runs quickly to build up and to build on what has already been built: systems of consciousness, civilized societies, schemas of knowledge, and deep evaluative divisions. Such a curiosity contributes to and maintains, however indifferently, the products of struggle: the distributions and effects of power. This is

Curiosity and Political Resistance 229

the "curiosity" of the general populace,[3] a "sober, pragmatic curiosity" that busies itself with the "curious investigation of . . . countless minutiae."[4] But there is another sort of curiosity, one vibrant enough to slip beneath civilization and slip through what has become so keenly conscious. This curiosity is eminently suspicious. It roots out illusions that maintain the current system, highlighting the greed and the hatred that fuels them. It is a "fateful curiosity"[5] that spells the demise of the status quo and present forms of existence. Nietzsche attributes this curiosity to the "free spirit" and "the great liberation."[6] This is the sort of curiosity Nietzsche himself endorses.

Much like Nietzsche, Foucault also conceives of two, warring curiosities in the political sphere.[7] Across his work, curiosity features first as an arm of institutions that identify, catalogue, control, and deploy persons and objects in the world. From *History of Madness* to *History of Sexuality,* one can trace the role of curiosity in the development of psychology and education, penal theory and punishment, and sexuality studies and the various professions of desire that mark the modern, liberal subject. Although this is patently clear conceptually, Foucault uses the term "curiosity" in this regard sparingly, although no less significantly. By contrast, Foucault's most extended and direct discussions of curiosity develop it as a practice of freedom, a tool by which people can resist objectification and subjectification. Curiosity, he says, refuses to be "immobilized" by reality and is instead determined "to throw off familiar ways of thought."[8] Curiosity resists the sedimentation of knowledge and power in particular institutions, working instead to make things "mobile" and "fluid."[9] He specifically explores this curiosity as a tactic of self-transformation,[10] as a characteristic of the *parrhesiastes* who speaks truth to power,[11] and as an impetus to critical or genealogical scholarship.[12] In each case, resistant curiosity relentlessly breaks up whatever is well-governed and allows people to think, imagine, and behave in counterdisciplinary ways.

For Derrida there are at least two different sorts of institutionalized curiosity against which resistant curiosity works.[13] In *The Beast and the Sovereign,* Derrida explores the culture of curiosity as exemplified in pre- and postrevolutionary France. On the one hand, there is a scientific curiosity that dissects an object in the service of knowledge, cleanly separating one thing from another. This curiosity fueled, for example, animal and human autopsies. On the other, there is a therapeutic curiosity that confines an object in the service of care, definitively isolating one thing from another.

230   Perry Zurn

This curiosity undergirds the menageries and asylums, which aimed "to treat, to care for, . . . to liberate by locking up differently."[14] Derrida argues that both are interconnected expressions of sovereignty. That is, they attempt to sovereignly control and deny the inherent instability of objects, divisions, walls, and procedures. And yet for Derrida there is a third kind of curiosity that capitalizes on precisely that instability. In *The Animal That Therefore I Am*, he explores a deconstructive curiosity that resists the sovereign impetus. Such a curiosity not only challenges the illusion of a clean dissection or safe confinement, the definitiveness of a position or the stability of an opposition, but also explores new, untested concepts and lines of argumentation. This curiosity is not invested in securing phallogocentric fantasies but aims "to track, to sniff, to trail, and to follow" what is as yet unrecognized.[15] Inherent in the structure of human language, as much as in the "exploratory behavior" of animals and plants,[16] this curiosity welcomes *l'avenir*.

A brief comparison of these accounts throws into relief the basic contours of politically resistant curiosity. For Nietzsche, resistant curiosity is eminently suspicious of civilization and rooted in the jubilant force of nature. It is fundamentally naturalistic. For Foucault, resistant curiosity is a counterforce to disciplinary isolation and biopolitical management, nurturing instead vibrant self-transformation and social activism. It is essentially historicized, insofar as it develops as counterpoint to contemporary configurations of power. For Derrida, resistant curiosity, regardless of time or place, attacks the illusion of sovereignty, with its absolute unities and divisions, and instead celebrates *la différance*. It is constitutive of symbolic systems. Thus, against civilization, discipline, and sovereignty, resistant curiosity is irreverent and courageous, experimental and tactical, responsive and integral. It comes from the bottom, from the marginalized, and from the constitutively excluded. It is disruptive. It is insubordinate. And it is this curiosity that each theorist endorses, in his own way, as a marker of his philosophical activity.

This essay is not concerned, however, with the role of resistant curiosity in philosophical work, as important as that is. Instead, in the following sections, three case studies of political activism will be analyzed in order to extract the anatomical structure of curiosity at work therein. These cases are Martin Luther King's nonviolent direct action, the Prisons Information Group's prison activism, and PISSAR's work for safe and accessible restrooms. In each case, activists deployed curiosity along several key tracks, asking (1) What is going on? (2) What do we need? and (3) What better

future can we imagine? These cases of resistant curiosity are in part eluci-
dated by Nietzsche, Foucault, and Derrida's theories, but they also expand
beyond those accounts. Ultimately, an analysis of resistant curiosity in these
specific, localized instances of political action emphasizes the otherwise
underthought sociality of curiosity. From the subsequent anatomy of resistant curiosity, then, can be drawn an ethics of communal curiosity.

The Civil Rights Movement and Nonviolent Action

Writing from jail during the Birmingham campaign in 1963, Martin Luther
King Jr. asserts that nonviolent action involves four basic steps: the collection of facts, negotiation, self-purification, and direct action.[17] Bookending
nonviolent action, then, are two distinct deployments of curiosity. There is
the curiosity it takes to gather relevant information: the brutal record of
injustice. This curiosity pits itself against forces of media and government
that refuse to tell these stories or collect this data. And then there is the curiosity that fuels protest. Activists wonder whether or not this will finally be
enough to change hearts and minds. More than this, activists engage protests as a tool to grip public attention, throw the status quo into question,
and generate public recognition that segregation is indeed a problem. Curiosity is therefore integral to pursuing an informed, creative reenvisioning of
a desegregated culture of equals.

King describes the first step of nonviolent action as the "collection of
facts to determine whether injustices are alive."[18] This is not the later work
of promulgating a nonviolent philosophy, expanding the existing network
of activists, tracking the boycotts, sit-ins, protests, and tabulating arrests.
Instead, this is the sort of information gathering that gets the movement
started, ignites it with the force of an unjust world that must be changed. The
Civil Rights Movement, in King's estimation here, begins by collecting facts
that indicate the absence of civil rights, the reality of discrimination and
segregation, and the brute force of violence against African Americans. This
is a commitment to curiosity, a desire to know the extent of pain and suffering, the effects of hatred and systemic injustice. Participants collected data
on the beatings, the sexual assaults, the lynchings, the burning or bombing
of African American homes and churches, as well as other activities of the
Ku Klux Klan and the White Citizens Council. They collected data on police
killings, unjust trials, voter registration restrictions and voter intimidation,

232   Perry Zurn

housing discrimination, school segregation rates, as well as statistics of unemployment and restricted employment. They mapped segregated spaces in downtown cities and identified merchants specifically responsible. They researched and evaluated current laws and policies, at once looking for legal resources to support their cause and lacunae where new legislation was needed. This is an agonizing curiosity, stemming from pain and met with greater pain at witnessing rampant inequality. But it is necessary. It comes first.

The fourth and final step of direct action—whether it involves protests, demonstrations, marches, sit-ins, or boycotts—also catalyzes curiosity. This is not the superficial curiosity of depoliticized young folk who join their friends at the picket lines on a whim and may or may not contract any real commitment.[19] It is instead a curiosity that generates and is generated by crisis. King states that the power of direct action lies in its ability to build a state of creative tension that breaks one's bondage to myth and prejudice, pushes one to rethink what is taken for granted, and fuels subsequent efforts at understanding.[20] King reminds his readers of Socrates, the nonviolent gadfly who aimed "to create a tension in the mind so that individuals could rise from the bondage of myths and half-truths to the unfettered realm of creative analysis and objective appraisal."[21] Being a gadfly, for Socrates, involved a meddlesome inquisitiveness directed at people of good standing[22] and about things one ought not to question.[23] It was Socrates's commitment to questions outside the confines of religion, politics, or established values that rattled the Athenian populace, opening up the possibility of radical intellectual and social change. Following King's line of comparison, then, the civil rights protests were arguably Socratic catalysts for public curiosity.

In *The Psychology of Nonviolence,* Leroy H. Pelton argues that the power of nonviolent protest, particularly that employed by the Civil Rights Movement, lies in its ability to ignite curiosity in the general public around heretofore unrecognized injustices.[24] Pelton relies heavily on Daniel Berlyne's classic study *Conflict, Arousal, and Curiosity.* Berlyne argues that conceptual conflict—or ideational incongruity—is the primary impetus to epistemic curiosity, which he defines as "the brand of arousal that motivates the quest for knowledge and is relieved when knowledge is procured."[25] For Pelton the protest form naturally creates conceptual conflict for the general public, which is presented with a manifestation of social and ideological discord. In order for that protest to best promote curiosity, and in turn facilitate attitudinal change, it needs to strike a careful balance. Its message must be complex enough to attract attention, but simple enough to defray natural resistance.[26] It must be novel enough to generate interest, but repeated often enough to increase the pleasure of familiarity.[27] While psychologists continue to debate the nature and causes of curiosity,[28] current theorists remain indebted to Berlyne's framework. Todd Kashdan's Curiosity and Exploration Inventory I and II,[29] for example, reinforces curiosity's attraction to novelty and complexity, as well as its willingness to endure the anxiety of conflict or uncertainty. While these elements may not be sufficient for curiosity in the final analysis, their importance underscores the continued relevance of Pelton's account of the efficacy of political protest.

The Civil Rights Movement, then, utilized curiosity as a fundamental tactic of political resistance from the earliest stages of nonviolent action to full-blown protests and decisive acts of noncooperation. W. E. B. Du Bois opens *Souls of Black Folk* with the remark that "between me and the other world there is always an unasked question . . . [:] How does it feel to be a problem?"[30] How does it feel to be Black in a white world? But the question is not asked honestly; it is never explicit. As Franz Fanon would later put it, the white man affords his Black counterpart "nothing but indifference, or a paternalistic curiosity."[31] For a group or an individual that is consistently the object of a gloating, a punishing, or a half-hearted question, it is immeasurably powerful to become the subject of questions, the source-point of curiosity. Part of the power of the Civil Rights Movement lies in the way African Americans took ownership of their own curiosity and demanded public recognition of it. They identified what institutions needed to be questioned, what information needed to be gathered, and what future needed to be imagined. The movement then worked to educate the curiosity, concern, and creativity of the broader public. In doing so it deployed inquiry and imagination—deployed curiosity—as a tactic of political resistance.

The Prisons Information Group and Prison Resistance Networks

It is a little-known fact that one of the foundational texts in critical prison studies, Michel Foucault's *Discipline and Punish,* was the product of three intense years of prison activism.[32] Foucault founded and led a movement called the Prisons Information Group (the GIP), active between 1970 and

1973. A vibrant coalition of prisoners, ex-prisoners, their families, doctors, lawyers, academics, and other professionals, this group worked to collect and share information about the prison gathered from prisoners themselves. The GIP deployed its resistance effort on multiple levels, not least of which was curiosity. For the GIP the prison must be made into a question.[33] And it is prisoners—not the penitentiary administration—who should be asked about it. Prison resistance in early 1970's France, then, was marked by a distinct war over curiosity.

The GIP's first act was to generate a questionnaire for dissemination to prisoners. Organizers were keen to insist, in the accompanying leaflet, "this is not a sociological inquiry, a curiosity-inquiry, it is an *intolerance-inquiry*."[34] What is the distinction here? In a similar statement published shortly thereafter, Foucault again characterizes the questionnaire as an "intolerance-inquiry." He explains, "We do not make our inquiry in order to accumulate knowledge, but to heighten our intolerance and make it an active intolerance."[35] The enterprise of gathering information from prisoners was not an academic one. It did not seek the acquisition of information for information's sake. Nor was the enterprise curious in a banal sense, attracted to the spectacle of the prison fetish. Instead, it was an act of intolerance. As Daniel Defert would put it two months later, distributing the questionnaires was "not sociological work" but "a political act."[36] It was the work of people with intimate ties to the prison and a staunch conviction of its intolerability. And it aimed to incite the public to recognize and treat the prison as "intolerable."[37] One might then say it was driven not by a banal but by an intolerant, already-politicized curiosity.

Fundamental to the GIP initiative was the practice of asking prisoners themselves to describe prison conditions, assess the penal system, and formulate necessary reforms. As the group repeatedly stated, it worked "*à donner la parole*," or "to give the floor," to prisoners.[38] From its outset, the GIP insisted that, despite official penitentiary reports, the prison remained a "black box,"[39] about which little if any truth was known. To rectify this situation, the GIP developed an investigation through which "questions were really addressed by detainees to detainees."[40] This meant that the center of curiosity shifted. Through the investigation's questionnaire, ex-prisoners asked current prisoners to report basic facts about their food, work, mail, medical care, visiting rights, and prison discipline.[41] But they also asked open-ended, evaluative questions: "Do you have any comments about the [prison] rules?"[42]

Curiosity and Political Resistance 235

"What comments do you have about this investigation or questionnaire?"[43] Furthermore, they asked politicized questions: "What is intolerable?"[44] "What is unbearable?"[45] and "What are the most scandalous aspects of penitentiary life you want people to focus on?"[46] The breadth of these questions positioned prisoners as the chief source of objective details and reflective assessments of the penitentiary system.

For three years, the GIP published pamphlet after pamphlet, disseminating the material gathered from prisoners to the wider world.[47] In doing so it aspired not only to enhance societal awareness of the prison but to force the broader public to recognize the prison as a problem and therefore take it as a question. According to Foucault's retrospective assessment, the GIP posed "the problem not of the political regime in prisons, but of the prison regime itself. . . . The problem was this: What is prison?"[48] This meant it laid bare the intolerable nature of incarceration not in order to instigate reform but rather to cast doubt on the entire institution. It asked, Why punish by confinement? Why exercise social control in this manner? For the GIP, "the existence of prisons posed problems, just as much as what happened there"; members therefore resisted making any proposals for reform, saying they "wanted no prescription, no recipe, and no prophecy."[49] The GIP problematized the prison. This is not yet the rich sense of problematization Foucault would later develop in his reflections on genealogy, but it does require the same "curiosity and scrutiny."[50] It does hang the same giant question mark over an accepted social institution. The political project of making the prison a question and centering prisoners' voices on that question was not a project of resolution. It was an enterprise to shift the center weight and the contours of curiosity.

The GIP's effort met with significant resistance from various quarters, perhaps chief among which were the police and the media. According to organizers, the French police were already part and parcel of the prison problem.[51] They targeted the poor, tortured racial minorities, beat detainees, killed protestors, and consistently used a heavy hand for slight infractions.[52] The police made special effort to combat the GIP's attempted shift of curiosity, breaking up groups of visitors, families, organizers, and protestors as they congregated outside prison doors.[53] They were also quick to confiscate lists of demands prisoners hurled over the walls and arrest anyone caught collecting them.[54] In its turn the media launched smear campaigns, taking swipes at GIP leaders and accusing them of self-aggrandizement.[55] It also levied accusations of deception and drunkenness against prisoners involved

236   Perry Zurn

in the GIP's various information campaigns.[56] And the media refused to publish journalistic submissions from prisoners themselves. As Foucault would remark with exasperation, "When detainees speak, it poses such a problem."[57] The police and the media together, therefore, worked to exclude prisons as well as prisoners from the realm of inquiry, from the purview of political curiosity.

The GIP provides a rich case study of the role of curiosity in the 1970's French prison resistance movement. For them, the prison must be a question, and it is prisoners who must be asked about it. The GIP's work cast a staple institution into doubt and recast the field of appropriate informants. It fought to make known what was hidden, to make heard those who were silenced. It cultivated in the French public a new, robust, and ethically informed desire to know what about the penal system remained unknown.

PISSAR and Queer/Crip Coalition

In the United States, bathrooms have always been a political space. As a historical centerpiece of segregation and unequal accommodation, bathrooms have been, by turns, targeted as a feminist issue, a race issue, a disability issue, and a transgender issue. Getting "ladies rooms" in the first place took political organizing, and today many people demand better provisions for menstruation and lactation. After the racial desegregation of restrooms, there remain significantly fewer public restrooms in low-income communities of color. ADA standards, while hard won, are unreliably met across U.S. accommodations. Transgender people consistently face discrimination and violence in whichever restroom they choose to use. Moreover, the inaccessibility of public restrooms for homeless people, low-income people, and street workers has been a sustained national problem. Given these various forms of inequality, scattered across multiple axes of oppression, the bathroom has been an inescapable source of agitation, locus of activism, and object of political resistance movements.[58] Curiosity has been a driving force and key tactic for these efforts. Organizers have utilized curiosity to collect necessary information, to make restrooms a question, and to shift the locus of inquiry in bathroom politics.

Curiosity was highly significant for a group called PISSAR (People in Search of Safe and Accessible Restrooms), active at the University of California, Santa Barbara, from 2003 to 2004.[59] For PISSAR, which was a coalition

Curiosity and Political Resistance   237

between disabled, trans, and/or genderqueer students, including and alongside those with menstruation and childcare needs, the structure of fully accessible public accommodations was unclear and therefore opened up for debate. This made the entire nexus of existing campus bathrooms a locus of politicized curiosity. Bathrooms had to become an issue in campus culture, while current bathrooms had to be mapped, evaluated, and ultimately changed.[60] PISSAR members—including undergraduates, graduate students, staff, and community members—started by posing questions to the student body:

> What do we need from bathrooms? What elements are necessary to make a bathroom functional for everyone? To make it safe? To make it a private and respectful space? Whose bodies are excluded from the typical restroom? More important, what kind of bodies are assumed in the design of these bathrooms? Who has the privilege (we call it pee-privilege) of never needing to think about these issues, of always knowing that any given bathroom will meet one's needs?[61]

By piquing public curiosity, PISSAR problematized the otherwise everyday institution of the bathroom.

The media campaign was only the first step. The second involved the aptly named "PISSAR patrols,"[62] which were groups of three people, ideally of varying genders, canvassing campus to catalogue and assess its bathrooms. All PISSAR patrols were equipped with team shirts, gloves, measuring tape, clipboards, and a checklist. Folks on PISSAR patrol were to be scientists, to be investigators and explorers, anthropologists and geographers. They recorded, in meticulous detail, the location, signage, urinal and stall measurements, latches, knobs, grab bars, flush levers, dispensers (toilet-seat covers, tampons, soap, paper towels), and changing tables of each restroom. Members retroactively characterized the four-page checklist as "a manifesto of sorts," because it modeled "queer coalition-building by incorporating disability, genderqueer, childcare, and menstruation issues into one document, refusing single-issue analysis."[63] Results from the patrols were collated into a map, which helped students locate more accessible restrooms on campus. The map was also, however, a "consciousness-raising tool" for those "who have never had to think about bathrooms."[64] PISSAR's cartographic effort was ultimately an advocacy effort. Not only did the patrols cultivate members' own "imagination" about the future of accessible restrooms,[65] but they

238   Perry Zurn

also got chancellors curious enough to ask, "What kind of bodies are we talking about here?"[66] and eventually led to renewed university commitments to accessibility.

Activism around restroom access is not alone in its deployment of curiosity. In fact, the culture of segregation and discrimination targeting variously gendered, raced, and abled bodies results repeatedly in the conversion of public accommodations into sharply guarded territories, policed with quick and cutting interrogations, in which accusatory questions are wielded as instruments of control and exclusion. One of the many ways people police restrooms is by inquisition: "Are you lost? Are you a . . . what the fuck are you? Where's your ID? What kind of plumbing you got, huh? What's in those pants!"[67] Sheila Cavanagh calls it "gender-based interrogation."[68] The Free to Pee group, started at George Brown College in 2012 and self-described as a PISSAR spin-off, highlights the complexity of this moment: "Discrimination comes in many forms, and it is not always easy to know why someone is asking you questions or telling you to leave the restroom."[69] Some may kindly pretend not to notice, while others will call security or attack you physically (sometimes with a weapon). And they may do so out of culturally, religiously, or ideologically bred attachment to this particular sanctuary of the gender binary. Curious stares and accusatory questions serve this end.

Restroom resistance movements have, by and large, worked against this use of the question to target, ostracize, and exclude, to rip away welcome and destroy belonging. Instead, they have deployed curiosity to ask honestly about the pain and institutional failure experienced so heavily by marginalized people. And they have also relied on curiosity to reignite and to reorganize their own political imagination.[70]

These three cases—the Civil Rights Movement, the Prisons Information Group, and PISSAR—provide material from which to draw an anatomy of politically resistant curiosity. As Nietzsche, Foucault, and Derrida's accounts suggest, curiosity in these cases is always a force on both sides of political struggle. Curiosity is not essentially insubordinate. Sometimes, and perhaps more often than not, it works in the service of established institutions, which predefine appropriate objects, subjects, and avenues of inquiry. Questions may be used to further this inquiry or to protect it from the threat of other knowledge formations. When curiosity's insubordinate potential is tapped, however, it investigates the suffering of the marginalized, it casts radical doubt on the status quo, and it fearlessly imagines new and better futures. Insubordinate curiosity also shifts who is consulted, who gets asked for their political wisdom. More than fleshing out the anatomy of resistant curiosity, moreover, these case studies launch a specific challenge to the accounts of canonical philosophers. Dispensing with any illusion of independent—let alone solitary—curiosity, political resistance movements illuminate the undertheorized sociality of curiosity. Curiosity is not, in these cases, the isolated characteristic of a genius or a rebel. It is collective and it is communal. What the anatomy of resistant curiosity produces, then, is a depiction of collective curiosity.

Curiosity in political resistance movements is first of all deployed against already-established configurations of knowledge and inquiry. In the Civil Rights Movement, stories and data of segregation were not being generated through the official channels and needed to be built by the Black community. Perhaps one of the most powerful exemplars of this work is the "Evidence" chapter in *We Charge Genocide* (1951), which insists that "this widespread failure to record crimes against the Negro people is in itself an index to genocide."[71] But conversely, conservative white media deployed questions in order to resist desegregation by fanning the flames of racism and red fear.[72] Likewise, for the GIP the official prison reports failed to represent prisoners' voices, and the media refused to incorporate them. But when Dr. Edith Rose, a prison psychologist, wrote a damning report of Toul prison in 1971, the penitentiary administration dismissed it with a question: Did you see all of this with your own eyes?[73] Restroom organizing, too, has developed hand in hand with data collection, from PISSAR's rudimentary map to extensive academic reports.[74] But questions about users' genders, moreover, are repeatedly used to police nonnormative bodies in restrooms.[75] It is not, therefore, the case that curiosity is absent from the status quo, but rather that it is governed and deployed in maintaining current political structures.

Against this established schematic of inquiry, resistance movements utilize curiosity insubordinately in at least four specific ways. First, they investigate the state of affairs for disempowered groups. What are the elements and effects of segregation, intolerable prison conditions, or inaccessible restrooms? An investigation of this sort asks targeted questions about marginalized experiences, questions that gather the information necessary to inform later strategies of struggle and reimaginations of the political landscape. Second, these resistance movements shifted not only the topic of inquiry but the

240 Perry Zurn

people being asked. The Civil Rights Movement asked the Black community about segregation, the GIP asked prisoners about prison conditions, and PISSAR asked genderqueer and disabled students about inaccessible bathrooms. In changing the directionality of curiosity, these movements changed who could speak and who could be heard. Insubordinate curiosity transforms the politics of voice and ear. Third, these movements launched major efforts to change what got recognized as a question or a problem. Targeting the government, the administration, and the public, they used questions not only to destabilize the unquestioned character of race, prisons, and restrooms but to make them questionable in their own right. While the formal effect of this effort was external consciousness raising, it also reconfigured the terrain of officially endorsed sites of inquiry. Fourth, they asked, "What do we need? What would a new future of care look like? And how can questions help us dream?" It is the courage to throw off familiar ways, to radically shift perspective, to believe change is possible, and to populate collective visions with the still unthinkable that fuels such movements. This is the anatomy of politically resistant curiosity.

The challenge that these cases pose to traditional theories of political curiosity is their inescapable qualification of curiosity as communal. If political thought is to adequately engage with resistance movements, it is critical that collective curiosity be theorized. Although Nietzsche places curiosity squarely in the midst of political struggle, his privileged figures of liberatory curiosity are himself,[76] his ideal reader—that "monster of courage and curiosity,"[77] and the free spirit of the future.[78] It is his rare references to curiosity as shared, for instance, among "we Europeans of the day after tomorrow,"[79] that must be theorized. Likewise, although Foucault describes a battle between institutionalized curiosity and resistant curiosity, his best-known paradigms of resistant curiosity are singular: himself, the *parrhesiastes,* and the intellectual.[80] More work must be done to wrest Foucauldian practices of freedom from the frameworks of solitary askesis and center them in communities of resistance. As Foucault says in a late interview, "What is good is something that comes through innovation. . . . The good is defined by us, it is practiced, it is invented. And this is a collective work."[81] Again, for Derrida, forms of curiosity by turns buoy and belie sovereign displays of power. He locates a curiosity coincident with deconstruction in himself and his cat, Lewis Carroll's Alice and Melville's Bartleby.[82] Relocating curiosity from the solitary philosopher to the crowd, from the intrepid animal to the packs and the herds, from a single plant to the network of organic life—that is what must be done. Collective curiosity is what we must now think.

Once the role of curiosity in political resistance movements is recognized, a whole series of questions follow relative to the ethics of curiosity. Even if one grants the claim that political resistance, on behalf of marginalized groups, is a good in itself, and the further claim that curiosity used in the service of such a good is ethical, a myriad of issues remain unresolved. What are the best ways to cultivate a collective curiosity? What is the responsibility of an individual to engage in collective curiosity in the service of political resistance? What are the strongest ethical criteria for collecting stories and data from marginalized communities? What are best protocols for facilitating the voices of those who are otherwise silenced? How can publicity be used responsibly in the effort to problematize current political institutions? And what are the constraints of an ethical imagination? Whatever the answers to these questions, ethical and epistemological debates about curiosity can no longer remain depoliticized. Instead, they must engage the undeniably vibrant role curiosity plays in insubordination.

Notes

1. Vladimir Nabokov, *Bend Sinister* (1947; New York: Vintage Books, 2012), 46.

2. Perry Zurn, "Busybody, Hunter, Dancer: Three Historical Models of Curiosity," in *Toward New Philosophical Explorations of the Epistemic Desire to Know: Just Curious about Curiosity*, ed. Marianna Papastephanou (Cambridge, U.K.: Cambridge Scholars Press, 2019), 26–49.

3. Friedrich Nietzsche, "On the Uses and Disadvantages of History for Life," in *Untimely Meditations*, ed. Daniel Breazeale (1874; Cambridge: Cambridge University Press, 1997), §7.

4. Nietzsche, "History for Life," §6.

5. Friedrich Nietzsche, "On Truth and Lies in a Non-moral Sense," in *The Birth of Tragedy and Other Writings*, ed. Raymond Geuss and Ronald Speirs (1873; Cambridge: Cambridge University Press, 2008), §1.

6. Friedrich Nietzsche, *Human, All Too Human*, trans. R. J. Hollingdale (1873; Cambridge: Cambridge University Press, 1996), preface §4 and §3.

7. Perry Zurn, "Curiosities at War: The Police and Prison Resistance after May '68," *Modern and Contemporary France* 26, no. 2 (2018): 179–91.

8. Michel Foucault, "The Masked Philosopher," in *Ethics: Subjectivity and Truth*, ed. Paul Rabinow, trans. Robert Hurley (New York: New Press, 1997), 325.

9. Michel Foucault, "Power, Moral Values, and the Intellectual," *History of the Present* 4 (1988): 1, 13.

242   Perry Zurn

10. Michel Foucault, *The Hermeneutics of the Subject: Lectures at the Collège de France, 1981–1982,* ed. Frédéric Gros, trans. Graham Burchell (New York: Picador, 2005), 260, 279; cf. Seneca, *Naturales Questiones* (Cambridge, Mass.: Harvard University Press, 1972), 1.12.

11. Michel Foucault, *The Courage of Truth: Lectures at the Collège de France, 1983–1984,* ed. Frédéric Gros, trans. Graham Burchell (New York: Picador, 2011), 125.

12. Michel Foucault, *The Use of Pleasure,* trans. Robert Hurley (New York: Vintage Books, 1990), 8.

13. Perry Zurn, "The Curiosity at Work in Deconstruction," *Journal of French and Francophone Philosophy* 26, no. 1 (2018): 65–87.

14. Jacques Derrida, *The Beast and Sovereign I,* ed. Michel Lisse, Marie-Louise Mallet, and Ginette Michaud, trans. Geoffrey Bennington (Chicago: University of Chicago Press, 2009), 299.

15. Jacques Derrida, *The Animal That Therefore I Am,* ed. Marie-Louise Mallet, trans. David Wills (New York: Fordham University Press, 2008), 33.

16. Jacques Derrida, "Séance 4," *Répondre du secret,* December 11, 1991, University of California, Irvine, Archives, MS-C001, box 21, folder 5, 8–9.

17. Martin Luther King Jr., "Letter from Birmingham Jail," in *A Testament of Hope: The Essential Writings and Speeches of Martin Luther King, Jr.,* ed. James M. Washington (New York: HarperOne, 1986), 290.

18. King, 290.

19. Dennis Chong, *Collective Action and the Civil Rights Movement* (Chicago: University of Chicago Press, 1991), 71.

20. King, "Letter from Birmingham Jail," 291.

21. King, 291.

22. Plato, *The Apology,* in *Euthyphro, Apology, Crito, Phaedo, Phaedrus* (Cambridge, Mass.: Loeb Classical Library, 2017), 31c. Here Plato uses one of the Greek cognates for the Latin *curiositas*: *polypragmosyne*.

23. Plato, 19b. Here Plato uses the other cognate: *periergon*.

24. Leroy H. Pelton, *The Psychology of Nonviolence* (New York: Pergamon Press, 1974).

25. Daniel Berlyne, *Conflict, Arousal, and Curiosity* (New York: McGraw Hill, 1960), 274.

26. Pelton, *The Psychology of Nonviolence,* 117.

27. Pelton, 119.

28. George Lowenstein, "The Psychology of Curiosity: A Review and Reinterpretation," *Psychological Bulletin* 116, no. 1 (1994): 75–98.

29. Todd Kashdan, Paul Rose, and Frank Fincham, "Curiosity and Exploration: Facilitating Positive Subjective Experiences and Personal Growth Opportunities," *Journal of Personality Assessment* 82, no. 3 (2004): 291–305; Todd Kashdan et al., "The Curiosity and Exploration Inventory-II: Development, Factor Structure, and Psychometrics," *Journal of Research in Personality* 43, no. 6 (2009): 987–98.

30. W. E. B. Du Bois, *The Souls of Black Folk* (1903; Radford, Va.: Wilder, 2008), 5.

Curiosity and Political Resistance   243

31. Franz Fanon, *Black Skin, White Masks* (1952; New York: Grove Press, 1967), 221.

32. Michel Foucault, "Toujours les prisons," *Dits et Ecrits II* (Paris: Gallimard, 2001), no. 282, 916. See also Perry Zurn and Andrew Dilts, eds., *Active Intolerance: Michel Foucault, the Prisons Information Group, and the Future of Abolition* (New York: Palgrave, 2016).

33. Louis Appert (Michel Foucault), François Colcombert, and Antoine Lazarus, "Luttes autour des prisons" (November 1979), *Dits et Ecrits II* no. 273, 813.

34. GIP, "Enquête Intolerance" (March 1971), *Le Groupe d'information sur les prisons: Archives d'une lutte, 1970–1972*, ed. Philippe Artières, Laurent Quéro, and Michelle Zancarini-Fournel (Paris: IMEC, 2003), 53. Hereafter *Archives d'une lutte*.

35. Michel Foucault, "Le GIP vient de lancer sa première enquête" (March 15, 1971), *Archives d'une lutte*, 52.

36. Daniel Defert, "Quand l'information est une lutte" (May 25, 1971), *Archives d'une lutte*, 72–73.

37. Foucault, "Le GIP," 52.

38. See, for example, Daniel Defert, "Sur quoi repose le système pénitentiare?" (November 11, 1971), *Archives d'une lutte*, 129.

39. GIP, "Nul de nous d'est sûr d'échapper à la prison" (February 8, 1971), *Archives d'une lutte*, 43.

40. Defert, "Quand l'information est une lutte," 69.

41. GIP, "Intolérable 1: Enquête dans vingt prisons," *Intolérable* (Paris: Verticale, 2013), 21–80.

42. GIP, "Intolerable 1: Investigation in 20 Prisons," in Marcelo Hoffman, *Foucault and Power: The Influence of Political Engagement on Theories of Power* (London: Bloomsbury, 2014), 160 (translation modified).

43. GIP, 166 (translation modified).

44. GIP, 174–75.

45. GIP, 181.

46. GIP, 166 (translation modified); cf. "What hazing do you stand ready to denounce?" (165).

47. Perry Zurn, "Publicity and Politics: Foucault, the Prisons Information Group, and the Press," *Radical Philosophy Review* 17, no. 2 (2014): 403–20.

48. Appert (Foucault), Colcombert, and Lazarus, "Luttes autour des prisons," 808.

49. Appert (Foucault), Colcombert, and Lazarus, 813.

50. Colin Koopman, *Genealogy as Critique* (Bloomington: Indiana University Press, 2013), 143.

51. For them, the penal system involved the police, the courts, and the prison. See Defert, "Quand l'information est une lutte," 73.

52. Michel Foucault, "Il y a un an à peu près . . ." (January 17, 1972), *Archives d'une lutte*, 195; Michel Foucault, "Le Discours de Toul" (January 5, 1972), *Dits et Ecrits I*, no. 99, 1105; Daniel Defert, "Sur quoi repose le système pénitentiare?" (November 11, 1971), *Archives d'une lutte*, 131; Michel Foucault and Pierre Vidal-Naquet, "Enquête sur les prisons: Brisons les barreaux du silence" (March 18, 1971), *Dits et Ecrits I*, no. 88, 1050.

53. Defert, "Quand information est une lutte," 69, 72–73; Appert (Foucault), Colcombert, and Lazarus, "Luttes autour des prisons," 816.

54. Foucault, "Il y a un an à peu près . . . ," 198.

55. Appert (Foucault), Colcombert, and Lazarus, "Luttes autour des prisons," 812; Michel Foucault and Paul Thibaud, "Toujours les prisons," *Dits et Ecrits II,* no. 282, 915–17.

56. Foucault, "Il y a un an à peu près . . . ," 195–96.

57. Michel Foucault, "Le grand enfermement" (March 25, 1972), *Dits et Ecrits I,* no. 105, 1170.

58. Perry Zurn, "Waste Culture and Isolation: Prisons, Toilets, and Gender Segregation," *Hypatia: A Journal of Feminist Philosophy* 34, no. 4 (2019): 668–89.

59. Simone Chess et al., "Calling All Restroom Revolutionaries!" *That's Revolting: Queer Strategies for Resisting Assimilation,* ed. Mattilda Bernstein Sycamore (Brooklyn: Soft Skull Press, 2004), 216–36. See also Isaac West's commentary in "PISSAR's Critically Queer and Disabled Politics," *Communication and Critical/Cultural Studies* 7, no. 2 (2010): 156–75.

60. Chess et al., "Calling All Restroom Revolutionaries!," 217.

61. Chess et al., 216–17.

62. The choice of "patrol" is perhaps more apt than members knew. It stems from the sixteenth-century French *patrouiller,* meaning to paddle or puddle in the mud. To patrol, then, is literally to muck about.

63. Chess, et al., "Calling All Restroom Revolutionaries!," 225. In this way, it modeled "theory" in action (226). Alison Kafer, in *Feminist, Queer, Crip* (Bloomington: Indiana University Press, 2013), urges subsequent coalitions to move their bathroom politics beyond architecture by integrating work for accessible catheters and diapers (154–57).

64. Chess et al., "Calling All Restroom Revolutionaries!," 219.

65. Chess et al., 227.

66. Chess et al., 228.

67. For a rich treatment of interviews on the topic, see Sheila Cavanagh, *Queering Restrooms: Gender, Sexuality, and the Hygienic Imagination* (Toronto: University of Toronto Press, 2010), chapter 2.

68. Cavanagh, 22.

69. George Brown College, Free to Pee Campaign, https://freetopeegbc.com/vic tories-2/.

70. For a broader account of trans and gender-nonconforming people's resistant curiosity, see Perry Zurn, "Puzzle Pieces: Shapes of Trans Curiosity," *APA Newsletter on LGBT Issues in Philosophy* 18, no. 1 (2018): 10–16.

71. William L. Patterson, ed., *We Charge Genocide* (Detroit: Civil Rights Congress, 1951), 57–192 (esp. 57).

72. See, for example, the John Birch Society flyer, "What's Wrong with Civil Rights?" *Palm Beach Post,* October 31, 1965, https://birchwatcher.files.wordpress.com/2015/03/ whats_wrong_with_civil_rights.png.

73. Michel Foucault, "Le Discours de Toul," 1106.

74. See, for example, Jody Herman, "Gendered Restrooms and Minority Stress: The Public Regulation of Gender and Its Impact on Transgender People's Lives," *Journal of Public Management and Social Policy* 19, no. 1 (2013): 65–80.

75. Herman, 72.

76. Friedrich Nietzsche, *Beyond Good and Evil,* trans. Walter Kaufmann (1886; New York: Vintage Books, 1989), §45; Friedrich Nietzsche, *On the Genealogy of Morals,* trans. Walter Kaufmann and R. J. Hollingdale (1887; New York: Vintage Books, 1989), preface, §3.

77. Friedrich Nietzsche, *Ecce Homo,* trans. Walter Kaufmann (1908; New York: Vintage Books, 1989), §3.

78. Nietzsche, *Human, All Too Human,* preface, §3.

79. Nietzsche, *Beyond Good and Evil,* §214.

80. Foucault, *The Use of Pleasure,* 8; Foucault, *The Courage of Truth,* 125; Foucault, "The Masked Philosopher," 325.

81. Foucault, "Power, Moral Values," 13.

82. Derrida, *The Animal That Therefore I Am,* 3, 4, 7; Jacques Derrida, "Séance 1," *Répondre du secret,* November 13, 1991, University of California, Irvine, Archives, MS-C001, box 21, folder 4.

14

Curiosity at the End of the World

Women, Fiction, Electricity

Hilary M. Schor

The end of inquiry is no longer to make wonder stop, but to let it begin.
—Lorraine Daston, "Wonder and the End of Inquiry"

It is possible to survive all this but not unaltered.
—Emily St. John Mandel, *Station Eleven*

Well, it's nice that at least the celebrity gossip survived.
—Emily St. John Mandel, *Station Eleven*

Who doesn't want to know how the world ends? A bang, a whimper, a flare of light, the growing cold. Meteors hurtle toward us, zombies attack us, we huddle once again by the campfire, but now grounded airplanes shimmer in the dark. Perhaps. But this is not an essay about the end of the world; rather, it is an essay about the beginning of a new form of curiosity, the reformulation of the central terms of the present volume. My primary text offers a particularly beautiful meditation on the end of the world as we know it. For in that fictional universe, as Emily St. John Mandel imagines it, "What was lost in the collapse: almost everything, almost everyone, but there is still such beauty." For her, as for me, curiosity itself becomes an object of inquiry around which readers and characters alike circle:

Twilight in the altered world, a performance of *A Midsummer Night's Dream* in a parking lot in the mysteriously named town of St. Deborah by the Water,

246

Lake Michigan shining a half mile away. Kirsten as Titania, a crown of flowers on her close-cropped hair, the jagged scar on her cheek-bone half-erased by candlelight. The audience is silent. Sayid, circling her in a tuxedo that Kirsten found in a dead man's closet near the town of East Jordan: "Tarry, rash wanton. Am I not thy lord?"[1]

Here, at our introduction to the new world of *Station Eleven,* more than just the town is "mysteriously named." Shakespeare has somehow survived; a woman with close-cropped hair has been scarred and transformed by candlelight, and we, like the audience, wait in silence. If the novel is to be more than a dead man's closet (and I believe it is), it, too, must tarry like a wanton, wandering and standing still at the same moment, ever curious.

Hence the question with which I must begin: What does curiosity have to do with the novel? To ask this question is immediately to fall into disreputable company, for no less a critic than E. M. Forster, in his justly famous *Aspects of the Novel,* scorned the curious reader as an idiot who asks only "And then? And then?"[2] And yet, without readerly curiosity, would anyone ever read a novel? For by curiosity, I do not mean merely what happened when and to whom. Rather, I take curiosity to be a world-building activity, one that catches readers in its grip. This sense of curiosity as a force that creates as well as interrogates reality, tying the world of the novel to that of the reader, has increasingly informed cultural criticism. Lorraine Daston and Katharine Park brilliantly expose the ways curiosity went from being a sin, a form of speculative spying that should belong only to God, to forming the roots of scientific inquiry.[3] Critics such as John Eisner, Mieke Bal, and Jean Baudrillard have re-limned the "culture of collecting";[4] Susan Stewart in *On Longing* has moved from Freud to Derrida to Bakhtin, reanimating "the secret life of things."[5] That secret life is the heart of the novel, a genre that grows up alongside virtuosi, *Wunderkammern,* micrography, and dollhouses. Without curiosity, no fiction; and in turn, every act of curiosity involves some act of fiction, some extension of the here and now into the "might have been" and "what if," a cloth-bound perspective box. As we look at the world, we are aware of ourselves looking at it, but to be curious is also to be committed to imagining another world, or at least worldview. If a "fiction" is literally a made thing (*fingere*: to form, to contrive), so too is curiosity (*cura*: to care, to cure, to be careful, to be odd and to look at oddities), and both unfold in time as well as space. Yet curiosity is not a way of seeing that unfolds entirely of our own making; it requires that we take a step backward and let the world work on us. Curiosity is a way of keeping the story going into the future.

As I turn to Mandel's version of curiosity, the curiosity at the end of the world (a world that may in fact have no future), my view grows out of my understanding of curiosity as a narrative mode deeply tied to the rise of feminism. In *Curious Subjects: Women and the Trials of Realism,*[6] I argue that the curious heroine serves as a kind of experimental thermometer for the novel, going beyond what her culture told her she needed to know, moving from the confines of the home and the marriage plot into the wider world. Starting with John Milton's Eve in *Paradise Lost,* the heroine's quest for knowledge shaped the novel as a genre and kept it fluent as culture changed. The novel is the definitive modern genre because it can incorporate not only new facts but new ways of organizing knowledge. It does not merely tell us stories, it prepares us to take the measure of the world. But if curiosity, women, and the novel were inseparably bound together at the rise of the novel, what has happened since then—and what will happen next? How will the novel stay curious; how will it again teach us how to be curious, when the world as we know it comes to an end?

The question is less odd than it seems. The novel is the cockroach of literary genres in part because it thrives at moments of cultural crisis. When the novel emerged from earlier forms of fiction, particularly the "romance," with its surreal heroes and heroines, it did so, as its name suggests, by purveying the news, or by making the "news" fictional.[7] The earliest novels in the English tradition were romans-à-clef, skirting libel laws by providing readers with the very choicest gossip in a variety of narrative forms: the epistolary novel, updated travel stories, current affairs of the court rendered by skeptical but eager narrators. All of these genres began by removing readers from what we might now call their "comfort zones." In a society where many were rising, so was the novel. Only gradually did the novel put its feet more firmly on the ground, introducing us to characters more like us: Robinson Crusoe, Pamela Andrews, Tom Jones, even the more bizarrely named Tristram Shandy. We can trust that no activity will be performed by these characters that we could not perform ourselves. No supernatural beings will intervene on their behalf, and they will walk in a world recognizably our own.

Yet despite this grounding in the real world, the novel traffics in new kinds of information and trains its heroine to recognize and interrogate new forms

Curiosity at the End of the World   249

of knowledge. When "a young female . . . makes . . . her first appearance upon the great and busy stage of life, with a virtuous mind, a cultivated understanding, and a feeling heart," as Frances Burney puts it, "her ignorance of the forms, and inexperience in the manners, of the world" also make for a great adventure.[8] To sort this new world, the heroine needs a kind of operational manual, and yet the guidebook to wonderland is never enough. As Evelina, Clarissa, Pamela, Justine, all encounter the world, they discover its rules, but they also prove themselves the exception. The novel flaunts its role as both conduct book and lab experiment, serving at one and the same time as a useful collection of maxims and a subversive prompt book for puckish bad students.

The nineteenth-century novel wonders something else and it walks down very different streets. So curious is the would-be Victorian novelist that he will venture beyond the limits of what has passed for knowledge even in these "novels of the present day." Charting an unknown territory, the novelist begins to wander like a "traveller in the poor man's country," as William Makepeace Thackeray put it.[9] This is a world, as Thackeray says, available to anyone willing to walk out his own front door. But most readers were not, and for them, there were always novels, particularly once Dickens took up his pen in the late 1830s. In the world of Charles Dickens, collections of curiosities abound, both in the form of strange objects and in inquiring characters. Dickens is clever enough to play with our interest in his sources: his prefaces revel in "real life" examples of phenomena he presents (collapsing houses, spontaneous combustion, governmental bureaucracies that inspired the Barnacles) and the pages draw us not into some teeming mass of "outcast London" but into particularized worlds curated by decidedly idiosyncratic speakers, each at home on his corner or in her alleyway, offering us far more information about their lives (and far more backstory hidden away till a suitable moment of revelation) than we could have thought possible.

Indeed, Dickens, that "special correspondent for posterity,"[10] was there before even Henry Mayhew, the intrepid author of *London Labour and the London Poor,* perhaps the greatest compendium of nineteenth-century daily life.[11] In Mayhew's four overstuffed volumes, the materials of Victorian life abound: the trinkets found by the Thames mudlarks; the dog dung collected by "pure-finders," both the high-price ones, who are paid to clean out kennels, and the scavengers who scour the streets; the whirling words and priceless patter of the ballad hawkers, rivaling the telegraph in their speed in

250 Hilary M. Schor

bringing the news to market; the girls yearning for sprats, girls not educated but canny, aware, and alert. What the novel adds to Mayhew's compelling inquiry is a plot: Dickens doesn't just continue to seek out new ways of interrogating the world, incorporating the anonymous interviewer who disappears silently into his investigations, but integrates our curious gaze with the fortunes of the plucky heroine who moves beyond her sphere and acts as a social investigator, entering the homes and hearts of the poor. In novels like *Dombey and Son, Bleak House,* and *Hard Times,* the heroines go beyond their assigned spheres, but the kind of "homework" they carry out transforms readers' hearts and heads, or so the theory of the realist novel at midcentury would argue. These texts take the curious heroine on a wandering path, carrying us far beyond the narrow walls of the miserable, lonely, cranky self.

The novel has in short always done double work: at once making the world familiar and estranging us from it, teaching us to see and giving us a sentimental education, offering us a coherent plot through which to organize the things and people we encounter, but also setting us a little off-balance as it takes us somewhere "new" and newsworthy. But if the eighteenth-century novel was a manual of conduct, telling the ambitious heroine how to behave as she aspired to a new social position, and the nineteenth-century novel brought us a museum, a wonder-house of previously unknown objects in a previously unknown world (Sprats! Purefinders! Statistics and stutterings!), what happens when the world is emptied of people, when objects are no longer recognizable, when the world, as we know it, comes to an end? What kind of curious readers and curious heroines will be possible at the end of the world?

This is the question Emily St. John Mandel takes up in her *Station Eleven,* a novel that begins in the world as we know it and turns that world into the world of *before* and *after,* killing off not only 99.9 percent of the population but all the statisticians prepared to tell us about it. Following a massive outbreak of the beautifully named "Georgian flu," "civilization [is] an archipelago of small towns [that] had fought off ferals, buried their neighbors, lived and died and suffered together in the blood-drenched years just after the collapse, survived against unspeakable odds and then only by holding together into the calm" (48). The novel, too, must find new ways of surviving against the odds, "holding together into the calm." After an event that shatters the conventional multiplot novel, disrupting entirely the relationships of people, objects, and plot on which the novel also depended, Mandel needs a

Curiosity at the End of the World   251

form of curiosity that will meld time frames, that will create networks without familiar webs, that can see the world in a snow globe—and she needs a very different form of the novel to depict it. While in some ways she stays true to my model of curiosity, continuing to focus on a single heroine whom we meet at the end of civilization and follow until the lights come back on (perhaps) at the end, she disrupts our idea of curiosity as well, making both readers and characters archeologists of the everyday. For, as Lorraine Daston once promised of the modern world, "The end of inquiry is no longer to make wonder stop, but to let it begin."

For that reason, the disruption of all we think we know, *Station Eleven* begins not with the plague but with a play, in a confetti of fake snow, on the stage of a Toronto theater, where King Lear is raging against the storm, as the three young actresses who played the younger versions of Goneril, Regan, and Cordelia once again sit on stage, playing a clapping game. The actor playing Lear, Arthur Leander, suffers a heart attack and reaches out blindly, striking the stage set as he misjudges his relationship to objects, dying in character but in a line from elsewhere in the play. "The wren goes to't," mutters Lear, and "Jeevan, who knew the play very well, realize[s] that the actor had skipped back twelve lines" (3). The curtain comes down abruptly, and Jeevan Chaudary, a former paparazzo turned entertainment reporter, now a trainee EMT, who has leapt onto the stage to try to resuscitate Arthur, finds himself in the uncanny space of the now bright-lit stage. "Not quite a room," he thinks, "too transitory, all those doorways and dark spaces between wings, the missing ceiling" (5). In a play on words that will echo throughout the novel, "It was more like a terminal, he thought, a train station or an airport, everyone passing quickly through." But he waits in the artificial light, comforting a child actress, Kirsten Raymonde, who played one of the daughters. The actors scatter, a few remaining, while the body is removed, and Jeevan walks away from the plastic snow into a real snowstorm in Toronto and, as he enters the park in the cold night, into the coming plague. While he has been in the theater, the Georgian flu has come to North America, and the disease is beginning to devastate the world. Or so we learn almost casually, as we return briefly to the theater, where the stage manager, Edgar, Gloucester, a makeup artist, Goneril, and an executive producer who had been in the audience, remain at the theater bar, toasting Arthur: "Of all of them there at the bar that night, the bartender was the one who survived the longest. He died three weeks later on the road out of the city" (15).

252   Hilary M. Schor

All of them dead, the last of them three weeks later on the road out of the
city. What to do? As Jeevan learns of the flu, he takes his lessons from his
literary training. "Jeevan's understanding of disaster preparedness was based
entirely on action movies, but, on the other hand he'd seen a lot of action
movies" (21). Fiction, even if lowbrow fiction, comes through. He knows
to buy lots of water, canned goods, toilet paper; only on his last trip to the
late-night grocery store does he buy flowers. That is all that happens. Or
more precisely, there are two things that do not happen at the beginning of
the novel: we do not see anyone die of the flu, and we do not hear from a
single medical expert or textbook or talking head. Such information as we
have in the moment of urgency is disseminated from Jeevan's best friend,
Hua, an emergency room doctor who calls to warn him: "You remember the
SARS epidemic? . . . You told me to call you if there was ever a real epidemic.
We've admitted over two hundred flu patients since the morning[,] . . . a
hundred and sixty in the past three hours. . . . You get exposed to this, you're
sick within hours" (18, 20). We hear Hua begin to cough, we see some people
expressing vague alarm on the television, and then we huddle with Jeevan
in an apartment with his crippled brother, as his brother ghostwrites the
autobiography of a celebrity philanthropist whose name he has vowed to
protect (and he does). And we also see the ramifications of the death of
Arthur Leander, the King who died onstage ("the wren goes to't"), as Arthur's
lawyer calls his best friend and his best friend calls his ex-wives. All these
characters are briefly gathered into "an incident," Arthur's death, the same
characters whom the rest of the novel will attempt to reconnect. Later in the
novel we will return to that quiet Toronto apartment and watch the lights
go out and the TV stations shut down; we will learn that if you got sick,
you were dead in forty-eight hours; we will watch, in keeping with the tradition of the novel, the end of "the news"—both the turning-off, forever, of
the cameras, and the web, and the grid, and the end of anything happening
but chaos. But now we watch the end of the world we recognize. As Mandel
puts it in the short chapter that ends part 1 of the novel:

AN INCOMPLETE LIST:
    No more diving into pools of chlorinated water lit green from below. No
more ball games played out under floodlights. No more porch lights with
moths fluttering on summer nights. No more trains running under the surface
of cities on the dazzling power of the electric third rail. No more cities. No

more films, except rarely, except with a generator drowning out half the dialogue, and only then for the first little while until the fuel for the generators ran out, because automobile gas goes stale after two or three years. Aviation gas lasts longer, but it was difficult to come by. (31)

The lists go on, until the chapter ends, and with it the first section of the book:

No more Internet. No more social media, no more scrolling through litanies of dreams and nervous hopes and photographs of lunches, cries for help and expressions of contentment and relationship-status updates with heart icons whole or broken, places to meet up later, pleas, complaints, desires, pictures of babies dressed as bears or peppers for Halloween. No more reading and commenting on the lives of others, and in so doing, feeling slightly less alone in the room. No more avatars. (32)

And with that (Why no more avatars? Why is that the last line?) the old world ends.

Or does it? Jeevan Chaudary's immediate thought had been that "this illness Hua was describing was going to be the divide between a *before* and an *after,* a line drawn through his life" (20). And in some ways that is true. The novel will pick up twenty years after that first night, and so many things will fall into the "no more" list. We are no longer in Jeevan's presence, no longer in the comforting space of a Toronto theater; instead, we are on the road with a group of musicians and actors, the "Traveling Symphony," in a caravan made up of repurposed pick-up trucks (all the automotive parts, those that needed fuel, are long gone), and only when we find Kirsten Raymonde, no longer a child but still an actress, do we know where we are:

'Enter Lear,' Kirsten said. Twenty years earlier, in a life she mostly couldn't remember, she had had a small nonspeaking role in a short-lived Toronto production of *King Lear.* Now she walked in sandals whose soles had been cut from an automobile tire, three knives in her belt. (35)

We are not used to "short-lived" being quite so literal, and it is with that hanging over us that we hear Kirsten continue, "Mad .... Fantastically dressed with wild flowers" (35). And if we, like Jeevan, are aficionados of

254   Hilary M. Schor

disaster, in our case fictional dystopias, we are fairly certain what we will read next: a short while down the road, we will stop exactly long enough for someone to tell us the story of "what went wrong." Exposition will briefly disrupt (or not so briefly, given the chattiness of such expository blowhards) the forward motion into more disaster, and then the talking will stop and we will get on with the apocalypse. Zombies will come, or violent refugees, or peaceful survivors lighting matches against the darkness, or canny peddlers, trading in news and sexual favors. (Yes, you read that novel, too.) Utopian novels, for what it is worth, follow a similar pattern: a resident of our world magically awakens in another world, wonders just how everyone became so peace-loving and well-fed, and The Oldest Inhabitant is dragged out to retell the founding story. We were violent; the world ended; we began again. Welcome to our paradise—and please, feel free to share our women! Dystopic or utopic, the future has a tendency to talk at us for a while and then get back to being the future.[12]

   That is not what happens here. Everything in this world has changed, and yet the world remains hauntingly familiar. This is still the world of realism with which I began. We still live in a world of ordinary people (no zombies will emerge in this apocalypse, nor any princesses, nor even a dragon), and we are still fascinated by the appearance of ordinary objects—if not sprats then dogs, abandoned classrooms, the remains of fast-food restaurants. And most important, the heroine remains the investigator, our passport into a world that remains curious (that is to say, unknown) to us. Kirsten must do what all heroines in curious novels do: she must traverse the landscape carrying her conduct book, testing its maxims and charting its variations. But the temporal chasm alters everything. If the eighteenth-century novel traces the "history of the young lady's entrance into the world," and the nineteenth-century novel is looking around the corner, down a darkened alley, searching for people at whose lives we can only guess, when we read *Station Eleven* we are trying to glimpse our own lives after apocalypse, reading about an event that could have happened yesterday (or that might happen for us tomorrow), and is, by the time the central portion of the book begins, only twenty years in the past. Futurist novels are always about what to them is the past, and to us is our present, and yet here this uncanny proximity comes at us with remarkable urgency. And that is because our heroine, Kirsten, is trying not just to survive in her world but to see *our* world. Like another Alice, she falls into the gap between the two worlds—

Curiosity at the End of the World   255

the world of the opening chapter, in which she moved about freely, just another child actress, and a world in which all remnants of that prior world are falling into decrepitude, and the markers no longer mean anything. She can, in short, see even her own life only in glimpses—as a younger character says, "I've read books. I even found a newspaper once. I know it all used to be different" (292). As Kirsten moves through the novel, she is doing two things: trying to survive and scouting out her own past.

If her journey is what we might expect, her conduct book most certainly is not. Nowhere in *Station Eleven* do we see any guides to living after a plague, nor even a road map of what the land around Lake Michigan used to be like. Mandel does not cite (not even in her acknowledgments) such bibles of plaguery as Richard Preston's *The Hot Zone* or Laurie Garrett's *The Coming Plague*; the only book to appear in those acknowledgments is an apocalyptic novel that features vampires, Justin Cronin's *The Passage*.[13] Even Shakespeare appears not as a guide to living nor as high art (the Symphony plays not only Beethoven but "classical, jazz, orchestral arrangements of pre-collapse pop songs" [37]), but as himself a product of the plague: "She remembered Dieter talking to her about Shakespeare, Shakespeare's work and family, Shakespeare's plague-haunted life. 'Wait, do you mean he had the plague?' she asked. 'No,' Dieter said, 'I mean he was defined by it. I don't know how much schooling you've had. Do you know what that means, to be defined by something?'" (308). And Kirsten thinks, "Yes. *There was a new heaven and a new earth.*" So no, not Shakespeare. Not the Bible, no apocalyptic fiction. Mandel's great trick of curiosity is that Kirsten's book of the world is a comic book, a graphic novel depicting another apocalypse "a thousand years in the future." It is that book that provides the aesthetic manifesto and the survival guide of our novel; it poses one of the chief mysteries of the plot, forging the chain that binds all the characters together; and it is also called "Station Eleven."

Or part of it is. "Station Eleven" is the first of two volumes of a graphic novel called "Dr. Eleven," depicting Station Eleven the place, a spaceship which is also a planet, one that has slipped through a rift in time and become a planet of night, covered by water, haunted by a part of the population that lives beneath the surface, in the "undersea." (To distinguish them in my essay, I will refer to *Station Eleven,* Mandel's novel, with italics; "Station Eleven," the volume of the graphic novel, with quotation marks; and Station Eleven the place as merely itself, but expect to lose your own place occasionally as you follow these complicated threads. Getting lost between worlds, remember, is the point.) The people in the graphic novel, those on the planet/spaceship, like the people in the world of *Station Eleven* after the disaster, are divided. Some live at peace in the new world, grown accustomed to the beauty of a world of perpetual twilight and sunsets; others live undersea and yearn only for the sweetness of the world they left behind. But here's the thing: this novel was written fifteen years before *our* apocalypse. It was written by Miranda Carroll, the first wife of Arthur Leander, the actor who died in the novel's first scene. (Miranda is one of the three ex-wives Arthur's best friend calls in the opening pages of the novel, after Arthur dies.) She was already working on it when she fell in love with Arthur and decided to leave her boyfriend for him. "It is sometimes necessary," she thought at that moment, "to break everything" (85). She "began thinking about the possibilities of the form, about spaceships and stars, alien planets, but a year passed before she invented the beautiful wreckage of Station Eleven" (88). It is what Miranda imagines when she begins her life with Arthur in Los Angeles: she thinks, "I could throw away almost everything . . . and begin all over again. Station Eleven will be my constant" (89). And at the same time, it is also the world through which we walk, what Kirsten calls "the beauty of this world where almost everyone was gone" (148), "beauty in the decrepitude," underwater and tarnished.

That sense of gorgeous estrangement is what makes Kirsten's book of the world so mysterious, so curious, so useful. At first we do not even know how Kirsten came to possess the book Miranda started so long ago. Indeed, it is a wonder she has any book at all, for very few written materials remain in the *after* world. There are *TV Guides,* which are treasured objects, even if they were already "mostly obsolete, but used by a few people right up to the end," and volumes of poetry, "even rarer than *TV Guide* copies" (40). Newspapers exist in a variety of forms, *before* and *after.* There are "old" newspapers—as one character asks ironically, "Do I have the second to last edition of the *New York Times?*" (184). which happens to be the newspaper that has Arthur's death in it—and there is a new newspaper, which is being typeset by hand by François Diallo, an editor in New Petoskey. The texts we spend the most time with are celebrity magazines: we watch Kirsten and her friend August hunt for them in the remaining houses, shops, ruins. But as Kirsten leafs through them, not just the past but alternative universes emerge: "August said that given an infinite number of parallel universes, there had to be one where there had been no pandemic and he'd grown up to be a physicist as planned" (200). In one magazine August finds a picture of a woman we know to be Miranda leaving the Toronto theater two weeks before Arthur's death, and says to Kirsten, "I mean, it *is* you in those pictures, in a parallel universe where the collapse didn't happen" (201). Kirsten stares at the magazine, and wonders: "I think I was there," Kirsten said. "I might've been in that building at that moment." Behind Miranda, "she saw only a steel door, the stone wall of a building. Had she passed through that door? She must have, she thought, and wished she could remember it" (201).

This is the uncanny status of curiosity in *Station Eleven*: Kirsten may wonder, but we know not only that she was there "at that moment" but that it is where her comics came from. Miranda was backstage at the theater, giving Arthur the finished copies of "Dr. Eleven," and Kirsten entered the dressing room. An entire parallel universe opens once we get the full "memory." As we learn late in the novel, when Miranda looked at the young Kirsten, two weeks before the end of the world in a theater in Toronto, she knew, instantly, that the girl was a child actor—although she "couldn't imagine what part there could possibly be in *King Lear* for a seven- or eight-year-old" (212):

> "Hello," Miranda said. The girl looked like a china doll, she thought. She looked like someone who'd been well-cared-for and coddled all her life. She was probably someone who would grow up to be like Miranda's assistant Laetitia, like Leon's assistant Thea, unadventurous and well-groomed. (212–13)

Miranda leaves the dressing room and Kirsten doesn't remember the encounter, knowing only that Arthur gave her the comics; the moment is lost. But another, "alternative" reality is lost as well. The girl that Miranda briefly conjures never comes into existence. The Kirsten we meet is still an actor, indeed, "the best Shakespearean actress in the territory" (120), but she bears two tattooed daggers on her wrist, the signs that she has killed two men. She is missing teeth, she has a scar for which she cannot account (it came in the first year, when she and her brother walked, and she remembers nothing), and she wears on her arm another tattoo, the motto of the Traveling Symphony, "Survival is insufficient." That adult woman is not in the least well-groomed and she is every bit of adventurous—but somewhere, in an alternative universe, another Kirsten has grown up like a china doll, coddled, cared for, and unmarked. That woman is lingering, ghostlike, just outside our text.

That is why "Dr. Eleven" is the only possible road map to the broken world, however surreal its intergalactic scenery. Its ghosts hold the clues to our novel. Kirsten cannot remember her parents' faces; her brother is dead; she remembers a scene backstage, and the actor dying, and a man (a man we know to be Jeevan) who was kind to her. She is looking for pieces of her own past—but they are also pieces of the other characters' past, and they allow the novel to move backward as well as forward, to assemble in fragments the pieces of a multiplot novel, that unified narrative no single character can (in this broken world) possess. But the book can, in the same way it can bridge the temporal disruptions. It gives us back what the characters have lost, in much the same way that when Arthur first sees the finished, published volumes of "Dr. Eleven," he remembers their creation: "The cover of the first one was on the studio wall in L.A., wasn't it?" It is an image, he once said, that was "like the establishing shot for a movie: the sharp islands of the City, streets and buildings terraced into the rock, high bridges between" (213–14).

By this time, of course, there are no more movies, and Arthur's analogy would mean little to someone actually in the world of the novel, yet the lost metaphor remains vital. That is in part because the creation of "Station Eleven" takes place in the world of the movies, giving those scenes much of their poignancy. The longest section of the novel is a single night in Hollywood, eleven years before the collapse, thirty years before the events of the present-day, a dreadful dinner party that brings together all the characters we have "already" met in the scenes after Arthur Leander's unexpected death. The guests are Elizabeth, the beautiful actress Arthur will marry next; Gary Heller, who is Arthur's lawyer; Heller's wife, whose name Miranda will forget "although she's heard it at least twice this evening" (92); a producer; an actor; and "a woman named Tesch," who "seems to be someone who mistakes rudeness for intellectual rigor" (93).

At first, this scene seems merely to provide the details of an impeccable realism, doing the work of the nineteenth-century novel by providing everything from Mayhewian social reportage to the Dickensian multiplot intricacy, offering that same proliferation of details. The conversation is brilliant, the satire pointed. Tesch, in a moment of dialectal delight, says that "Station Eleven" reminds her "'of a documentary I saw last month, a little Czech film about an outsider artist who refused to show her work during her lifetime. She lived in *Pra*ha, and—' 'Oh,' Clark says, [interrupting her] 'I believe when you're speaking English, you're allowed to refer to it as Prague'" (95). Mandel reports quietly that "Tesch appears to have lost the power of speech." At this moment Miranda realizes, "It's too late, and it's been too late for a while," and her marriage is over (98). But the night continues. Her picture is taken outside by Jeevan the paparazzo, her house is in silence, the opening shot of "Station Eleven" is on an easel in her room, and Miranda, sitting by the swimming pool, says to her dog Luli ("shining like a ghost," (91) about to make her way into "Station Eleven" and hence into the *after*world), "This life was never ours. . . . We were only ever borrowing it" (101). Miranda realizes that "she is marooned on a strange planet" (92), and "Station Eleven is all around [her]" (107), but so are all the "damaged homes": the silent house of their ruined marriage, the ravaged ruins of the world after the plague, the painting on the easel where Dr. Eleven ("a man from the future who does not whine") stands on a rock with a Pomeranian by his side: "Text: *I stood looking over my damaged home and tried to forget the sweetness of life on earth*" (214). No wonder the comic book is a guide to the apocalypse. It knew the end before we did, and it survived.

For Kirsten, who is herself "marooned on a strange planet," this is the book she needs, not "Apocalypse for Dummies" or "Beloved Back-Roads of Central Michigan." Like Benjamin's angel, she is always looking back at what is lost while fighting for survival amid what is broken, and for her, "Station Eleven" is both a piece of the lost world and a guide to bridging the temporal gap, a stopgap, allowing her to construct a life at the intersection. Mandel, too, in a world without planes, trains, and automobiles, without bridges and tunnels and railways, without the usual mechanisms (quite literally) of plot, must hold together her fictional universe. But how? For after all, in the realist novel, so much depends on the network, the familiar grooves along which a reader's curiosity can travel.

Here we rejoin the curiosity of the world of Dickens and Mayhew, the world in which "sprats" became magical, and Florence Dombey and her slipshod sisters trod the world of homeless London, every object illuminated. How much more so is that true after the collapse, in the "orangeless world," where it is the objects, far more than the people, that travel, radiant in their very ordinariness. Kirsten's copy of "Station Eleven" is one of those objects and, as we shall see, a crucial one, but almost any object will do—a souvenir, a haunted teacup, a photograph, any object of a certain weight. Or more accurately, one kind of weight, for "You're still the only person I know who carries a paperweight in her backpack," the journalist in the *after*world says

260 Hilary M. Schor

to Kirsten (184). The paperweight marks out its own network in the novel. It was given by Clark to Arthur on the night of that dreadful dinner party in Los Angeles; Miranda takes it when she leaves the house in LA and only years later, two weeks before the apocalypse, does she return it to Arthur in a theatre in Toronto, where it will be handed to Kirsten, after Arthur's death, by Tanya, the "wrangler" of the child actors, to comfort her in the fake snow and the bright light of the theater: "Kirsten, teary-eyed and breathless, a few days shy of her eighth birthday, gazed at the object and thought it was the most beautiful, the most wonderful, the strangest thing anyone had ever given her. It was a lump of glass with a storm cloud trapped inside" (15). And that is eerily what Miranda thought when she first saw it, that night in Los Angeles: "A paperweight of clouded glass[,] . . . when she holds it, it's a pleasing weight in the palm of her hand. It's like looking into a storm. She tells herself as she switches off the light that she's only taking the paper-weight back to her study to sketch it, but she knows she's going to keep it forever" (104). Miranda doesn't, of course, but the novel does.

The novel is the place where objects go to die and to live forever: one character, on being told of the "Museum of Civilization," "a place where arti-facts from the old world are preserved," laughs, "a sound like a bark." "Arti-facts from the old world," he says. "Here's the thing, kids, the entire world is a place where artifacts from the old world are preserved. When was the last time you saw a new car?" (146). But that world is fast decaying: as Kirsten herself reflects, when asked how she bears it, "We stand it because we were younger than you were when everything ended, Kirsten thought, but not young enough to remember nothing at all. Because there isn't much time left, because all the roofs are collapsing now and soon none of the old build-ings will be safe. Because we are always looking for the former world, before all the traces of the former world are gone" (130). The novel needs to create—rather, people need to create—a holding place for the traces of the former world. The novel needs to design a place where objects come back to life.

That place is, ironically, truly a "terminal," the airport of Severn City, where Clark Thompson, Arthur Leander's best friend, is diverted midflight on his way to Arthur's funeral—no one, despite Jeevan's earlier metaphor, is moving "quickly" through this airport. This is where Clark realizes, in the book's most haunting sentence, "I was here for the end of electricity." In the sudden darkness, "the stars were a cloud of light across the breadth of the sky, extravagant in their multitudes," and Clark thinks he is hallucinating, but his friend Dolores says no, it is not his imagination; he is actually seeing the sky that Galileo saw, now that "the era of light pollution had come to an end" (251). Yet in this permanent layover, the "darkness pooling over the earth [as] the grid was failing," Clark creates a *Wunderkammer* of curiosities. Out of the beautiful empty shelves of the Skymiles Lounge, he forges a museum: He places his useless iPhone on the top shelf, adds an Amex card and a driver's license belonging to a woman who died, and while he mentions it to no one, "when he came back a few hours later, someone had added another iPhone, a pair of five-inch red stiletto heels, and a snow globe" (255).

This moment transforms the novel. Until then, the novel's only verb has been "to walk." As one character says, "All of the Symphony's stories were the same, in two variations. Everyone else died, I walked, I found the Symphony. Or, I was very young when it happened, I was born after it happened, I have no memories or few memories of any other way of living, and I have been walking all my life" (266), but the novel now offers a new verb: "to museum," to form a collection, to say that we (not I, we) were here. These objects have become curious: they bear the traces of care, they have the power to cure, and they are beautiful:

> There seemed to be a limitless number of objects in the world that had no practical use but that people wanted to preserve: cell phones with their delicate buttons, iPads, Tyler's Nintendo console, a selection of laptops. There were a number of impractical shoes, stilettos mostly, beautiful and strange. There were three car engines in a row, cleaned and polished, a motorcycle composed mostly of gleaming chrome. Traders brought things for Clark sometimes, objects of no real value that they knew he would like: magazines and newspapers, a stamp collection, coins. There were the passports or the driver's licenses or sometimes the credit cards of people who had lived at the airport and then died. Clark kept impeccable records. (258)

It is no accident that the passage describing the beauty of objects takes up, of all things, the snow globe. "Clark had always been fond of beautiful objects, and in his present state of mind, all objects were beautiful," and he goes on to "consider the snow globe": the mind that invented it; the factory worker "who turned sheets of plastic into white flakes of snow, the hand that drew the plan for the miniature Severn City," the assembly-line worker who watched the globe glide past on a conveyer belt somewhere in China (255).

The gloves on the hands of the woman who shipped it, the ship that carried it, the signature on the shipping manifest, the secret hopes of the UPS man. The whole of the world really is contained in a single object, and it is the mass-market twin of the paperweight that Kirsten carries in her backpack, both objects a novel unto themselves. In that doubling, our novel has seemingly done its curious work: it has brought the heroine to the edge of the known world, and it has assembled its own collection of objects in the wonder house, a museum that is itself a "terminal."[14]

But this "terminal" is not the end of the novel, nor is it the novel's final word on curiosity. That word might actually be borrowed by a theorist at the other end of the ecological spectrum, Anna Lowenhaupt Tsing, in *The Mushroom at the End of the World: On the Possibility of Life in Capitalist Ruins.* Tsing has gone so far as to suggest that in bringing back the world, "our first step is to bring back curiosity."[15] What she has in mind is the matsutake, an exotic mushroom, blooming rarely, with a legendary, piquant, "woodsy" odor redolent of the autumn in which it grows, the first thing to grow after the atom bomb in Hiroshima. Her response to the ruins of capitalism is to return to the precarious, the organic, the rare, and the meaningful, something we hunt out, something that is precisely not ruined.

And yet, unexpectedly, it is Tsing who gives me back the language with which I began, for she, too, imagines that this "curiosity" grows out of destruction, that life as we know it is always a state of "disturbance." As she says, at the moment of precarity, the matsutake grows only in "deeply disturbed forests."[16] What she does not mean is an empty airport terminal, obviously, or the "archipelago" of civilization, inhabited by ferals, but what she does mean are the increasingly messy networks, the "patches" of social organization, which require "the magic of translation,"[17] the "searching" for the matsutake,[18] the translation which is "the drawing of one world-making project into another,"[19] the "under-ground," "world-building" networks of fungi that happen "after progress."[20] As Tsing claims, "radical curiosity beckons."[21]

And that is the work of *Station Eleven,* where curiosity is explicitly made world (re)building, and the heroine is remade from the actress into the explorer, the "searcher," setting out for another world armed with, of course, her guidebook: the novel of the impossible future made up of the beautiful fragments of the lost world. So consider again the snow globe, that elegant, ubiquitous, mass-produced, infinitely disposable object, truly a *multum in parvo.* The novel began in a flurry of fake snow in a theater in Toronto; Jeevan steps out of the theater into a real snowstorm, which conjures the joys of his childhood; Kirsten travels with a paperweight that contains a storm within it; at the end of the novel, Clark, now a very old and frail man, is contemplating the wonders of another fake snowstorm, this one inside a snow globe of the Severn City Airport, a place he will never leave.

This is the way *Station Eleven* finally remodels curiosity, as itself a model of how the world is to continue: not just the snow globe but Kirsten's backpack filled with celebrity clippings, fragments, a reminder that "once, when she was sixteen years old, . . . she found her past" in a magazine (40), a reminder that we leave a record behind us—even if that record is a thousand years in the future. "I collect celebrity gossip clippings. . . . I understand something about permanent records" (268).

The novel creates its own collection. It holds the world together as Elaine Scarry promises of what the Swiss do in practicing, repeatedly, for nuclear war. Each member of a village has a task, down to collecting "the statue of Saint Roch with the accompanying statue of Saint Roch's dog, who in turn holds in his mouth a ceramic Eucharist wafer."[22] This is no trivial act, for "in saving any one precious object, what is preserved is not only that object but the population's link, through that object, to many kindred objects outside of Switzerland, which may or may not survive a nuclear war."[23] This is Scarry's account in *Thermonuclear Monarchy,* but she argues something even more powerful in *Rule of Law, Misrule of Man.* She argues that even (or especially) in war, "the most fundamental norms are not to be violated": "The creation of an accurate record is the work of many people."[24] She says explicitly, "Some small pieces of language in war must remain wholly intact, uncompromised, unwavering, undiluted in their meaning. These few insignia [white flags, red crosses, ambulances, and hospitals] are placed *hors de combat,* or 'out of combat': they constitute a civil structure that remains in place in the international sphere in the same way that inside a country the military is kept inside a civil frame."[25] She goes on: "Unless certain pieces of language remain uncontaminated by war, no international framework of trust remains available for a truce or peace accord. These small pieces of language must be kept intact because they provide a bridge back to civilization."[26]

For Mandel this is not a "civil frame" as much as it is an imaginative frame. "A location from which other true sentences can be spoken"[27] is what the curious heroine both seeks and provides. This was suggested as early as Miranda's death, which we only read at the end of the book, for although

264   Hilary M. Schor

Miranda dies of the plague, she dies into her own novel. As she dies the whole world turns into "Dr. Eleven": "A wash of violent color, pink and streaks of brilliant orange. . . . The seascape bleeding into confused visions of Station Eleven, its extravagant sunsets and its indigo sea" (228). We think this is the last of Miranda, but she comes back again later, at the very end, when we return to the scene in Toronto when she first sketched what will become Dr. Eleven's ship:

> Miranda is drawing Leon Prevant's reception area before she realizes what she's doing. The prairies of carpet, the desk, Leon's closed office door, the wall of glass. The two staplers on her desk—how did she end up with two?—and the doors leading out to the elevators and restrooms. Trying to convey the serenity of this place where she spends her most pleasant hours, the refinement of it, but outside the glass wall she substitutes another landscape, dark rocks and high bridges. (86–87)

As it first appeared, this was classic realism, the connection of characters and things, the second stapler like Barthes's barometer, the sign of a realism that is "enough" by being "too much," superfluous to requirement.[28] But when she dies, that scene comes back, magically illuminated:

> In *Dr. Eleven,* Vol. 1, No. 2: *The Pursuit,* Dr. Eleven is visited by the ghost of his mentor, Captain Lonagan, recently killed by an Undersea assassin. Miranda discarded fifteen versions of this image before she felt that she had the ghost exactly right, working hour upon hour, and years later, at the end, delirious on an empty beach on the coast of Malaysia with seabirds rising and plummeting through the air and a line of ships fading out on the horizon, this was the image she kept thinking of, drifting away from and then toward it and then slipping somehow through the frame: the captain is rendered in delicate watercolors, a translucent silhouette in the dim light of Dr. Eleven's office, which is identical to the administrative area in Leon Prevant's Toronto office suite, down to the two staplers on the desk. (330)

When Dr. Eleven is visited by his mentor's ghost, he asks him what dying was like: "It was exactly like waking up from a dream," he says. But Miranda's dream is precise, careful, a refurnishing of the world. Gil argued that the Traveling Symphony should perform "'*A Midsummer Night's Dream,*' Gil

Curiosity at the End of the World 265

said, breaking an impasse. 'I believe the evening calls for fairies'" (44). But this "evening," this interlude in the archipelago of civilization, also requires gadgets, objects, staplers. If we are going to have electricity again, we will need not "enough" objects but too many—not one stapler, but two: "How did she end up with two?"

This is the way *Station Eleven* becomes once again curious. It reassembles the fragments of our culture, lost and disused ("When was the last time you saw a new car?") so that Kirsten can walk bravely into a new world. Miranda and the landscape of "Station Eleven" and *Station Eleven* come together at the end, when Kirsten carries "Station Eleven" into the museum, where it meets its final and best reader: Clark. And what he finds, when Kirsten hands him the novel, is a drawing of an undersea world, which is actually a representation of that infamous dinner party he attended thirty years before in Los Angeles. In both, there is a dog called Luli, a wavery figure who resembles Clark himself, and a pretentious woman in glasses reminiscing about life on Earth. "'I traveled the world before the war,' she says. 'I spent some time in the Czech Republic, you know, in *Pra*ha . . . ,' and tears come to his eyes because all at once he recognizes the dinner party; he was *there*" (332). Suddenly, we, too, are there, and we hear the echo of that ironic comment, all those years ago: the wavery figure in our memory says, "I believe when you're speaking English you're allowed to refer to it as Prague." "Once Clark sat with all of them in Los Angeles, at a table under electric light. On the page, only Miranda is missing, her chair taken by Dr. Eleven" (332). He feels "such affection for them," and he remembers Miranda slipping out the door, into the night, when he followed her, because he was "curious about her" as she sits outside with the dog who looks like a cloud, as Jeevan, the paparazzo, waited by her front door, waiting to snap her, unawares, for the gossip pages. "At least celebrity gossip survives"—it survives, and with it, the world.

E. M. Forster was wrong. Curiosity, our desire to know "and then . . ." does hold the world together. Throughout the book, we have done the work of curiosity. We have placed the fragments back together, we have found the objects and mapped their trajectories, we have made a coherent narrative where there were only ghosts. We have built the bridge on which Kirsten will walk away from "the terminal" and into the new world. Having seen the glimmer of the internet beginning again and lights in the distance, in a new city, she goes bearing her guidebook, her novel, or rather, only one of her

266 Hilary M. Schor

novels. One volume of "Dr. Eleven" goes with her; the other stays behind, in the museum, so that one will always be safe. "And if Clark hadn't come to know her a little, over the weeks when the Symphony had lived in Concourse A and performed music or Shakespeare every night, he might not have caught the excitement in her voice. She was beside herself with impatience to see the far southern town with the electrical grid," the town they have only glimpsed (is it again Galileo, a new age of enlightenment?) through a telescope (332).

> Perhaps vessels are setting out even now, traveling toward or away from him, steered by sailors armed with maps and knowledge of the stars, driven by need or perhaps simply by curiosity: whatever became of the countries on the other side? If nothing else, it's pleasant to consider the possibility. He liked the thought of ships moving over the water, toward another world just out of sight. (332–33)

Perhaps. And perhaps in that new world, "just out of sight," people will again sit under an electric light, gossiping and flirting and being ordinary. "Simply by curiosity"? Nothing simple here, and yet what Mandel is offering us is what the anthropologists, the epidemiologists, the documentarians, and the fantasists want but only the novel can provide: a ship made of paper, in which we can sail into the curious unknown.

Notes

1. Emily St. John Mandel, *Station Eleven* (New York: Knopf, 2014), 57. Further page citations are in the text.

2. E. M. Forster, *Aspects of the Novel* (New York: Harcourt, Brace and World, 1927), 86–87.

3. Lorraine Daston and Katharine Park, *Wonders and the Order of Nature, 1150–1750* (New York: Zone Books, 1998).

4. John Eisner and Roger Cardinal, *The Culture of Collecting* (Cambridge, Mass.: Harvard University Press, 1994); Mieke Bal, "Telling Objects: A Narrative Perspective on Collecting," in Eisner and Cardinal, *The Culture of Collecting*; Jean Baudrillard, "The System of Collecting," in Eisner and Cardinal, *The Culture of Collecting*; and Jean Baudrillard, "A Marginal System: Collecting," in *The System of Objects*, trans. James Benedict (1968; London: Verso, 1996).

5. Susan Stewart, *On Longing: Narratives of the Miniature, the Gigantic, the Souvenir, the Collection* (Durham, N.C.: Duke University Press, 1992), 54.

6. Hilary M. Schor, *Curious Subjects: Women and the Trials of Realism* (New York: Oxford University Press, 2013).

7. My account of the rise of the novel follows Ian Watt's classic *The Rise of the Novel* (London: Chatto and Windus, 1957); for further discussions of the relationship of the "news" to the novel, and the rise of the heroine as "nobody," see Lennard Davis, *Factual Fictions: The Origins of the English Novel* (Philadelphia: University of Pennsylvania Press, 1983); Catherine Gallagher, *Nobody's Story: The Vanishing Acts of Women Writers in the Marketplace, 1760–1920* (Berkeley: University of California Press, 1994).

8. Frances Burney, *Evelina, or The History of a Young Lady's Entrance into the World* (Oxford: Oxford University Press, 1982), 7.

9. William Makepeace Thackeray, "Waiting at the Station," from *Punch,* March 9, 1850, reprinted in *Punch's Prize Novelists, The Fat Contributor and Travels in London* (New York, 1853).

10. This most perfect phrase is Walter Bagehot's, in his "Charles Dickens," *National Review,* 1858, reprinted in *Literary Studies*, vol. 2, ed. Richard Holt Hutton (London: Thomas Greene, 1895), 141.

11. *London Labour and the London Poor* began as a series of articles by Henry Mayhew published in the 1840s in a newspaper, *The Morning Chronicle.* They were collected into three volumes in 1851; they are largely organized by profession, but they also feature a dizzying array of objects, statistics, and interviews.

12. The novel is *California,* by Edan Lepucki (New York: Little, Brown, 2014)—a very good novel, despite my teasing. The literature on dystopia and utopia is too vast to collect here, but readers will also recognize my allusion to William Morris's *News from Nowhere.*

13. These were the two books on my shelf as I was writing this essay: Laurie Garrett, *The Coming Plague: Newly Emerging Diseases in a World Out of Balance* (New York: Penguin, 1994) and Richard Preston, *The Hot Zone: The Terrifying True Story of the Origins of the Ebola Virus* (New York: Random House, 1994). *The Passage* (New York: Ballantine Books, 2010) is invoked in the novel by Arthur's second wife, Elizabeth, as proof that the rest of the world could actually still exist and they simply not know it (as happens in *The Passage*, where vampires have taken over North America and a quarantine is imposed), and that civilization could survive. Clark doubts her— but she might, in fact, be right; civilization might survive after all.

14. Barbara Stafford has argued that curiosity cabinets find their modern equivalent in the computer, another kind of "terminal." *Devices of Wonder: From the World in a Box to Images on a Screen* (Los Angeles: Getty Research Institute, 2001).

15. Anna Lowenhaupt Tsing in *The Mushroom at the End of the World: On the Possibility of Life in Capitalist Ruins* (Princeton, N.J.: Princeton University Press, 2015), 7.

16. Tsing, 50.

17. Tsing, 123.

18. Tsing, 77.

19. Tsing, 62.

20. Tsing, 139, 139, 66.

21. Tsing, 144.

22. Elaine Scarry, *Thermonuclear Monarchy: Choosing between Democracy and Doom* (New York: Norton, 2014), 356.

23. Elaine Scarry, *Thinking in an Emergency* (New York: W. W. Norton, 2011), 55.

24. Elaine Scarry, *Rule of Law, Misrule of Man* (Cambridge, Mass: MIT Press, 2010), 65, 74.

25. Scarry, 66.

26. Scarry, 67.

27. Scarry, 66.

28. Roland Barthes, "The Reality Effect," in *The Rustle of Language* (Berkeley: University of California Press, 1989).

Conclusion

On Teaching Curiosity

Arjun Shankar and Perry Zurn

> Curiosity as restless questioning, as movement toward the revelation of something hidden, as a question verbalized or not, as search for clarity, as a moment of attention, suggestion, and vigilance, constitutes an integral part of the phenomenon of being alive.
>
> —Paulo Freire, *Pedagogy of Freedom*

We want to begin with a story from a teacher training session, entitled "Curiosity in the Classroom," that Arjun Shankar and Mariam Durrani ran with New York City school teachers in 2013. The teachers were from all over the city, old and young, more experienced and less experienced, and each had found out about this workshop through different networks—a fellow teacher, an email chain, a Facebook group, and so on. What they had in common was an unquestioned enthusiasm about curiosity. Before entering the room, they all already believed in its value and felt, like most teachers, that it was an essential component of any classroom experience.

Yet these teachers were also suspicious. They had been to too many professional development workshops in the past, each of which had advertised itself as the next big thing for their classrooms. And, over the course of the workshop, the teachers began to voice their concerns about a curiosity-centric pedagogy. As any teacher will tell you—whether in K-12 or higher education—bureaucratic stipulations, requirements, state objectives, and grading put heavy constraints on how and what teachers can teach.[1] Most of the teachers were overwhelmed by it all. Yes, they loved to teach and wanted to do right by their students, but at the same time they felt there were competing priorities they could not neglect. Given that most of them were working in some of the most underresourced schools in the city, with students who needed a great amount of attention, curiosity seemed like a privilege they could not afford. In other words, they were grappling firsthand with the system of racial capitalism[2] that continues to produce schools "not concerned with curiosity," as Ta-Nehisi Coates puts it, "but [with] compliance."[3]

For these teachers, curiosity was an exception and exceptional. They began to tell stories about fleeting instances of curiosity in the classroom, moments when an especially curious student would question, explore, and discover without any extra help. They recalled a time when a twelve-year-old boy raised his hand more often than usual or when a ten-year-old girl decided to research a subject she had learned about just a few days earlier. In these cases, teachers knew that students were demonstrating curiosity in their classrooms. Sometimes they even felt that they did things to produce this curiosity in the students. But they didn't have a critical awareness of *why* it was happening and, therefore, could not go about systematically facilitating a curiosity-based classroom. Instead, they relied on narratives that continued to suggest curiosity was ad-hoc, usually based on the "natural curiosity" of a special student.

The New York City teachers workshop thus raised several fundamental questions: Why do we as educators—whether in K-12, college, or other educational settings—know that curiosity is central to education but not know how to cultivate it? Is curiosity naturally vibrant in all students or more robust in exceptional students? Can students be taught to be curious (and, for that matter, can teachers be taught how to teach students to be curious)? How can curiosity be cultivated within and despite the bureaucratic structures and pragmatic requirements so pronounced in most twenty-first-century educational institutions and contexts? Finally, how do we cultivate a curiosity that is politically vibrant rather than harmlessly compliant?

In what follows, we offer a preliminary account of why and how to consciously cultivate curiosity in contemporary learning environments. First, we begin by discussing some of the educational theory upon which curiosity-centric classrooms might be built: experiential learning pedagogy, feminist pedagogy, critical pedagogy, and abolitionist pedagogy. Second, recognizing that our social, cultural, political, and economic processes all shape who can be curious, about what, and when, we then formulate what we call a *critically curious pedagogy*. Critically curious pedagogy aims to stay accountable to the complex sociopolitical processes in and against which curiosity is either cultivated or suppressed. Such pedagogy relies on the affective practices of reflexivity, mindfulness, empathy, uncertainty, and transformative questioning. Third, we identify several key elements of curiosity-based assignments by which teacher–learners from all disciplinary backgrounds—whether they be mathematicians, engineers, anthropologists, psychologists, or philosophers—can facilitate the growth of critical curiosity in their students. These elements include student leadership, a research mindset, collaborative environments, multimodal outputs, real-life applications, and community engagement. Finally, we reflect on future directions in the theory and praxis of curiosity-centric learning environments. It is our hope that this chapter provides a framework for members of teacher–learner communities of all sorts to become aware of and cultivate their own curiosity with one another.

Education and the Politics of Curiosity

Many, if not most, K-12 and college educators typically think of curiosity simply as a natural and cultivatable capacity in their students. This conception stems from a long tradition in the philosophy and psychology of education that treats curiosity as a universal human characteristic, subject to standard behavioral development and training. This conception originates in the modernist intellectual tradition, with the likes of Francis Bacon and Thomas Hobbes, and later incorporates ideologies regarding "fixed" capacities that emerged as part of scientific racism's lasting legacy. John Locke, perhaps one of this tradition's more eloquent spokesmen on the subject of curiosity, states quite plainly that curiosity is "the great instrument nature has provided to remove . . . ignorance," and as such "ought to be encouraged" in children through various means, including the incremental complexification of questions, the identification of reliable sources of information, and the importance of trial and error in the search for knowledge.[4]

While widely influential, this modernist perspective has certain important limitations. First, it assumes a unified concept of curiosity and therefore fails to diversify curiosity into curiosities. If they are not careful, practitioners may well miss curiosity as it modulates across students of different personalities and capabilities, especially among neuroatypical learners,[5] as well as across social identities and cultural contexts. Second, it often replicates dated techniques for cultivating curiosity, failing not only to account for neuroflexibility but to attend to curiosity in its ecological contexts.[6] Many practitioners reproduce learning environments in which rote memorization, lecturing, strict rules and procedures, and exam-based evaluation are the norm. These approaches may carefully attend to pedagogical questions such as how to learn the facts or content of a subject, but they do very little to address *the very pedagogy of questioning*—that is, how to ask questions and what questions to ask. Third, these simplistic pedagogical strategies have especially failed minoritized populations. Students of color, for example, have been assumed as less curious, and less capable, given the white-Western heritage of mapping intellectual capacity on to imaginary typologies of racial difference. Some practitioners, perhaps subconsciously and because of implicit biases, predetermine what types of student can be curious and therefore delimit their students' opportunities for educational attainment and mobility. As such, the traditional educational framework does little to democratize, deepen, and diversify our understanding of how curiosity manifests itself—and how it can be cultivated—in people's everyday lives.

How do we make space for curiosity in its multiplicity, across the human experience, while also framing its manifestations within social processes? And how do we organically cultivate such a curiosity in children, young adults, and beyond? To tackle these questions, we turn to four powerful pedagogical traditions that counter the hegemonic system of educational praxis: (1) experiential learning pedagogy, (2) feminist pedagogy, (3) critical pedagogy, and (4) abolitionist pedagogy. These traditions not only reiterate the natural and developmental character of curiosity but supplement the modernist framework with a functional understanding of curiosity as environmentally interconnected, socially embedded, and politically dynamic. It is upon these traditions that we then build our own account of a *critically curious pedagogy,* which places curiosity squarely within an innovative, materialist framework requisite for our hyperconnected and yet fractured world.

Experiential learning pedagogy stems primarily from the work of John Dewey. Against the reigning educational theory and customs of his time, which conceptualized the student atomistically as an isolable individual with potentialities all his or her own, Dewey insisted that learning is a dynamic, experiential process, rooted in the learner's physical and social environments and integral to the construction of democracy.[7] Dewey's philosophy was predicated on the concept of "flexible aims," which allowed for a range of interpretations of information and the ability to shift the direction of one's actions based on new information. Thus learners learn not according to ideological principles, canons, or schemas of truth but according to what works in the everyday process of inquiry and experimentation, adaption, and cooperation.[8] For Dewey this activates what is always a multidimensional intelligence and a vibrant imagination.[9] It also builds on curiosity. Curiosity is a naturally occurring openness to experience that develops in three stages: (1) physiological curiosity, (2) social curiosity, and (3) intellectual curiosity.[10] Children effortlessly move from poking at something, to asking someone what it is, and to finally considering the thing itself in connection with other problems they have solved and conceptual material they have acquired. Because curiosity can be "fossilized" through routine and dogmatic instruction, however, not only must education be reimagined to organically nurture curiosity, but teachers themselves must be wary of their own waning interests and capacity for openness. "With respect to curiosity," Dewey sagely notes, "the teacher usually has more to learn than to teach."[11] If learning is experiential, so must curiosity be.

Feminist pedagogy—or, perhaps more appropriately, feminist pedagogies—begins with the recognition that classical educational theory and practice was developed by and for certain groups of people and not others: chiefly, women and girls. Feminist pedagogy focuses on who is in the classroom and how that should or could change the learning process. Against Dewey's abstract notions of the individual and community, feminist pedagogues ask, "Which individual? Which community? And what are the complex and sometimes inconsistent relationships between them?"[12] Taking patriarchy as paradigmatic of unjust hierarchies (and therefore taking gender justice as a springboard to social liberation writ large), feminist pedagogy aims to decolonize curriculum, invest in antiracist praxis, implement universal design, and queer the classroom.[13] It also aims to fundamentally disrupt the teacher/student dyad by treating learners as whole persons, engaging learners in the process of knowledge creation, developing real world applications, and maintaining community accountability.[14] Granting the situatedness of curiosity, feminist pedagogues work to identify and critically engage the different positionalities from which questions are inherited, generated, pursued, or suppressed.[15] A "feminist curiosity," as Cynthia Enloe puts it, therefore involves not only "taking women's lives seriously" but taking seriously a whole slew of things that have been "infantilized, trivialized, ignored," or left "unquestioned"—including curiosity itself.[16]

Critical pedagogy, and the critical Marxist tradition from which it emerged, counteracts the forces of systemic economic and political oppression by critically attending to—and getting curious about—how hegemonic power relations, and the economic bases for these relations, inform educational environments.[17] For critical pedagogues, intellectuals and teachers have traditionally been a part of the control apparatus, generating and promulgating knowledge that works at the behest of capitalist interests and therefore maintains social hegemony. For Antonio Gramsci, the traditional intellectual ought to be replaced by the organic intellectual, whose knowledge and interests are based on their everyday experience and consciousness of class position and class oppression.[18] Likewise, for Paulo Freire, teachers must develop methods and strategies by which to resist political and economic inequities in the classroom.[19] From a critical pedagogical perspective, "education can only be liberatory when everyone claims knowledge as a field in which we labor,"[20] and claims curiosity as a tool by which we labor in that field. While Freire grants a certain "common sense" curiosity, present in all learners, he aims to facilitate a "critical" curiosity. Critical curiosity is a movement of "attention, suggestion, and vigilance" vital to the "construction and reconstruction" of history and society, as led by Global South communities.[21] Through it, instrumental rationality and mechanized education, so central to capitalist colonial interests, are deconstructed through the ethical commitments, aesthetic creation, and affective praxis of teacher–learner communities at the margins.[22] Curiosity, in this context, is viewed within a political–economic frame: What kind of curiosity, exploration, and questioning is valued because it works toward capitalist interests, and what kind of curiosity is seen as subversive precisely because it seeks to challenge hegemonic power relations?[23]

Finally, abolitionist pedagogy takes seriously a curiosity embedded in the pedagogical strategies and tactics that antiracist pedagogues have deployed in order to begin the work of freeing all of us from racism's violent effects. Emerging from the Du Boisian and the Black feminist traditions, these pedagogues argue that critical perspectives are incomplete without a simultaneous recognition of our racist histories and remind us that one of the greatest problems of the twenty-first century continues to be the "global color line."[24] This global color line has structured and continues to structure curiosity, determining who can and should be curious and who is, at best, an object of racist curiosity. As such, abolitionist pedagogies reintroduce histories that

Conclusion 275

have been systematically erased—those of indigenous and formerly enslaved peoples—and forcefully demystify the mythologies of race that continue to undergird our public discourses. They also seek to bring to the fore educational models that actively challenge the pedagogies of whiteness that have subsumed children's curiosity, revealing how certain assessments, standards, and teaching methodologies work to maintain white supremacy. Carter G. Woodson, author of *The Mis-Education of the Negro* and staunch advocate for "Negro History week" (the precursor to Black History month), argued that schooling cultivated an anti-Blackness that was inextricably linked to the violence Black people experienced, and, as such, developing curricula that makes all of us sincerely curious about the Black experience is one step toward liberation for all.[25] In this context curiosity must be seen as part of an antiracist struggle, continuously cracking open those narratives that maintain supremacy and superiority, and hail genocidal histories as "destiny."[26] Drawing on the concept of "fugitive pedagogy," developed by historian Jarvis R. Givens and rooted in "the subversive intellectual and embodied acts African Americans employed to navigate anti-Black constraints within the American schooling project,"[27] we might develop tactics of *fugitive curiosity*. These subversive lines of questioning challenge the racist constraints on learning and draw us toward a model of curiosity that is liberatory rather than oppressive.

Today the abolitionist framework has developed beyond its roots in emancipation and has become a clarion call for liberation more generally, "an immoderate rejection of white supremacy, patriarchy, heteronormativity, ableism, settler-colonialism, border imperialism, political hierarchy, and the rule of capital."[28] As Angela Davis insists, abolition is both the work of tearing down and building up, critiquing all nodes of systemic oppression and creating rich, community-based care systems in their place.[29] As such, abolitionist pedagogy is experiential, feminist, critical, and more. Responsive to the flexible aims of diverse learning communities, it is committed to two fundamental questions: "What do we need? And how do we get there?" Abolitionist pedagogy stands ready to abolish the academy as it is and cultivate something else, as it might be. A learner who is empowered to hear themselves and their communities speak. A teacher who is willing to be disoriented by the collective work of critical curiosity and political imagination.[30] A society always poised to unravel its present state. A university that does not incorporate and confine difference but reimagines itself from the inside out in response to social unrest and political resistance.[31] A learning community that courts new modes and methods of study, in and outside the classroom.[32] Abolitionist pedagogy—and indeed the future of critically curious pedagogy—involves radically reimagining the very possibilities and potentialities of learning.

Taken together, these four pedagogical traditions—experiential learning pedagogy, feminist pedagogy, critical pedagogy, and abolitionist pedagogy— provide a challenging new framework through which to understand and cultivate curiosity in the classroom. They push pedagogues to think beyond particular content-based rules, concepts, or principles, to reconceptualize learning as a dynamic learner-driven process, and to identify and resist the hierarchies implicit in traditional classrooms and systems of knowledge. They underscore that curiosity is a natural capacity, subject to developmental training and growth, but they also emphasize that curiosity is environmentally interconnected, socially embedded, and politically dynamic. Curiosity is capable of being trained in ways that reinforce established patterns of thought, including those that subtend social inequalities, or in ways that are truly innovative, pursuing the most pressing scientific and political questions of our times in ways that radically reconfigure our collective values and imagination. It is the pedagogues' calling to facilitate precisely this work. When they root what is to be learned and how it is to be learned in the students themselves—asking who they are, what they know, and where they come from—students' own curiosity can beget insights that can change how we understand the concepts under study. By situating student curiosity within multiple ecologies—of the mind, the classroom, the society, and beyond— teachers can lay the groundwork for a critically curious pedagogy.

Toward a Critically Curious Pedagogy

Building on these rich resources in educational theory, we turn our attention now to what we call a *critically curious pedagogy*. A critically curious pedagogy necessarily reshapes our educational praxis on the bedrock of a different type of learning, one that not only resists the rigid regimens of traditional instruction and the brittle distinction between teacher and learner but also embraces the socially embedded and political character of transformative learning.[33] Paulo Freire argues that such an approach to life equips people to explore humanity in its totality: asking questions of one another, voicing their opinions, developing new perspectives, and co-constructing and

Conclusion 277

expanding their realities.[34] Therefore, challenging our assumptions about what learning is, where it happens, and from whom we can learn is a prerequisite for a critically curious pedagogy. All of this requires a change of habits and even a change in feeling. In what follows, we propose several key affective practices that are fundamental to a critically curious pedagogy. These include the following: (1) practicing sincere self-reflexivity; (2) developing an empathic stance; (3) creating and enjoying uncertainty rather than resolving or resisting it; and (4) questioning sociocultural norms and challenging structures and institutions of power.

Reflexivity, in its simplest form, involves self-consciously interrogating the relationship between teachers and their students. It means asking questions regarding how we might alter ongoing scientific and sociocultural investments that reproduce reductive hypotheses, neoliberal academic priorities, supremacist logics, and colonial social relations in our teaching methodologies. We draw specifically from the discipline of anthropology for this discussion because anthropologists have had longstanding debates regarding reflexivity, given their methodological investment in ethnography and the discipline's history of facilitating (settler)colonial governance.[35] In response, many anthropologists have sought to find means by which to enact a *sincere* reflexivity.[36] A sincere reflexivity takes seriously intersubjectivity, coevalness, and our interlocutors as complete, agential, affective beings like ourselves. As such, sincerity foregrounds our shared humanity and ensures we are not constructing "objects of curiosity" as we enter into research relationships.[37] All too often, researchers allow their inherited assumptions to go unidentified, their biases to go unchallenged, and therefore their subjects of research are impoverished, objectified, and even dehumanized. We can extend this idea of reflexivity beyond the confines of research into our teaching and learning practices as well. When we are sincerely self-reflexive, we are able to undertake self-critique and we allow for our own fallibility when living and working in the midst of those who are as human as we are. This humility, in turn, provides openings for genuine simultaneity of teaching and learning that, in turn, can become the basis for cultivating a critical curiosity.

And as a sincere reflexivity seems to imply, openness to another also involves empathic communication, including the ability to listen, whether another person is right in front of us or far away in space or time. Certain practices of curiosity reinforce existing beliefs, manage to dehumanize Others, and even prevent the symbiotic relations within and between human and nonhuman ecologies.[38] An empathic curiosity begins with a form of questioning that sincerely shows interest in ideas, feelings, states, and circumstances beyond oneself and one's beliefs, whether expressed in words or not.[39] Even when those we seek to relate to are not human, we can still bring an empathy to our endeavor, thinking with questions such as, "Why is the cat looking at me?" "How does a forest think?" or "What does a picture want?"; such questions open up the possibility that these things may not exist solely for the purpose of our discovery.[40] To engage in a critical curiosity, then, involves a conscious communication of empathic inquiry that, and this is essential, is ideally registered as such by the listener, the species companion, the collaborator, the patient, or the research subject.[41] The critically curious classroom is marked by a culture of questioning that stems from an emotional place of care and signals interest rather than unproductive criticism. In practice this also means that critically curious learners must not only take into account their own positions but the positions of those they encounter. Gender, race, ethnicity, sexual orientation, nationality, and the like change how inquiry is *felt* and, in turn, we must continuously shift how we inquire to take the communicative differences of our listeners and collaborators seriously.

In order for a critically curious pedagogy to emerge, however, all those involved must also be willing to create and enjoy an environment of uncertainty rather than resolve or resist it.[42] In much of our current educational system, uncertainty has been all but eradicated as we teach students that they should not take risks and should only ask questions for which answers are easily available. Indeed, much of our standardized testing model exacerbates this issue, creating a culture of fact seeking that does little to cultivate in students the ability to suspend themselves in the unknown. In fact, students are taught to avoid such situations and begin to link the experience of uncertainty with negative emotions: fear, anxiety, and the like. They refrain from raising their hands because of the risk of getting wrong answers or asking a question that will reveal their lack of knowledge. But uncertainty and the experience of not knowing can be enjoyable and exciting, spurring on our creative inquiry rather than foreclosing it when appropriately cultivated. When we cultivate in students the ability to live with the unknown and remain flexible in their stances, we equip them to engage with their environments without the fear of losing their sense of self when faced with differences, unknowns, or uncertainties, all of which facilitate critical curiosity.

Conclusion 279

Finally, and perhaps most important, a critical curiosity unsettles taken-for-granted theorems, power structures, and social norms, thereby producing the possibility of local struggles that might dislodge hierarchies that would otherwise remain entrenched.[43] When the "truths" of the past—who we are as a people, culture, nation, society—are open to continuous critical inquiry and reconstruction, we will interrogate what we have learned like the best scientific researchers do, reminding us that any theory is valuable only insofar as it is open to its own disproof. Indeed, if Kuhn's *Structure of Scientific Revolutions* tells us anything, it is this: when we begin to challenge our basic assumptions, incorporate perspectives and ideas that may seem outside of what we have taken for granted scientifically, politically, and socio-culturally, we open the space to discover that the time and the space we live in are not quite as self-evident as we may have once believed. We might begin to incorporate new histories and pedagogies that come out of the indigenous and Black radical traditions, for example, which challenge our dearly held assumptions, critique white imperial legacies, and push our curiosity in new directions.[44]

To be truly critically curious, then, will also by definition lead us to question the status quo, its existing dogmas and longstanding investments, not only in light of the search for truth but also in light of ongoing efforts to achieve environmental, social, and cognitive justice. In his *Talk to Teachers,* James Baldwin writes:

> The paradox of education is precisely this—that as we become conscious one begins to examine the society in which he is being educated. The purpose of education, finally, is to create in a person the ability to look at the world for himself, to make his own decisions. . . . To ask questions of the universe, and then learn to live with those questions . . . . But no society is really anxious to have that kind of person around. What societies really, ideally, want is a citizenry which will simply obey the rules of society. If a society succeeds in this, that society is about to perish. The obligation of anyone who thinks of himself as responsible is to examine society and try to change it and to fight it—at no matter what risk. This is the only hope society has. This is the only way societies change.[45]

This paradox is precisely the space in which critical curiosity functions, supporting society by continuing to challenge its structures of power and knowledge. For a critically curious person and one who believes in a critically curious pedagogy, there are no sites that are not open to questioning and, therefore, sites of power and knowledge are as much open to questioning as any others.

Engaging actively in challenging power/knowledge structures is not easy. An *affective praxis* of critical curiosity is a much harder thing to enact, relying on each of the fundamental characteristics discussed above and forcing us to reckon with the fact that our personal lives are political and our silences (what we do not question) are as much an act of political decision-making as what we voice. In some ways, we see critical curiosity as an *ideal*,[46] a never-ending process of unfolding that involves sincerity and the ability to admit wrong and struggle for change no matter how hard or how long it takes. Most of us who have lived on this planet have had our minds colonized, infused with sexist and homophobic ideologies, burdened by capitalist desires, trained by ableism to stigmatize mental unwellness, and so on. Given these starting points, it makes sense that the kind of change we are advocating for here will take time, energy, and the ability to at once take responsibility for our roles in exacerbating and upholding structures of violence while also finding ways to be fair and forgiving to ourselves. Most of all, what a critical curiosity relies on, as Perry Zurn reminds, is a *hopefulness*: a hope that we can change, that the world around us can change, and that we might be capable of something else. This hope, Sandy Grande cautions, must not fall into a future-orientation that erases our past but instead must be "a hope that lives in contingency with the past."[47] This process necessarily results in a radical reshaping of ourselves and our worlds.[48] It is in this sense that a critical curiosity is also a *radical curiosity*.

Curiosity in the Classroom: Developing Assignments

Thus far we have sought to outline some of the fundamental precepts of an educational model founded on critical curiosity. But how does this look in practice, in our differing classroom settings or even more broadly in our labs, libraries, social media discussions, interfaith community dialogues, and the like? What kinds of activities and assignments might we develop and deploy and to what end? Indeed, our claim is that a critically curious pedagogy, because it allows for multiplicity and sociocultural contextualization, is as important for professors in the natural sciences as it is for those in the humanities and social sciences. And while there will be inevitable differences that emerge based on our specific content-foci and community of practice, the kinds of shifts in pedagogical approach we advocate for here can be implemented in any of these contexts. Furthermore, while we will use the vocabulary of the classroom—teacher/student, and so on—we trust that those in other social contexts will also find the suggestions below useful and applicable.

Some have continued to propagate the myth that cultivating curiosity is simply about asking more and better questions. But the truth is, cultivating curiosity is not easy and involves much more than asking many questions or the "right question." We have found several practices especially useful when seeking to infuse curiosity into our classrooms: (1) bringing students into the process of deciding on assignment goals and content, (2) making curiosity an explicit part of the assignment prompt, (3) cultivating a research mindset in students through the assignment protocol, (4) providing multimodal variations to assignment structure, (5) linking assignments to students' experiences outside of class, and (6) creating a collaborative environment in which assignment outputs can be discussed. Insofar as these practices aid in critical questioning, dialogical engagement, democratizing the classroom, and overturning ideological schemas and social hierarchies, they together reflect the first steps toward integrating experiential, feminist, critical, and abolitionist pedagogical commitments into the classroom. We recognize, however, that this process—and, indeed, the further work of decolonizing pedagogical praxis—is continuous and iterative.

First, an assignment might begin with curiosities voiced by students or, perhaps more appropriately, through dialogue not only between teacher and student but between all participants in a (class)room. Indeed, if instructors want to cultivate curiosity in their students, they must resist the urge to develop assignments that provide too many prescriptive objectives. While all courses will have subject-specific concepts that students are required to learn, instructors can always find ways to allow students to set areas of inquiry within these subjects that reflect their own interests and questions. For example, in a course on urbanization, students might choose a city or an aspect of urban planning that they find most interesting. And, when they articulate their choice, they could frame their decisions using the rhetoric of curiosity. Instructors might even require that students write a short statement in which they explicitly describe why they are curious about this subject based on personal experience, previous research, and the like. You may find that some students resist this more "open" and student-driven approach to assignments, seeking to receive simple yes/no, right/wrong, teacher-driven questions, assignments, and protocols. When students express resistance, these moments can become essential opportunities to reflect on how and why their educational socialization may have delimited their ability for curious exploration.[49]

Second, the assignment should make curiosity explicit rather than implicit. While it may seem simple, articulating that an assignment is intended to provide a framework to discuss and invoke curiosity helps to direct students' attention to curiosity as its own site for cultivation. In our classroom experiences, we have found that students remark over and over again that they had no idea just how differently they would approach their learning when they approached it through the lens of curiosity. All too often they remark that they now "see curiosity everywhere." In other words, they are becoming mindful of curiosity in their everyday lives. The results of this new mindfulness can be extremely empowering for students who have had so many classroom experiences that dismiss their curiosity or erase the cultivation of curiosity from classroom objectives.

Third, the assignment should cultivate a research mindset in the student, while perhaps gaining an awareness of the pitfalls of many traditional research paradigms. We all have many questions that briefly flit through our minds and that we leave unexplored. This is natural given the inexhaustibility of potential avenues for inquiry and the limitations on our time. But when we are especially curious, we are in fact driven to ask a question and seek its answer.[50] Yet this process of inquiry is not quite as simple as asking and answering. In fact, many students lose their curiosity not because they don't want to ask questions but *because they have been dissuaded from satiating their curiosity and, in turn, have not been taught how to satiate their curiosity.* When students develop the skills by which to satiate their curiosity, they are likely to continue on their own, well beyond the confines of the classroom. As such, assignments must draw students into the basic precepts of inquiry: How do I ask questions? Where do I go to answer questions? What research methodologies might I employ to discover an answer? How do I deepen my site of inquiry? In answering these questions, we might utilize elements of a Participatory Research framework,[51] which specifically focuses on research toward collective action and decenters any single researcher's expertise when deriving these insights. At the same time, research methods should attend to the problematics of the research process: When students

Conclusion 283

analyze and present data, how varied are their results and why? What does this tell us about how we experience reality and, in turn, the way that our objects of curiosity are shaped by how we approach questioning?

Fourth, the assignment should provide multimodal variations. All too often, even when instructors seek to cultivate curiosity, they focus on the content of a course rather than the form of an assignment. And in so doing, instructors continue to rely on traditional writing assignments or exams. However, form and content are inextricably linked[52] and, when students are provided different methods and forms of exploration, their curiosity can go in multiple, unique directions. For example, when a student is invited to make a film on a concept rather than write an essay or take a test, they become curious about film technology, editing, and a whole slew of other aspects of form even as they ask ever deeper questions about the course's content. But the exploration of form allows a kind of critical awareness that otherwise might not be possible: when we see how things are made, we begin to understand that all of our productions, whether in film, focus group, text, formula, or experimental design, have been created by someone to tell a particular story for a particular audience with a particular ideology.[53] And this awareness is part and parcel of a critical curiosity. Providing assignments using multiple modalities and research methods has the added benefit of facilitating learning based on a student's varying intelligences and strengths.[54] If, for example, a student is more comfortable working in sound, they are more likely to explore their curiosity if provided this platform rather than the traditional essay or exam.

Fifth, assignments should be linked to experiential moments: a walk down the street, a TV show, an engineering problem, or even a close relationship could be fodder for our curiosity.[55] Such approaches build upon educational discourses that ask teachers to facilitate students' ability to make text-to-text, text-to-world, and text-to-self connections. What we know is also part and parcel of expanding our spheres of curiosity. This model can be easily applied to those working in higher education as well. Civil engineering professors can animate the models, equations, and theories learned in class through experiential assignments—or better yet, makerspaces—that get students to engage a real-world physical problem they encounter. In so doing, professors can get students to critically assess their physical environments, learn the mathematical bases for human-made constructions, while also seeing that such decision-making has social implications for the movement of people through space. Professors in mathematics, neuroscience, anthropology, philosophy, and the like can all create similar assignments, providing students the opportunity to think with concepts beyond the classroom and have problems emerge from their movement in the world(s) they inhabit.

Finally, the assignment must live within a collaborative environment in which discussion and co-creation is encouraged. Sharing work, redrafting, asking questions about the choices made and the discoveries begot is as important as the work itself. Peer-to-peer and university–community dialogue helps students to understand that curiosity is multiple and can move in different directions. And in this environment students will begin to deepen their understanding of curiosity, incorporating new types of curiosity into their praxis based on their exposure to the types of curiosity demonstrated by their classmates and community partners.[56] As such, instructors should embed peer-to-peer engagement and community engagement into their courses, signaling to students that they will be sharing and co-creating work at various moments during the semester. At first, such exposure may be anxiety producing for students who are not used to co-creating or sharing work frequently. However, for students to become still more deeply curious, they must begin to feel comfortable with sharing their ideas, taking risks, and reveling in the uncertainty of knowing that their ideas are always unfinished and can be further improved with the critical curiosity of their peers and community members. Peer-to-peer and community engagement permits ideas and innovations to be sharpened with and alongside the people for whom they most matter.

Together, these shifts in how we conceive of our classroom assignments can lay the groundwork for a richer curiosity-based praxis and, we believe, a more curious future. We now turn to precisely that future. Where might all of this newfound curiosity take us as we imagine new research sites, pedagogical possibilities, institutional restructurings, and transformative relationships?

Future Directions

As we close we recall something John L. Jackson Jr. will often reiterate: "Every film always begets its sequel." This framing is an especially fitting characterization for an essay on teaching curiosity. Curiosity is nothing else if not an infinite regress toward evermore expansive sites of inquiry, connections between ideas, and reconstructions of our realities. And so we cannot help but acknowledge the questions we have left unanswered and the many insights yet to emerge from our curious readers.

By way of conclusion, we want to explore, for a moment, where we think a critically curious pedagogy could and should go in the future. First, all too often curiosity has been overdetermined by an attention to children and primary educational contexts. While it is true that children's curiosity and the continued exploration of its manifestation is quite important, we would like to see more attention paid to curiosity across the lifespan. Indeed, it is our conviction that curiosity continues to emerge in unique forms throughout our lives, and that part of the "politics of curiosity" is this continued and persistent narrative that sees adults and the elderly as less able or unable to be curious. This is a space that curious pedagogy would do well to explore further. How does curiosity change over the lifespan, and how might we learn to facilitate curiosity differentially in people of all ages?

Second, we would like curious pedagogy to focus on specific institutional settings—in education, medicine, law, and so on—assessing the ways that the rules, procedures, stipulations, power relations, and values of these institutions predetermine the types of curiosity that individuals can pursue. At the same time, we would like to see more empirically grounded studies that do not analyze curiosity as a generalizable concept within these institutional spaces but rather reveal its contingent manifestations based on one's socioeconomic status, gender, race, sexuality, neurodiversity, and so on. In this vein, we would like to see scholars take a far more intersectional approach to curiosity, drawing from the many insights of Black feminist, decolonial, and queer scholars who have shown us that all knowledge—and, therefore its impetus: curiosity—is contingent on our sociocultural positions and the power relations therein.

Third, and perhaps most important, further praxis-based research should focus on the question of how to cultivate a culture of curiosity. While we have attempted to lay the groundwork for this inquiry, much more must be done to understand the specific and unique tools to induce curiosity in city planners and bus drivers, doctors and therapists, park rangers and lawyers, poets and philosophers. Indeed, if curiosity might also be a means by which to do these jobs better, it behooves us to focus more energy on determining the benefits of curiosity as they relate to the goals and motivations specific to each of these communities of practice.

At this final juncture, we have but one hope: that each of us and all of us together take what we have learned through engaging with this text to practice a more radical curiosity in our everyday lives.

Notes

1. Pam Grossman et al., "The Test Matters: The Relationship between Classroom Observation Scores and Teacher Value Added on Multiple Types of Assessment," *Educational Researcher* 43, no. 6 (2014): 293–303.

2. Cedric Robinson, *Black Marxism: The Making of the Black Radical Tradition* (Durham, N.C.: University of North Carolina Press, 2000).

3. Ta-Nehisi Coates, *Between the World and Me* (New York: Random House, 2015), 26.

4. John Locke, *Some Thoughts Concerning Education,* ed. John William Adamson (1693; New York: Dover, 2007), §118, 93.

5. See Johnson, this volume.

6. See Bassett, this volume.

7. Jim Garrison, Stefan Neubert, and Kersten Reich, *John Dewey's Philosophy of Education: An Introduction and Recontextualization for Our Times* (New York: Palgrave Macmillan, 2012).

8. Carol Dweck's growth-mindset theory is indebted to Dewey. For Dweck, students who see the brain as a muscle, subject to challenge and growth, see their own intelligence as malleable and open to change. See Carol Dweck, *Mindset: The New Psychology of Success* (New York: Ballantine Books, 2007).

9. We do find that thinking of intelligence as multimodal is critical to recognizing curiosity across the learner spectrum. See Howard Gardner's classic, *Frames of Mind: The Theory of Multiple Intelligences* (New York: Basic Books, 1983), and the long scholarly discussion that follows in its wake.

10. John Dewey, *The Middle Works of John Dewey, 1899–1924,* vol. 6, *How We Think* (Carbondale: Southern Illinois University Press, 2008), 205–7.

11. Dewey, 207; cf. John Dewey, *The Middle Works of John Dewey, 1899–1924,* vol. 9, *Democracy and Education* (Carbondale: Southern Illinois University Press, 2008), 55.

12. Cf. Nel Noddings, "Dewey's Philosophy of Education: A Critique from the Perspective of Care Theory," in *The Cambridge Companion to John Dewey,* ed. Molly Cochran (Cambridge: Cambridge University Press, 2010), 265–87. Reflecting upon Dewey's emphasis on "problem-solving," Noddings also insists on asking, Whose problem? Solved with and for whom?

13. Renée Bondy, Jane Nicholas, and Tracy Penny Light, "Introduction: Feminist Pedagogy in Higher Education," in *Feminist Pedagogy in Higher Education: Critical Theory and Practice* (Waterloo, Ont.: Wilfrid Laurier University Press, 2015), 1–10.

14. Bondy, Nicholas, and Light, 1–10.

Conclusion 287

15. Donna Haraway, "Situated Knowledges: The Science Question in Feminism and the Privilege of Partial Knowledge," in *Feminist Theory Reader*, ed. Carole R. McCann and Seung-Kyung Kim (1988; New York: Routledge, 2013), 412–23.

16. Cynthia Enloe, *The Curious Feminist: Searching for Women in a New Age of Empire* (Los Angeles: University of California Press, 2004), 5.

17. Henri Giroux, "Critical Pedagogy in Dark Times," in *On Critical Pedagogy* (New York: Continuum, 2011), 3–16.

18. Antonio Gramsci, "The Intellectual," *The Prison Notebooks,* in *An Anthology of Western Marxism,* ed. Roger Gottlieb (Oxford: Oxford University Press, 1989), 113–19.

19. Paulo Freire, *Pedagogy of the Oppressed* (New York: Continuum, 1970).

20. bell hooks, "Engaged Pedagogy," in *Teaching to Transgress* (New York: Routledge, 1994), 14.

21. Paulo Freire, *Pedagogy of Freedom: Ethics, Democracy, and Civic Courage* (Lanham, Md.: Rowman and Littlefield, 1998), 37–38.

22. Freire, 38.

23. See Shankar, this volume.

24. Zeus Leonardo, "The Souls of White Folk: Critical Pedagogy, Whiteness Studies, and Globalization Discourse," *Race Ethnicity and Education* 5, no. 1 (2010): 29–50.

25. Carter Woodson, *The Mis-Education of the Negro* (Dreweryville, Va.: Khalifah's Booksellers, 1933).

26. Howard Zinn, *A People's History of the United States* (New York: HarperCollins, 2009).

27. Jarvis R. Givens, *Fugitive Pedagogy: Carter G. Woodson and the Demands of Black Education* (Cambridge, Mass.: Harvard University Press, forthcoming); and "'There Would Be No Lynching If It Did Not Start in the Schoolroom': Carter G. Woodson and the Occasion of Negro History Week, 1926–1950," *American Educational Research Journal* (2019), https://doi.org/10.3102/0002831218818454.

28. Andrew Dilts, "Abolition Statement," *Abolition: A Journal of Insurgent Politics* (2015), https://abolitionjournal.org/abolition-statements-a-collection/.

29. Angela Davis, *Abolition Democracy* (New York: Seven Stories Press, 2005), 73.

30. Dylan Rodriguez, "The Disorientation of the Teaching Act: Abolition as Pedagogical Position," *Radical Teacher* 88 (2010): 7–19.

31. Roderick Ferguson, *The Reorder of Things* (Minneapolis: University of Minnesota Press, 2012).

32. Eli Meyerhoff, *Beyond Education: Radical Studying for Another World* (Minneapolis: University of Minnesota Press, 2019); cf. Philip Schmidt's Peer2Peer University (P2PU) project, https://www.p2pu.org/en/about/.

33. See Benedict, this volume.

34. Paulo Freire writes: "The process of learning, through which historically we have discovered that teaching is a task not only inherent to the learning process but . . . also characterized by it, can set off in the learner *an ever-increasing creative curiosity*" (*Pedagogy of Freedom*, 32).

35. See Swanson, this volume.

36. In many anthropological spaces, the idea of reflexivity has become a tool to deflect one's own culpability: by listing one's identities (white, male, etc.), one undercuts the more rigorous consideration of how our positions affect the kinds of knowledge we produce, disseminate, and teach. Sincere reflexivity is a response to this tendency. See John L. Jackson Jr., "On Ethnographic Sincerity," *Cultural Anthropology* 51, no. S2 (2010): 279–89.

37. See Marvin, this volume.

38. We also turn to Anna Tsing's work on Matsusake mushrooms, in which she asks us to consider just this relationship between the human and nonhuman, writing while thinking about the ruins of lifeworlds laid to waste: "Global landscapes today are strewn with this kind of ruin. Still, these places can be lively despite announcements of their death. . . . In a global state of precarity, we don't have choices other than looking for life in this ruin. Our first step is to bring back curiosity." *Mushroom at the End of the World: On the Possibility of Life in Capitalist Ruins* (Princeton, N.J.: Princeton University Press, 2015), 6.

39. See Pegi M. McEvoy et al., "Empathic Curiosity: Resolving Goal Conflicts That Generate Emotional Distress," *Journal of Psychiatric and Mental Health Nursing* 20, no. 3 (2013): 273–78.

40. See, for example, Timothy Mitchell, *Rule of Experts: Egypt, Techno-Politics, Modernity* (Berkeley: University of California Press, 2002); Donna Haraway, *When Species Meet* (Minneapolis: University of Minnesota Press, 2008); Eduardo Kohn, *How Forests Think: Toward an Anthropology beyond the Human* (Berkeley: University of California Press, 2013); W. J. T. Mitchell, *What Pictures Want: The Lives and Loves of Images* (Chicago: University of Chicago Press, 2006). Also see Swanson, this volume.

41. See Keval, this volume.

42. Helga Nowotny, *The Cunning of Uncertainty* (Boston: Polity, 2017).

43. See Zurn, this volume.

44. Sandy Grande's *Red Pedagogy: Native American Social and Political Thought* (New York: Rowman and Littlefield, 2004) charts a new terrain that integrates critical pedagogy with Native American epistemological traditions. She writes, "What distinguishes Red pedagogy is its basis in hope. Not the future-centered hope of the Western imagination, but rather, a hope that lives in contingency with the past—one that trusts the beliefs and understandings of our ancestors as well as the power of traditional knowledge. A Red pedagogy is, thus, as much about belief and acquiescence as it is about questioning and empowerment, about respecting the space of tradition as it intersects with the linear time frames of the (post)modern world. Most of all, it is a hope that believes in the strength and resiliency of indigenous peoples and communities, recognizing that their struggles are not about inclusion and enfranchisement to the 'new world order' but, rather, are part of the indigenous project of sovereignty and indigenization" (28–29).

45. James Baldwin, *James Baldwin: Collected Essays* (New York: Library of Americas, 1998), 678–79.

46. Cf. Yarimar Bonilla, "Unsettling Sovereignty," *Cultural Anthropology* 32, no. 3 (2017): 330–39: "I believe it is worth exploring what a decolonial, rather than postcolonial, notion of sovereignty—and of anthropology itself—might mean. However, I prefer the term unsettling to decolonizing not only because it privileges the perspective of settler colonialism (which has often held a backseat within postcolonial studies) but also because I remain skeptical as to whether one could truly decolonize either sovereignty or anthropology, given that there is no precolonial status to which either could return. Unsettling avoids the telos of decolonization. What is unsettled is not necessarily removed, toppled, or returned to a previous order but is fundamentally brought into question" (335).

47. Grande, *Red Pedagogy,* 28.

48. See Schor, this volume.

49. Anton Tolman and Janine Kremling, eds., *Why Students Resist Learning: A Practical Model for Understanding and Helping Students* (Sterling, Va.: Stylus, 2016).

50. See Engel, this volume.

51. Arjun Shankar et al. "Anthropology, Film, Pedagogy, and Social Change," *American Anthropologist* 119, no. 1 (2017): 147–53.

52. We draw from McLuhan's famous phrasing, "The medium is the message." See Marshall McLuhan, *The Medium Is the Message: An Inventory of Effects* (New York: Penguin Books, 1967).

53. Arjun Shankar, "Toward a Critical Visual Pedagogy: A Response to the End of Poverty Narrative," *Visual Communication Journal* 13, no. 3 (2014): 341–56.

54. In Shankar's classrooms, for example, students are always provided opportunities to work in photography, film, and/or sound in addition to text, each of which allows students different avenues by which to explore their curiosity. And in Zurn's classroom, students are often invited to develop a multimodal portfolio for their final project.

55. Arjun Shankar, "A (Gentle) Critique of the Photovoice: Case Study from Karnataka, India," *Visual Anthropology Review* 32, no. 2 (2016): 157–66.

56. Perry Zurn, "Busybody, Hunter, Dancer: Three Historical Models of Curiosity," in *Toward New Philosophical Explorations of the Epistemic Desire to Know: Just Curious about Curiosity,* ed. Marianna Papastephanou (Cambridge, U.K.: Cambridge Scholars Press, 2019), 26–49.

Afterword

Helga Nowotny

Curiosity is a strange phenomenon. It is inscribed in all living organisms, pushing them to explore their habitat and learn how to survive in it. Children continue to amaze and delight us with their inborn curiosity. They also let us witness the later waning of their curiosity or its diversion into what adults call pure distraction. Looking back in history, we can see the enormous variations across time and space—in the ways in which curiosity expresses itself, the changes in the primary objects of its attention, and especially how different kinds of curiosity were either cultivated or repressed in varying contexts. In my book *Insatiable Curiosity*, I show how society—any society or collectivity—cannot tolerate unchecked curiosity. Curiosity is loaded with too much of a subversive potential to let it flourish without societal intervention or censure. If left completely free, it becomes utterly transgressive. Not only does it not respect established boundaries by moving into directions for which it has not received directions, it explores wildly and often erratically whatever it finds without knowing what it will find. It does not follow any preset script, nor does it have a built-in moral compass. For these reasons, society seeks to *tame* curiosity; it strives to channel it into approved directions and to induce it to explore preset goals. By cultivating certain forms of curiosity and not others, society largely succeeds in instrumentalizing curiosity and fitting it into the dominant economic, cultural, and political context.

Yet precisely at the moment when curiosity appears domesticated, tamed, and instrumentalized, it may flip and display its subversive force. It resists being taken hostage or being moved in one direction only. It succeeds in finding escape routes and does so either playfully or in a more transgressive mood. It becomes unpredictable again, percolating through structures that seem firmly established and finding novel and subversive forms of expression. This is where the present volume, *Curiosity Studies,* enters. At a time when corporate capitalism, so the argument presented here goes, is channeling the inherent curiosity of the young generation exclusively and obsessively toward its own anticipated goals, we are challenged to revisit curiosity. If the only goal that matters in education is to equip students with the aspiration "to get a job," the scope is dangerously narrowed, leading some who witness the negative downsides to accuse the system of "being broken."

When reading the contributions brought together in this volume, I was most struck by the urgent, passionate, and, at least to me, novel emphasis on (re)introducing the study of curiosity into the classroom and academia in the United States. Apparently, the authors are hitting a raw nerve with their insistence on the subversive and insubordinate potential of curiosity in teaching and education. By making this the focus of the book, *Curiosity Studies* breaks new ground. It challenges the academic and educational establishment to grant open spaces for a double intervention: to explore the many-layered facets of curiosity from a genuine multi- and interdisciplinary perspective and to conduct teaching and research experiments in the classroom that let students *practice* their own curiosity while guiding them to reflexively analyze where it leads and what might follow.

The book excels in bringing out the persisting ambivalence of curiosity, the "frivolous" and "serious" side of its double nature. It is this inherent ambivalence that needs to be linked back to education and to the teaching of curiosity, making students fully aware of it. They need to relearn to be curious but also be taught how easily they can be seduced to engage in "mere" curiosity. They need to learn to recognize and accept the ambivalence of curiosity. In the end, they should learn how to cope with it. This includes teaching the younger generation to identify, acknowledge, and judge the two sides of curiosity as they manifest themselves in the various real-life contexts explored in this volume. They have to learn to decide what matters to them individually and what is good for a better society. In other words, the book is unique in offering guidance on how to develop curiosity-informed judgments of curiosity in contexts that span a broad swath of contemporary society and the anxieties it produces. Students should be enabled to cope with the ambivalence of curiosity by learning how to become aware and self-reflexive.

Reading the book was a joyful experience for me, offering many gems of novel and surprising insights. It convinced me that the editors have succeeded in bringing together the material for making a strong case for *curiosity studies*—not only as a field of scholarship but as *a way of studying curiosity* in the classroom and outside. As such, the book offers the opportunity to produce resonance with a readership "out there" that is eager to fill the current void or that actively and strategically seeks to resist what I have called the *taming of curiosity* and its one-dimensional instrumentalization in contemporary society. If academia and schools, as the last bastions of providing space for seemingly idle curiosity, are now under relentless assault from corporate capitalism that channels curiosity in one and one direction only, namely profit and success as defined by markets, then the call for subversive resistance has a chance to be heard.

Acknowledgments

Any project on curiosity worth its salt must owe an unusual number of debts to people, places, and things. This book is no exception. We want to begin with a warm thanks to the Center for Curiosity, in conjunction with the University of Pennsylvania's School of Social Policy and Practice, for providing both of us with academic homes, financial support, and intellectual inspiration as we conceived and executed much of this project. Special thanks to Kushal Sacheti, founder and director of the Center for Curiosity, whose continued and vigorous belief in all things curiosity spurred this project forward. We would also like to thank the participants of several symposia we organized under the auspices of the Center for Curiosity—the Curiosity: Emerging Sciences and Educational Innovations symposium at the University of Pennsylvania (December 2018), the Reimagining Education: Curiosity and Mental Health symposium at American University (April 2018), the Network Neuroscience of Curiosity symposium at the University of Pennsylvania (November 2017), and, especially, the Curiosity across the Disciplines symposium at the University of Pennsylvania (December 2016). Not only did symposia participants enrich our understanding of curiosity, many of their talks grew into chapters for the present volume. On that note we owe a huge thanks to all of our contributors, for their prompt, fearless, and eminently curious work. Thanks also to our anonymous reviewers and to the enthusiastic support of our editors at the University of Minnesota Press: to Danielle Kasprzak, who saw the promise of the project and shepherded it through review, and to Pieter Martin, who oversaw the later stages of development.

Perry Zurn owes a tangible debt to a few rooms of his own that made both the mundanities and the electric moments of this project possible: G11 Franklin Patterson, 316 Hayden, and 112 Battelle-Tompkins. In recognizing the material conditions of my own curiosity—and signaling the historically unequal distribution of those conditions—I also want to acknowledge the Nonotuck people, the Lenni-Lenape people, and the Piscataway people, on whose traditional territories I undertook this work. Many thanks to American University for research leave to accept the postdoctoral fellowship at Penn's Center for Curiosity. I also thank the students in "The Ethics of Curiosity" course at Hampshire College (Spring 2016) and "The Philosophy of Curiosity" course at American University (Spring 2018) for getting curious about curiosity in a more expansive sense than I could ever have imagined. Thanks to generous audience members where I presented my curiosity-related work, including attendees at the American Philosophical Association, Critical Genealogy Workshop, Derrida Today, Diverse Lineages of Existentialism, philoSOPHIA, the Society for Phenomenology and Existential Philosophy, and the Trans Philosophy Project conferences, as well as audiences at Academic Programs International, Adelphi University, American University, Appalachian State University, DePaul University, Hampshire College, Haverford College, MIT Media Lab, the University of Colorado Denver, the University of North Carolina at Charlotte, the Imagination Institute, the Penn Network Visualization program, Lea Elementary, Open Connections, and Westtown School. Special thanks also to my grandmother, Sara Atlee, and mother, Holly Zurn, for modeling and facilitating my raucous and self-reflective curiosity from a young age. And big thanks to Arjun for being my co-conspirator in curiosity studies these past few years!

Arjun Shankar knows that his meandering, tangential, idiosyncratic journey down this intellectual path has been made possible only through the trust, friendship, and belief of many who have supported him along the way. Many thanks to the Center for Curiosity in conjunction with the School of Social Policy and Practice at the University of Pennsylvania for providing the space and resources necessary to think with curiosity from 2016 to 2018. I owe much to Dean John L. Jackson Jr., whose advocacy, enthusiasm, and intellectual support has been essential to seeing this project through. Kushal Sacheti's belief in this project, along with his rigorous critique, has made it possible for me to think curiously, expansively, and across disciplines. Thanks to the students in my class "Curiosity: An Ethnographic Approach"

Acknowledgments 297

(Spring 2018) for listening to early drafts of chapters and providing enthusiastic criticism. Thanks to those who have offered their feedback on my curiosity-related work, including audiences at the American Anthropological Association, Hamilton College, American University, Goldsmiths, Aarhus University, the University of Pennsylvania, Penn's Netter Center for Community Engagement, the Penn Network Visualization program, and Westtown School. Thanks to my former ninth-grade students at the Academy for Social Action in New York City, who taught me so much about what teaching and learning is and the struggles that come when challenging a system that oppresses young people of color; they led me to dedicate my life to education. Special thanks to my mother, Kamala Shankar, who encourages my curiosity even when she is unsure what it means or where it is going, and my sister, Priya Shankar, who is an endless ball of enthusiasm and hope. Thank you, Mariam Durrani, who inspired me with her ceaseless reminders that no work is worth anything if it does not push us to challenge the patriarchal and racist systems that continue to oppress all of us. I hope this work contributes in a small way to that project. Finally, thanks to Perry Zurn, for being the collaborator I did not know could be. Let this be the beginning of many curious collaborations.

To curiosity studies. To radical curiosity. And to all those whose curiosity has brought us to this moment.

Contributors

DANIELLE S. BASSETT is J. Peter Skirkanich Professor in the Department of Bioengineering and the Department of Electrical and Systems Engineering, as well as affiliate faculty in the Department of Physics and Astronomy, the Department of Neurology, and the Department of Psychiatry, at the University of Pennsylvania.

BARBARA M. BENEDICT is Charles A. Dana Professor in the Department of English at Trinity College. She is author of *Framing Feeling: Sentiment and Style in English Prose Fiction, 1745–1800, Making the Modern Reader: Cultural Mediation in Early Modern Literary Anthologies,* and *Curiosity: A Cultural History of Early Modern Inquiry.*

SUSAN ENGEL is senior lecturer in the Department of Psychology and founding director of the Program in Teaching at Williams College. She is author of *The Stories Children Tell: Making Sense of the Narratives of Childhood, Context Is Everything: The Nature of Memory, Real Kids: Creating Meaning in Everyday Life, Red Flags or Red Herrings? Predicting Who Your Child Will Become, The Hungry Mind: The Origins of Curiosity in Childhood,* and *The End of the Rainbow: How Educating for Happiness (Not Money) Would Transform Our Schools.*

ELLEN K. FEDER is William Fraser McDowell Professor in the Department of Philosophy and Religion at American University. She is author of *Family*

Bonds: Genealogies of Race and Gender and *Making Sense of Intersex: Changing Ethical Perspectives in Biomedicine.*

PAM GROSSMAN is dean of the Graduate School of Education and George and Diane Weiss Professor of Education at the University of Pennsylvania.

JOHN L. JACKSON JR. is Walter H. Annenberg Dean of the Annenberg School for Communication and Richard Perry University Professor at the University of Pennsylvania. He is author of *Harlemworld: Doing Race and Class in Contemporary Black America, Real Black: Adventures in Racial Sincerity, Racial Paranoia: The Unintended Consequences of Political Correctness,* and *Thin Description: Ethnography and the African Hebrew Israelites of Jerusalem.*

KRISTINA T. JOHNSON is a PhD candidate in the Affective Computing Group in the Media Lab at the Massachusetts Institute of Technology.

NARENDRA KEVAL is a therapist and clinical psychologist at Cardinal Clinic. He is author of *Racist States of Mind: Understanding the Perversion of Curiosity and Concern.*

CHRISTINA LEÓN is assistant professor of English at Princeton University.

TYSON E. LEWIS is associate professor in the College of Visual Arts and Design at the University of North Texas. He is author of *The Aesthetics of Education: Theatre, Curiosity, and Politics in the Work of Jacques Rancière and Paulo Freire, On Study: Giorgio Agamben and Educational Potentiality,* and *Inoperative Learning: A Radical Rewriting of Educational Potentialities.*

AMY MARVIN is an independent scholar. She earned her PhD in philosophy from the University of Oregon and has served as a lecturer in both the Department of Philosophy and the Department of Women's, Gender, and Sexuality Studies at the University of Oregon.

HELGA NOWOTNY is professor emerita in the Department of Social Studies at the Swiss Federal Institute of Technology in Zurich (ETHZ) and president of the European Research Council. She is author of *Time: The Modern and Postmodern Experience, The Public Nature of Science under Assault: Politics,*

Markets, Science, and the Law, Cultures of Technology and the Quest for Innovation, Insatiable Curiosity: Innovation in a Fragile Future, The Cunning of Uncertainty, and *An Orderly Mess.*

HILARY M. SCHOR is professor of English and comparative literature at the University of Southern California. She is author of *Scheherezade in the Marketplace: Elizabeth Gaskell and the Victorian Novel, Dickens and the Daughter of the House,* and *Curious Subjects: Women and the Trials of Realism.*

ARJUN SHANKAR is visiting assistant professor in the Department of Sociology and Anthropology at Colgate University.

SEETA SISTLA is assistant professor in the Department of Natural Resources Management and Environmental Sciences at California State Polytechnic University, San Luis Obispo.

HEATHER ANNE SWANSON is associate professor in the Department of Anthropology at Aarhus University. She is coeditor of *To See Once More the Stars: Living in a Post-Fukushima World, Arts of Living on a Damaged Planet: Ghosts and Monsters of the Anthropocene* (Minnesota, 2017), and *Domestication Gone Wild: Politics and Practices of Multispecies Relations.*

PERRY ZURN is assistant professor in the Department of Philosophy and Religion at American University. He is coeditor of *Active Intolerance: Michel Foucault, the Prisons Information Group, and the Future of Abolition.*

Index

Aarhus University Research on the Anthropocene (AURA), 16, 18, 23; members, 27, 28, 29, 30, 31, 32, 33–34
abiding, 92, 99, 100, 101, 103, 104
absentmindedness, 99, 103, 104
accommodation, 150, 151, 238
action: collective, 282; direct, 231, 232; nonviolent, 231–33
activism, 38, 171, 190, 230, 233, 236, 238
Addison, Joseph, 213
aesthetics, xiv, xxii, xxiii, 169, 173, 174, 184, 193, 221; Latina/o, 168; minoritarian, 168, 170, 183
African Americans, 6, 154, 231, 233, 275
Age of Curiosity, xii
Age of Science, 209
agriculture, 19, 24, 30
Ainsworth, Mary, 83
Alice's Adventures in Wonderland (Carroll), 219, 220, 221, 254; curiosity and, 209
alterity, 176, 177, 180, 182; Latina/o, 169
ambiguity, 80, 89, 94; learning and, 85; moral, 209; phenomenological, 209
American Geophysical Union, 9
Andrews, Pamela, 248
Animal That Therefore I Am (More to Follow), The (Derrida), 22, 230

Anthropocene, 15, 16, 25
anthropologists, 27; biologists and, 17–18; multispecies, 23
anthropology, xii, 27, 28, 31, 33, 34, 277; co-analysis/dialogue and, 29; curiosity and, 15, 18–21, 25, 29, 108–12; dialogic commitments of, 32; multispecies, 15, 33; natural history and, 17; natural sciences and, 15
anxiety, xix, 108, 111, 121, 122, 148, 153, 159, 160, 162; excess, 106; managing, 147, 158
Anzaldúa, Gloria, 203
Aquinas, Thomas, xiv
Archaeology of Knowledge, The (Foucault), 187n23
Aristotle, 53n38; curiosity and, xiii, 37–38; knowledge and, 49
ars apodemica, xix
artificial intelligence, xxiv, 142
ASDs. *See* autism spectrum disorder
Aspects of the Novel (Forster), 247
assessments, xiii, 63, 141; developmental, 138; retrospective, 235; standardized, 137
assignments: curiosity-based, 271; developing, 280–84; experiential, 283–84

303

304 Index

Athenian Mercury, The, 218
attachment theory, 84
attention, xix, 97, 98, 142; more-than-human, 24–25
attention deficit/hyperactivity disorder (ADHD), 134–36
attentiveness, 97, 99, 102, 104; being attentive to, 92–96
attunement, 24, 28, 33, 94, 95, 184
Auerbach, Nina, 219, 220
Augustine, xiii–xiv, 91, 97, 102, 103; belief systems and, 93; curiosity and, 93; Heidegger and, 94; phenomenology of, 92
AURA. *See* Aarhus University Research on the Anthropocene
autism spectrum disorder (ASD), 130, 131, 133
awareness, xxii, 122, 149, 292; critical, 270, 283; cultural, 189; demographic, 174; sensory, 137; societal, 235

Bacon, Francis, 271
Bagehot, Walter, 267n10
Bais, Sander, xviii
Bakhtin, Mikhail, 247
Bal, Mieke, 247
Baldwin, James, 279
Ball, Philip, xviii
Banks, Sir Joseph, 212
Barabási-Albert model, 64, 65
Barthes, Roland, 264
Bartleby, the Scrivener (Melville), 240
Basic Questions of Philosophy (Heidegger), 95
Bassett, Danielle S., xxii
Bateson, F. W., 215
Bateson, Gregory, xxviin23
Baudrillard, Jean, 247
Beast and the Sovereign, The (Derrida), 229
Beethoven, Ludwig van, 255

behavior, xiv, xvii, 22, 27, 32, 130, 143, 229; competitive, 119; controlling, 159; curiosity, 137, 142, 221; exploratory, 131, 136, 140, 141, 144; information-seeking, 57, 61; learned, 68; naturalistic, 142; proactive, 159; sexist/xenophobic, xii
Behn, Aphra, 217
Beltrán, Cristina, 170, 171
Benedict, Barbara, xx, xxiii
Benjamin, Walter, 96, 100, 259
Berlyne, Daniel, xix, 130, 132, 138, 232, 233
Bernard of Clairvaux, xiv
Bettcher, Talia, 189
Big Lebowski, The (film), xxii, 92, 98, 102, 193
Binova, Daniel, 221
biodiversity, 7, 8
biology, 17–18, 43, 47, 57
biomedicine, xii, 6, 202
biopolitics, 176, 177, 230
Black community, 239; segregation and, 240
Bleak House (Dickens), 250
Blue Razz, xi
body, 151–54; cis, 201; intersex, 37, 38, 39, 40, 42; normal/abnormal, 49; trans, 201
Body Worlds, 193
Bonawitz, Elizabeth, 85
Bouncing Raisins, 86, 87
boundaries, 152, 291; gender, 223; geographical, 150; physical/conceptual, xviii
Bowie, David, 198
Bowlby, John, 83
Boyle, Richard, 213
Boyle, Robert, 211, 212
breastfeeding, trans women, 199, 200, 201
Brexit, 148, 155, 156
British Museum, 214

Index

305

Brooks, Peter, 217
brown coal beds, 18, 26–27, 30, 31; enacting curiosities at, 23–25
Bubandt, Nils, 17, 34n7
Bullough, Vern, 46, 47
bureaucracy, 5, 122, 227
Burney, Frances, 249
Butler, Judith, 173
Butler, Samuel, 212
Buzard, James, 221

Cadet, Peggy, 44, 45, 46, 50, 52n25
Can You Forgive Her? (Trollope), 221
capitalism, xvi, 113, 121, 125n12, 275; curiosity and, 292; gendered, 110; hermeneutics of, 185; mental unwellness and, 108; neoliberal, 110, 111; racialized, 110; transnational, 202
carbon footprint, 4, 8, 10
Carroll, Lewis, 209, 219, 220, 221, 240
cats, curiosity and, 147–48
Cavanaugh, Sheila, 238
Center for Curiosity, viii, 124n12
change, xviii–xxi, 158; abiotic/biotic, 7
Changing Sex (Hausman), 195
Charles II, 211
Chigurh, Anton, 101
CHILDES, 82
Chouinard, Michele, 78
Chow, Rey, 187n23
Christen, Pat, 13
Chronicle of Higher Education, The, 11
cinema, 100, 101, 103, 104
cissexuals, 195
civilization, 229, 250, 262, 263, 265, 267n13; consciousness and, 228; end of, 251
civil rights, 231, 232
Civil Rights Movement, 238, 239, 240; curiosity and, 228, 231–33
classrooms, 269; contemporary conceptions of, 86; curiosity in, 167–68

cleansing, racist phantasies of, 154–57
Cloud, Dana, 111
coal mining, damage from, 16
co-analysis, 25, 29, 31, 33, 34
Coates, Ta-Nehisi, 270
Coen Brothers, 92, 98–99, 100, 101, 102, 103, 104
Colapinto, John, 41, 42
collaboration, 17, 22–23, 161; curiosity and, 21; intradisciplinary, 16, 27
colonialism, xvi, 20, 33, 277; appropriation of, 192; settler, 275, 289n46
Coming Plague, The (Garrett), 255
commodity, 210; curiosity as, 114
communication, 130, 193; conscious, 278; nonfunctional, 142
community: biological, 7; Black, 239, 240; dialogues, 280; engagement, 284; environmental science, 11; individual and, 273; intersex, xxi; scientific, 5, 10; teacher–learner, 271, 274
complexity, 46, 62, 89, 122, 132, 137, 141, 150, 163, 183, 198, 233, 238; historical, xxiii
complexity theory, xv
concepts, 68, 97; disconnected, 61; majority of, 62; relationships between, 69
concern, 23; collapse of, 151–54; corrupting, 154–57; curiosity and, 23, 160–64; race and, 149–51
Confessions (Augustine), 92
Conflict, Arousal, and Curiosity (Berlyne), 232
connections, 61, 66; across difference, 197; global, 110; long-distance, 62; networks of, xvi; scientific, 10
Conrad, Joseph, 220
Cornell University, suicide at, 107
corruption, 154–57, 161, 218
Cottegnies, Line, xx
Crapanzano, Vincent, 20, 23

306 Index

creativity, xix, 31, 61, 66, 113; curiosity and, viii–xix; development of, 149–50
Cronin, Justin, 255
culture, 96, 108, 109, 120, 159, 168, 180, 192, 209, 291; binding, 113; campus, 237; curiosity, 113, 285; European, 169; mass, 189, 191, 201; nature and, 22; as product, 113; signifiers of, 171; trans, 202; visual, 170, 177
cura, 181, 210, 247
curio, 181, 191–94, 198
curiosi, xix
curiositas, xiii, xiv, xix, 16, 242n22; displays of, 210; enacting, 23–25; multispecies, 21, 25; multivalent, 191
curiosity: acts of, 69; analyses of, xv, xxiv–xxv, 92, 285; appetite for, 76–77; attention for, 93, 104, 285; bringing back, 262, 288n38; collapse of, 151–54, 162; collective, 240, 241; commodification of, 108, 112–21; common sense, 274; compromising, 11; corrupting, 154–57; critical, 271, 275, 277, 278–79, 280; criticism of, 92, 157–60; cultivating, 270, 271–72, 281, 282, 283; demonstrating, ix, 77, 270; dimension of, 96–97; encouraging, 86, 217; end of, 49–50; epistemic, 138, 139; expansive, 17, 19, 21; exploring, xiv–xv, xvii; expressing, 85, 87, 109, 116; individualized, 32; institutionalized, 240; intellectual, 273; manifestations of, 132, 140–41; measuring, 130; modeling, 88; modes of, 21, 28; morbid, 193; more-than-human, 18; natural, xiv, 91, 210, 270; objects of, 37, 39, 67, 69, 195, 277, 283; politics of, 202, 228–31, 240, 271–76; practice of, xv, xix, 33, 58, 59, 66, 67, 68, 69, 70; promise of, 38, 50; promoting, 232–33; public, xxiii, 189, 200, 232; radical, xiii, xxi, 114, 280, 286; resistant, 239, 240, 244n70; scientific, xxi–xxii, xxiii, 4, 5,

6, 11, 219; social, 231, 273; structuring, 274; student, 108, 121, 122; studying, xii, xiii, xv, xvi, xviii, xxvn1, 293; subjects of, xx, 38–41, 198; taming, xxi, 291, 293; theory of, 97, 130; therapeutic, 229–30; understanding of, 144, 248
Curiosity: An Ethnographic Approach (class), 107
Curiosity (Mars Rover), xi
curiosity about, xxi; curiosity with and, 20
Curiosity and Exploration Inventory I and II (Kashdan), 233
curiosity cabinets, 136, 210, 217, 221, 267n14
Curiosity Cola, xi
Curiosity.com, xi
Curiosity in Early Modern Europe (Kenny), xviii
"Curiosity in the Classroom" (training session), 269
curiosity studies, xii, 136, 292, 293; ecologically informed, xvii; establishing, xii; neurodiverse, 130–33, 138, 143
curiosus, 181
curiotization, 190, 191; form of, 196–97; process of, 194, 196, 199; tipping points and, 199–202; trans, 194–98, 201; world-traveling and, 198
Curious George, xi
"Curious Is Calling," xi
"Curious Maid" poems, 213
Curious Subjects (Schor), xviii, 248
"curious under fire," 160

Daily Mail, 199
Darling, Candy, 203
Dartle, Rosa, 219
Darwin, Charles, 75–76, 89, 219
Daston, Lorraine, 246, 247, 261
data, 6, 80, 81, 82; analysis, 10, 132, 142; collecting, 136, 239; ethnographic, 19;

informative, 4; interview, 108; relational, 59

David Copperfield (Dickens), 219

Davis, Angela, 275

Dead Subjects (Viego), 171

de Bury, Richard, xiv

Deccan Chronicle, 199

Deferred Action for Childhood Arrivals (DACA), 177

Defert, Daniel, 234

Defoe, Daniel, 217

de Man, Paul, 175–76

Democracy and Education (Dewey), 57

demography, 19, 168, 172, 174, 175; lens of, 170

depression, 106, 108, 121, 123n3

Derrida, Jacques, 186n5, 231, 238, 240; criticism of, 22; curiosity and, 228; sovereignty and, 230

Descartes, René, xiv, 37, 38

desegregation, 236, 239

de Silva e de Menezes, Jean, 153

desire, 110, 174; curiosity and, 20, 37, 49, 50

de Sousa Santos, Boaventura, xvi

development, xix, 133, 150, 193; age, 138; cognitive, 58; curiosity and, 88, 89, 130, 131, 151; emotional, 149; professional, 269

Devore, Tiger, 44, 50; curiosity of, 45–46; Money and, 45, 46, 48

Dewey, John, 57, 272, 286n8; curiosity and, xix, 273; problem-solving and, 286n12

Diallo, François, 256

Diamond, Milton, 52n19

Dickens, Charles, 217, 219, 221, 249, 250, 259

difference, 170; cultural, xx; curio of, 185; curiosity and, xi–xii; generalizations and, 168; intradisciplinary, 16–18; relation and, 173

disabled people, 154, 240

Discipline and Punish (Foucault), 233

discourse: achievement, 111; educational, 283; political, 163; public, 275; social, 110

discovery, 147, 278; appetite for, 76–77; gratification in, 93

Discovery Channel, xi

discrimination, 231, 232, 236, 238

Disney, Walt, 193, 194

distraction, xv, 94, 98–104, 193; cinema and, 100–101; curiosity and, 92, 97, 99, 104; rethinking, 96–98

diversity, xvi, 130, 132, 163, 174, 175

DNA, 5, 26–27, 36n28, 135; analyzing, 26–27, 36n28

Dombey and Son (Dickens), 250

Drabinski, John, 182

Dr. Eleven, 264

"Dr. Eleven," 255, 257, 258, 264, 266

Dr. Money and the Boy with No Penis (documentary), 41–42

Du Bois, W. E. B., 233, 274

"Dude Looks Like a Lady" (Aerosmith), 196

Durkheim, Emile, 109

Durrani, Mariam, 269

Dvorak, Antonin, 140

Dweck, Carol, 286n8

dystopias, 254, 267n12

eastern hemlock *(Tsuga canadensis),* 3

ecology, xii, xv, xxi, 4, 8, 17, 21, 23; complex, 24; curious, 34; epistemic, xviii; forest, 26; human/nonhuman, 277–78

economics, 107, 108, 121, 270, 291

ecosystem, 3, 6; conception of, 8; preservation of, 7

education, xii, xviii–xxi, 96, 106, 107, 250, 278, 291; aesthetic, 184, 185; curiosity and, vii, xi, xxii, xxiii, 92, 93, 95, 104, 122, 270, 271–74; daydreaming and, 92; higher, xxii, 110, 283; neoliberal, 115–21; philosophy of, 92,

104; purpose of, 279; reconstruction of, 96

educational theory, 59, 270, 272

Eisner, John, 27

Elegy Department Spring (Gabriel), 188

Elephant in the Moon, The (Butler), 212

empiricism, 212, 214, 218

endocrinology, 44, 52n25, 203

engagement, 113, 184, 191; abrasive, 159; dialogical, 281; peer-to-peer, 284

Engel, Susan, xix, xxii

Enlightenment, xix, 209, 218, 223

Enloe, Cynthia, xx, 273

entanglements, 31, 33, 203; curiosity and, 181–85

entrepreneurship, 23, 113, 114

environment, xv, 9, 66, 85, 108, 142, 143; collaborative, 271, 281, 284; learning, 84, 271, 272

environmental damage, 8, 10, 11, 15, 16

environmental scientists, 3, 4, 7, 8, 9, 11

Epcot. *See* Experimental Prototype Community of Tomorrow

epistemology, 16, 79, 170, 173, 176, 228, 241; Native American, 288n44

Epistle (Pope), 213

Epistle I: To Richard Temple, Viscount of Cobham (Pope), 215

Epistles to Several Persons (Pope), 214

Epistle to Dr. Arbuthnot (Pope), 215

Erhardt, Anke, 46, 47–48, 53n38

Essay Concerning Human Understanding, An (Locke), 214

ethics, 9, 37, 40, 42, 169, 171, 173, 176, 228; connection to, 6; curiosity and, 168, 170, 172, 180, 241; ecological, 7, 8; politics and, 174, 183, 185n1; professional, 7; violations, 49

ethnic cleansing, 153

ethnicity, 148, 152, 177, 180, 278

European Union, 31, 148, 156

Eve, xx, 209, 248

Evening Standard, 199

"Evil Deceivers and Make-Believers" (Bettcher), 189

experience, 57, 61, 89, 141; class, 117, 269; educational, 67, 70; lived, 195, 196; sociopolitical, 156; student, 112; trans, 201

Experimental Prototype Community of Tomorrow (Epcot), 193, 198

exploration: basal sensory, 138; interest/motivation in, 85; methods/forms of, 283; potential for, 149; risks/rewards of, 83–89; security and, 84; spontaneous, 141

Fanon, Franz, 233

Fargo (film), 100

fatalism, 115, 125n22

Feder, Ellen, xxi

feedback, 43, 86, 88, 141

Feeling in Theory (Terada), 175–76

Feinberg, Leslie, 203–4

feminism, xvii, 187n27, 203, 248, 274

fieldwork, 7, 15, 24, 25–29, 30, 32; anthropological, 23, 31; conducting, 16–17; curiosity and, 17, 19

fingere, 247

forests, 262; clear-cutting, 9; industrial, 24

Forster, E. M., 247, 265

Foucault, Michel, 124n12, 176, 187n23, 231, 233, 236, 238; curiosity and, 228, 229, 230, 240; GIP and, 235; intolerance-inquiry and, 234; knowledge and, 110

"Four Ways to Cultivate a Culture of Curiosity" *(Harvard Business Review),* 112–13

Fowler, Harry, xix

frameworks, 6, 282; abolitionist, 275; conceptual, 61; educational, 272; knowledge, xii, xv–xviii; modernist, 272; theoretical, 44

Frankenstein (Shelley), 218

Index

Frankenstein, Victor, 209, 218
free association, 63, 101, 102
Free to Pee group, 238
Freire, Paulo, xx, 125n22, 269, 274; curiosity and, xix; on process of learning, 287n34; transformative learning and, 276
Freud, Sigmund, 149, 213, 247
Fried, Dana, 200–201, 210
Frye, Marilyn, 197, 198
Fuchs, Jacob, 225n14
Fuckology (Morland, Downing, and Sullivan), 46, 47–48
Fungible Truth, 10–11
fungus, 25, 26, 27, 28–29, 31, 32; photo of, 26
Future World, 193, 194, 198

Gabriel, Kay, 188
Galileo, 261
Gan, Elaine, 25
Gärdenfors, Peter, 68
Garland-Thomson, Rosemarie, xx, 177
Garrett, Laurie, 255
gaze, 142, 177, 181; colonial, 184; curious, 250; medical, 39; violent, 180
gender, 19, 46, 47, 121, 152, 278, 285; assigned, 39; binary, 238; conformity, 194; inconsistencies of, 195; nonconformity, 194; norms, 189
genderqueer people, 176, 237, 240
genetics, 5, 59, 129, 130, 135
GIP. *See* Prisons Information Group
Givens, Jarvis R., 275
Giving an Account of Oneself (Butler), 173
Glanville, Joseph, 212
Glissant, Édouard, 168, 172, 182, 183
globalization, xix, 154, 157, 185
goals, 116, 117, 119, 135, 292
Godwin, William, 218
Goldstein, Zil, 199
Gottlieb, Jacqueline, xix

Graeber, David, 109
Gramsci, Antonio, 274
Grande, Sandy, xxiv, 280
Gray, Dorian, 183
Green, Jamison, 195
Gregory the Great, xiv
group-think, 5, 9
growth, 63; modeling, 59; network, 69; physical, 83; psychological, 83; technological, 4
Gulliver's Travels (Swift), 212, 223

Hamilton College, 106–7, 119; curiosity and, 114; mental health at, 123; sickness at, 120–21; student experiences at, 112
Hamilton College Career Center, 116
Hamilton News, 118
Hampson, Joan, 41, 43
Hampson, John, 41, 43
Haraway, Donna, 18, 23, 28, 33, 203; curiosity and, 21–22; on Derrida, 22
Hard Times (Dickens), 250
Harney, Stefano, 122, 124n12
Harris, Paul, 79, 80
Hart, Roger, 85
Harvard Business Review, 112–13, 115
Hausman, Bernice, 101, 195
Hearne, Thomas, 213
Heart of Darkness (Conrad), 220
Hegel, G. W. F., 202
Heidegger, Martin, 91, 95, 103; Augustine and, 94; curiosity and, 97; phenomenology of, 92
Heisenberg, Werner, 129
Heller, Gary, 258
Hemingway, Ernest, 183
hemlock woolly adelgid *(Adelgis tsugae),* 3, 7
Henderson, Bruce, 86
hermaphroditism, 42–43
Hervey, Lord, 215
heterogeneity, xviii, 18, 62

310 Index

Hillel the Elder, Rabbi, 10
Hills, Thomas T., 65–66
history, xii, xv, 182, 202, 279; colonial, 20; cultural, 223; literary, 223; multi-species, 31; specularization of, 201; trans, 196–97
History of Madness (Foucault), 229
History of Sexuality (Foucault), 229
Hobbes, Thomas, xiv, 271
Holmes, Sherlock, 99, 209
homosexuality, 43, 44
hope, xviii, 123, 227, 271, 280, 286, 288n44
HopeLab, 113, 114
hormones, 42–43, 52n19, 203
Hot Zone, The (Preston), 255
Hughes, Martin, 78, 80
humanities, 21–22, 280
humanity, xxiii, 163, 196; curiosity and, 95; uprootedness of, 94
Hume, David, xiv
humiliation, 152, 156, 158, 160
Hurston, Zora Neale, vii
hypospadias, 44, 45, 52n27

ideas, xvii; democracy of, xvi; probing, 80–83; questions and, 81
identity, 133, 148, 153, 204; self and, 155; sexual, 52n19; social, xii, 271; telos of, 186n5; transgender, 190
ideology, xiii, 271, 283; homophobic, 280; sexist, 280
imagination, 237, 288n44; curiosity and, viii–xix; ethical, 241; poetic vision of, 183; political, 239; private/public, 153; racist, 157
"I'm Curious" (Spears), xi
imperialism, xix, 111; border, 275
information, 10, 78, 88, 99, 118, 176, 217; anthropological, xix; assimilation of, 143; biological, 27; collecting, 78, 80, 81, 214, 234; data of, 176; features of, 132; geographical, xix; pursuit, 81–82; seeking, 8, 58–59, 79

innovation, viii; curiosity and, vii, 113
inquiry, 83, 131–32, 251; appetite for, 88; curiosity and, 284–85; intolerance, 234; language of, 77–78; masculin-ized, 220; neoliberal system of, 118; process of, 282; provoking, 209; schematic of, 239; sustained, 76
Insatiable Curiosity (Nowotny), 291
insubordination, curiosity and, 228, 238–39, 240, 241
intellectual capacity, growth of, 12
intellectual disability (ID), 133
interests, xix, 84, 85, 135; emergence of, 89; personal, 144; sustained, 86, 191
interrogation: cross-disciplinary, xii; gender-based, 238
intersex, 40, 44, 45; medical manage-ment of, 39; medicalization of, 38
intersex people, xxi, 44, 45, 49
Intersex Society of North America, 47
intervention, 37, 49; aesthetic, 168; double, 292; hormonal/surgical, 40
investigation, 40, 149; curiosity and, 37, 229; gratification in, 93; physical, 77
Irving, Dan, 190
Isaacs, Nathan, 78
Isidore of Seville, xiv

Jackson, John L., Jr., 284
James, William, xix, 130
Jenner, Caitlyn, 189
John/Joan case, 41, 46, 49
Johns Hopkins University, 44, 49; Money and, 41, 42, 43, 45, 48
Johnson, Kristina, xxii
Jones, Tom, 248
Jorgensen, Christine, 201
Journal of Ethnobiology, 16
Journal of the Plague Year, A (Defoe), 218
judgments, curiosity-informed, 45, 292
"just curious," xi, 91, 92, 96, 98, 104

Kang, Min Jeong, xviii
Kansas Republican Party, transgender identity and, 190
Kashdan, Todd, xix, 233
Kenny, Neil, xviii, xx
Keval, Narendra, xx, xxii–xxiii
Khan, Chengez, 151, 153
Kidd, Celeste, xix
Kimmerer, Robin Wall, xxiv
King, Martin Luther, Jr., 230, 231, 232
King Lear (Shakespeare), 253, 257
Kinks, 196
Kipling, Rudyard, 219
Klein, Melanie, 37
Kleinman, Arthur, 123n3
knowing, xxi; aesthetic sphere of, 182; familiarity of, 147
knowledge, xv, xxi, 28, 57, 62, 78, 88, 93, 147, 176, 215, 276, 280; acquiring, 39, 58–59, 68, 92, 109, 115, 149, 182, 183; alternative, 175; anthropological, 32; colonial, 183; concrete, 78; core, 5; curiosity and, xiv, xviii, 68, 138, 229; decolonial, 175; demographic, 169; desire for, 37, 49, 50; discrete, 168; innovative, 113; lack of, 278; mastery and, 174; nature of, 61–62; network of, xxii, 61–63, 64, 66, 67, 68, 69, 70; plurality of, xvi; postcolonial, 175; production of, xv, xvi, xviii, 5, 111, 168, 288n36; schemas of, 228; scientific, xiv, xix, 32; sociological, 170; structures of, 279; technologization of, xxiv; value and, 110, 111–12, 121; wholeness and, 171
knowledge-emotion, 108, 109
knowledge-making, 23, 28, 30
Kockelman, Paul, 109
Kreitler, Hans, 134, 135
Kreitler, Schulamith, 134, 135
Kroeber, Alfred, 19, 20
Kroeber, Karl, 19, 20
Ku Klux Klan, 231
Kuhn, Thomas, 279

landscapes, 23; dynamics of, 28; economic, 107; global, 288n38; industrial, 31; more-than-human, 25; political, 228, 239
language, 61–62, 83, 134; abilities, 133; abstract, 142; curiosity and, 77, 78–79; degradation of, 156; first-person, 132; identity-first, 132–33; lack of, 137; receptive, 136
Latina/os, 167, 169, 173, 174, 175; category of, 170; wholeness/agentiality and, 171
Latina/o studies, 168–69, 185n1
latinidad, xxii, 167, 173, 174, 175, 185; curiosity and, 168–70; engagement with, 184; ethical relation to, 168–69; ethical work of, 185n1; sign of, 171–72; transparency and, 170–71
learning, xxi, xxii, 67, 80, 86, 87, 149, 291; capacity, 70; character development and, 37; curiosity and, xxii, 37, 116, 278; machine, 140, 142; promoting, 184; statistical, 68; theories of, 59; transformative, 276
learning disabilities, 134–36
learning platform, photo of, 135
Leask, Nigel, 169
Lee, Erica Violet, xxiv
León, Christina, xxiii
Leroi, Armand Marie, 53n38
Levinas, Emmanuel, 175, 176, 182
Lewis, Tyson E., xxii, 169
literature, xii, 168, 169, 174, 209
Little Mermaid, The, 194
Llewelyn, Clara Jean, 101
Locke, John, xiv, 214, 224n10, 271
logos, xv, 176
"Lola" (Kinks), 196
London Labour and the London Poor (Mayhew), 249
Lowenstein, George, xix
Lubchenco, Jane, 11
Lugones, María, 191, 197, 198

312 Index

MacWhinney, Brian, 82
Mandel, Emily St. John, 246, 252–53, 255, 258–59, 263, 266; curiosity and, 248; work of, 250–51
Man Who Would Be King, The (Kipling), 219
marginalized groups, xxiii, 21, 133, 167, 230, 238, 241
Marvin, Amy, xxiii
masculinism, 33, 120
Mayhew, Henry, 249, 250, 259, 267n11
McDougall, Joyce, 149
McLuhan, Marshall, 289n52
meaning-making/meaning-building, xxi
media, 23, 148, 189, 199, 200, 227; curiotization and, 191; trans and, 202
Melville, Herman, 240
memory optics, 201–2
Mendieta, Ana, 177; work of, 178–79, 180, 181
mental health, xxii, 21, 63, 66–67, 106, 121, 123; anthropology of, 108–12; capitalism and, 108; cultural values and, 107
Metaphysics (Aristotle), 37
Midsummer Night's Dream, A (Shakespeare), 246, 264–65
Miller's Crossing (film), 100, 102
Milton, John, 248
mindfulness training, xxiv, 66
mining, 23–24, 25, 26, 27
Mis-Education of the Negro, The (Woodson), 275
models, 59; educational, 275; generative, 58; growth, 64, 65, 69; mathematical, 69; mental, 77; preferential attachment, 64
modernity, xiv, 150, 185
Moll Flanders (Defoe), 217
Money, John, 41, 50, 53n38; criticism of, 42, 48; Devore and, 45, 46, 48; dissertation of, 43; Erhardt and, 48; intersex

bodies and, 42; investigating, 44–49; legacy of, 44, 48, 49; reassignment and, 46; standard of care and, 38; theories of, 42, 43
"Monk" (TV show), 99
monopragmosune, xiii
Montague, Lady Mary Wortley, 215
Moral Epistles (Pope), 214
morality, 9, 163, 213, 214, 228
Morning Chronicle, The, 267n11
Morris, William, 267n12
Moss, Llewelyn, 101
Moten, Fred, 122, 124n12
motivations, xix, 41, 43, 45, 57, 85, 109, 136, 137, 139, 152, 217, 219, 285
Muldaur, Jenni, 197, 198
Mulvey, Laura, xx
"Museum of Civilization," 260
Mushroom at the End of the World, The (Tsing), 262
music, 140, 141
Mütter Museum, 192, 193
Mysteries of Udolpho, The (Radcliffe), 218
myth, xx, 93, 149, 150, 162, 212, 232, 275, 281

Nabokov, Vladimir, 223, 228
Nair, Mira, 151
Namaste, Viviane, 189, 195
narratives, 38, 101, 151, 152, 154, 155, 248; failure, 119; false, 164; intersex, 39; racist, 150
National Oceanic and Atmospheric Agency, 11
natural history, 17, 24
naturalia, 214
natural sciences, 9, 15, 17, 28, 53n38, 280
nature: culture and, 22; questioning, 129; valuation of, 7
necropolitics, 176
Negro History week, 275

neoliberalism: curiosity and, xxi, xxii, 107–8, 113; hermeneutics of, 185

Neoplatonism, xiv

networks, 227; brain, 61; building, 59, 63–66, 67; concept, 59, 65; co-occurrence, 63; defining, 59–61; geometry of, 68; graph of, 60; growth of, 59, 63–66, 67; knowledge, xxii, 63, 64, 66, 67, 68, 69, 70; language, 59; mathematical, 69; multiscale, 61; prison resistance, 233–36; representation of, 60; scientific, 12; semantic, 59, 62, 63, 66, 69; social, 61; structure of, 62, 65; transport, 65; world building, 262

neurodevelopment, 58

neurodiversity, 138, 139, 143, 285

neuroscience, xii, 57, 58, 59

News from Nowhere (Morris), 267n12

Newton, Isaac, 211

New York Post, 199

New York Times, 123, 200, 256

New York University, suicide at, 107

Nicholson, Marjorie Hope, 214

Nietzsche, Friedrich, xx, 231, 238, 240; curiosity and, 228, 229, 230

No Country for Old Men (film), 101, 102

nodes, 60, 63, 64; connections to, 64–65; network, 59, 60, 62

nonhuman species, 17, 24, 32, 34

North, Paul, 92, 97, 99, 101, 104

Nowotny, Helga, xxi

Obama, Barack, xi, xvii

objectification, 174, 195, 196, 198

objects, 68, 85, 210, 267n11

O'Brien, Michelle, 202–3

oddities, 80, 120, 209, 217, 222, 247; medical, 192–93

Odysseus, xx

Oedipus, 149, 209

oikos, xv

Old Curiosity Shop, The (Dickens), 217, 221

"On Cartography and Dissection" (Rose), 102

On Longing (Stewart), 247

opacity, 177, 182; aesthetic, 170, 181; attunement to, 184; curiosity and, 168–70, 174; ethics of, 172, 173; relationality and, 172; term, 171–73

openness, xi, 27, 39, 61, 273, 277

Operation Peter Pan, 180

organisms, 16, 24, 130, 291; classifying, 28; collecting, 7; genetic modification of, 6; nonhuman, 7, 28

Origin of Species, The (Darwin), 219

Oroonoko, or the Royal Slave (Behn), 217

Other, 109, 149, 171, 174, 177; nonhuman, 34; racial/ethnic, 147, 154; real, 147

paleoclimatology, 9

Pandora, xx, 209

Paradise Lost (Milton), 248

Park, Katherine, 247

parrhesiates, 229, 240

Parrish, Judith Totman, 10

Participatory Research framework, 282

Passage, The (Cronin), 255, 267n13

Patria Potestad law, 180

patriarchy, xvi, 273, 275

Paxillus involutus, 25, 27, 29, 31, 32, 33; photo of, 26

pedagogy, 167, 168, 183, 184, 279, 284; abolitionist, 270, 272, 274–75, 276, 281; critical, 270–71, 272, 274, 276, 277, 281; curious, 269, 270–71, 276, 277, 278, 280, 285; experiential, 270, 281; feminist, 270, 272, 273, 276, 281

Pedagogy of Freedom (Freire), 269

Pelton, Leroy H., 232, 233

"People Are Talking," 45

People in Search of Safe and Accessible Restrooms (PISSAR), 230, 236–41; patrols, 237–38

314 Index

perceptions, xix, 57, 61, 62, 134, 152, 197, 198, 214
periergia, xiii
phallogocentric fantasies, curiosity and, 230
phantasies, 153, 163; primal scene, 150; racist, 148, 150, 154–57, 164
Philobiblon (de Bury), xiv
philosophy, xii, 91, 92, 211, 228, 271; curiosity and, xxvin6, 95, 96; educational, 95, 104; experimental, 214
physiology, 132, 139, 140, 273
Piaget, Jean, 130
Pindar, Peter, 212
PISSAR. *See* People in Search of Safe and Accessible Restrooms
Plato, xiii, 242n22
"Playfulness, 'World'-Travelling, and Loving Perception" (Lugones), 197
poetics, 172, 183
Poetics of Relation (Glissant), 172, 182
political life, triangulation/strangulation of, 160–64
political protest, efficacy of, 233
politics, xix, 18, 107, 123n3, 156, 169, 172, 176, 189, 231, 239, 240, 270, 291; American, 148; curiosity and, 182; deformation of, 163; demands of, 171; ethics and, 174, 183, 185n1; identity, 153; programmatic, 172
polypragmosyne, xiii, 242n22
Pope, Alexander, 213, 214, 215, 216, 220, 224n10, 225n14
popular culture, curiosity and, xi
poverty, 154–55, 156
power, 240, 280; curiosity and, 229; effects of, 228; hegemonic, 274; institutions of, 277; systems of, 121, 279
powerlessness, 152, 156, 161
praxis, xii, xiii, 271; affective, 274, 280; antiracist, 273; curiosity-based, 284,

285; educational, 272, 276; pedagogical, 281
Preston, Richard, 255
Prevant, Leon, 264
Prisons Information Group (GIP), 230, 233–36, 238, 239
prison studies, 233–36, 240
production: aesthetic, 169; cultural, 110, 169, 175, 191, 194, 196; knowledge, xv, xvi, xviii, 168, 288n36
professionalization, 5, 122, 124n12
Prometheus, xx
Prosopopoeia, 175, 186n17
protocols, xxii, 7, 38, 42, 47, 49, 151, 241, 281, 282
psyche, 151–54, 209
psychoanalysis, xii, 43, 147, 149
psychoendocrinology, 46, 47, 48
psychology, xii, 57, 58, 107, 156, 271; academic, 48; developmental, 83; traditional, 109
Psychology of Nonviolence, The (Pelton), 232
psychopathology, 43
psychosexual orientation, 42, 43

Queer/Crip coalition, 236–46
queer scholars, 285
queer theory, 111
questions, xii, 30, 96, 129; critical, 281; culture of, 278; curiosity and, xix, 89, 173–74, 269; ethical, 6; fundamental, 150; nature of, 80, 81; pedagogy of, 272; politicized, 235; quality of, 88; related, 79; right, 281; sociopolitical, xvii; why, 78
Quintana, Jesus, 100

race, 121, 177, 180, 240, 278, 285; concern and, 149–51; curiosity and, 149–51
Rachmaninoff, Sergei, 140
racial difference, typologies of, 272
racial profiling, 169

Index

racism, xxiii, 148–49, 151, 155, 156, 158, 159–60, 162, 163, 189, 239; scientific, 271; sexism and, 180
Radcliffe, Ann, 218
"Radiant Opacity," 168
Ranganath, Charan, xviii
Rape of the Lock, The (Pope), 216, 220
realism, 254, 258, 264
reassignment, 41, 46
Recruiter.com, 115
Redick, Alison, 42, 43
Reed, Lou, 196, 197, 198, 203
reflexivity, xxii, 271, 277, 288n36
Reimer, Brenda (Joan/David), 41, 46
Reimer, David, 52n19, 53n38; suicide of, 41–42, 46
Reisman, Tamar, 199
relations: class-inclusion, 62; difference and, 173; ethics of, 172, 173; more-than-human, 27, 30, 32; radical, 173; semantic, 62; symbiotic, 277–78
relationships, xviii–xxi, 67–68, 141, 149; building, 10; measuring, 69; nuanced, 143; productive, 150
Reluctant Fundamentalist, The (film), 151
Renaissance, 209, 214
representation, 173; crisis of, 20; ideational, 150; network, 62; politics of, 169
research, 4, 29, 32; biological, 17; empirical, 69; environmental, 6, 7; ethnographic, 20; financial investment in, 5; interdisciplinary, vii, xvii, xxvn5; methods, 6, 282–83; more-than-human, 24–25; protocols, xxii; scientific, xxi, 5, 7, 12; sex, 47
resistance: curiosity and, xx, xxi, 228, 230, 239–40, 241; political, 233, 239, 241, 275; prison, 234; restroom, 238; subversive, 293
restoration, racist phantasies of, 154–57
rhetoric, 111, 114, 162, 174, 216, 281; political, 156; sexist/xenophobic, xii

Robinson Crusoe (Defoe), 217
Rolling Stone, 41
Rose, Edith, 239
Rose, Elena, 192
Rosenberg, Charles, xv
Rousseau, Jean-Jacques, xiv
Royal Society for the Advancement of Learning, 211, 212, 214
rubber boots method, 16, 17, 34n7
Rule of Law, Misrule of Man (Scarry), 263
"Ruling Passions" (Pope), 215

safety: curiosity and, 83; emotional, 152–53, 157
Sanskrit poems, curiosity in, xxxn68
Scarry, Elaine, 263
Schepher-Hughes, Nancy, 124n4
scholarship, xiii, xx, 21; curiosity and, viii; more-than-human, 18; multispecies, 22–23; trans, 202
Schor, Hilary, xviii, xxiii
Schulz, Laura E., 85
science, xviii–xxi, 16, 38, 57, 137; climate, 10; curiosity and, xi, xxi–xxii, xxiii, 4, 5, 6, 11, 219; democratization of, 5; environmental, 7, 8, 9, 11, 12; ethical conduct in, 9, 12; feminist, xxiv; learning about, 87; modern, 8; network, xv, 61, 69–70; neutral, 20; professionalization of, 5; technology and, 5
Science and Technology Studies (STS), 23
security, 84, 148, 150, 162; curiosity and, 83; exploration and, 84; risk and, 117
Sedgwick, Eve, 185
segregation, 232, 236, 238, 239, 240
self: annihilation of, 148; identity and, 155; tearing from, 115
"Self-portrait as a Karen" (Gabriel), 188
self-reflexivity, xxii, 277, 292
semantics, 59, 62, 63, 65, 66, 67, 69, 133

316 Index

Seneca, curiosity and, xiii
Serano, Julia, 194–95, 198, 201
sex, 46, 177; inconsistencies of, 195
sex anatomies, 38, 41, 42, 45, 47
sex difference, 37, 40, 43
sexism, racism and, 180
sexology, 48
sexuality, 46, 111, 121, 149, 152, 278, 285
sex workers, 189
Shadwell, Thomas, 211
Shakespeare, William, 247, 255, 266
Shandy, Tristram, 248
Shankar, Arjun, viii, xxii, 269, 289n54
Shelley, Mary, 218
signifiers: chain of, 176; dead, 171, 180
Sistla, Seeta, xxi
Sloane, Sir Hans, 214–15
Snorton, Riley, 201
Snow, Catherine, 82
Soap Lady, 192–93
social: groups, xv, 60; implications, 119,
    283–84; inequalities, xx, 227, 276;
    institutions, 110, 235; interaction, 83,
    109; life, xx, 109; media, xv, 253;
    mores, 210, 213, 221, 227; order, 20,
    218, 223, 262; practice, xvi, 23, 270;
    relations, 112, 118; sciences, 6, 21–22,
    280; situations, 110, 143; unrest, 148,
    275
sociocultural systems, xix, 108
Socrates, 232
Sommer, Doris, 174
Souls of Black Folk (Du Bois), 233
space, 68; binary, 153; for curiosity, 272,
    293; geographical, 150; mental, 150,
    162; regressive, 12; social, 150, 156, 162;
    thinking/breathing, 160; totalitarian,
    162; triangulated, 150, 151
Spears, Britney, xi
speech, 129, 130, 134
Spielberger, Charles, xix
Spivak, Gayatri Chakravorty, 184–85,
    186n5

SPRING, 136; photo of, 135
Springer, Jerry, 189
Stafford, Barbara, 267n14
standard of care, 38, 40, 41–44
Starr, Laura, xix
Station Eleven (Mandel), 246, 247,
    250–51, 254–59, 262–65
Steele Reserve, xi
Steintrager, James, 224n10
stereotypes, xxiii, 180, 181
Stewart, Susan, 247
Steyvers, Mark, 65
Stiegler, Bernard, 91, 95, 96, 97, 99, 103
Stoller, Robert, 44–45
Stone, Sandy, 203
Stranger, The, 200–201
stress, 58, 106, 107, 111, 120; political, 158;
    social, 158
Structure of Scientific Revolution
    (Kuhn), 279
Stryker, Susan, 203
student life, curiosity and, 115–21
studiositas, xiv
success, 39, 108, 112; job, 121; present/
    future, 117; student, 118
suicide, 106, 121, 123n3; clusters, 107
suprasyllabic objects, 62
Swanson, Heather, xxi
Swift, Jonathan, 212, 213, 223

Talk to Teachers (Baldwin), 279
technology, xv, xxi, 227; curiosity and,
    xi, 143; development of, 6; embrac-
    ing, 10; film, 283; future, 193; science
    and, 5
telos, vii, 176, 186n5, 289n46
temporalities, 29, 61, 171
Tenenbaum, Joshua B., 65
Terada, Rei, 175–76
terrorism, 151, 152, 153, 162
Thackeray, William Makepeace, 249
Thermonuclear Monarchy (Scarry), 263
Things as They Are (Godwin), 218

Index

Thompson, Clark, 258, 260, 261, 263, 265, 266

Thoresby, Ralph, 214–15

thought: capacity for, 149; curious, 57–58; dualistic, 172; patterns of, 276

Tillerson, Rex, 163

Time, 189; Money and, 42

Tizard, Barbara, 78, 80

Tomkins, Silvan, 176

"To Mr. Addison, Occasioned by his Dialogues on Medals" (Pope), 213

Topham, Richard, 213

"Tracing this Body" (O'Brien), 202

transexuality, 189, 202, 203–4

transformation, xxv, 198; artificial, 195; body, 195; technological, vii

Transformer (Reed), 197

Transgender Health, 199

transgender issue, 202, 236

transgender tipping point, 194, 196, 198; curiosity and, 188–91, 197, 199–202

"Transgender Tipping Point" *(Time),* 189

Transgender Warriors (Feinberg), 204

transparency, 172; latinidad and, 170–71; problem of, 170–71

trans people, 176, 189, 195, 196, 199, 200, 236, 237; curiosity and, 194; historical pathways and, 204; poor/homeless, 189

transphobia, 197, 200

transsexuality, 44, 190, 195, 202, 203; curiosity and, 194

trans studies, curiosity in, 190–91

transvestism, 202

travel, environmental costs of, 11, 12

Traveling Symphony, 253, 261, 264, 266

Trollope, Anthony, 221

Trouble with Unity, The (Beltrán), 170

Trump, Donald, 148, 154, 156, 157; curiosity and, xii, xvii; extreme vetting and, 162; travel ban and, 163

Truth, 102; attentiveness to, 94; curiosity and, 92–93; God's, 93, 94

Tsing, Anna Lowenhaupt, 16–17, 25, 262, 288n38; AURA and, 16; radical curiosity and, xxi

Tulane University, suicide at, 107

"Tumbling Tumble Weeds" (Sons of the Pioneers), 98

TV Guide, 256

Twin Towers, attack on, 151, 152

uncertainty, xxiii, 84, 85, 88, 89, 130, 156, 233, 271, 278, 284; creating/enjoying, 277

understanding, 37, 158; drive for, 79; hierarchy of, 20–21

ungendering, 195, 196

University of Pennsylvania, viii, 113, 114; suicide at, 107

Untitled (Glass on Body Imprints—Face) (Mendieta), 177, 178–79

U.S. Public Health Service, 6

value, 109; anthropology of, 108–12; collective, 276; knowledge and, 110, 111–12, 121; statistical, 176

Veblen, Thorstein, 107, 119

Velvet Underground, 196

Verran, Helen, 23

Viego, Antonio, 171, 175

violence, 123n3, 189, 190, 202; curiosity and, 176, 177; structures of, 280

visibility, 172, 173, 177, 201

von Hagens, Gunther, 193

vulnerability, 162; emotional, 148; human, 163–64

Wagner, Roger, xviii

"Walk on the Wild Side" (Reed), 191, 196, 198, 199, 201, 203

Walt Disney World, 193

wandering, xi, xiv, 92, 93, 101, 102, 103, 147, 247

318 Index

Warhol, Andy, 196–97
War on Drugs, 202
Washington Post, 10, 11
Watt, Ian, 267n7
We Charge Genocide (Patterson), 239
Whalley, Angelina, 193
When Species Meet (Haraway), 21
Whipping Girl (Serano), 194–95
White Citizens Council, 231
Whyte, Kyle, xxiv
Wilkins, Lawson, 43, 49
Winfrey, Oprah, 45, 189
Winter, Sarah, 217
"Wonder and the End of Inquiry"
  (Daston), 246
wonderment, 88, 99, 103

Woodlawn, Holly, 203
Woodson, Carter G., 275
"Work of Art in the Age of Mechanical
  Reproduction, The" (Benjamin), 196
workshops, 269, 270, 296
worlds, more-than-human, 21, 28, 31, 33
Wunderkammern, 210, 247, 261

xenophobia, 148, 174, 189

Young, Iris Marion, 39

Zigler, Edward, 134
Zurn, Perry, viii, xxiii, 102, 123, 191, 193,
  280, 289n54

CPSIA information can be obtained
at www.ICGtesting.com
Printed in the USA
BVHW041207110920
588046BV00022B/137